George Eliot

Also by K.K. Collins

IDENTIFYING THE REMAINS: GEORGE ELIOT'S DEATH IN THE LONDON RELIGIOUS PRESS

George Eliot

Interviews and Recollections

Edited by

K.K. Collins
Southern Illinois University Carbondale

First published 2010 by
PALGRAVE MACMILLAN

Palgrave Macmillan in the UK is an imprint of Macmillan Publishers Limited, registered in England, company number 785998, of Houndmills, Basingstoke, Hampshire RG21 6XS.

Palgrave Macmillan in the US is a division of St Martin's Press LLC, 175 Fifth Avenue, New York, NY 10010.

Palgrave Macmillan is the global academic imprint of the above companies and has companies and representatives throughout the world.

Palgrave® and Macmillan® are registered trademarks in the United States, the United Kingdom, Europe and other countries.

ISBN 978–0–333–99363–7   hardback

This book is printed on paper suitable for recycling and made from fully managed and sustained forest sources. Logging, pulping and manufacturing processes are expected to conform to the environmental regulations of the country of origin.

A catalogue record for this book is available from the British Library.

A catalog record for this book is available from the Library of Congress.

10   9   8   7   6   5   4   3   2   1
19 18 17 16 15 14 13 12 11 10

Transferred to Digital Printing 2011.

For Margie

Contents

Acknowledgements

In the course of working on this collection I have come under many pleasant obligations. Among my colleagues at Southern Illinois University Carbondale I wish to thank Scott McEathron, George Goodin, Michael Molino, Beth Lordan, John Hooker, and Frederick Williams for their good advice. David Gobert and Véronique Maisier helped with French, Frederick Betz and Martin Petith with German, and Frederick Williams with Greek and Latin. I am grateful to them all. From the staff of SIUC's Morris Library, I am especially indebted to Deborah Cordts, Marta Davis, Loretta Koch, David Bond, Harry Davis, Charles Flagg, and Roland Person.

Travel to other libraries and archives was made possible by financial support from Southern Illinois University Carbondale, for which I thank Michael Molino, Michael Humphries, John A. Koropchak, and Alan C. Vaux. I am also grateful to Prudence M. Rice for timely counsel.

Colleagues at other universities provided generous assistance: Christina Bashford, University of Illinois at Urbana-Champaign; Francesca D'Alessandro Behr and Clinton Brand, University of St Thomas; Daniel Brewer, University of Minnesota; Roger Cooke, University of Vermont; Cliff Eisen, King's College London; Kate Flint, Rutgers University; Margaret Harris, University of Sydney; Kerry McSweeney, McGill University; Suzanne Kaufman, Loyola University Chicago; Gerlinde Röder-Bolton, University of Surrey; David Sutton, University of Reading; Angus Trumble, Yale Center for British Art; Alan Walker, McMaster University; and Phyllis Weliver, St Louis University.

In London thanks are due to Stephen Humphrey, Southwark Local History Library, and to the staffs of the British Library's Reading Rooms and Manuscripts Reading Room, especially Cynthia Mary Goodwin, Auste Mickunaite, Joe Maldonado, Sandra Powlette, and Bart Smith. In Oxford Penelope Bulloch, Alan Tadiello, and Jeremy Hinchliff of the Balliol College Library went far out of their ways to assist me, and I thank them most heartily. I am also grateful to Anne Walters of Oxford's Library Services, as well as to Colin Harris of the Bodleian Library and his staff in the Special Collections Reading Rooms. In Cambridge warm thanks are due to Richard Andrewes, Patrick Zutshi, and Godfrey Waller of the University Library, and the staff of its Manuscripts Reading Room; Elizabeth Ennion-Smith and Patricia McGuire of the King's College Archive Centre; Anne Pensaert of the Pendlebury Library of Music; Nicholas Robinson and Marit Gruijs of the Fitzwilliam Museum; and Anne Thomson of Newnham College.

The staffs of the following libraries also provided valuable help: Olin Library, Gaylord Music Library, and West Campus Library, Washington

University in St Louis; the Music Library and the University Library, University of Illinois at Urbana-Champaign, especially Scott Mann; the New York Public Library, especially David Smith; the Houghton Library, Harvard University, especially Heather Cole, Mary Haegert, and Leslie Morris; the Firestone Library, Princeton University; and the Beinecke Rare Book and Manuscript Library, Yale University, especially Anne Marie Menta, Morgan Swan, Ellen R. Cordes, and Taran Schindler. Moira Fitzgerald, also of the Beinecke, deserves special mention here.

A deeply gratifying part of preparing this volume has been corresponding, by email and post, with so many welcoming persons associated with libraries and archives. I here thank them en bloc for not pressing 'Delete', or turning to the shredder, when my queries appeared.

From collections in the United States, I am obliged to Cheryl Adams, Library of Congress; Susan Boone, Neilson Library, Smith College; Tina Marie Doody, Montclair (New Jersey) Public Library; Edward Gaynor, Small Special Collections Library, University of Virginia; Teresa L. Gipson, Miller Nichols Library, University of Missouri Kansas City; Sarah Hartwell and Jay Satterfield, Dartmouth College Library; Declan Kiely, Morgan Library and Museum, New York; Jennifer B. Lee, Butler Library, Columbia University; Pat Lyons, Doheny Libraries, St John's Seminary; Lisa Moellering, Fondren Library, Rice University; Amanda Price, Ransom Humanities Research Center, University of Texas; Catherine Reed, Swem Library, College of William and Mary in Virginia; and Gayle M. Richardson, Huntington Library.

From collections in Britain, I am obliged to Patricia Collins, Richard Bond, and George Turnbull, Manchester Central Library; Stephen Curry, Surrey Libraries; Andrew Mealey, Coventry History Centre; Michael Meredith, Eton College Library; Carol Robinson, Central Library, Coventry; and Linda Young, Kenilworth Library. For handling my requests with such courteous dispatch, and for supplying copies of materials, I am especially grateful to Sally Harrower, Sheila Mackenzie, and Iain G. Brown, National Library of Scotland; Rayanne Byatt, Coventry Libraries; Alison Brisby, Castle Howard Archives; and Grace Timmins, Tennyson Research Centre. Finally, Jane Sutton of the Nuneaton Library provided extraordinary help. I am deeply indebted to her.

Other correspondents to whom I am grateful are Donna Anstrey, Yale University Press; Mary Cobeldick, National Library of New Zealand; John Collins, formerly of Maggs Bros; Bill Harding; Emma Whitney Hennessey, Wiley-Blackwell; Angie R. Hogan, University of Virginia Press; Sarah Lewis, Curtis Brown Group; Jennifer Marshall, Inveroran; Anette Müller, Robert-Schumann-Haus, Zwickau; Zdzisław Pietrzyk, Anna Kozlowska, Joanna Kopacz, and Joanna Jaskowiec, Jagiellonian Library, Cracow; Jeff Roth, *New York Times*; Patricia Schultz and Iona Williams, Mellen Press; Mary Siegel, Alexander Street Press; Michelle Sikkes and Jeanne Holierhoek, Montesquieu Institute; Stewart Spencer; the Hon. Oliver Walston; Maria Wiemers, Greg

James, and Kevin Leamon, State Library of New South Wales; the Revd Danny Wignall, St Stephen's Shottermill; and Charlotte Yeldham.

To the following copyright holders and authorities I gratefully acknowledge permission to publish manuscripts in their rights and possession: Lord Acton; Fr Charles Dilke; Camilla Hornby; the Hon. Simon Howard; the British Library Board; the Houghton Library, Harvard University; the Jagiellonian Library; the Jowett Copyright Trustees; the Provost and Fellows of Eton College; the Sophia Smith Collection, Smith College; the Southwark Local History Library; the State Library of New South Wales; the Syndics of Cambridge University Library; the Syndics of the Fitzwilliam Museum; the Tennyson Research Centre; and the Trustees of the National Library of Scotland.

To the following copyright holders I gratefully acknowledge permission to publish printed texts: William Baker; Margaret Harris; Christopher Stray; Cambridge University Press; Coventry History Centre; the Trustees of the National Library of Scotland; the University of Virginia Press; and Blackwell Publishing Ltd.

I am especially grateful for permissions granted by Jonathan Ouvry, G.H. Lewes's great-great-grandson and holder of the George Eliot copyright. His co-operation has been invaluable to me for over thirty years.

While every effort has been made to trace copyright holders for the material in this volume, any further information would be welcomed.

In the midst of this project I was long delayed by a series of eye operations. M. Gilbert Grand of the Barnes Retina Institute, School of Medicine, Washington University in St Louis, saved me from total eclipse. I cannot put into words my debt to him.

One consequence of these delays has been the opportunity of working with more than the usual number of editors at Palgrave Macmillan. Each has been exemplary. For their time and trouble – and their patience – I thank my two past editors, Eleanor Birne and Emily Rosser, and especially my present editor, Paula Kennedy. I am also indebted to their assistants: Becky Mashayekh, Christabel Scaife, Steven Hall, and especially Benjamin Doyle.

Warm thanks are due as well to my copy editor, Barbara Slater, for her meticulous care with the text, her constructive criticism, and her helpful suggestions. She has been extraordinary.

To Paul Elledge of Vanderbilt University, who assisted with this book from its proposal stage forwards, I owe more than I can say or repay.

My wife Margaret spent several of her summers alongside me searching archives and transcribing manuscripts. But my greatest debt to her is for seeing me through when I thought I had no choice but to throw the whole thing over. She saved this book. My dedicating it to her is the merest token of my gratitude.

Abbreviations

[ ]	Matter supplied by the editor, unless otherwise noted
< >	Overscored but recoverable
<[?]>	Overscored and not recoverable
Ashton	Rosemary Ashton, *George Eliot: A Life* (London: Lane, 1996)
BL	British Library
Blind	Mathilde Blind, *George Eliot*, new edn (London: Allen, 1888)
Browning	Oscar Browning, *Life of George Eliot* (London: Scott, 1890)
Companion	*Oxford Reader's Companion to George Eliot*, ed. by John Rignall (Oxford: Oxford University Press, 2000)
Critical Heritage	*George Eliot: The Critical Heritage*, ed. by David Carroll (London and New York: Routledge, 1995)
CUL	Cambridge University Library
Essays	*Selected Essays, Poems and Other Writings*, ed. by A.S. Byatt and Nicholas Warren (London: Penguin, 1990)
GE	George Eliot, by any and all of her names: Mary Anne, Mary Ann, Marianne, Marian, Marian Evans Lewes, and Mary Ann Cross
GE-GHLS	*George Eliot–George Henry Lewes Studies*
GHL	George Henry Lewes
Haight	Gordon S. Haight, *George Eliot: A Biography* (Oxford: Oxford University Press, 1968)
Journals	*The Journals of George Eliot*, ed. by Margaret Harris and Judith Johnston (Cambridge: Cambridge University Press, 1998)
Letters	*The George Eliot Letters*, ed. by Gordon S. Haight, 9 vols, I–VII (New Haven: Yale University Press; London: Oxford University Press, 1954–5), VIII–IX (New Haven and London: Yale University Press, 1978)
Life	*George Eliot's Life as Related in Her Letters and Journals*, ed. by J.W. Cross, 3 vols (Edinburgh and London: Blackwood, 1885)
Life new edn	*George Eliot's Life as Related in Her Letters and Journals*, ed. by J.W. Cross, new edn (Edinburgh and London: Blackwood, 1887)
NLS	National Library of Scotland
NPG	National Portrait Gallery, London

ODNB   *Oxford Dictionary of National Biography* (Oxford University
                Press, 2004) [http://www.oxforddnb.com]
Shirtmaker   *A Monument to the Memory of George Eliot: Edith J. Simcox's
                'Autobiography of a Shirtmaker'*, ed. by Constance M.
                Fulmer and Margaret E. Barfield, Literature and Society
                in Victorian Britain, 4 (New York and London: Garland,
                1998)
Writings   *Selected Critical Writings*, ed. by Rosemary Ashton
                (Oxford: Oxford University Press, 2000)
Yale   MS, Section III, George Eliot and George Henry Lewes
                Collection, Beinecke Rare Book and Manuscript Library,
                Yale University

Chronology

1819	Nov 22	GE born Mary Anne Evans at South Farm, Arbury, Warwickshire.
1820		Moves to Griff House, outside Nuneaton.
1824		At Mrs Moore's dame school, across from Griff House.
1825–27		At Miss Lathom's School, Attleborough.
1828–32		At Mrs Wallington's School, Nuneaton.
1832–35		At Misses Franklin's School, Coventry.
1836	Feb	Her mother dies.
1837		Her sister marries. GE now manages her father's household.
1838–40		Reads widely and studies hard, adding Italian and German to her French, and continues her music lessons. Undertakes charity work and publishes poem in *Christian Observer*.
1841	Mar	Moves with her father to Foleshill, Coventry, where she later begins Latin and Greek.
	Nov	Meets Charles and Caroline Bray and Sara Hennell.
1842	Jan–May	Refuses to attend church.
1844	Jan	Begins translation of Strauss's *Das Leben Jesu*.
1846		*The Life of Jesus* published anonymously. GE writes for Bray's Coventry *Herald and Observer*.
1849	May	Her father dies.
	June	GE goes abroad with Brays and spends winter in Geneva.
1850	Nov	Visits John Chapman's at 142 Strand, London.
1851	Jan	Publishes first review essay in *Westminster Review*. Goes to live at 142 Strand.
	Mar	Leaves.
	Sept	Returns as assistant editor of *Westminster Review*, which Chapman now owns.
	Oct	Meets Herbert Spencer, who introduces her to GHL.
1852	June–July	Rumoured engaged to Spencer, who in fact rejects her.
1853	Oct	Moves to 21 Cambridge St, having been intimate with GHL probably since spring.

1854	July	Feuerbach's *Essence of Christianity* published with 'Marian Evans' as translator. Goes to Germany with GHL for seven months.
1855	Mar	Returns to England to live with GHL as his wife.
	Apr–Sept	GE and GHL at 8 Victoria Grove Terrace, then 7 Clarence Row, East Sheen, then Worthing.
	Oct	To 8 Park Shot, Richmond, for three years four months.
1856	Sept	Begins 'Amos Barton', first of *Scenes of Clerical Life*.
1857	Jan–Nov	*Scenes* appears anonymously in *Blackwood's Edinburgh Magazine*.
	Oct	Begins *Adam Bede*.
1858	Jan	*Scenes of Clerical Life*, 'By George Eliot', 2 vols, published.
	Feb	Reveals her identity to her publisher John Blackwood.
	Apr–Aug	In Munich and Dresden with GHL, the second of their 18 European journeys.
1859	Jan	Begins preliminary work on *The Mill on the Floss*.
	Feb	*Adam Bede*, 3 vols, published. GE and GHL move to Holly Lodge, South Fields, Wandsworth, for 19 months.
	June	Acknowledges to friends that she wrote *Adam Bede*.
	July	'The Lifted Veil' appears in *Blackwood's*. GE and GHL go to Switzerland for a week.
1860	Apr–June	In Italy, returning via Switzerland with Charles Lee Lewes, who joins household for five years. GE meditating a historical novel set in Italy (GHL's suggestion), which will become *Romola*. *The Mill on the Floss*, 3 vols, published in April.
	Sept	GE, GHL, and Charles move to 10 Harewood Sq. for three months. She begins *Silas Marner*.
	Dec	GE, GHL, and Charles move to 16 Blandford Sq. for three years.
1861	Apr	*Silas Marner*, 1 vol., published. GE and GHL go to France and Italy, returning in June. In Florence GE makes notes for *Romola*, which she starts writing in October. It proves profoundly difficult.
1862	July	*Romola* begins in *Cornhill Magazine* and concludes in August 1863 with fourteenth part. Published, 3 vols, in July 1863.
1863	Aug	GE and GHL buy the Priory, 21 North Bank, Regents Park, their principal residence from now on.
1864	May–June	In Venice, accompanied by Frederic Burton.

	June	Begins *The Spanish Gypsy*.
	July	'Brother Jacob' appears in *Cornhill*.
	Oct	Begins to study Spanish.
1865	Jan	In Paris for ten days.
	Mar	Begins *Felix Holt, the Radical*.
	Aug	To Normandy and Brittany for a month.
1866	June	*Felix Holt*, 3 vols, published. To Holland, Belgium, and Germany, returning early August.
	Aug	Resumes work on *The Spanish Gypsy*.
	Dec	To southwest France and Spain, returning in March.
1867	Aug–Sept	In Germany. Writes 'O May I Join the Choir Invisible'.
1868	Feb	First of three visits to Cambridge.
	May	*The Spanish Gypsy* published. To Switzerland and Black Forest for two months.
1869	Mar–Apr	In Italy. GE introduced to John Walter Cross.
	May	'How Lisa Loved the King' appears in *Blackwood's*. Thornton Lewes returns ill from Natal, and dies in October.
	Aug	'Agatha' appears in *Atlantic Monthly*. GE begins *Middlemarch*.
1870	Mar	To Berlin and Vienna, returning in May.
	May	'The Legend of Jubal' appears in *Macmillan's*. First of six visits to Oxford.
1871	Feb–Mar	Interested in buying a country house.
	May–Sept	At Shottermill, with Tennyson as neighbour. 'Armgart' appears in *Macmillan's* in July. GE severely ailing after returning to London.
	Dec	*Middlemarch*, Book I appears. The novel concludes with Book VIII in December 1872, when it is published, 4 vols.
1872	May–Aug	At Redhill, Surrey.
	Sept	First of several visits to Six Mile Bottom. Then to Germany for three weeks at Bad Homburg.
1873	June	To France and Germany for two months, with two weeks at Bad Homburg. GE visits synagogues and continues reading books on Jewish subjects in preparation for *Daniel Deronda*.
	Sept–Oct	At Blackbrook, near Bickley, still wanting a country house.
1874	Feb	First episode of renal pain afflicting GE until her death.
	May	*The Legend of Jubal and Other Poems* published.

	June–Sept	At Earlswood Common, Redhill.
	Oct	In Paris and Brussels for two weeks.
1875	June–Sept	At Rickmansworth, Herts.
1876	Jan	*Daniel Deronda*, Book I, appears. The novel concludes with Book VIII in September and is published in 4 vols in late August.
	June	To France and Switzerland through August.
	Dec	GE and GHL buy the Heights at Witley.
1877	June	Last visit to Cambridge, then to Witley through late October.
1878	Jan	Publication of Cabinet Edition of GE's works begins.
	June	Last visit to Oxford, then to Witley through mid-November, GE writing *Impressions of Theophrastus Such*.
	Nov 30	GHL dies at Priory of enteritis, 61 years of age.
1879	Jan	GE begins work on remaining manuscripts of GHL's *Problems of Life and Mind*, which she will publish in two volumes.
	Feb	Sees Cross for first time since GHL's death.
	May	*Theophrastus Such* published. GE goes to Witley through October.
	Nov	In London again, sees Cross frequently over next few months.
1880	May	Marries Cross in St George's, Hanover Square.
	June	In Venice, on their honeymoon, Cross leaps into canal.
	July	They return to Witley and move to 4 Cheyne Walk, Chelsea, in early December.
	Dec 22	GE dies at 4 Cheyne Walk of renal failure, 61 years of age. Buried in Highgate Cemetery one week later.

Portions of this Chronology draw upon Gordon S. Haight's 'Chronology of George Eliot's Life', *Letters*, I, pp. xxiii–xxxiv, and John Rignall's 'Time Chart', *Companion*, pp. 472–7.

Introduction

Visits from friends and from those who are likely to
become friends I am very fond of, but I have a horror of
being interviewed and written about ...

George Eliot to Lord Houghton, 9 April 1878[1]

This book brings together recollections of a reclusive Victorian giant. George
Eliot (Mary Anne Evans, 1819–80) was certainly not the only famous writer
of her time to protect her privacy, but she may have been alone in guarding
it so fiercely that meeting her seemed an event of mythic proportions. There
was no way to prepare. Apart from the 'apocryphal stories' *The Times* would
mention in its obituary,[2] only her novels and poetry were available – and
these, rumour had it, she never allowed to be mentioned in her presence. So
completely did George Eliot distance herself from 'newspaper chit-chat', as
she called it, so consistently did she withhold information even from standard reference sources, that she managed to ensure distrust of everything
printed about her personal life by declining to offer anything in its place.[3]
For those accomplished or important enough to hope for an introduction,
it was safest to assume nothing. This axiomatic ignorance is what gives
so many recollections of George Eliot their special quality: a reverent but
eager curiosity, mixed with a delighted capacity for surprise. It makes them
uncommonly appealing.

The selections in this volume range in length from a few words to a few
pages, in tone from gushing adoration to biting condemnation, and in
origin from manuscript letters and diaries to published works of all sorts:
histories, correspondence, memoirs, 'literary lives', biographies, autobiographies, periodicals, and newspapers. The aim of this eclectic approach has
been to provide as richly detailed a record as possible of the experience of
meeting, or in a few cases merely seeing, George Eliot. The comparison to a
picture-gallery is tempting here, but since this particular gallery is devoted
to one sitter, its attractions lie nearly as much in what the portraits reveal
of their diverse creators as in what they convey of their common subject.
Accordingly, head-notes typically indicate the connection between the
author of an entry and George Eliot, with subsequent notes adding any
further recollections of her from this author, clarifying allusions and background, and filling in relevant contexts.

As a rule, modern biographies of George Eliot quote, or quote from, about
forty recollections of her. These vary in nature; some are remarks, others
essays; some are observations, others explorations. Altogether, however,
they have formed nothing less than a canon of reminiscence: the basis,

along with her letters and journals, of our current perceptions of George Eliot's distinctive personal character. These documents have had staying-power for good reasons. Some describe George Eliot at times in her life about which relatively little material remains: Charles Bray's account of her at twenty-two, for example, or John Chapman's diary entries when she lodged with him after moving to London. Others have become classics by virtue of their intimacy, poignancy, warmth, wit, personal devotion, vivid detail, and quality of witness – with credit due respectively to John Walter Cross, William Hale White, Lucy Clifford, Nina Lehmann, Edith Simcox, Mary Augusta Ward, and Henry James. These writers' recollections, along with the other standards, are fully represented here.[4]

This volume also features a large assortment of recollections which appear to have remained outside the biographical tradition. It would be an exaggeration to say that these unfamiliar sources demand a radical revision of the George Eliot, complex and contradictory, who emerges from the familiar ones. But they do complicate her character and cir-cumstances even further, often in richly modulated ways. We now have more detailed pictures both of her unhappiness as a schoolgirl and of her popularity among her classmates. Her time as a London journalist also comes into different focus; she seems already to have been think-ing of herself as a novelist-to-be, and she appears not only as the mod-est young woman known for her prodigious learning but also as a sharp observer on the margins, listening, analysing, taking mental notes. In Germany, her scandalous elopement with a married man seems to have hardened her defences (they put even Franz Liszt on his guard). But now the translator of Strauss and Feuerbach and the editor of the *Westminster Review* – for that is how she was introduced in Weimar and Berlin – comes more into her own conversationally and socially, almost as if she is rehearsing in a foreign tongue for her impending role as one of the most private of public figures back home. The dozens of fresh recollections of George Eliot in her years of fame range too widely for easy summary, but a few striking perspectives may be noted here: her subtle, incomplete replacement of outspoken revolt by patient kindliness, spiced with a per-fect contempt for feigning, fawning or flattery; her interest in fashion and fashionable gossip, tempered with indifference to both; her pain in being recognized, offset by her pleasure in being appreciated; her joking laughter, which quite suddenly unseats her self-conscious gravity; her distinctly non-imperial respect for alien social traditions; the room in her heart for the transparent needs of children, with freezing retraction from any presump-tion of entitlement; and above all, the way her plaguing lack of self-con-fidence moves in step with an endlessly energetic, assured, and daunting *focus*. 'She received me with dignity' recalls the American playwright Steele MacKaye, took my letter, read it deliberately, and then for the first time looked intently at my face, at the same time extending her hand to me with charming frankness. In another moment I was perfectly at home and forgot everything in the presence of this charming woman, for she is the most fascinating and the ugliest woman that I ever saw in my life.[5]

It is a defining moment. With George Eliot there is such concentration, such attention with concentration, that everything becomes important. Nothing escapes. Her interlocutor can forget everything – not uncommon in these recollections – because George Eliot forgets nothing. Some found this stifling, insufferable. For others it was transcendent.

In the official *Life*, J.W. Cross disallows 'remembered sayings by George Eliot, because it is difficult to be certain of complete accuracy, and everything depends upon accuracy'.[6] As it happens, one noticeable feature of recollections of George Eliot is how seldom they include direct quotations. Indeed several persons mention that, contrary to their expectations, she said nothing memorable. Even so, Cross's idea that everything depends upon accuracy is scarcely an enabling principle for a volume of this sort. Did George Eliot really tell Charlotte Eastman, in the garden of a Swiss hotel, that she would rather hear her voice complimented than hear *Romola* complimented? Possibly: Lord Acton notes her 'suspiciousness of accustomed praise' (for her susceptibility to unaccustomed praise, see Candace Wheeler Stimson's recollection).[7] Did George Eliot really rise at a London dinner party and recite, in tears, John Hay's ballad 'Jim Bludso', after pronouncing it 'one of the finest gems in the English language'? It seems less than likely; but we do hear (at third-hand, unluckily) that she asked after Hay when she met Bret Harte, saying that one of his poems 'was the finest thing in our language'.[8] The similar phrasing suggests textual transmission; but the problem lies in what is being transmitted, and independent evidence is wanting. Andrew Carnegie, who never met George Eliot, quotes her as saying,

I can imagine the coming of a day when the effort to relieve human beings in distress will be as involuntary upon the part of the beholder as to clasp this mantel would be this moment on my part were I about to fall.

This comment also appears in the periodical press, but there a vase topples from the mantel and, after involuntarily catching it, George Eliot draws a hopeful analogy: a future when people involuntarily catch each other. Ten years later this second version surfaces again, but now the vase is 'a costly bit of Sèvres china'.[9] From such iterations we can at best infer that George Eliot may have expressed the fundamental idea common to both versions, which is, from other evidence, characteristic of her thinking.

Problems of accuracy also arise outside the scope of 'remembered sayings'. In some cases (chiefly inconsistencies in dates), history can correct memory. Others are less clear – for instance, several conflicting versions of what 'usually' happened at George Eliot's famous Sunday gatherings. Here it may be reasonable to conclude that since no one report is likely to be definitive, they are all true in the sense that if her receptions followed some basic script, it simply changed in details from time to time. (James Sully, a careful observer and long-term Sunday guest, suggests as much.[10]) In any case, when a significant problem of historical accuracy arises, I have noted it; when it does so in contexts amenable to evidence, I have addressed it. Within the realm of personal recollections, however, historical accuracy can be chimerical. What 'really happened' is that a certain person met George Eliot and formed a certain impression. That accepted, the very lack of uniformity can be compelling. It affords an amplitude of perspectives on the mysteries of genius, highly individual and idiosyncratic, with great varieties of colour and interest, by those who had the privilege to witness it and took the trouble to share what they saw.

Many of course did not, including some of George Eliot's most famous (and talkative) acquaintances. If Charles Dickens wrote an account of his meetings and meals with her, someone else must find it; his entry here consists of comments others said he made. Anthony Trollope refrained on principle; his entry too is a token, but still revealing.[11] John Ruskin's diary for 9 February 1874 laconically reports, 'Called on George Eliot, but felt wretchedly exhausted and ill.' Matthew Arnold, who met her two years later, made no entry at all. Clara Schumann played several times with George Eliot in attendance, and they dined together; but of her surviving diary entries, none mentions George Eliot. H. Rider Haggard remarks that Nicholas Trübner (who knew George Eliot quite well) had an 'extremely epigrammatic and amusing' description, but he does not repeat it. Nor does Mary Collier recount Lewis Pelly's 'good stories'. The usually voluble Mary Clarke Mohl records only that 'Mr. and Mrs. Lewes have been to dine and breakfast here. She is the George Eliot who wrote "Adam Bede." We are excellent friends. Adieu.' An even briefer glimpse comes from Margaret Warren, who in the Dulwich Gallery saw 'George Eliot (alive) looking at the pictures.' (Her brother John may or may not have shared news of his Sunday call in July 1865; her diaries do not say.) But absolutely the least helpful reference appears in relation to the notorious forger T.J. Wise: 'He clearly remembers his meeting with George Eliot.'[12]

If these and other losses are matters for regret, it is also true that the greatest challenge of compiling this volume was deciding what to leave out. That process brought me to a new understanding of the moment in *Barchester Towers* when Anthony Trollope, faced with 'disposing' of so many characters in the third and final volume, half blames his publisher for the problem: 'Oh, that Mr Longman would allow me a fourth! It should transcend the other three as the seventh heaven transcends all the lower stages of celestial bliss.'[13] My one volume stretched its contractual seams early on. Mr Palgrave forbidding me a second, the notes now refer to those recollections which did not seem quite so sublime until falling under the axe. Especially difficult has been disposing – in Trollope's sense now – of George Henry Lewes. Although long passages devoted solely to Lewes have been omitted, he plays an integral part in many others focused on George Eliot, just as he did in the fabric of her life. Finally it seemed unfair to fill his place with ellipses, so he has remained a constant presence in these pages.

The problem of what to exclude came up too with certain features of George Eliot's person, behaviour, and surroundings. Readers will hear more than once that she resembled a horse (or Dante or Savonarola), sat in an armchair to the left of the fireplace (with Lewes to the right), had a musically enchanting voice, and lived in a charming villa set apart from the road by a high wall. Occasionally a repetition is informative: Lucy Clifford finds a subtle link to Jonathan Swift's Houyhnhnms; T.A. Trollope recalls that George Eliot herself 'playfully disclaimed any resemblance to Savonarola'; Charles Warren Stoddard and James Sully mention that the gate in the high wall, once the bell was rung, mysteriously unlocked on its own.[14] Even when repetitions are merely repetitious, however, it proved impossible to prune them all without inserting even more clumsily interfering ellipses than were already present. I have also left intact a few recollections' introductory paragraphs, even when they do not feature George Eliot, if they help stage the drama of meeting her.

Part IV covers George Eliot's twenty years of productive fame. Here the problem of omission was compounded by one of arrangement. Recollections of George Eliot in this period far outnumber those before and after it combined – and their authors' personal or social connections with her vary proportionately. Arranged chronologically, as in the other parts, the recollections in Part IV seemed disjointed, an effect of their multiple settings (personal meetings, receptions, dinner parties and musical events, university visits, and so on). After several experiments, they ended up in sections organized mainly around these settings. This arrangement gives Part IV needed continuity, but it also produces three other conspicuous results. First, the chronology resets with each new section (acceptable, I believe, because the span of years in this part is smaller than its range of relations and locales). Second, some entries qualify for inclusion in more than one section. Nina Lehmann would fit into 'Some Younger Women', but meeting George Eliot in France has put her in 'The Continent'. Similarly, an occasional entry in 'Eton, Cambridge, and Oxford' or 'The Countryside' would fit in 'A Few Good Friends', since George Eliot visited good friends in these places (and is sometimes with them, too, in 'Out and About in London'). Third, most recollections with multiple settings have been split up, with cross-references; the ones left intact could not be easily divided. In other words, the arrangement of entries in Part IV has not been haphazard, but it has also resisted perfect consistency.

Some slight variation also occurs in assigning responsibility for second-
and third-hand recollections. The name of the person assigned responsibility
appears in italic above the recollection itself. Usually this person is the
author of the book or article from which a recollection is taken, even if this
author did not meet George Eliot but instead reports upon someone who
did. Thus William Moore's brief description of George Eliot as a teenager
(in Part I) appears in an entry by Edgar Wakeman, who quotes Moore in his
article. Similarly, a recollection from an anonymous 'American lady' (in 'The
Continent' in Part IV) appears under Andrew Carnegie, who got the story
from this lady's friend. However, when a reported recollection is extensive
and allegedly verbatim (as with Mary Sibree Cash and Susanna Chapman
in Parts I and II), the reported speaker, not the author, has been assigned
responsibility. Here the actual author appears in the source-reference following the recollection, with the relation between author and reported speaker
clarified in the head-note. (For convenience this arrangement is also used in
a few entries in 'Vignettes' in Part IV.)

The index in this volume functions as a partial glossary by briefly
annotating any substantive reference in a recollection not glossed in the
notes. Accordingly, a reader who wants to know who Charles Lewes was,
or whether and where he appears in a recollection, will simply look under
'Lewes, Charles'.[15] The same rule applies to places, organizations, titles of
books and periodicals, pieces of music, and works of art. Principal entries
usually appear under the names of authors, composers, and artists, with
cross-references from the named works, unless that introduces an unnecessary step in reference. Occasionally notes have been needed to provide leads
to index headwords. A recollection by Bessie Rayner Parkes Belloc in Part II
refers to several portraits of George Eliot but does not mention the artists
who made them, so a note was required; information about the portraits,
however, appears in the index under the artists' names. More than a few
notes also cite secondary recollections not included as main entries in this
volume. The first note under Eliza Lynn Linton's recollection in Part IV cites
both Theodore Watts-Dunton, who agreed with Linton on George Eliot's
manner, and Henry Buxton Forman, who did not. Since neither Watts-
Dunton nor Forman has a main-entry recollection here, the index alone will
lead a reader to what they – or any other author of a secondary recollection –
said about George Eliot.

Finally, a few editorial principles. (1) In transcribing manuscript sources,
I have tried to keep in mind the reader's convenience, but also to convey
some flavour of the original (as when Mary Gladstone Drew misspells
someone's name, ends a sentence without a full point or begins one with
a lower-case letter) without taking recourse to different fonts and typo-
graphical oddities. With M^r and M^{rs} I have brought down the superscript
letters. Dashes that replace full points at ends of sentences have remained.

Insertions are not noted, but strike-outs with replacements appear in angular brackets (this and related practices are noted in Abbreviations). I have added a paragraph indention when a space after a sentence clearly indicates a break, and underlining in manuscripts appears as italics in the text. (2) Since the *Oxford Dictionary of National Biography* is widely available online, relevant persons cited in a recollection's head-note – but only there – are tagged with the abbreviation *ODNB* if they have a main entry in the *ODNB*. (3) A parenthetical page number in a head-note refers to the source of the recollection, cited just above the head-note. (4) *Sic* has been omitted when *Eliot* has been misspelled as *Elliot* or *Lewes* as *Lewis*. (5) All ellipses are mine unless otherwise noted. Since most entries are excerpts, I have avoided opening and closing ellipses unless I have omitted words from the first or last sentence itself. (6) To prevent confusion, in a few recollections I have silently removed embracing quotation marks in the source text.

NOTES

1. *Letters*, VII, 19.
2. 'George Eliot', 24 December 1880, p. 9. As the *Literary World* wittily put it, in George Eliot's case the record seemed to be 'unusually incorrect' ('Literary Table-Talk', 31 December 1880, pp. 457–8 (p. 458)).
3. For the 'chit-chat', see *Letters*, v, 239. As for inquirers denied answers, the single exception was the American writer Elizabeth Stuart Phelps, for whom George Eliot clarified a few points from her past (VI, 163–4; IX, 355). 'I believe that I have in no other instance', she noted, 'given any other reply to biographical questions than, that I decline to furnish personal information' (VI, 68).
4. Two significant exceptions: John Chapman and Edith Simcox. Chapman's entries on George Eliot in his 1851 diary (see *n.* 4 of Charles Bray's recollection in Part I) are so interlocking and localized day-by-day that they finally seemed inappropriate for this collection, even had limits on space permitted reprinting them. Taking their place is a hitherto unknown recollection by Chapman's wife Susanna (Part II). Simcox's 'Autobiography of a Shirtmaker' (see Abbreviations) is more detailed yet, and counts in and of itself as a volume of recollections of George Eliot. It has been used in the annotations and for one main-entry recollection (in Part III). The two other recollections by Simcox (in 'Vignettes' in Part IV, and in Part VII) come from her obituary of George Eliot.
5. See 'Other Personal Meetings' in Part IV.
6. I, p. vii.
7. See respectively Emma Nason in 'The Continent', Acton in 'Vignettes', and Stimson in 'The Continent', all in Part IV.
8. See 'An English Gentleman' in 'Out and About in London' in Part IV.
9. Andrew Carnegie, *An American Four-in-Hand in Britain* (New York: Scribners, 1883), p. 143; [John Clifford], 'Scraps from the Editor's Waste Basket: XIII: Stretch out a Helping Hand', *General Baptist Magazine*, 83 (1881), 309; and Carlos Martyn, *William E. Dodge: The Christian Merchant* (New York and London: Funk & Wagnalls, 1890), p. 96.
10. See 'Sunday Gatherings at the Priory' in Part IV.

11. See respectively 'Vignettes' in Part IV, and Part V.
12. *The Diaries of John Ruskin*, ed. by Joan Evans and John Howard Whitehouse, 3 vols (Oxford: Clarendon Press, 1956–59), III, 773; William Bell Guthrie, 'Matthew Arnold's Diaries: The Unpublished Items' (unpublished doctoral thesis, University of Virginia, 1957), p. 1058 (Arnold dined with her on Boxing Day 1876; see *Letters*, IX, 184 *n.* 2); Berthold Litzmann, *Clara Schumann: Ein Künstlerleben nach Tagebüchern und Briefen*, 4th edn, 3 vols (Leipzig: Breitkopf and Härtel, 1910–12); H. Rider Haggard, *The Days of My Life: An Autobiography*, ed. by C.J. Longman, 2 vols (London: Longmans, Green, 1926), I, 210–11; *A Victorian Diarist: Extracts from the Journals of Mary, Lady Monkswell 1873–1895*, ed. by E.C.F. Collier (London: Murray, 1944), pp. 109–10; M.C.M. Simpson, *Letters and Recollections of Julius and Mary Mohl* (London: Kegan Paul, Trench, 1887), p. 228; Margaret Leicester Warren, *Diaries*, 2 vols ([Taunton]: n.p., 1924), II, 245; and Wilfred Partington, *Forging Ahead: The True Story of the Upward Progress of Thomas James Wise, Prince of Book Collectors, Bibliographer Extraordinary, and Otherwise* (New York: Putnam, 1939), p. 233, where Partington quotes this statement only to doubt its veracity.
13. Ed. by Michael Sadleir and Frederick Page (Oxford: Oxford University Press, 2009), p. 178 (Chapter 43).
14. All in Part IV: Clifford, Stoddard, and Sully in 'Sunday Gatherings at the Priory', Trollope in 'The Countryside'.
15. Anyone familiar with Margaret Harris and Judith Johnston's splendid edition of *The Journals of George Eliot* will see that I have taken it as my model both for an explanatory index and for my explanation of how such an index works.

Part I
Mary Anne Evans
1819–49

THE LITTLE GIRL

J.W. Cross

The little girl very early became possessed with the idea that she was going to be a personage in the world; and Mr Charles Lewes has told me an anecdote which George Eliot related of herself as characteristic of this period of her childhood. When she was only four years old she recollected playing on the piano, of which she did not know one note, in order to impress the servant with a proper notion of her acquirements and generally distinguished position. ... She was not in these baby-days in the least precocious in learning.[1] In fact, her half-sister, Mrs Houghton – who was some fourteen years her senior – told me that the child learned to read with some difficulty; but Mr Isaac Evans says that this was not from any slowness in apprehension, but because she liked playing so much better. ...

... During one of our walks at Witley, in 1880, my wife mentioned to me that what chiefly remained in her recollection about this very early school-life was the difficulty of getting near enough the fire in winter, to become thoroughly warmed, owing to the circle of girls forming round too narrow a fireplace. This suffering from cold was the beginning of a low general state of health: also at this time she began to be subject to fears at night – "the susceptibility to terror" – which she has described as haunting Gwendolen Harleth in her childhood.[2] The other girls in the school, who were all naturally very much older, made a great pet of the child, and used to call her "little mamma," and she was not unhappy except at nights; but she told me that this liability to have "all her soul become a quivering fear," which remained with her afterwards, had been one of the supremely important influences dominating at times her future life. Mr Isaac Evans's chief recollection of this period is the delight of the little sister at his homecoming for holidays, and her anxiety to know all that he had been doing and learning. ...

The first book that George Eliot read, so far as I have been able to ascertain, was a little volume published in 1822, entitled 'The Linnet's Life,' which she gave to me in the last year of her life, at Witley.

1

It bears the following inscription, written some time before she gave it to me:–

"This little book is the first present I ever remember having received from my father. Let any one who thinks of me with some tenderness after I am dead, take care of this book for my sake.[3] It made me very happy when I held it in my little hands, and read it over and over again; and thought the pictures beautiful, especially the one where the linnet is feeding her young."

It must, I think, have been very shortly after she received this present, that an old friend of the family, who was in the habit of coming as a visitor to Griff from time to time, used occasionally to bring a book in his hand for the little girl. I very well remember her expressing to me deep gratitude for this early ministration to her childish delights; and Mr Burne Jones has been kind enough to tell me of a conversation with George Eliot about children's books, when she also referred to this old gentleman's kindness. They were agreeing in disparagement of some of the books that the rising generation take their pleasure in, and she recalled the dearth of child-literature in her own home,[4] and her passionate delight and total absorption in Æsop's Fables (given to her by the aforesaid old gentleman), the possession of which had opened new worlds to her imagination. Mr Burne Jones particularly remembers how she laughed till the tears ran down her face in recalling her infantine enjoyment of the humour in the fable of Mercury and the Statue-seller.[5] Having so few books at this time, she read them again and again, until she knew them by heart. One of them was a Joe Miller jest-book, with the stories from which she used greatly to astonish the family circle.[6]

Life, I, 14–15, 16–17, 19–20

NOTES

John Walter Cross (1840–1924), a banker, married GE on 6 May 1880, a little over seven months before her death. Other recollections by him appear below in this part, in 'The Continent' in Part IV, and in Parts V and VI.

1. According to Grace Gilchrist Frend, however, GE's 'grave intensity of thought was early evinced; for it is related of her that as a little girl at school, bidden to write an essay on God, the child sat down and drew for her sole essay a large eye' ('Great Victorians: Some Recollections of Tennyson, George Eliot and the Rossettis', *Bookman*, 77 (1929), 9–11 (p. 9)).

2. Cross quotes from *Daniel Deronda*, where Gwendolen's 'helpless fear' is compared to 'a brief remembered madness, an unexplained exception from her normal life' (ed. by Graham Handley (Oxford: Oxford University Press, 1988), p. 51 (Book I, Chapter 6)).

3. It is now in the Beinecke Rare Book and Manuscript Library, Yale University.

4. Not necessarily a complaint, since GE objected to didacticism. She criticized Hannah More for it (*Letters*, I, 245), found Thomas Hughes's *Tom Brown's Schooldays* (1857) 'an unpleasant, unveracious book' (*Journals*, 81), and took

exception to *Westward Ho!* (1855) because Charles Kingsley liked to deduce morals ('Belles Lettres', *Westminster Review* (1855), repr. in *Essays*, pp. 311–19, and in *Writings*, pp. 110–18). But *The Child's Own Book* (1830) – with its traditional fairy tales and legends, well-known poems and nursery rhymes – she remembered fondly (*Shirtmaker*, p. 21), and Mary Sibree Cash heard GE declare in 1842 of Shakespeare that 'in educating a child his would be the first book she would place in its hands' (*Life* new edn, p. 51). The Evans household had *The Pilgrim's Progress, The Vicar of Wakefield, The History of the Devil*, and of course Aesop (Haight, p. 7).

5. It is uncertain which version of Aesop GE read as a child, but the only one she mentions specifically (in 1840) is by Jefferys Taylor (*Letters*, I, 38): '*Mercury*, wishing much to know | How he was liked by men below | Disguised himself in shape of man, | As well we know such beings can; | And to a sculptor's shop descended, | Where statues of the gods were vended: | There *Jupiter* and *Juno* stood, | In bronze, in marble, and in wood; | *Mars* and *Minerva* richly drest, | And *Mercury* amongst the rest. | Then said he to the sculptor, | "Sir, Pray what's the price of *Jupiter*?" | The sum was named without delay: | "And what dy'e ask for *Juno*, pray?" | "A trifle more," the man replied; | "She's more esteem'd than most beside:" | "And what for *that* upon the shelf?" | Said *Mercury*, nodding at himself. | "O!" said the man, "his worth is small; | I never charge for him at all; | But when the other gods are bought, | I always give him in for nought"' (*Æsop in Rhyme, with Some Originals* [1820], 3rd edn (London: Baldwin and Cradock, 1828), p. 31).

6. The best known eighteenth-century jestbook. Originally it had considerable erotic content, but later editions were milder (Robert Hutchinson, 'Introduction', *Joe Miller's Jests: or, The Wits Vade-Mecum*, comp. by John Mottley (1739; repr. New York: Dover, 1963), pp. v–xix).

ON READING NOVELS AS A CHILD

George Eliot

I shall carry to my grave the mental diseases with which they have contaminated me. When I was quite a little child I could not be satisfied with the things around me; I was constantly living in a world of my own creation, and was quite contented to have no companions that I might be left to my own musings and imagine scenes in which I was chief actress. Conceive what a character novels would give to these Utopias. I was early supplied with them by those who kindly sought to gratify my appetite for reading and of course I made use of the materials they supplied for building my castles in the air.

To Maria Lewis, formerly her teacher, 16 March 1839, in *Letters*, I, 22

NOTE

GE (*ODNB*) was nineteen years old when she wrote this letter to the friend who was probably the most important influence upon her at the time, a strictly evangelical governess at Mrs Wallington's school, which GE had left seven years before. Another recollection by GE appears in Part III.

'SHE ALWAYS CRIED WHEN THE HOLIDAYS CAME'

'An old schoolmate'

She and I were school-fellows at Mrs. Wallington's boarding school, Nuneaton. There were about forty pupils, and Marianne Evans joined us at the age of thirteen.[1] Although two or three years the younger, I can recall many little incidents with regard to her. She was of moderate height, neither stout nor thin, with fair hair and complexion. She was decidedly not a pretty girl, but she certainly could boast of a beautiful set of white, even teeth. I am very fond of music, and soon after her arrival I was attracted towards the drawing room, where she was practising, by the air of Bishop's 'Bid me discourse,' which I then heard for the first time, and which, child as I was, I knew was being played with the greatest taste and feeling. But what called forth my childish admiration and wonder the most was the amazing rapidity with which she mastered all her lessons, the contents of pages being made her own by simply reading them once or twice over. She was ever at the head of her class, and certainly loved learning for learning's sake; so devoted, indeed, was she to it that, to the aston-ishment and perhaps disgust of her schoolfellows, she always cried when the holidays came. She learned, besides English and music, dancing and French, and was considered a good French scholar.[2] She was of quiet, studious habits, and, though generally preferring book to play, was nevertheless a favorite among us. She stayed with Mrs. Wallington two years.[3]

'George Eliot', *Woman's Journal*, 23 April 1881, p. 131 (writer untraced)

NOTES

1. She came in 1828, eight years old.
2. Baptized *Mary Anne*, GE was still spelling her name *Marianne* in a school notebook six years later (Haight, pp. 3, 552).
3. She stayed four years. A Miss Shaw recalled GE around this time 'at a children's party at her mother's – about 9 or 10 years old, she thinks. M.A. sat apart from the rest, and Mrs. Shaw went to her and said, "My dear, you do not seem happy; are you enjoying yourself?" "No, I am not," said M.A. "I don't like to play with children; I like to talk to grown-up people"' (*Letters*, I, 41 *n.* 3). Compare a neighbour's impres-sion of GE at twelve: '"a queer, three-cornered, awkward girl," who sat in corners and shyly watched her elders' (Blind, p. 16). In 1885 Maria Lewis described GE at Mrs Wallington's as 'so very loveable, but unhappy, given to great bursts of weeping; finding it impossible to care for childish games and occupations' (*Shirtmaker*, p. 223).

'THE "CLEVER GIRL" OF THE SCHOOL'

Alfred L. Scrivener

There are some of "George Eliot's" schoolfellows living among us now, but their recollection is somewhat vague. From those whom we have questioned, we gather that their famous schoolfellow was a shy and reserved girl, with a profusion of light hair, puffed in front, above strongly lined, almost masculine features. One recalls that the first time she sat down to the piano, Mary Ann Evans astonished her companions by her knowledge of music, and her command of the instrument. She mastered her lessons with an ease which excited wonder. She read with avidity. She joined very rarely in the sports of her companions. A reserve, which was not the result of pride in her intellectual superiority, but rather of modest diffidence and shrinking sensibility, prevented her from forming any close friendship among her schoolfellows.

She was the "clever girl" of the school, "but" says one of her schoolfellows "We never thought –" what? that her true rank would be among England's greatest.

'George Eliot', *Nuneaton Observer and District Advertiser*,
31 December 1880, p. 5

NOTE
This unsigned article is almost certainly by Alfred Lester Scrivener (1845–86), who edited the *Nuneaton Observer* from 1877 to 1881 and was noted as writing on GE in this paper after her death (*Shirtmaker*, p. 142).

MUSIC AND TEARS

The child of a schoolmate

My mother was a little girl at school in Coventry[1] when Mary Ann Evans was one of the older pupils, and long before "George Eliot" became famous, had constantly related to her children traits in the character of a school-fellow whom, even then, her comrades felt to be quite different from themselves. ... In her classes for English composition, Mary Ann Evans was, from her first entering the school, far in advance of the rest, and while the themes of the other children were read, criticised, and corrected in class, hers were reserved for the private perusal and enjoyment of the teacher, who rarely found anything to correct. Her enthusiasm for music was already very strongly marked, and her music master, a much-tried man, suffering from the irritability incident to his profession, reckoned on his hour with her as a refreshment to his wearied nerves, and soon had to confess that he had no more to teach her. In connection with this proficiency in music, my mother recalls her sensitiveness at that time as being painfully extreme. When there were visitors, Miss Evans, as the best performer in the school, was sometimes summoned to the parlour to play for their amusement, and, though suffering agonies from shyness and reluctance, she obeyed with all readiness, but, on being released, my mother has often known her to rush to her room and throw herself on the floor in an agony of tears.

Her schoolfellows loved her as much as they could venture to love one whom they felt to be so immeasurably superior to themselves, and she had playful nicknames for most of them. My mother, who was delicate, and to whom she was very kind, was dubbed by her "Miss Equanimity." A source of great interest to the girls, and of envy to those who lived further from home, was the weekly cart which brought Miss Evans new laid eggs and other delightful produce of her father's farm.

'Our Monthly Letter to Friends Abroad', *Our Times*, 1 (1881), 290–6
(pp. 293–4; writer untraced)

NOTE

1. Run by sisters Mary and Rebecca Franklin; GE boarded there in 1832–35, aged twelve to fifteen. Gillian Sutherland describes the curriculum as 'the conventional female one: English, arithmetic, history, and drawing, with French, German, and music as extras' ('Franklin, Mary (1800–1867)', *ODNB*); Audrey Anderson adds geography, catechism, and 'scientific dialogues', with strong emphasis upon French ('The Franklins and George Eliot', *George Eliot Fellowship Review*, 12 (1981), 15–17 (p. 16)). Strong emphasis should fall also upon catechism. Patty Jackson, a schoolmate, recalled that the girls had 'very thorough Scriptural instruction. We were taught to regard the Divine Word as worthy of our unreserved reliance and to know that only as we kept close to its vital truths could we hope to avoid the snares & temptations that might openly or insidiously beset our path through life' (letter from Martha (Mrs Henry) Barclay to Charles Lewes, 3 June 1884, Yale). GE herself recalled that 'the girls used to get up prayer-meetings in which she took a leading part, reproaching herself when she found she could not be carried away like the others' (*Shirtmaker*, p. 152).

MINERVA, IN NEED

Mathilde Blind

One of her schoolfellows, who knew her at the age of thirteen, confessed to me that it was impossible to imagine George Eliot as a baby; that it seemed as if she must have come into the world fully developed, like a second Minerva. Her features were fully formed at a very early age, and she had a seriousness of expression almost startling for her years. ...

... She stood aloof from the other pupils, and one of her schoolfellows, Miss Bradley Jenkins, says that she was quite as remarkable in those early days as after she had acquired fame.[1] She seems to have strangely impressed the imagination of the latter, who, figuratively speaking, looked up at her "as at a mountain." There was never anything of the schoolgirl about Miss Evans, for, even at that early age, she had the manners and appearance of a grave, staid woman; so much so, that a stranger, happening to call one day, mistook this girl of thirteen for one of the Misses Franklin, who were then middle-aged women.[2] ... Being greatly in advance of the other pupils in the knowledge of French, Miss Evans and Miss Jenkins were taken out of the general class and set to study it together;[3] but, though the two girls were thus associated in a closer fellowship, no real intimacy apparently followed from it. The latter watched the future "George Eliot" with intense interest, but always felt as if in the presence of a superior, though socially their positions were much on a par. This haunting sense of superiority precluded the growth of any closer friendship between the two fellow-pupils. All the more startling was it to the admiring schoolgirl, when one day, on using Marian Evans's German dictionary, she saw scribbled on its blank page some verses, evidently original, expressing rather sentimentally a yearning for love and sympathy. Under this granite-like exterior, then, there was beating a heart that passionately craved for human tenderness and companionship!

Blind, pp. 14, 17–18

NOTES

Mathilde Blind (1841–96, *ODNB*), a poet, published in 1883 the first full-length biography of GE, 'pioneering, sensitive, uneven and sympathetically feminist' (Graham Handley, 'Mathilde Blind', *George Eliot Review*, 29 (1998), 65–9 (p. 65)).

1. She may however have played with other pupils here more than she had at Mrs Wallington's. A schoolmate reported that 'she was always interested in their childish games and sports on the lawn' (Blanche Colton Williams, *George Eliot: A Biography* (New York: Macmillan, 1936), pp. 23–4).
2. Both were under thirty-five. Their niece Rebecca Franklin Sharp, a pupil at the time, later described Mary Franklin as 'motherly, warm-hearted, businesslike, bustling, and self-sacrificing in the extreme', but Rebecca as 'quite in the clouds. ... A sort of intangible, diffusive, and yet exquisite elaboration of diction clothed all her ideas ... as made it a perfect puzzle to catch her real meaning. ... Aunt Mary said to me one day, you may be sure not boastingly, "My dear, I have always endeavoured from my youth up to live to the glory of God." Aunt Rebecca, being asked by my mother if she minded getting old, replied, "I do not think of anything so paltry"' (Irene Morris, 'George Eliot Reminiscences', *Coventry Herald*, 7–8 November 1919, suppl., p. 5).
3. 'We sat side by side on the same form', GE wrote in 1879, 'translating Miss Edgeworth into French when we were girls' (*Letters*, VII, 197; see also I, 213–14).

WALKING BY THE ALPHABET

'A fellow-pupil'

She learned everything with ease ... but was passionately devoted to music, and became thoroughly accomplished as a pianist. Her masters always brought the most difficult solos for her to play in public, and everywhere said she might make a performer equal to any then upon the concert stage. She was keenly susceptible to what she thought her lack of personal beauty, frequently saying that she was not pleased with a single feature of her face or figure. She was not especially noted as a writer, but so uncommon was her intellectual power that we all thought her capable of any effort; and so great was the charm of her conversation, that there was continual strife among the girls as to which of them should walk with her. The teachers had to settle it by making it depend upon alphabetical succession.

George Willis Cooke, *George Eliot: A Critical Study of Her Life, Writings and Philosophy* (Boston: Osgood, 1883), pp. 8–9 (quoted source untraced)

'A BEING BORN TO INSPIRE LOVE'

Elizabeth M. Bruce

Going one day in an omnibus from Highgate to Ludgate Hill, we chanced to occupy a seat opposite a lady who remarked upon the beauty of some green leaves that were peeping from between the lids of the sketch-book which we held in our hand. We replied that these leaves were brought from the grave of George Eliot, which we had just visited. Her face brightened instantly, and she said:

"Ah, she was a friend of mine. Our youth had the same surroundings. We were schoolmates in the long ago."

None save those as enthusiastically eager as we regarding the life of this great novelist, can judge the delight with which we caught this statement and proceeded to avail ourselves of the opportunity thus opened to us. We asked the privilege of sitting by the lady who had become suddenly of such interest in our eyes, and proceeded with a list of questions which she most freely and cheerfully answered.

"Was Mary Ann Evans a precocious child – did she give evidence in those beginning years of the great mental faculties which afterward distinguished her?"

"No; she was not distinguished at school. She did not pass for a child of more than usual mental ability."[1]

"Was she a child of cheerful disposition?"

"She was unusually so. Our memory of her in those years is of an exceedingly bright and happy child, who lived in the light of her own cheerful spirit, and made sunshine for all who surrounded her."[2]

"Was she beautiful?"

"No, she would not have been called beautiful in the sense in which this world judges. But she had beautiful laughing eyes, and no one could look into them without being made happier. Do you remember how she describes Dinah in 'Adam Bede'? 'There was such kindness in the eyes.[3] They seemed rather to be shedding love than making observations.' That is a perfect description of the mission to which her own beautiful eyes seemed devoted."

"Was she a favorite among her companions?"

"Yes; eminently so. This was true, not alone of her childhood, but of all the afterward of her life. She was a being born to inspire love to all by whom she was surrounded."

"Did this peculiarly happy spirit of her childhood continue with her in her later life?"

In answer to this question a look of sadness overspread the kind face of our companion and a mournful shake of the head made us sure that the story of her childhood was a disconnected fragment of joy broken from the after part of an existence in which life's great intense tragedy began.

'Communications: England's Holy Ground', *Christian Leader*,
27 October 1881, p. 3

NOTES

Elizabeth Meugens (Mrs James E.) Bruce, née Hurd (1830–1911), was an American writer of juvenile fiction, a Universalist pastor, and an advocate for the higher education of women. Another recollection by her appears in Part VII.

1. Explicitly at odds with the three preceding recollections. See also Charles D. Lockwood in 'The Countryside' in Part VI.
2. Of these years GE later mentioned '"the absolute despair I suffered from of ever being able to achieve anything"' (*Life*, I, 36).
3. An error for 'There was no keenness in the eyes' (*Adam Bede*, ed. by Carol A. Martin (Oxford: Oxford University Press, 2008), p. 21 (Book I, Chapter 2)).

BUTTER AND CHEESE

Frederic R. Evans

After leaving school Mary Anne Evans returned to her father's house at Griff, and diligently continued her studies. There may have been some sense of loneliness at times after her mother's death,[1] through the frequent absence of her father and brother on business, and from lack of companions of similar tastes to her own, but she was well supplied with books,[2] had masters in foreign languages and music,[3] and was given to sitting up late absorbed by her work, so much so that on one occasion the house was entered and robbed without her being any the wiser. Presently, on her elder sister's marriage [in May 1837], she became manageress of her father's house. One rather imaginative biographer says that she became "dairy woman as well, and that her right hand being larger than her left was accounted for by her labours in crushing the curd."[4] Whereas my father's account was that "she could never be persuaded to touch a cheese, and never made a pound of butter in her life."

'George Eliot Centenary', *Coventry Herald*, 7–8 November 1919,
suppl., p. 10; also in *Coventry Standard*, 7–8 November 1919, p. 9

NOTES

The Revd Canon Frederic Rawlins Evans (1842–1927) was GE's nephew, her brother Isaac's eldest son. He never met her, prevented by the estrangement between father and aunt, but was quoted 'as saying it would be a life-long regret not to have known her' (*Shirtmaker*, p. 232).

1. She returned to Griff in spring 1835, twelve years old; Christiana Evans died on 3 February 1836. Two years later, asking Maria Lewis to pay a visit, GE described her situation as 'most inattractive', promising 'no amusement farther than a book, a walk, and a dialogue' (*Letters*, I, 4). Maria Congreve, who visited there *c.*1834, remembered 'how she heard the piano approaching the house, the contrast between the open piano and books and her father's appearance' (*Shirtmaker*, p. 147).

2. What we know of GE's reading during her six years at Griff comes from some four dozen letters to only five people (*Letters*, I, 3–86). Nearly two-thirds are to Maria Lewis, whose evangelical fervour GE had shared since her days at Mrs Wallington's. All the letters tend to display books for the recipients' approval, so the picture they give of GE's reading is probably incomplete – perhaps seriously so, since reading can be a relatively easy and safe means of secret transgression. The list includes canonical prose and poetry in English, Greek, Latin, French, and Italian; ecclesiastical histories, sermons, and religious essays, as well as biographies and autobiographies of Evangelicals and missionaries (but also of Samuel Johnson, Sir Walter Scott, and Louis XIV); a few scientific treatises; plus the Bible, studied daily with a concordance and commentaries. See Avrom Fleishman, 'George Eliot's Reading: A Chronological List', *GE-GHLS*, 54–5 (2008), suppl., pp. 1–76, esp. pp. 5–7.

3. Joseph Brezzi, a local language teacher, gave weekly lessons in Italian and (from March 1840) in German.

4. Exact quotation untraced, but the anecdote is in Blind, p. 20, and repeated by GE's cousin William Mottram in *The True Story of George Eliot in Relation to "Adam Bede," Giving the Real Life History of the More Prominent Characters* (London: Unwin, 1905), p. 78.

'"A PLAIN SORT O' HANGEL"'

Edgar L. Wakeman

My own discoveries of those who had lived about Griff when the members of George Eliot's family were all together here, include John Marston, an old wheelwright, whose smithy still stands near the steading; "Bill" Jaques, seventy-seven years of age, a schoolmate of Isaac Evans and a playmate of the novelist; the old man Crabstock, whose generosity with a single turnip lost him his place at Griff; Richard Emmons, living at Stockingford, now a very old man, and reputed by the peasantry to have "hatfuls of sovereigns," who was, in turn, field labourer, house servant, and footman at Griff, footman at "Birds Lodge,"[1] and finally house servant back at Griff for Isaac Evans, until his death in 1890; and William Moore, now seventy-three years of age, who lives at Collycroft, a little miners' hamlet between Bedworth and Griff.

The latter is the son of the veritable Dame Moore, who kept the Dame's School opposite Griff's gates.[2] It was in his mother's cottage that George

Eliot, then a maiden of fifteen, gathered together the children of the miners and cottiers about Griff, and taught them, for several years, for an hour or two each Sunday morning, and then took her ragged charges to Chilvers Coton Church.[3] In the afternoon they all came together again, when she taught them from Scriptures and some simple melodies of the time.

"God bless ee, sir!" said old William Moore, the tears trickling down his wrinkled face. "I can see 'er hangel face – she wor a plain sort o' hangel, sir – this minute afore my eyes. Mary Ann teached t' class fur nigh onto five year. She wot a great scholard, sir, an' a 'ooman true!"

'George Eliot's Early Home', *Leeds Mercury*, 18 May 1895, suppl., p. 1

NOTES

An American journalist, Edgar L. Wakeman (1848–1934?) searched out GE's old home about 1892–93. He was so critical of her remaining relations that the *Leeds Mercury* printed an apology praising them for all the good they had done ('The Family of "George Eliot"', 1 June 1895, suppl., p. 4).

1. That is, Bird Grove, Foleshill, Coventry, where GE and her father moved in March 1841, when he retired.
2. GE was there in 1824.
3. *c.*1834; Bernard Taylor, a Nuneaton silk-weaver, recalled of GE later that she 'used to come Sunday mornings to Chilvers Coton Church with her father and sister in a carriage. They were the only family that came in a carriage at that time, 1839 to 1840' ('George Eliot: Recollections of Her Early Life', *New-York Daily Tribune*, 26 February 1899, suppl., p. 13).

A VISIT TO LONDON

J.W. Cross

Mr Isaac Evans himself tells me that what he remembers chiefly impressed her was the first hearing the great bell of St Paul's. It affected her deeply.[1] At that time she was so much under the influence of religious and ascetic ideas, that she would not go to any of the theatres with her brother, but spent all her evenings alone reading.[2] A characteristic reminiscence is that the chief thing she wanted to buy was Josephus's 'History of the Jews'; and at the same bookshop where her brother got her this, he bought for himself a pair of hunting sketches.

Life, I, 39–40

NOTES

For John Walter Cross, see above. Other recollections by him appear below in this part, in 'The Continent' in Part IV, and in Parts V and VI.

1. The service less so: she was indignant with the chanters, 'for it appears with them a mere performance, their behaviour being that of schoolboys, glad of an

opportunity to titter unreproved' (*Letters*, I, 7). The great bell (5.7 tons), cast in 1709, was 'remarkably fine and clear in its tone', producing 'the musical note A, concert pitch' (E.M. Cummings, *The Companion to St. Paul's Cathedral* ..., 35th edn (London: Author, 1869), p. 35). The visit was in August 1838, when GE was eighteen years old.

2. In the daytime, however, she and Isaac 'worked hard at seeing sights' (*Letters*, I, 6). Greenwich Hospital interested her particularly, perhaps because of its charitable role; she saw it with its full complement of 2,710 old or disabled seamen. (John H. Brady's *New Pocket Guide to London and Its Environs* (London: Parker, 1838), pp. 288–92, devotes more space to the Hospital Chapel than to any other feature.) At this time, Mary Sibree Cash recalled, GE's piety 'led her to visit the poor most diligently in the cottages round her own home. Many years after, an old nurse of mine told me that these poor people had said after her removal, "We shall never have another Mary Anne Evans"' (*Life*, I, 156).

WRITING POETRY

Robert Evans

My Aunt Mary Ann (Geo Eliot) was staying with her half sister (Mrs Houghton) at Bagginton near Coventry in 1839 at the same time there was visiting my Uncle Henry Houghton his Sister then unmarried, during this visit writing poetry had been a topic of conversation Aunt Houghton produced a "scrap book" and in it M.A.E. wrote three pieces – "A Sonnet" – "The Song" and the "Farewell" alluded to[1] – the authoress remarked how badly she had written them and either then or soon after the leaves were cut out and Miss Houghton was allowed to take them ...

Letter to John Walter Cross, 1 March 1881, Yale

NOTE

Robert Evans (1832–1911) was GE's nephew, also visiting Frances Houghton at this time, mid-July.

1. Earlier in the letter Evans mentions this poem, GE's first published work, which appeared in the *Christian Observer*, January 1840 (see Haight, pp. 25–6). As soon as she wrote 'Farewell', GE sent her 'doggerel lines, the crude fruit of a lonely walk last evening' (*Letters*, I, 27) to Maria Lewis, who urged her to submit it for publication.

THE POWER OF SOUND

J.W. Cross

[Her] remarks on oratorio[1] are the more surprising, because two years later, when Miss Evans went to the Birmingham festival in September 1840, previous to her brother's marriage, she was affected to an extraordinary degree, so much so that Mrs Isaac Evans – then Miss Rawlins – told me that the attention of people sitting near was attracted by her hysterical sobbing. And in all her later life music was one of the chiefest delights to her, and especially oratorio.

Life, I, 44

NOTE

For John Walter Cross, see above. Other recollections by him appear in 'The Continent' in Part IV and in Parts V and VI.

1. Early in November 1838, just short of nineteen years old, GE declared it 'little less than blasphemy' that the tenor John Braham, presumed at this time to be Jewish, was in Mendelssohn's *St Paul* (1836) – adding that she would hardly regret it 'if the only music heard in our land were that of strict worship' (*Letters*, I, 13). By October 1840, again writing to Maria Lewis, she was praising Handel's and Haydn's oratorios, and recommending that her friend read Wordsworth's poem 'On the Power of Sound' (pub. 1835) (I, 68).

AT FOLESHILL, COVENTRY, WITH THE BRAYS

'A correspondent'

In this somewhat more populous neighbourhood she soon became known as a person of more than common interest, and, moreover, as a most devoted daughter and the excellent manager of her father's household.[1] There was perhaps little at first sight which betokened genius in that quiet gentle-mannered girl, with pale grave face, naturally pensive in expression; and ordinary acquaintances regarded her chiefly for the kindness and sympathy that were never wanting to any. But to those with whom, by some unspoken affinity, her soul could expand, her expressive grey eyes would light up with intense meaning and humour, and the low, sweet voice, with its peculiar mannerism of speaking – which, by-the-way, wore off in after years[2] – would give utterance to thoughts so rich and singular that converse with Miss Evans, even in those days, made speech with other people seem flat and common. Miss Evans was an exemplification of the fact that a great genius is not an exceptional, capricious product of nature, but a thing of slow laborious growth, the fruit of industry and the general culture of the faculties. At Foleshill, with ample means and leisure, her real education began. She took lessons in Greek and Latin from the Rev. T. Sheepshanks,[3] then head master of the Coventry Grammar School, and she acquired French, German, and Italian from Signor Brezzi. An acquaintance with Hebrew was the result of her own unaided efforts. From Mr. Simms, the veteran organist of St. Michael's, Coventry, she received lessons in music, although it was her own fine musical sense which made her in after years an admirable pianoforte player. Nothing once learned escaped her marvellous memory; and her keen sympathy with all human feelings, in which lay the secret of her power of discriminating character, caused a constant fund of knowledge to flow into her treasure-house from the social world about her. Among the intimate friends whom she made in Coventry were Mr. and Mrs. Charles Bray – both well known in literary circles. In Mr. Bray's family she found sympathy with her ardent love of knowledge and with the more enlightened views that had begun to supplant those under which (as she described it) her spirit had been grievously burdened.[4] Emerson, Froude, George Combe, Robert Mackay, and many other men of mark, were at various times guests at Mr. Bray's house at Rosehill while Miss Evans was there either as inmate or occasional visitor; and many a time might have been seen, pacing up and down the lawn, or grouped under an old acacia, men of thought and research, discussing all things in heaven and earth, and listening with marked attention when one gentle woman's voice was heard to utter what they were quite sure had been well matured before the lips opened. Few, if any, could feel themselves her superior in general intelligence, and it was amusing one day to see the amazement of a certain Doctor, who, venturing on a quotation from Epictetus to an unassuming young lady, was, with modest politeness, corrected in his Greek by his feminine auditor.[5] One rare characteristic belonged to her which gave a peculiar charm to her conversation. She had no petty egotism, no spirit of contradiction: she never talked for effect. A happy thought well expressed filled her with delight; in a moment she would seize the point and improve upon it – so that common people began to feel themselves wise in her presence, and perhaps years after she would remind them, to their pride and surprise, of the good things they had said.

'George Eliot's Early Life', *Pall Mall Gazette*, 30 December 1880, p. 10
(author untraced)

NOTES

1. They moved to Foleshill on 17 March 1841, when GE was twenty-one. Sara Hennell later reported that GE 'felt it a meager life': '... all the entertaining at home – farmers and so on – was most irksome to her, though she did it all scrupulously ...' (*Shirtmaker*, p. 144); but compare Matilda Betham-Edwards's recollection, *n.* 2, in 'The Countryside' in Part IV. At Foleshill GE's charitable work continued; Mary Sibree Cash wrote that 'on her first visit to us [early in 1841] I well remember she told us of a club for clothing set going by herself and her neighbour Mrs Pears, in a district to which she said "the euphonious name of the Pudding-Pits had been given"' (*Life* new edn, p. 47; for further activities, see pp. 56–7). An unidentified friend of GE's at this time later remarked to Rose G. Kingsley that '"she was the most devoted daughter for those nine years that it is possible to imagine"', to which Kingsley adds, paraphrasing the friend: 'Her father always spent three days in the week away from home and those three days were Miss Evans's holidays, given up to her work and her friends. But on the evenings he was at home, not the most tempting invitation in the world would induce her to leave him' ('George Eliot's County', *Century Magazine*, 30 (1885), 339–52 (p. 351)). In a rare glimpse of GE's father, this friend is also quoted as saying that Robert Evans 'would often

open the front door himself if she chanced to come on the last day of the week. His gruff welcome of "Come to see Mary Anne?" though kindly meant, never failed to make her quake in her shoes, from its grave, severe tone' (p. 351).

2. A mystery. Charles Bray, just below, mentions her 'measured, highly-cultivated mode of expression' at this time, but by most accounts that did not wear off. For GE herself on 'the effect of a peculiarity of speech in conversation', see the recollection by A.G.C. Liddell in 'Eton, Cambridge, and Oxford' in Part IV.

3. He was later asked what sort of pupil GE had been: '"She got on very well for a young lady," he replied, "very well, indeed; but I think if she had been a little longer under my care, it would have done her no harm"' ('George Eliot's Classical Tutor', *Disciple*, 1 (1881), 48–52 (p. 52)).

4. Mary Sibree Cash wrote that the Brays 'were her world, and on my saying to her once, as we closed the garden door together, that we seemed to be entering a Paradise, she said, "I do indeed feel that I shut the world out when I shut that door"' (*Life* new edn, p. 60).

5. Later GE told Oscar Browning that she had '"to comprehend every word"' before she could '"understand anything of a Greek writer"' (Browning, p. 26). The 'Doctor' has remained untraced.

SUN AND SHADE

Charles Bray

I consider my intimate friendship of nine years with Miss Evans (George Eliot) among the bright spots of my life. I saw a great deal of her, we had long frequent walks together, and I consider her the most delightful companion I have ever known; she knew everything. She had little self-assertion; her aim was always to show her friends off to the best advantage – not herself. She would polish up their witticisms, and give them the credit of them. But there were two sides; hers was the temperament of genius which has always its sunny and shady side. She was frequently very depressed – and often very provoking, as much so as she could be agreeable – and we had violent quarrels; but the next day, or whenever we met, they were quite forgotten, and no allusion made to them. Of course we went over all subjects in heaven or earth. We agreed in opinion pretty well at that time, and I may claim to have laid down the base of that philosophy which she afterwards retained.[1] ... At that time we were both very much interested in Phrenology, and in 1844 she had a cast taken of her head by Deville, in the Strand, which is still in my possession. We afterwards took lessons of Mr. Donovan, on Organology, when he was staying at Coventry and converting all the leading men of the city to the truth of the science by the correctness of his diagnosis of character. Miss Evans's head is a very large one, 22 1/4 inches round; George Combe, on first seeing the cast, took it for a man's. The temperament, nervous lymphatic, that is, active without endurance, and her working hours were never more than from 9 a.m. till 1 p.m. The 3rd Volume of Strauss was very heavy work to her, and she required much encouragement to keep her up to it.[2] In her brain-development the Intellect greatly predominates; it is very large, more in length than in its peripheral surface. In the Feelings, the Animal and Moral regions are about equal; the moral being quite sufficient to keep the animal in order and in due subservience, but would not be spontaneously active. The social feelings were very active, particularly the adhesiveness.[3] She was of a most affectionate disposition, always requiring some one to lean upon,[4] preferring what has hitherto been considered the stronger sex, to the other and more impressible. She was not fitted to stand alone. Her sense of Character – of men and things, is a predominatingly intellectual one, with which the Feelings have little to do, and the exceeding fairness, for which she is noted, towards all parties, towards all sects and denominations, is probably owing to her little feeling on the subject, – at least not enough to interfere with her judgment. She saw all sides, and they are always many, clearly, and without prejudice. ...

Although I had known Mary Ann Evans as a child at her father's house at Griff, our real acquaintance began in 1841 ... She was then about one-and-twenty, and I can well recollect her appearance and modest demeanour as she sat down on a low ottoman by the window, and I had a sort of surprised feeling when she first spoke, at the measured, highly-cultivated mode of expression, so different from the usual tones of young persons from the country. We became friends at once. We soon found that her mind was already turning towards greater freedom of thought in religious opinion, that she had even bought for herself Hennell's "Inquiry,"[5] and there was much mutual interest between the author and herself in their frequent meeting at our house. She said of him, "Mr. Hennell seemed to me a model of moral excellence."[6]

> *Phases of Opinion and Experience During a Long Life: An Autobiography*
> (London: Longmans, Green, 1884), pp. 72–6

NOTES

Charles Bray (1811–84, *ODNB*) was a ribbon manufacturer, social reformer, and philanthropist. He and his wife Caroline or 'Cara', née Hennell (1814–1905, *ODNB*), a children's writer, with her sister Sara Sophia Hennell (1812–99, *ODNB*), who wrote on theology, were GE's friends from her Coventry days until the end of her life – the only disruption arising when Cara objected to GE's union with GHL in 1854. 'With all three it is a beautiful and consistent friendship', Cross notes, 'running like a thread through the woof of the coming thirty-eight years' (*Life*, I, 114).

1. Bray takes credit for GE's interest in the unforgiving consequences of human actions, and the moral dangers of orienting those actions towards some reward in a future life. His *Philosophy of Necessity; or, the Law of Consequences; as Applicable to Mental, Moral, and Social Science* (1841) argued for a mental determinism which, once accepted, would compel widespread social reform.

2. For two years GE translated from the German *Das Leben Jesu* by David Friedrich Strauss, who 'proceeds to investigate every episode as told in all four Gospels,

looking first at traditional interpretations, then at historical explanations, and finally offering an argument for reading each episode mythically' (Ashton, p. 52). In February 1846 Cara Bray described GE as 'Strauss-sick' (*Letters*, I, 206); the work appeared anonymously in June. 'She told me', Oscar Browning says, 'that her greatest difficulty was to find the exact English equivalents for German particles' (Browning, 26).

3. 'I am pronounced to possess a large organ of "adhesiveness," a still larger one of "firmness," and as large of conscientiousness' GE wrote in February 1842; 'hence if I should turn out a very weather cock and a most pitiful truckler you will have data for the exercise of faith maugre common sense, common justice, and the testimony of your eyes and ears' (*Letters*, I, 126).

4. One of the most influential statements ever made about GE, and a key motif of Haight's biography. One wonders how specific the comment was, in Bray's mind, to GE's character, since the idea is so commonplace. Compare John Chapman: 'It is the order of nature that women should lean on men, but men have none to lean upon ...' (Gordon S. Haight, *George Eliot & John Chapman: With Chapman's Diaries* (New Haven: Yale University Press; London: Oxford University Press, 1940), p. 158). For the idea in a religious context, see J. Hain Friswell, *The Gentle Life: Essays in Aid of the Formation of Character* (London: Low & Marston, 1870), p. 93; for its (conservative) political expression, see *Victorian Women's Magazines: An Anthology*, ed. by Margaret Beetham and Kay Boardman (Manchester: Manchester University Press, 2001), p. 152.

5. *An Inquiry Concerning the Origin of Christianity* (London: Smallfield, 1838), by Cara's brother Charles Christian Hennell, argues that Christ's life and the spread of Christianity contain 'no deviation from the known laws of nature, nor ... require, for their explanation, more than the operation of human motives and feelings' (2nd edn (1841), p. iv).

6. According to Mary Sibree Cash, GE described him as '"a perfect model of manly excellence"' (*Life* new edn, p. 60).

SCENES OF COVENTRY LIFE

Mary Sibree Cash

I

It was not until the winter of 1841, or early in 1842, that my mother first received (not from Miss Evans's own lips, but through a common friend) the information that a total change had taken place in this gifted woman's mind with respect to the evangelical religion which she had evidently believed in up to the time of her coming to Coventry, and for which, she once told me, she had at one time sacrificed the cultivation of her intellect and a proper regard to personal appearance.[1] 'I used,' she said, 'to go about like an owl, to the great disgust of my brother; and I would have denied him what I now see to have been quite lawful amusements.'

My mother's grief on hearing of this change in one whom she had begun to love was very great; but she thought that argument and expostulation might do much, and I well remember a long evening devoted to it by my father. The discussion is now vividly present to my mind. There was not only on Miss Evans's part a vehemence of tone, startling in one so quiet, but a crudeness in her objections, an absence of proposed solution of difficulties which partly distressed and partly pleased me (siding as I did mentally with my father), and which was in strange contrast to the satisfied calm which marked her subsequent treatment of religious differences.

Upon my father's using an argument (common enough in those days) drawn from the present condition of the Jews as a fulfilment of prophecy,[2] and saying, 'If I were tempted to doubt the truth of the Bible, I should only have to look at a Jew to confirm my faith in it' – 'Don't talk to me of the Jews!' Miss Evans retorted, in an irritated tone; 'to think that they were deluded into expectations of a temporal deliverer, and then punished because they couldn't understand that it was a spiritual deliverer that was intended!' To something that followed from her, intimating the claim of creatures upon their Creator, my father objected, 'But we have no claim upon God.' 'No claim upon God!' she reiterated indignantly; 'we have the strongest possible claim upon Him.'

I regret that I can recall nothing more of a conversation carried on for more than two hours but I vividly remember how deeply Miss Evans was moved, and how, as she stood against the mantelpiece during the last part of the time, her delicate fingers, in which she held a small piece of muslin on which she was at work, trembled with her agitation. ...

II

She attended the service at the opening of a new church at Foleshill[3] with her father, and remarked to me the next day, that looking at the gaily dressed people, she could not help thinking how much easier life would be to her, and how much better she should stand in the estimation of her neighbours, if only she could take things as they did, be satisfied with outside pleasures, and conform to the popular beliefs without any reflection or examination. Once, too, after being in the company of educated persons 'professing and calling themselves Christians,' she commented to me on the *tone* of conversation, often frivolous, sometimes ill-natured, that seemed yet to excite in no one any sense of impropriety.

III

As I knew Miss Evans, no one escaped her notice. In her treatment of servants, for instance, she was most considerate.[4] 'They come to me,' she used to say, 'with all their troubles,' as indeed did her friends generally, – sometimes, she would confess, to an extent that quite oppressed her. When any object of charity came under her notice, and power to help was within her reach, she was very prompt in rendering it. Our servant's brother or sister, or both of them, died, leaving children dependent on friends themselves poor. Miss Evans at once offered to provide clothing and school-fees for one of these, a chubby-faced little girl four or five years of age. Unexpectedly, however, an aunt at a distance proposed to adopt the child. I recollect taking her to say good-bye to her would-be benefactress, and can see her now standing still and subdued in her black frock and cape, with Miss Evans kneeling down by her, and saying, after giving her some money, 'Then I suppose there is nothing else we can do for her.'

IV

In treating of love and marriage, Miss Evans's feeling was so fine as to satisfy a young girl in her teens, with her impossible ideals. The conception of the union of two persons by so close a tie as marriage, without a previous union of minds as well as hearts, was to her dreadful. 'How terrible it must be,' she once said to me, 'to find one's self tied to a being whose limitations you could see, and must know were such as to prevent your ever being understood!' She thought that though in England marriages were not professedly 'arrangés,' they were so too often practically: young people being brought together, and receiving intimations that mutual interest was desired and expected, were apt to drift into connections on grounds not strong enough for the wear and tear of life; and this, too, among the middle as well as in the higher classes. After speaking of these and other facts, of how things were and would be, in spite of likelihood to the contrary, she would end by saying, playfully, 'Now remember I tell you this, and I am sixty!'[5]

She thought the stringency of laws rendering the marriage-tie (at that date) irrevocable, practically worked injuriously;[6] the effect being 'that many wives took far less pains to please their husbands in behaviour and appearance, because they knew their own position to be invulnerable.' And at a later time she spoke of marriages on the Continent, where separations did not necessarily involve discredit, as being very frequently far happier.

Life new edn, pp. 48–9, 54, 55–6, 58

NOTES

The daughter of Charlotte and John Sibree, a dissenting minister, Mary Sibree (1824–95), later Mrs John Cash, became GE's friend soon after GE moved to Foleshill. She sent her extensive recollections to Cross after he published the first edition of the *Life*. In his subsequent one-volume edition, he quoted them under the heading 'Communication from Mrs Cash', pp. 46–60.

1. Apart from GE's letters at the time, this is the only first-hand account of her religious turmoil, which led her in January 1842 to refuse to attend church with her father (she resumed going in May). She was twenty-two years old. For a detailed analysis of the ways GE expressed and controlled this crisis, see Rosemarie Bodenheimer, *The Real Life of Mary Ann Evans: George Eliot, Her Letters and Fiction* (Ithaca and London: Cornell University Press, 1994), pp. 57–84.

2. For example in Thomas Hartwell Horne, *An Introduction to the Critical Study and Knowledge of the Holy Scriptures*, 7th edn, 5 vols (London: Cadell, 1834): 'The prophecies of the Old Testament distinctly announced that the MESSIAH WAS TO

COME, when the government should be utterly lost from Judah. ... The tribe of Judah is no longer a political body; it has no authority or magistrates of its own, but is dispersed and confounded among the other tribes of Jews; its present condition, therefore, is an evident mark that Shiloh, or the Messiah, is already come' (I, 293).

3. St Paul's District Church, 'a neat brick edifice, in the modern style of architecture, situate on the heath, erected by subscription, and a grant from the church building society, in 1843' (Francis White & Co., *History, Gazetteer, and Directory, of Warwickshire* ... (Sheffield: White, 1850), p. 582).

4. A unidentified friend from this time later said that GE never allowed a maid to tend her drawing-room fire: 'She always had a man-servant in to do it, for she could not bear, she said, to see a woman putting on coals' (Kingsley, 'George Eliot's County', p. 351).

5. She was about twenty-three, Mary about sixteen.

6. A point of delayed and momentous significance. After falling in love with GE, GHL could not divorce his wife Agnes, since legally he had condoned her adultery by registering under his own name her children by another man (Ashton, p. 102).

MEETING RALPH WALDO EMERSON

Moncure Daniel Conway

Emerson remembered well that visit to the Brays at Rosehill [on 13 July 1848], when he sat with them under the beautiful acacia, and talked with Charles Bray on the "Philosophy of Necessity," which had reached him in Concord and spoke to his mind. George Eliot was then Miss Evans of Birdgrove, where Emerson's essays were among her friends in loneliness. When Emerson had talked a few moments with her he suddenly said, "What one book do you like best?" She instantly answered, "Rousseau's Confessions." He started, then said, "So do I. There is a point of sympathy between us."[1] George Eliot cherished the remembrance of meeting Emerson under these happy auspices, and also in London, where she played the piano at evening, in Dr. Chapman's house, without perhaps knowing that Emerson's ear for such music was what he used to call "marble."[2]

Emerson at Home and Abroad, English and Foreign Philosophical Library, 19 (London: Trübner, 1883), p. 275

NOTES

An American freethinker and social reformer who for many years preached at London's South Place Chapel, Moncure Daniel Conway (1832–1907, *ODNB*) knew Emerson well and met GE a few times. Other recollections by him appear in 'A Few Good Friends' and 'Out and About in London' in Part IV. Conway has a brief description of one of GE's Sunday gatherings in his *Autobiography: Memories and Experiences*, 2 vols (Boston and New York: Houghton, Mifflin, 1904), II, 164–5.

1. An exchange spawning at least three additional versions. (a) From Conway himself, just after he published this account: 'I have been informed by one who was present

that Emerson's question was not "What one book do you like best?" but "What one book do you find the most interesting?" To this she answered, "Rousseau's Confessions," and he agreed with her in the words I have used' ('Emerson and George Eliot', *The Times*, 31 January 1883, p. 7). (b) From Mary Sibree Cash, *c.*1886: 'She told us that he had asked her what had first awakened her to deep reflection, and when she answered, Rousseau's "Confessions," he remarked that this was very interesting, inasmuch as Carlyle had told him that very book had had the same effect upon his mind' (*Life* new edn, p. 104). (c) From 'a private journal page of April 1901', recording Cara Bray's recollection of the incident: 'A mild exclamation made Mrs. Bray inquire what had surprised him. "I was asking Miss Evans what work had most impressed her, and she tells me 'Rousseau's Confessions,' and I exclaimed that it was strange, as that had been my own experience"' (Warwick H. Draper, 'George Eliot's Coventry Friends', *Cornhill Magazine*, n.s. 20 (1906), 225–36 (p. 235)). For Rousseau as GE's 'great inspiration', see Barbara Hardy, *George Eliot: A Critic's Biography* (London: Continuum, 2006), pp. 37–44.

2. Emerson stayed with John Chapman at 142 Strand from March to July 1848, before GE moved there. GE did see Emerson later in London, but in April 1873 (*Letters*, IX, 113). At Rosehill he struck her as 'the first *man* I have ever seen'; Emerson, in turn, 'expressed his admiration many times to Charles – "That young lady has a calm, serious soul ..."' (Cara Bray in *Letters*, I, 271 *n*. 6). Mary Sibree Cash heard the remark (from GE herself) differently: '"That young lady has a calm, clear spirit"' (*Life* new edn, p. 104).

CROSSING THE COL DE BALME

Mathilde Blind

So they started on their travels, going to Switzerland and Italy by the approved route, which in those days was not so hackneyed as it now is. To so penetrating an observer as Miss Evans there must have been an infinite interest in this first sight of the Continent. But the journey did not seem to dispel her grief, and she continued in such very low spirits that Mrs. Bray almost regretted having taken her abroad so soon after her bereavement.[1] Her terror, too, at the giddy passes which they had to cross, with precipices yawning on either hand – so that it seemed as if a false step must send them rolling into the abyss – was so overpowering that the sublime spectacle of the snow-clad Alps seemed comparatively to produce but little impression on her. Her moral triumph over this constitutional timidity, when any special occasion arose, was all the more remarkable.[2] One day when crossing the Col de Balme from Martigny to Chamounix, one of the side-saddles was found to be badly fitted, and would keep turning round, to the risk of the rider, if not very careful, slipping off at any moment. Marian, however, insisted on having this defective saddle in spite of the protest of Mrs. Bray, who felt quite guilty whenever they came to any perilous places.

Blind, pp. 50–1

NOTES

For Mathilde Blind, see above. She had this story from Cara Bray.

1. GE's father died in the night of 30 May 1849. On 12 June the Brays took her abroad, returning in July and leaving GE in Geneva. She returned in March 1850.
2. When GE first came to look at her Geneva lodgings, 'she was so horrified with the forbidding aspect of the stairs, that she declared she would not go up above the first floor; but when she got inside the door she was reconciled to her new quarters' (*Life*, I, 232).

'QUEL ESPRIT VIGOUREUX'

Louis Wuarin

Un petit détail qui montre bien quel esprit vigoureux c'était que George Eliot:

Un jour elle imagina un moyen de soulager son esprit "en proie à la pensée", et pour se calmer, pour oublier un moment les graves problèmes ou les visions d'avenir qui la hantaient[1] (mais dont elle gardait le secret pour elle, aimant à se tenir le plus possible dans l'ombre), elle se remit à ses mathématiques qu'elle avait autrefois poussées assez loin. Elle prit un professeur,[2] mais bientôt celui-ci se retira, déclarant qu'elle était assez avancée pour se tirer d'affaire toute seule.

[A small detail which shows well what a vigorous mind George Eliot had:

One day she devised a way to relieve her mind 'racked with thought', and to calm down, to forget for a moment the serious problems or the visions of the future which haunted her (but which she kept to herself as a secret, since she liked to remain in the shadow as much as possible), she started doing mathematics again which she had formerly studied rather far. She hired a professor, but soon the latter withdrew, claiming that she was advanced enough to manage on her own.]

'Correspondence Étrangères: Suisse', *Livre*, 3 (1881), 198–203 (p. 201);
translated by Véronique Maisier

NOTES

Louis Wuarin (1846–1927), a Swiss sociologist and economist, was a professor at the University of Geneva. He presents this recollection as told to him by François D'Albert Durade, with whose family GE lodged in Geneva.

1. 'When I was at Geneva', GE told D'Albert Durade after returning to England, 'I had not yet lost the attitude of antagonism which belongs to the renunciation of *any* belief – also, I was very unhappy, and in a state of discord and rebellion towards my own lot' (*Letters*, III, 230–1).
2. Untraced. Cross says that 'inspired by Professor de la Rive's lectures, she had been greatly interested in mathematical studies', especially geometry (*Life*, III, 423). During GE's stay, Arthur Auguste de la Rive gave a course of lectures on experimental physics intended especially for women (*Letters*, I, 325).

'UNDERSTOOD EVERYTHING WONDERFULLY'

Lord Acton

M. d'Albert Durade. Geneva October 30, 1884[1]
She was charming and aff[ection]nate. Clung to Mme. d'Albert.[2] Sought
work to distract her from violent emotion.
Never betrayed authorship.
Spoke French badly, but knew it well, & could hardly go back to English.
Understood everything wonderfully
Pantheistic.[3] Spinoza. never sp[oke] of Comte.
Spiritualist – always disputing with him never with his wife.[4]
Sometimes heard Meunier.
Translated Latin & Greek for occupation.
Her master of math found that she was in the integral calculus.
Her eye sometimes flashed but never spoke with passion.
Remarkable for intelligence, not yet for imagination.
Appears as Lewes's wife at Geneva [in June 1860] –

> CUL, Add. MS 5627, fol. 61[r]; reproduced with kind permission of
> Lord Acton and the Syndics of Cambridge University Library

NOTES

The historian John Emerich Edward Dalberg Acton, 1st baron (1834–1902, *ODNB*),
came to know GE in 1878 and deeply respected her place in the history of ethical
thought. While reading the proofs of Cross's *Life* and preparing his review of that
work for *Nineteenth Century*, Acton discovered that D'Albert Durade was still alive,
paid him a visit, and made these notes. Another recollection by Acton appears in
'Vignettes' in Part iv.

1. Acton later used some of this material: 'At Geneva she is still remembered with
   affection. Her days were spent obscurely, in the hard work which was her refuge
   from loneliness, from despondency, from the absence of a woman's joys and
   cares. She kept the secret of her authorship, and avoided aggressive speech; but
   those whom she trusted knew her as a pantheist and a stubborn disputant. She is
   described as talking well but showily ...' ('George Eliot's "Life"', *Nineteenth Century*,
   17 (1885), 464–85 (p. 470)).
2. 'She kisses me like a mother', GE told the Brays, 'and I am baby enough to find
   that a great addition to my happiness' (*Letters*, i, 322; GE has a warm reminiscence
   of 'Maman' in v, 393). D'Albert Durade recalled in a letter to Cross 'comment Miss
   Evans se trouvait à l'aise dans l'intimité de notre intérieur de famille [how much
   Miss Evans felt at ease in the intimate life of our family]' (15 February 1885, Yale).
3. 'For years of my youth,' GE wrote in 1869, 'I dwelt in dreams of a pantheistic sort,
   falsely supposing that I was enlarging my sympathy' (*Letters*, v, 31).
4. Something not conveyed to her friends back home. She found the D'Albert
   Durades 'evangelical and conservative', but admired their breadth of culture,
   and soon loved Monsieur 'as if he were father and brother both': 'His conversation is charming. I learn something every dinner-time' (*Letters*, i, 314,
   316, 317).

'THE VERY LEARNED SCHOLAR, MISS EVANS'

Bessie Rayner Parkes Belloc

Driving from Warwick through the arching elms of that embowered nook of the Shires, with a very dear and gifted companion[1] (a descendant of Oliver Cromwell), we reached Coventry ... There, being at the time myself just two-and-twenty,[2] I was taken to make the acquaintance of the very learned scholar, Miss Evans. Not Abelard in all his glory, not the Veritable Isaac Casaubon of French Huguenot fame, not Spinosa in Holland or Porson in England, seemed to my young imagination more astonishing than this woman, herself not far removed from youth, who knew a bewildering number of learned and modern languages, and wrote articles in a first-class quarterly.[3]

I remember the scene vividly, though, unfortunately, after so long an interval of time I can remember none of the conversation. George Eliot had a bad headache, and received us kindly and politely, but with an air of resigned fatigue. Mr. Bray himself was a great talker; always full of ideas, somewhat vigorously expressed. I do not remember that Miss Evans said any noteworthy thing,[4] but I looked at her reverently, and noticed her extra-ordinary quantity of beautiful brown hair (always to the last a great charm), and that we all went out and stood on a sort of little terrace at the end of the garden, to see the sunset, and that the light fell full on her head and was reflected from her kind blue eyes. And as night fell, my companion and I were driven back to Warwick, and I did not see the learned scholar again till the next year in London, the year 1851.

'Dorothea Casaubon and George Eliot', in *In a Walled Garden* (London: Ward and Downey, 1895), pp. 1–24 (pp. 4–6); first publ. in *Contemporary Review*, 65 (1894), 207–16

NOTES

Bessie (Elizabeth) Rayner Parkes (1829–1925, *ODNB*), later Mme Louis Belloc, was a journalist and campaigner for women's rights. After meeting again in London, she and GE were close friends for several years. Another recollection by her appears in Part II.

1. Sara Hennell, who introduced her to GE (Joanne Shattock, *ODNB*).
2. Some confusion here. Parkes was twenty-two on 16 June 1851, but later refers to 1851 as 'the next year', even though GE did not debut in a 'first-class quarterly', the *Westminster Review*, until 1851. GE returned to Rosehill from Geneva in late March 1850, went away in April, and came back in June for seven months. If this meeting did not take place in 1850, and if indeed it was at Rosehill, it occurred sometime between late March and late September 1851.
3. Each figure in the list was in some respect controversial or unorthodox, so it con-veys Parkes's idea of GE as a person with both rare erudition and daring independ-ence of thought.
4. A point made several times in recollections of GE, although variously stated. William Bell Scott found her 'the most bland and amiable of plain women, and most excellent in conversation, not finding it necessary to be always saying fine

things' (*Autobiographical Notes of the Life of William Bell Scott*, ed. by W. Minto, 2 vols (New York: Harper, 1892; repr. New York: AMS Press, [1970]), II, p. 71). Charles Dilke confided to his 'Memoirs' that although he worshipped GE's books, she 'never says anything in conversation' (BL, Dilke Papers, Add. MS 43932, fol. 115, reproduced with kind permission of Fr Charles Dilke and the British Library Board). Similar remarks come from Noah Porter (Part II), Charles Godfrey Leland, and Edward Dowden (both in 'Sunday Gatherings at the Priory' in Part IV).

Part II
An Anonymous London Journalist 1850–53

'UNDER-BRED AND PROVINCIAL'

Eliza Lynn Linton

It was at John Chapman's [on 29 November 1850] that I first met George Eliot – then Marian Evans, having adopted neither her pseudonym nor her style and title of George Lewes's wife.[1] "Confession is good for the soul," they say; and I will candidly confess my short-sighted prejudices with respect to this – to be – celebrated person. These were her undeveloped as well as her insurgent days.[2] She was known to be learned, industrious, thoughtful, noteworthy; but she was not yet the Great Genius of her age, nor a philosopher bracketed with Plato and Kant,[3] nor was her personality held to be superior to the law of the land, nor was she recognised as a conventional gentlewoman: – in those days, indeed, she was emphatically not that! She was essentially under-bred and provincial; and I, in the swaddling-clothes of early education and prepossession as I was, saw more of the provincial than the genius, and was repelled by the unformed manner rather than attracted by the learning. She held her hands and arms kangaroo fashion; was badly dressed; had an unwashed, unbrushed, unkempt look altogether; and she assumed a tone of superiority over me which I was not then aware was warranted by her undoubted leadership. From first to last she put up my mental bristles, so that I rejected then and there what might have become a closer acquaintance had I not been so blind, and so much influenced by her want of conventional graces.[4]

'A First Meeting with George Eliot', in *My Literary Life*
(London: Hodder and Stoughton, 1899), pp. 85–103 (pp. 94–6);
first publ. in *The Woman at Home*, 4 (1895), 443–7

NOTES

Like GE, Elizabeth Lynn Linton (1822–98, *ODNB*) had come to London to live by her pen. She published her best-known novels in the 1870s and 1880s. Other recollections by her appear in Part III and in 'Sunday Gatherings at the Priory' in Part IV.

1. Rosemarie Bodenheimer dates GE's insistence upon being called *Mrs Lewes* from June 1857, when 'family excommunication' resulted from GE's explanatory letter,

signed *Marian Lewes*, to her brother Isaac's lawyer (*The Real Life of Mary Ann Evans: George Eliot, Her Letters and Fiction* (Ithaca and London: Cornell University Press, 1994), p. 129). 'Our marriage is not a legal one', she wrote, 'though it is regarded by us both as a sacred bond' (*Letters*, II, 349).

2. Ten years before this essay appeared, William Hale White classed GE as one of 'the Insurgents' (see his recollection below). Similarly, George Smith remarks that when GE 'first knew Lewes she was a member of a coterie of clever men and women who were supposed to look down on "society" and on the ordinary woman. George Eliot herself, at that stage, affected to despise the weaknesses of her sex, and the relationship between men and women' ('Recollections of a long and busy life', NLS, MS 23191, fol. 217).

3. Ironic, but not untrue. At the height of her fame and just after her death GE was widely considered a serious philosopher; Frederic Harrison, for example, indirectly compares her in 'knowledge, philosophic power, and moral seriousness' to Kant while drawing an explicit parallel between GE's and Plato's epigrammatic 'golden words of wisdom'(*The Choice of Books and Other Literary Pieces* (London: Macmillan, 1886), p. 220).

4. According to GE, however, Linton declared when they first met that 'she was "never so attracted to a woman before as to me" – I am "such a loveable person"' (*Letters*, I, 337).

GRAND AND SMALL

Elsie Draper

I have a very happy recollection of George Eliot. I was very young, three or four years of age, and was staying with the Brays. George Eliot was then paying a visit to her old friends soon after or about the time she removed to London. There was a grand piano in the room, the Brays being very musical, and as I was playing with another child George Eliot went before me and guided me so I should not bump against the instrument and hurt myself. She was always very kind to children and was trying to save my head.

'Reminiscences of George Eliot and the Brays', *Coventry Herald*,
7–8 November 1919, suppl., p. 3

NOTE

Elsie (Mrs E. Herbert) Draper, née Hennell (*c*.1849–1924), was the daughter of a Coventry ribbon manufacturer related to Sara Hennell and Caroline Bray. The occasion recalled here was probably in early January 1851.

142 STRAND

Susanna Chapman

When I first saw George Eliot ... it was one evening at the house of a lady who had asked us to meet at tea.[1] She was about twenty-four at that time, and I had been told that she was very plain, but when I saw her she did not give me that impression.[2] She had such fine eyes, and the upper part of her face was so good, that it quite redeemed the lower part, which was large for a woman, and heavily set. I remember being struck to find how short she was when she rose from the tea-table, for I had imagined a tall woman as I saw her seated. She was very quiet in her manner, and although she had given no promise then of her doings in the future, she was always spoken of as being clever and well-read. We lived at that time in the Strand, where we had a large house.[3] My husband, as you know, was the editor of a quarterly review, in which everything tending towards advanced thought appeared. Our house was frequented by the rising literary lights of the day – Herbert Spencer, George Henry Lewes, and others; while many leading Americans made it their headquarters, among them Emerson, but he had left before George Eliot came to stay with us. To give you an idea of how literary was our set, I can remember being in my drawing-room of an evening when I was the only one out of forty people who had not written a book! George Eliot, living then in the country, longed to see more of life, and we invited her to spend a fortnight with us. She found our house and the friends who surrounded us so congenial to her tastes, that she arranged to make her home with us, and we were glad to have her.[4] The great charm of our house to her was its wealth of books, in which she revelled. For a short time she assisted my husband in editing the review, but to this work she never took very kindly.[5] She had then done nothing beyond translating Strauss, for which she was paid the sum of £20. But there is very little doubt that she was meditating her future work. It was slowly fermenting in her mind, as she used often to say to me that it was the great ambition of her life to write a good *novel*, and when any book was under discussion she would remark, 'I hope I may do better than that!'

How well I can see her now; small in person, and always beautifully neat in her dress. She used to say she loved my breakfast-table, it was so bright and cheery, such a contrast to those in Germany.[6] It was a joke between us when she came to breakfast, that she used too much soap, wasted it, I said, for I used to tell her she seemed to have washed all the colour out of her face! Meal-time was always a cheerful one with us, the conversation that enlivened it was often of the best, as you may imagine, but occasionally George Eliot was the victim of a fool; and I remember her disgust one day when an American gentleman detained her just as she was leaving the room to ask her a riddle, the *first,* as he said, he had ever made. So standing with her back to the door she waited with patience while he very gravely asked her the following –

'Why is *Punch* a dealer in hardware?'

The subtle wit of even a George Eliot was not equal to the burden of a reply; so, with much delight at his own ingenuity, the American gave the profound answer – 'Because he deals in *irony*!'

This was too much for George Eliot, and she fled from the tormentor.[7] But she never forgot to inquire of me if he had perpetrated a *second* riddle.

My aunt was living with me at the time, and during her last illness I was much occupied and fatigued nursing her.[8]

'Ah,' said George Eliot to me one day, 'you will never regret your labour of love. The greatest consolation I have now is in looking back at the time when I nursed my father in his last illness. There was much weariness and fatigue in all I underwent then; but I am glad to think that I was able to do it.' ...

I remember once two friends of mine coming to stay with me, an old lady and her daughter, simple, gentle-hearted people, and not at all cultured in the sense of being well-read. To them George Eliot took immediately. She played beautifully on the piano, and my friends were delighted; so she said, 'I have not very much time, but if you enjoy my playing I shall be glad to play to you whenever you can come to my room.'[9] After my friends left us George Eliot said to me, 'If I were not myself, I would rather be Miss — (the daughter) than any one I know. Intellectuality is all very well, but there is something beautiful in the love of that girl for her mother, and the sincere simple natures of those two women are delightful.' ...

It was at our house that George Eliot first knew Herbert Spencer and George Henry Lewes.[10] We often went to the theatre together, as Mr. Lewes was at that time theatrical critic for the *Leader*. George Eliot's long and faithful friendship for Lewes began at first in fun. He was one of the most good-tempered, amiable, wittiest of men – and the vainest. He had written a novel called 'Rose, Blanche, and Violet.' One of the characters in this novel, described as a very vain and very ugly man,[11] so resembled himself that George Eliot asked me to put the question to him, 'Who was the original?' I felt sure he meant it for himself; but no, he gave me the name of another gentleman who was equally as plain, and not half so amiable.[12] ...

She lived with us for two years, and when we changed our house she arranged to come with us.[13] In the meantime, however, other complications arose. I heard that she meditated a visit to Germany, in company with Mr. Lewes, and we lost sight of each other after that.

J.J.P., 'Memories of George Eliot', *Burlington*, 1 (1881), 364–68
(pp. 365–8)

NOTES

The person whose memories are quoted here is never identified, but she is obviously Susanna Chapman, née Brewitt (1808–92), who married the physician and publisher John Chapman (1821–94, *ODNB*) in 1843. Five years after this recollection appeared, she was reported to be 'putting together materials for a life of George Eliot' ('Notes on Authors', *Publishers' Weekly*, 30 October 1886, p. 619). J.J.P. has remained untraced.

1. Presumably Sara Hennell, whom GE visited in Clapton in spring 1846, when the Chapmans lived nearby (*Letters*, I, 219 n. 4).

2. If they met in spring 1846, GE was twenty-six.

3. An elision. The Chapmans moved to 142 Strand in July 1847.

4. Yes and no. After visiting from 18 November to 2 December 1850, GE moved in on 8 January 1851, having decided to pursue a career in journalism. In March she returned to Rosehill, driven away by the jealousy of Susanna Chapman and Elisabeth Tilley, John Chapman's live-in mistress, who believed some intimacy had occurred between him and GE (Rosemary Ashton, *142 Strand: A Radical Address in Victorian London* (London: Chatto & Windus, 2006), pp. 88–90). GE returned on 29 September 1851 as the *Westminster Review*'s 'assistant editor' (really the editor, uncredited). For rich daily detail on GE in the midst of this domestic tangle, see Haight, *George Eliot & John Chapman: With Chapman's Diaries* (New Haven: Yale University Press; London: Oxford University Press, 1940), esp. pp. 128–49, 171–5.

5. GE assisted with the *Westminster* until 1854, although her last contribution appeared in January 1857. She felt both an intense personal interest in the magazine and the occasional impulse to run away from it (see *Letters*, ii, 47–50, 88).

6. She had not yet visited Germany, but rather France, Italy, and Switzerland.

7. Untraced. In January 1851 GE mentioned 'a Mr. Jarvis, an American, evidently a noodle', and in June 1852 she reported the house as 'brimful of Americans with varying degrees of disagreeableness' (*Letters*, i, 341; ii, 31). What did not vary was the house's agreeableness to Americans. Visiting London in 1851, Horace Greeley advised travellers from the States 'never [to] think of stopping at a London hotel this summer unless you happen to own the Bank of England. If you know any one here who takes boarders or lets rooms at reasonable rates, go directly to him; if not, drive at once to the house of Mr. John Chapman, American Bookseller, 142 Strand, and he will either find you rooms or direct you to some one else who will' (*Glances at Europe: In a Series of Letters from Great Britain, France, Italy, Switzerland, &c.* (New York: Dewitt & Davenport, 1851), p. 46).

8. A Miss Bellamy (*Letters*, i, 375; viii, 31).

9. She seems also to have performed at Chapman's gatherings (*Philip Gilbert Hamerton: An Autobiography 1834–1858 and a Memoir by His Wife 1858–1894* (London: Seeley, 1897), p. 160). The two friends have remained untraced.

10. John Chapman introduced GE to GHL in a Burlington Arcade bookshop on 6 October 1851; she had met Spencer in August (Haight, pp. 127, 112).

11. Julius St John, ugly (as the narrator tirelessly points out), but not vain. *Rose, Blanche, and Violet* appeared in 1848. GE read its first two volumes in July 1852, but did not finish it (*Letters*, viii, 51).

12. Untraced.

13. The Chapmans moved to Blandford Square in June 1854 (Ashton, *142 Strand*, p. 253), but GE had determined to leave them by January 1853, and did so in October.

'A VERY LARGE BRAIN'

George Combe

I

Miss Evans is the most extraordinary person of the party.[1] She translated Strauss's work "Das Leben Jesu" from the German, including the Hebrew,

Greek, & Latin quotations in it, without assistance; and it is said to be admirably executed. She has a very large brain, the anterior lobe is remarkable for length, breadth, & height, the coronal region is large, the front rather predominating; the base is broad at Destruc: but moderate at Aliment. & the portion behind the ear is rather small in the regions of Comb. Amat. & and Philopro.[2] Love of approb. and and [*sic*] Concentrativeness are large. Her tempera. is nervous lymphatic.[3] She is rather tall, near 40 apparently, pale & in delicate health.[4] She is an excellent musician. She read the Letter of Henry Atkinson on new organs in his & Miss Martineau's Book, & we discussed them.[5] She shewed great analytic power & an instinctive soundness of judgment. We had a great deal of conversation on religion, political economy, & political events, and altogether, with the exception perhaps of Lucretia Mott, she appeared to me the ablest woman whom I have seen, & in many respects she excells Lucretia. She is extremely feminine & gentle; & the great strength of her intellect combined with this quality renders her very interesting.

> Journal, 29 August 1851, NLS, Combe Papers, MS 7428, fols 11ᵛ–12ʳ, reproduced with kind permission of the Trustees of the National Library of Scotland

II

Miss Marian Evans, aged 32, who assists Mr. John Chapman in editing the Westminster Review, has been our guest for a fortnight,[6] & has left us this day. She is a distinguished linguist, including Greek Latin & Hebrew, German, French & Italian; an admirable musician; and is mistress of all the philosophies of modern times; & is a good political economist; also knows art well. She is thoroughly feminine, refined, & Lady-like. Her brain is large, the anterior lobe & coronal region predominating. Tempr. nervous lymphatic: pleasing but not pretty.

> Journal, 20 October 1852, fol. 57ʳ

NOTES

George Combe (1788–1858, *ODNB*) was a phrenologist and social reformer, a supporter of Chapman's new *Westminster Review*, and a great admirer of GE until he discovered that she was living with GHL in Germany.

1. At Rosehill, on 29 August 1851. The group consisted of Combe and his wife Cecilia, Charles and Caroline Bray, Sara Hennell, and GE.
2. According to Combe's system, brain size, other things being equal, is 'a measure of power' and 'the degree of mental energy possessed', while the size of the anterior lobe is 'the measure of intellect' (*Elements of Phrenology*, 7th edn (Edinburgh: Maclachlan and Stewart; London: Simpkin, Marshall, and Longman, 1850), pp. 178, 20). The coronal region is the seat of moral sentiments, and Combe's comments reveal GE's large organ of Benevolence, said to produce the desire of happiness for others as well as compassion, mildness, cheerfulness, and charity (pp. 29, 93). Combe puts Destructiveness with Alimentiveness because the former is the instinct that

leads us to kill to eat. The former, in GE the stronger, 'gives weight to injunction' and 'is essential to satire' (p. 74). Combativeness, Amativeness, and Philoprogentiveness, all 'rather small' in GE, would signify a relative inability to resist hostility as well as lack of sexual feeling and 'instinctive love of the young' (pp. 72–3, 62–3, 65). At this point in his journal, three years later, Combe added a note at the bottom of the page: 'This was written from eye-observation. She has gone off as the mistress of Mr. Lewes, a married man with 6 children. July 1854.'

3. Love of Approbation 'produces the desire of the esteem of others' and the desire to please them; Concentrativeness (and here Combe admits to hypothesizing) gives 'continuity to impressions' and protects one from distractions (pp. 88, 67). He says that 'the different temperaments are rarely found pure', with nervous-lymphatic a common mixture combining the 'proportionally vivacious' with 'proportionally sluggish and weak' mental manifestations (pp. 22, 21).

4. She was thirty-one.

5. *Letters on the Law of Man's Nature and Development* (1851), published by John Chapman. 'Whatever else one may think of the book', she wrote, doubtless of its open atheism, 'it is certainly the boldest I have seen in the English language' (*Letters*, I, 364). Atkinson's experiments in mesmerism revealed 'new organs', most important '"the Eye of the Mind"' or 'the Intuitive faculty; for it is this which is chiefly concerned in *clairvoyance*' (p. 76). In his *On Force, Its Mental and Moral Correlates* (1866), Charles Bray thought this organ's existence highly probable, and it surfaces ten years later in *Daniel Deronda*: '"Second-sight" is a flag over disputed ground. But it is a matter of knowledge that there are persons whose yearnings, conceptions – nay, travelled conclusions – continually take the form of images which have a foreshadowing power' (ed. by Graham Handley (Oxford: Oxford University Press, 1988), p. 404 (Book V, Chapter 38)).

6. From 7 to 20 October 1852: 'The Combes are all kindness and I am in clover – an elegant house, glorious fires, and a comfortable carriage ...' (*Letters*, II, 59).

'THE MOST ADMIRABLE WOMAN, MENTALLY, I EVER MET'

Herbert Spencer

A letter to Lott on the 23rd April [1852] speaks of: –

'Miss Evans whom you have heard me mention as the translatress of Strauss and as the most admirable woman, mentally, I ever met. We have been for some time past on very intimate terms.[1] I am very frequently at Chapman's and the greatness of her intellect conjoined with her womanly qualities and manner, generally keep me by her side most of the evening.' ...

In physique there was, perhaps, a trace of that masculinity characterizing her intellect; for though of but the ordinary feminine height she was strongly built. The head, too, was larger than is usual in women. It had, moreover, a peculiarity distinguishing it from most heads, whether feminine or masculine; namely that its contour was very regular. Usually, heads have here and there either flat places or slight hollows; but her head was everywhere convex. Striking by its power when in repose, her face was remarkably transfigured by a smile. The smiles of many are signs of nothing more than amusement; but with her smile there was habitually mingled an expression of sympathy, either for the person smiled at or the person smiled with. Her voice was a contralto of rather low pitch and I believe naturally strong. On this last point I ought to have a more definite impression, for in those days we occasionally sang together; but the habit of subduing her voice was so constant, that I suspect its real power was rarely if ever heard. Its tones were always gentle, and, like the smile, sympathetic.

These traits of manner resulted from large measures of both the factors which prompt altruistic feeling – the general sympathies and the domestic affections. The activity of these last largely conduced to the leading incidents of her subsequent life. That from her general sympathies resulted a great deal of the enthusiasm of humanity, scarcely needs saying. They also caused a desire to feel at one with society around. The throwing off of her early beliefs left her mind in an attitude of antagonism which lasted for some years; but this was only a temporary feeling: her natural feeling was a longing to agree as far as possible. Her self-control, leading to evenness of temper was marked. Only once did I see irritation, not unjustified, a little too much manifested. Conscientious and just in all relations and consequently indignant against wrong, she was nevertheless so tolerant of human weaknesses as to be quickly forgiving; and, indeed, was prone to deprecate harsh judgments. This last trait was I doubt not in part caused by constant study of her own defects. She complained of being troubled by double consciousness – a current of self-criticism being an habitual accompaniment of anything she was saying or doing; and this naturally tended towards self-depreciation and self-distrust.[2] ...

In early days she was, I believe, sometimes vivacious; but she was not so when I first knew her, nor afterwards. Probably this was the reason why the wit and the humour which from time to time gave signs of their presence, were not frequently displayed. Calmness was an habitual trait. There was never any indication of mental excitement, still less of mental strain; but the impression constantly produced was that of latent power – the ideas which came from her being manifestly the products of a large intelligence working easily. And yet this large intelligence working easily, of which she must have been conscious, was not accompanied by any marked self-confidence. Difference of opinion she frequently expressed in a half apologetic manner.

It was, I presume, her lack of self-confidence which led her, in those days, to resist my suggestion that she should write novels.[3] I thought I saw in her many, if not all, of the needful qualifications in high degrees – quick observation, great power of analysis, unusual and rapid intuition into others' states of mind, deep and broad sympathies, wit and humour, and wide culture. But she would not listen to my advice. She did not believe she had the required powers.

An Autobiography, 2 vols (London: Williams and Norgate, 1904), I, 394–8

NOTES

Herbert Spencer (1820–1903, *ODNB*), the founder of evolutionary philosophy, met GE in October 1851 and remained her friend until her death. Another recollection by him appears in 'A Few Good Friends' in Part IV.

1. In June 1852 a rumour spread that GE and Spencer were engaged; after GE's death it went the rounds again, but with the addition that she had jilted him for GHL (*Letters*, I, xxiv, lxxv). In fact GE fell in love with Spencer, who rejected her. Her wrenching plea at least for his companionship, if that's all she can have, is in *Letters*, VIII, 56–7. Towards the end of his *Autobiography*, Spencer, now a bachelor of seventy-three, obliquely remarks upon the incident: 'Physical beauty is a *sine quâ non* with me; as was once unhappily proved where the intellectual traits and the emotional traits were of the highest' (II, 445). Another indirect reference to GE occurs in his *Study of Sociology* (London: King, 1873), p. 376 – a passage that she herself copied on a leaf now in the Parrish Collection, Princeton University (her ellipses):

    > One further ability may be named as likely to be cultivated and established – the ability to distinguish quickly the passing feelings of those around. ... Ordinarily, this feminine faculty, showing itself in an aptitude for guessing the state of mind through the external signs, ends simply in intuitions formed without assignable reasons; but when, as happens in rare cases, there is joined with it skill in psychological analysis, there results an extremely-remarkable ability to interpret the mental states of others. Of this ability we have a living example never hitherto paralleled among women, and in but few, if any, cases exceeded among men.

2. Both of which she turned to for support in her sorrow. A week or so after being rejected, GE told Spencer that her own imperfections were a greater source of misery for her than what he had done (see *Letters*, VIII, 61).

3. Sir Edmund Gosse, who served in 1883 with Spencer on the Committee of the London Library, says that Spencer thought fiction inappropriate for its collections, and suggested 'that in future no novels, "except of course those of George Eliot," should be purchased for the Library' (Evan Charteris, *The Life and Letters of Sir Edmund Gosse* (London: Heinemann, 1931), pp. 497–8). Spencer's estimation of GE's verse was not so high. Rosaline Masson, visiting him in the winter of 1886–87, found in his bookcase a volume of her poems with 'a long inscription to him in her handwriting ... uncut beyond the seventh page!' (*Poets, Patriots, and Lovers: Sketches and Memories of Famous People* (London: Clarke [1933]), p. 191).

VEILED POWER

Bessie Rayner Parkes Belloc

And indeed it requires touch upon touch to render such a personality living to those who never saw her, for her power was in some sense a veiled one. In the first place, none of her portraits appear to me to be like her. The one in a hooded bonnet, said to have been sketched in St. James's Hall, is a monstrous caricature and accidental impression of her face, which was neither harsh nor masculine. The one which prefaces her life is too sentimental. The early photograph, on sale at Spooner's in the Strand, is very like, but not favourable, and absolutely without any art in the arrangement. It is, however, the only real indication left to us of the true shape of the head, and of George Eliot's smile and general bearing.[1] In daily life the brow, the blue eyes, and the upper part of the face had a great charm. The lower half was disproportionately long. Abundant brown hair framed a countenance which was certainly not in any sense unpleasing, noble its general outline, and very sweet and kind in expression. Her height was good, her figure remarkably supple; at moments it had an almost serpentine grace. Her characteristic bearing suggested fatigue; perhaps, even as a girl, she would hardly have been animated; but when she was amused her eyes filled with laughter. She did not look young when I first saw her, and I have no recollection of her ever looking much older.

The effect of her presence – it was peculiarly impressive. Her great weight of intellect told in all circles. My father[2] was much attached to her, and whenever any special celebrity was invited to dinner, such as Thackeray, Grote the historian, or old Mr. Warburton (one of the principal founders of the London University), he was never content unless he had also secured his young countrywoman Marian Evans, for he himself was a Warwickshire man. On these occasions, from 1851 to 1855, she used to wear black velvet, then seldom adopted by unmarried ladies. I can see her descending the great staircase of our house in Savile Row (afterwards the Stafford Club), on my father's arm, the only lady, except my mother,[3] among the group of remarkable men, politicians, and authors of the first literary rank. She would talk and laugh softly, and look up into my father's face respectfully, while the light of the great hall-lamp shone on the waving masses of her hair, and the black velvet fell in folds about her feet. But for the deliberate casting away of her social chances when she left for Germany with Mr. Lewes, she would undoubtedly have achieved a very great position in the London world quite independently of her novels. In those years not a soul suspected her of a tinge of imaginative power. A real, deep thought and quiet wit were the characteristics of her talk. Most interesting as it was, I should hesitate to call it charming. There was always a want of brightness in her conversation.[4] Her nature smouldered deeply and occasionally glowed with interior fire; to the outward eye it never burst into a quick flame.

'Dorothea Casaubon and George Eliot', in *In a Walled Garden* (London: Ward and Downey, 1895), pp. 1–24 (pp. 16–18); first publ. in *Contemporary Review*, 65 (1894), 207–16

NOTES

For Bessie Rayner Parkes Belloc, see Part I.

1. Respectively, one of two pencil sketches by Laura Alma-Tadema; the engraving by Paul Adolphe Rajon; and the photograph by J.J.E. Mayall. Leonée Ormond surveys GE's portraits in *Companion*, pp. 309–10.
2. Joseph Parkes, a lawyer, politician, and reformer.
3. Elizabeth Rayner Parkes.

4. 'She said the other day', Bessie Parkes wrote in 1853, 'having made me sit close to her, and looking full into my eyes: "I thought when I first knew you, you had a great deal of self-esteem in the sense of putting forth your own opinions, but I have quite lost the impression. I suppose when we love people, we lose the sense of their faults." I was inexpressibly touched. I nearly cried. The odd mixture of truth and fondness in Marian is so great. She never spares, but expresses every opinion, good and bad, with the most unflinching plainness, and yet she seems able to see faults without losing tenderness' (*Letters*, II, 87).

THREE MEMORIES

William Hale White

I

As I had the honour of living in the same house, 142, Strand, with George Eliot for about two years, between 1851 and 1854,[1] I may perhaps be allowed to correct an impression which Mr. Cross's book may possibly produce on its readers. To put it very briefly, I think he has made her too 'respectable'. She was really one of the most sceptical, unusual creatures I ever knew, and it was this side of her character which to me was the most attractive. She told me that it was worth while to undertake all the labour of learning French if it resulted in nothing more than reading one book – Rousseau's 'Confessions'. That saying was perfectly symbolical of her, and reveals more completely what she was, at any rate in 1851–54, than page after page of attempt on my part at critical analysis. I can see her now, with her hair over her shoulders, the easy chair half sideways to the fire, her feet over the arms, and a proof in her hands, in that dark room at the back of No. 142, and I confess I hardly recognize her in the pages of Mr. Cross's – on many accounts – most interesting volumes. I do hope that in some future edition, or in some future work, the salt and spice will be restored to the records of George Eliot's entirely unconventional life. As the matter now stands she has not had full justice done to her, and she has been removed from the class – the great and noble church, if I may so call it – of the Insurgents, to one more genteel, but certainly not so interesting.

'Literary Gossip', *Athenæum*, 28 November 1885, p. 702

II

She occupied two dark, but very quiet rooms at the end of a long passage which runs back from the front and at right angles to the street;[2] but she had her meals with the family. She was then not quite what she appeared to be in later years. She never reserved herself, but always said what was best in her at the moment, even when no special demand was made upon her. Consequently, she found out what was best in everybody. I have not heard better talk than hers, even when there was nobody to listen but myself and the ordinary members of the Chapman household.

'Dr. John Chapman', *Athenæum*, 8 December 1894, pp. 790–1 (p. 790)

III

I remember vividly the day on which I came to No. 142, and had lunch there. Miss Evans sat opposite to me. I was a mere youth, a stranger, awkward and shy. She was then almost unknown to the world, but I had sense enough to discern she was a remarkable creature. I was grateful to her because she replied even with eagerness to a trifling remark I happened to make, and gave it some importance. That was always her way. If there was any sincerity (an indispensable qualification) in the person with whom she came into contact she strove to elicit his best, and generally disclosed to him something in himself of which he was not aware. I have never seen anybody whose search for the meaning and worth of persons and things was so unresting as hers. The traveling American was not very interesting, but even from him she managed to extract whatever gave him a title to existence. She had little notebooks, in which she jotted down whatever struck her. Passages she had read which she had not been able to understand were also put down and looked up at her leisure. These notebooks, many of them at any rate, are still in existence.[3] The style of Miss Evans's conversation was perfect; it was quite natural, but never slipshod, and the force and sharpness of her thought were never lost in worn phrases. She was attractive personally. Her hair was particularly beautiful, and in her grey eyes there was a curiously shifting light, generally soft and tender, but convertible into the keenest flash.[4] The likeness by Sir Frederick Burton is good, but it gives permanence to that which was not permanent in her face. It lacks the generality combined with particularity which we find in portraits by the greatest masters.

I fancy that one of the reasons why she and Chapman did not agree was that she did not like his somewhat disorderly ways.[5] She has been accused of 'respectability.' Even Sir Leslie Stephen in his scholarly essay describes her as 'eminently respectable.'[6] It is not very easy to understand what is meant by this word. If there is any meaning in it worth preservation it is conformity to usage merely for the sake of conformity, and perhaps, more precisely, it is mental compromise. I deny that in either of these senses George Eliot was 'respectable.' She never terminated inquiry till she had gone as far as her powerful intellect permitted her to go, and she never refused to act upon her investigation. If she did not outrage the world by indecency it was not because she was 'respectable' but because she had not deduced indecency as the final outcome of thinking or the highest achievement of art. She delighted in music, and played Beethoven, one evening, as I shall never forget, to me alone.[7] She was not, I suppose, a first-rate performer, but she more than satisfied me, and I was, I am afraid, a little incoherent in my thanks.

A favourite composer with her was Gluck, and it was she who introduced me to Orfeo.[8] She was generous to a degree which nobody now living can measure, and she not only gave money to necessitous friends, but took pains to serve them. Years after I had left Chapman's I wrote to her asking if she could assist a poor man of letters whom we both knew, and she got work for him.[9] It was foolish of me to let my intercourse with her drop. Its cessation was mainly due to that careless, wasteful indifference of youth which leads us to neglect the most precious opportunities. Towards the close of a long life there is nothing more painful than the recollections of those many tides in our affairs which would have led on to fortune but were omitted.[10]

'George Eliot as I Knew Her', in *Last Pages from a Journal with Other Papers* [ed. by Dorothy V. White] (London: Oxford University Press, 1915), pp. 131–7 (pp. 131–4); first publ. in *Bookman*, 22 (1902), 159–60

NOTES

William Hale White (1831–1913, *ODNB*), a civil servant, wrote a series of autobiographical novels 'by Mark Rutherford' and 'edited by his friend Reuben Shapcott'.

1. White arrived in October 1852, and GE left a year later.
2. In March 1853 GE changed from one room at Chapman's to another but described the new (single) room as 'very light and pleasant' (*Letters*, II, 93).
3. Margaret Harris surveys GE's known notebooks in *Companion*, pp. 288–9.
4. In *The Autobiography of Mark Rutherford, Dissenting Minister* (London: Trübner, 1881), these qualities (plus the generosity with money mentioned in the next paragraph) appear in Theresa, a character with whom the narrator falls in love, and who is often said to be based upon GE.
5. GE ended her friendship with Chapman because he would not respect her desire to remain anonymous after she published *Scenes of Clerical Life*.
6. *George Eliot* (London: Macmillan, 1902), p. 135.
7. She delighted especially in Beethoven, who is mentioned in her letters and journals more often than any other composer. In *Mark Rutherford* White has some fun with this connection; when the narrator asks Theresa to play a piece by Beethoven, she replies, 'You like Beethoven best. I knew you would. He encourages a luxurious revelling in the incomprehensible and indefinably sublime. He is not good for you' (p. 160).
8. She later uses the aria 'Che Farò senza Euridice' from *Orfeo* in 'Mr Gilfil's Love Story' in *Scenes of Clerical Life*.
9. William Maccall. GHL, not GE, got work for him, and GHL answered the letter White wrote to her in May 1876 on Maccall's behalf (*Letters*, VI, 248). In appreciation White sent GE a likeness of himself, which GHL, not GE, acknowledged (VI, 279).
10. An allusion to Shakespeare's *Macbeth*, IV, iii: 'There is a tide in the affairs of men, | Which, taken at the flood, leads on to fortune.' In 1898 rereading GE's novels revived White's 'old passion', and he wrote that on the whole he still thought the same of her as when he knew her (*Letters to Three Friends*, ed. by Dorothy V. White (London: Oxford University Press, 1924), p. 180). 'Of George Eliot he spoke with such devotion, such humility, such peace', his wife Dorothy remarks. 'He said she was a sweet, gentle creature; he said: "I could worship that woman"' (*The Groombridge Diary* (London: Oxford University Press, 1924), p. 72).

'HER HEAD WAS AMONG THE STARS'

Grace Greenwood

I had the happiness of knowing George Eliot in London many years ago, meeting her occasionally at the house of Mr. Chapman – then, I think, her home. She was at that time known only as Miss Evans, a young lady of remarkable intellect and acquirements. I did not divine her absolute genius. She was not brilliant in the ordinary sense; yet she made a deep impression upon me, and I have yet a distinct recollection of her. She was fair, and struck me as slight and thin for an English woman; perhaps because of the unusual size of her head and the massive character of her features. Her hair, which I have seen described as "auburn," was almost blonde and very abundant. She wore it, after what was then an English fashion, in large clusters of curls on either side of her face. I must still think that a beautiful mode for beautiful hair. It certainly served to soften the lady's heavy jaw and somewhat too prominent nose and cheek-bones, as a similar arrangement served to richly frame the small, pale face of Elizabeth Barrett Browning.

Miss Evans certainly impressed me at first as exceedingly plain, with her aggressive jaw and her evasive blue eyes. Neither nose, nor mouth, nor chin were to my liking; but, as she grew interested and earnest in conversation, a great light flashed over or out of her face, till it seemed transfigured, while the sweetness of her rare smile was something quite indescribable. It is over the massive or craggy features so often belonging to men and women of genius that the sunlight of a great soul plays most gloriously. She was then, as I have heard she always continued, singularly modest in regard to her own work and aims; but she could no more hide her prodigious learning than an Egyptian obelisk, carved from base to summit with hieroglyphic lore, could present a blank face to the world. I remember I was a little afraid of her erudition, and kept in the very outer circles of the after-dinner discussions on scientific or ethical questions, in which she was at home. Still, she was very considerate, and more than once shifted the conversation to topics more familiar to me, showing a generous and intelligent interest in our American institutions and literature. Slavery was then "the burning question," and I was grateful to find her more tolerant of our great inherited national sin than most English people, as she more clearly comprehended our great national difficulty.[1] That unhappy "institution" was then a great barrier, a sort of sea of ice, between the English and American mind. They pitied and they reprehended us. Perhaps it was because of my too sensitive Americanism; but Miss Evans seemed to me to the last lofty and cold. I felt that her head was among the stars – the stars of a winter night. This was before "Adam Bede" had revealed to us the heart of fire under the snows of Hecla.

Her low, soft voice, which is now spoken of as "sweet and exquisitely modulated," seemed to me wanting in that something sympathetic and endearing which such voices usually possess. It was not exactly indifferent; but it seemed to have no vibrations of human weakness, whatever later sorrow and passion may have imparted to it. Subdued as it was, it was the voice of a strong woman; of one who needed not to assert herself and cared not for recognition.[2]

'Three Great Women', in *Stories and Sketches* (New York: Tait, 1892), pp. 38–49 (pp. 40–3); first publ. in *Independent*, 17 February 1881, pp. 1–2, then as 'An American Picture of English Celebrities', *Congregationalist* (London), 10 (1881), 293–9

NOTES

Grace Greenwood, the pseudonym of Sarah Jane Lippincott, née Clarke (1823–1904), was an American journalist who first met GE on 28 June 1852 at one of Chapman's gatherings. 'We had quite a constellation', GE wrote the next day, 'a beautiful American authoress, Miss Sara Clarke, alias Grace Greenwood, being the greatest star' (*Letters*, II, 40).

1. 'More tolerant' probably means that GE did not immediately insist upon some one view and asked questions rather than offering answers. We know that she admired William Edward Forster's pro-Northern 'American Slavery, and Emancipation by the Free States', *Westminster Review*, 59 (1853), 125–67. 'I hope you are interested in the Slavery question', she wrote to a friend after the article appeared, 'and in America generally – that cradle of the future. I used resolutely to turn away from American politics. ... But I am converted to a profound interest in the history, the laws, the social and religious phases of North America, and long for some knowledge of them' (*Letters*, II, 85). Greenwood herself had been fired from *Godey's Lady's Book* in 1850 for publishing letters in the *National Era*, an anti-slavery weekly.

2. Visiting Chapman in November 1852, William Cullen Bryant seems barely to have noticed her, mentioning only that he met 'a blue-stocking lady, who writes for the "Westminster Review"' (Parke Godwin, *A Biography of William Cullen Bryant*, 2 vols (New York: Appleton, 1883), II, 66).

'LIVING APART IN HER OWN WORLD'

Noah Porter

In the year 1853 the writer saw George Eliot – then called Miss Marian Evans by universal consent – for several days at the house of John Chapman in the Strand, London. ...[1] At this time she was thirty-three years old, with plain but interesting features, of a little above medium size, of a very quiet and almost timid bearing, most noticeable for her singularly refined voice, her clear thoughts, her choice yet by no means stilted diction, and above all for her fervid yet unaffected sensibility. She was free and affable with the family and guests, but unmistakably wore the air of a person preoccupied with many engagements, and living apart in her own world of elevated thoughts and intense feeling. The writer remembers once being greatly moved at seeing her, after having come late to the breakfast table and being left almost alone, give way to a mood of abstraction during which the tears flowed in streams over her strong yet gentle face. It was delightful to hear her converse, and yet I recall little or nothing of a long conversation with her as once we sat opposite one another at the table, and were left to ourselves.

> 'George Eliot: Personal Recollections with Comments', *Christian Union*,
> 26 January 1881, pp. 80–1 (p. 80); 'the writer' is Porter

NOTE

Noah Porter (1811–92) was an American Congregational minister, college president, and philosopher.

1. In a long passage omitted here, Porter describes 142 Strand and the 'ban of social ostracism' that lay on Chapman: 'He printed only 650 copies of the "Review," and he said with some bitterness that it was not "taken in" at any reputable reading-room in the United Kingdom.' When he bought it, he hoped it would continue at its circulation of 1000 (*Letters*, VIII, 29). Porter also remarks that GE 'was spoken of as perhaps the most learned and cultured lady in the kingdom'.

'A FLOOD OF TEARS'

A Victorian lady

I saw dear old Miss Anna Swanwick the other day ... and she told me that a lady she knew was in the same lodging with George Eliot long ago.[1] One day the landlady came up to her and said that the lodger in the rooms below, a Miss Evans by name, seemed in great trouble, and she thought she stood in need of a friend.[2] A Mr. Lewes, she said, called there every day, and always after his visits Miss Evans was in a flood of tears.

The lady replied that as she did not know Miss Evans, such a visit might be considered an intrusion, so she did not call on her. A week later George Eliot left England with Mr. Lewes.[3]

> *Echoes of the 'Eighties: Leaves from the Diary of a Victorian Lady*,
> intro. by Wilfred Partington (London: Nash, 1921), p. 15

NOTES

The diarist here is Lucy B. Walford's 'cousin Mary' (surname untraced), cross-identified through Walford's telling an anecdote also in *Echoes* (p. 14); see *Memories of Victorian London* (London: Arnold; New York: Longmans, Green, 1912), pp. 145–6, VI. A recollection by Walford appears in 'Out and About in London' in Part IV.

1. 21 Cambridge Street, Hyde Park, where GE moved in October 1853; the co-lodger has remained untraced.
2. GE consulted her friends Barbara Leigh Smith and Bessie Rayner Parkes. See Matilda Betham-Edwards, 'Madame Bodichon: A Reminiscence', *Fortnightly Review*, n.s. 51 (1892), 213–18 (esp. pp. 213–14); Parkes's *Reminiscences*, new rev. edn (London: Unit, 1903), p. 141); and *Diaries and Letters of Marie Belloc*

Lowndes 1911–1947, ed. by Susan Lowndes (London: Chatto & Windus, 1971), p. 100.

3. For Germany, on 20 July 1854. Rosemary Ashton surveys the most important stories swirling round their elopement (*G.H. Lewes: A Life* (Oxford: Clarendon Press, 1991), pp. 153–9). Many persons were intolerant; others tried platonically to salvage things – Richard Charles Jackson, for example, told Walter Pater that GE and GHL 'never occupied together the same bed-room', and that their closeness began when GE heard at a dinner party that GHL was ill, rushed to his lodgings, and cried from the street: '"I have come to nurse you. Let me in, and I won't leave the house till you are better"' (Thomas Wright, *The Life of Walter Pater*, 2 vols (London: Everett; New York: Putnam, 1907), II, 179). Still others thought that GHL abandoned his wife and family for GE, an error repeated half a century later by *The Times* in its obituary of Agnes Jervis Lewes, 24 December 1902, p. 8. It was E. Katharine Bates who set the record straight by asking Charles Lewes for the truth and reporting his reply: '"My mother had left my father before he and George Eliot had ever met each other. George Eliot found a ruined life, and she made it into a beautiful life. She found us poor little motherless boys, and what she did for us no one on earth will ever know"' ('George Henry Lewes and George Eliot: To the Editor of The Times', *The Times*, 27 December 1902, p. 8). Ashton believes that GHL left home in the summer or autumn of 1852, and became GE's lover probably in the following spring (*G.H. Lewes*, p. 132; Ashton, p. 102).

Part III
Mrs Lewes Abroad and at Home 1854–58

'NOT TOO ENGLISH IN HER VIEWS AND OPINIONS'
Franz Liszt

I knew George Eliot and her husband very well ... and they were a remarkably ugly couple. Mr. Lewis, the author of "The Life of Goethe," called on me first, alone, telling me, in the course of conversation, that he was at Weimar, with Miss Evans, the translator of "The Life of Jesus," by Strauss; but that he did not know whether he could present himself with her, as they were living together in a manner inadmissible in society.[1] I gave him to understand that I cared very little whether people's relations were regular or not, and though people said "shocking"[2] in Weimar, as they did elsewhere, I gave them a hearty welcome and invited them to come and dine with me.[3] Princess de Wittgenstein, who had long preferred to interest herself in religious and philosophical questions, took a great interest in Miss Evans, and got on capitally with her. Ugly though she was, Miss Evans had a charm, and knew how to captivate those around her. At times her way of listening reminded me of Madame Sand. She seemed to absorb like a sponge everything she saw and heard. Her long, ill-favoured face put on an expression of attention so rapt that it became positively interesting. But Madame Sand was composed while listening, and she made one more eloquent; Miss Evans, on the other hand, seemed to be jealous of what one said, and put one on one's guard.[4] I have always noticed that the men, in these sort of "irregular positions," are the more uncomfortable. Mr. Lewis visibly suffered under it, especially when he had to introduce Miss Evans;[5] she, on the contrary, walked with her head erect. She had plenty of ease of manner, and, in fact, was not too English in her views and opinions. Mr. Lewis was a very able man. One day when I came in I found Mr. Lewis's card, and those of three other Englishmen. When I met him shortly afterwards, I said to him:

"There are some of your countrymen here, I see."

"Mine? Not that I know of!"

"But I found your card at my house together with three others with English names on them." Mr. Lewis laughed. "They are all myself, only myself," said he. "Those are my three *noms de plume* under which I work at different branches of literature.[6] It is a little plan by means of which, in my opinion, I secure to myself the attention of four different groups of the public. It suits me very well, and it appears to suit the public also."

Janka Wohl, *Francois Liszt: Recollections of a Compatriot*, trans. by B. Peyton Ward (London: Ward & Downey, 1887), pp. 120–3; first publ. as *François Liszt: souvenirs d'une compatriote* (Paris: Ollendorff, 1887)

NOTES

Franz Liszt (1811–86), Hungarian pianist and composer, was at this time Kapellmeister in Weimar. For GE he was 'the first really inspired man' she had ever seen: 'Genius, benevolence and tenderness beam from his whole countenance, and his manners are in perfect harmony with it' (*Letters*, ii, 171; *Journals*, p. 21).

1. They arrived on 3 August 1854 and left for Berlin on 3 November; GHL called on 9 August. GE's Weimar diary and her 'Recollections of Weimar 1854' are in *Journals*, pp. 19–29, 218–40. She also published 'Liszt, Wagner, and Weimar' in *Fraser's Magazine* (1855), repr. in *Writings*, pp. 82–109. For a detailed account of her stay, see Gerlinde Röder-Bolton, *George Eliot in Germany, 1854–55: 'Cherished Memories'* (Aldershot: Ashgate, 2006), pp. 41–104.
2. In English in the original as well (p. 138).
3. Liszt too was in an irregular domestic arrangement with Carolyne Sayn-Wittgenstein, at this time still married (but divorced in 1855). She later published works on the history of Catholicism and on Buddhism and Christianity.
4. 'Semblait convoiter les énonciations et vous mettait sur vos gardes' (p. 139). Recollections of GE later in her life tend to emphasize how much she put others at ease.
5. Compare Sir J.D. Hooker, who met GHL in September 1865 and thought that a connection like his 'must tend to destroy a man's manners in public; the very sense of its exciting prejudice must insensibly react in a man's manners' (*The Correspondence of Charles Darwin*, ed. by Frederick Burkhardt and others (Cambridge: Cambridge University Press, 1985–), xiii (2003), p. 241).
6. 'Slingsby Lawrence' and 'Frank Churchill' when he translated or adapted French plays, 'Vivian' when he wrote theatre criticism in the *Leader* (see Ashton, *G.H. Lewes: A Life* (Oxford: Clarendon Press, 1991), p. 360).

'A SENSIBLE, UNDERSTANDING WOMAN'

Karl August Varnhagen von Ense

[7 November 1854] Miss Evans. Wir sprachen über Carlyle; er sei ein Kind, sagte Lewes von ihm, und ein Prophet; er habe meistens kantischen Geist, aber ein demokratisches Herz; es sei wunderbar, wie gewaltig Goethe auf in eingewirkt habe. Und doch versteht er Goethe'n so wenig. Und welche Vorurteile er hat! [Miss Evans. We talked about Carlyle; he's a child, Lewes said of him, and a prophet; he generally has a Kantian mind, but a democratic heart; it is marvelous, how powerfully Goethe has influenced him. And yet he understands Goethe so little. And what prejudices he has![1]]

[9 November] Miss Evans ein verständiges, einsichtsvolles Frauenzimmer. Wirt über Goethe gesprochen, über Heinrich von Kleist, Mad. Vogel, Mad. Sander &c. Alle schienen zufrieden. Man trennte sich erst nach 8 Uhr. [Miss Evans a sensible, understanding woman. We spoke about Goethe, about Heinrich von Kleist, Madame Vogel, Madame Sander etc. Everyone seemed satisfied. We parted company only after 8 o'clock.]

[14 November] Mit Miss Evans über Hegel, Mangel an Geschmack, an Welt, Karakterschwäche, Imponiertsein, Ranke &c.[2] [[Talked] with Miss Evans about Hegel, the lack of taste, of life-experience, weakness of character, being impressed, Ranke etc.]

[19 November] Mit Frln Evans[3] viel gesprochen, über die Schriften von Strauss, deutsche Philosophen &c. [Talked at length with Miss Evans, about the writings of Strauss, German philosophers etc.]

[24 November] Unterhaltung mit Lewes und Miss Evans über litterarische Gegenstände; Miss Evans ist belesen in römischen Schriftstellern. [Conversation with Lewes and Miss Evans on literary matters; Miss Evans is well-read in Latin authors.]

[4 December] Nachmittags Kaffeegesellschaft bei Ludmilla. ... Sehr belebt. Es sollte nur französisch gesprochen werden, aber man fiel aft, und zuletzt ganz in's Deutsche. Lewes gab artige Geschichten zum Besten und anregende Streitereien. Fanny Lewald und Miss Evans, die beiden freigeisterischen Schriftstellerinnen, hatten einander viel zu sagen.[4] [This afternoon a coffee reception at Ludmilla [Assing's]. ... Very lively. We were supposed to converse only in French, but we fell out of it and ended up talking only in German. Lewes told good stories very well and [there were] stimulating arguments. Fanny Lewald and Miss Evans, the two freethinking authors, had much to say to each other.]

MS Diary, Varnhagen Collection, Case 255,
Jagiellonian Library, Cracow, reproduced with kind permission
of the Jagiellonian Library; translated by Frederick Betz

NOTES

Karl August Varnhagen von Ense (1785–1858) was a German diplomat who wrote, among other books, a biography of Goethe. He met GE and GHL out walking on 5 November (*Journals*, p. 33).

1. I wish to thank Dr Michael Petith for deciphering Varnhagen's *Frakturhandschrift*. For a detailed account of GE's stay in Berlin, 3 November 1854–10 March 1855, see Röder-Bolton, *George Eliot in Germany*, pp. 105–69.

2. Note the colourful string of varied topics, suggesting that Varnhagen enjoyed his own and GE's wide-ranging information.

3. Dr Petith points out that Varnhagen's (temporary) substitution of 'Fräulein' for 'Miss' Evans indicates quite an acceptance, and that although he is never short of harsh words for politics, people, and ideas he dislikes, he has no such language for GE.

4. Fanny Lewald lived with Adolf Stahr; they would be married in February 1855, 'after 9 years of waiting' (*Journals*, p. 45). GE wrote two articles on Stahr's *Torso: Kunst, Künstler und Kunstwerk der Alten* (1854): 'The Art of the Ancients', *Leader*, 6 (1855), 257–8, and 'The Art and Artists of Greece', *Saturday Review*, 2 (1856), 109–10.

DIE CAST

Eliza Lynn Linton

When they returned home, I called on them by their joint request. They were in lodgings in St. John's Wood,[1] and the aureole of their new love was around them. There was none of the pretence of a sanctioned union which came afterwards – none of the somewhat pretentious assumption of superior morality which was born of her success. She was frank, genial, natural, and brimful of happiness. The consciousness that she had finally made her choice and cast the die which determined her fate, gave her a nobility of expression and a grandeur of bearing which she had not had when I first knew her. Then my heart warmed to her with mingled love and admiration, and I paid her the homage she deserved. I felt her superiority, and acknowledged it with enthusiasm. Had she always remained on that level, she would have been the grandest woman of this or any age.

'A First Meeting with George Eliot', in *My Literary Life* (London: Hodder and Stoughton, 1899), pp. 85–103 (pp. 96–7)

NOTE

For Eliza Lynn Linton, see Part II. Another recollection by her appears in 'Sunday Gatherings at the Priory' in Part IV.

1. 8 Victoria Grove Terrace (now Ossington Street), Bayswater, from 18 April to 1 May 1855.

WANDERERS

Janet Ruutz-Rees

They came to our neighbourhood at Wandsworth, in the suburbs of London, and took a small detached villa with a garden of half an acre around it.[1] George Eliot thought much of this garden, and I remember seeing her often there. They were both very unattractive people to look upon, and they used to wander about the neighbourhood, the biggest pair of frights that ever was, followed by a shaggy little dog who could do tricks. Their villa was the centre of the literary coterie of English Liberals, like Frederick Harrison, Miss Martineau and such, and it was the rendezvous of scientists like Huxley and Herbert Spencer – all the so called broad thinkers of the times. I was at the house several times. She had a sort of double parlors, communicating rooms, where she mostly received guests. Here Emerson visited her at that time.[2] I remember well how she looked. She had a dull sort of brown hair, which she combed smoothly straight down over her forehead, temples and ears, about as unbecoming as could be.

'"A Pair of Frights"', *Boston Daily Globe*, 9 January 1881, p. 6, an anonymous article in which Ruutz-Rees (here spelled Runtz-Rees) gives her recollections to a newspaper correspondent

NOTES

Janet Emily (Mrs Louis Emile) Ruutz-Rees, née Meugens (b.1842), was an English journalist and writer on religion. At the time of GE's death, when this recollection appeared, she was living in New York City.

1. Holly Lodge, South Fields, where they lived from 11 February 1859 to 23 September 1860.
2. I have found no evidence that Emerson visited them in Wandsworth, or that Harriet Martineau did so (she had been on good terms with GE in the early 1850s, but disapproved of her connection with GHL).

BREAD AND BUTTER

Edith Simcox

January 18, 1881
Went yesterday to see Mrs. Congreve. ... She only saw Her once at Coventry.[1] ... Then she did not see Her till 22 years ago when both were married and living at Wandsworth. She remembered hearing her father say, and understanding by a kind of intuition, when people were speaking unkindly of her and Mr. Lewes, that he was certain by what he had seen of Miss Evans that she had done no wrong, that she could not have done anything she did not in her conscience feel to be right. She spoke of that as the time when friends wrote you letters of six sheets to remonstrate with you for going to see her. In those days they were very poor; she said they had not even enough food and then explained it by a story that one day when they were having luncheon, – for economy bread and butter only, their landlady who had had a present of game sent them up some partridges, and after eating it they felt so much better they agreed they could not be having enough to eat. ... One thing else she said that seemed to help my vision; that her vehemence in those days made her formidable to many women – one can understand her passionate utterances – repented when unanswered; and if not shy, she was very timid and the "appealingness" of her look, which in later years had turned to graciousness was, she said unutterably touching. And even then, in those earlier years of the marriage, she had a look of sadness, like discontent "though one knew she was only discontented with herself."

Shirtmaker, pp. 146–7

NOTE

Edith Jemima Simcox (1844–1901, *ODNB*), an essayist and social activist, met GE in 1872 and recorded her adoration in profound detail in *The Autobiography of a Shirtmaker*. As 'H. Lawrenny' she also reviewed *Middlemarch* in the *Academy* (1873), repr. in *Critical Heritage*, pp. 322–30. Other recollections by her appear in 'Vignettes' in Part IV and in Part VII.

1. See both Frederick R. Evans's recollection, *n.* 3, in Part I, and Frederic Harrison's recollection in 'A Few Good Friends' in Part IV.

'HOW I CAME TO WRITE FICTION'

George Eliot

September 1856 made a new era in my life, for it was then I began to write Fiction. It had always been a vague dream of mine that some time or other I might write a novel, and my shadowy conception of what the novel was to be, varied, of course, from one epoch of my life to another. But I never went farther towards the actual writing of the novel than an introductory chapter describing a Staffordshire village and the life of the neighbouring farm houses,[1] and as the years passed on I lost any hope that I should ever be able to write a novel, just as I desponded about everything else in my future life. I always thought I was deficient in dramatic power, both of construction and dialogue, but I felt I should be at my ease in the descriptive parts of a novel. My "introductory chapter" was pure description though there were good materials in it for dramatic presentation. It happened to be among the papers I had with me in Germany and one evening at Berlin, something led me to read it to George. He was struck with it as a bit of concrete description, and it suggested to him the possibility of my being able to write a novel, though he distrusted, indeed disbelieved in, my possession of any dramatic power. Still, he began to think that I might as well try, some time, what I could do in fiction, and by and bye when we came back to England and I had greater success than he had ever expected in other kinds of writing,[2] his impression that it was worth while to see how far my mental power would go towards the production of a novel, was strengthened. He began to say very positively, "You must try and write a story," and when we were at Tenby he urged me to begin at once. I deferred it, however, after my usual fashion, with work that does not present itself as an absolute duty. But one morning as I was lying in bed, thinking what should be the subject of my first story, my thoughts merged themselves into a dreamy doze,[3] and I imagined myself writing a story of which the title was – "The Sad Fortunes of the Reverend Amos Barton". I was soon wide awake again, and told G. He said, "O what a capital title!" and from that time I had settled in my mind that this should be my first story. George used to say, "It may be a failure – it may be that you are unable to write fiction. Or perhaps, it may be just good enough to warrant your trying again". Again, "You may write a chef-d'oeuvre at once – there's no telling". But his prevalent impression was that though I could hardly write a *poor* novel, my effort would want the highest quality of fiction – dramatic presentation. He used to say, "You have wit, description and philosophy – those go a good way towards the production of a novel. It is worth while for you to try the experiment."

We determined that if my story turned out good enough, we would send it to Blackwood, but G. thought the more probable result was, that I should have to lay it aside and try again.

But when we returned to Richmond I had to write my article on Silly Novels and my review of Contemporary Literature for the Westminster; so that I did not begin my story till September 22.[4] After I had begun it, as we were walking in the Park, I mentioned to G. that I had thought of the plan of writing a series of stories containing sketches drawn from my own observation of the Clergy, and calling them "Scenes from Clerical Life" opening with "Amos Barton". He at once accepted the notion as a good one – fresh and striking; and about a week afterwards when I read him the early part of 'Amos', he had no longer any doubt about my ability to carry out the plan. The scene at Cross Farm,[5] he said, satisfied him that I had the very element he had been doubtful about – it was clear I could write good dialogue. There still remained the question whether I could command any pathos, and that was to be decided by the mode in which I treated Milly's death.[6] One night G. went to town on purpose to leave me a quiet evening for writing it. I wrote the chapter from the news brought by the shepherd to Mrs. Hackit, to the moment when Amos is dragged from the bedside and I read it to G. when he came home. We both cried over it, and then he came up to me and kissed me, saying "I think your pathos is better than your fun".

Dec.6.57[7]

Journals, pp. 289–91 (pp. 289–90). Another recollection by
GE appears in Part I

NOTES

1. This piece may date from 1846 (Haight, p. 206).
2. Since publishing her translation of Strauss, GE had translated Ludwig Feuerbach's *Das Wesen des Christenthums* (1841), which appeared in 1854 as *The Essence of Christianity*. Further, between leaving for Germany with GHL and September 1856, she published fifty periodical essays and reviews, thirteen of them extensive, on a great variety of subjects – some 380 pages in two years (see *Essays of George Eliot*, ed. by Thomas Pinney (London: Routledge and Kegan Paul; New York: Columbia University Press, 1963), pp. 453–4). In this period she also translated Spinoza's *Ethics*, finally published in 1981.
3. At the end of Chapter 1 of *The Mill on the Floss*, the narrator slips into a similar condition, associated in this novel with both creativity and danger.
4. Probably the 23rd (*Letters*, II, 407 *n*. 3).
5. Chapter 1.
6. Chapter 8.

7. By this date *Scenes of Clerical Life* had been published anonymously in monthly instalments, January through November, in *Blackwood's Edinburgh Magazine*. It would appear in two volumes, 'By George Eliot', in January 1858. Placing 'How I came to write Fiction' within its context of diary entries, Harris and Johnston argue that it is about the making of George Eliot (*Journals*, pp. 283–6).

HOW SHE CAME TO WRITE FICTION

I
Charles Eliot Norton

Oxford. August 1868.
Mr. Lewes came to Oxford to the Meeting of the British Medical Ass[ociation] and staid with Dr. Ackland.[1]

He gave us an account of his wife's beginnings in novel writing. Often, he said, <to sas[?]> she had been asked to write, "and often friends had said to me – your wife ought to write."[2] "I always answered, 'there's no question she has more talent than any of us, but whether in that direction, I don't know.'"

"Moreover, we were very poor, (living at Wimbledon in one room, where I had my little table with my microscope making my observations, and my wife another, close at hand, where she wrote) we were trying to pay off debts;[3] and were so poor, that I remember well as we crossed the Common one morning saying to her 'You and I ought to live better than we do, we'll begin to have beer for lunch'. A little after this, I said to her, 'suppose you should try and write a story,' and some <time> days later she showed me the first pages of 'Amos Barton'. 'That's very nice as far as it goes, but you've got yet to show what you can do in pathos,' I said to her. But one day when I was going up to London, and just as I was leaving, my wife said to me, 'I wish you would not come back till night', and so of course, I did not go back till night, and that evening she read to me the account of Milly's death. 'That will do', I said to her, 'there's no doubt any longer as to what you can accomplish.'"

Telling this Mr. Lewes's eyes filled with tears, and through all this talk he seemed as sensitive and quick in his emotions as a woman.

Journal, Houghton Library, Harvard University,
bMS Am 1088.5, Box 15, fols 1–2, reproduced with kind permission
of the Houghton Library; publ. with alterations in *Letters of Charles Eliot
Norton*, ed. by Sara Norton and M.A. DeWolfe Howe, 2 vols (London:
Constable; Boston and New York: Houghton Mifflin, 1913), I, 307–8

II
Benjamin Jowett

G.H.L. spoke to me of her [on 4 October 1877]. Her mind had been injured in early life by morbid self-consciousness. She had a natural tendency to criticize herself & her writing which was greatly increased by any external criticism – had it not been for his sympathy she would never have written anything.[4]

One day he said to her ("We were very poor at that time") my dear try & write a novel. So she produced the first pages of Amos Barton. He said this is well, but there is nothing dramatic in <all this> what you have written: she added a dramatic sketch' 'Good' – 'Now try the pathetic' – She did so & introduced the death of Millie. Thus the question of her power to write a novel was solved

Notwithstanding her great knowledge & enormous intellectual force he thought that sensitivity and self-criticism would have prevented her from writing. Great labour & study given to de Ronda – translated into Hebrew. This gave her great pleasure.

Notebook, *10 – April 1877*, Balliol College Library,
Oxford University, MS I/H31, fol. 81ᶠ, reproduced with
kind permission of the Jowett Copyright Trustees

III

Margaret Holland

Pinewood October 7th 1877.

Mr. Lewes came in to see me today. The conversation falling on Mrs. Lewes's writings he said, as far as I recollect, "The extraordinary thing is that I never discovered this power in her – that she never should have written a line till her 35th year. Our friends – Herbert Spencer – and others used to say to me – Why doesn't she write a novel? and I used to reply that she was without the creative power. At last – we were very badly off – I was writing for Blackwood – I said to her 'My dear – try your hand at something. Do not attempt a novel – but try a story. We may get 20 guineas for it from Blackwood and that will be something.'[5]

"Well she did try, and she began and then she read me the first chapter of 'Amos Barton' (Scenes of CL.) Well, this was all descriptive and I doubted. 'We want something dramatic,' I said to her. She shook her head and seemed to say that was hopeless. The next thing she read to me was the scene in Widow Hackitt's cottage.[6] 'Come' said I 'this will do. Now for the pathos – unless you can manage that we shall not get on.' But she seemed to think that quite hopeless, that there was no power of pathos in her. However one day when I was going to town she said 'I wish you would dine in London today.' I was all astonishment to hear such an extraordinary wish expressed as that we should be apart and eagerly enquired the reason – but she would not answer. Presently she said again 'I *wish* you would stay and dine in town today.' And then on my pressing for a reason, it came out. She said she felt she had something she must write that evening. And I always objected to her working at night. But so it was this time – she said she felt she *must*.

And that evening she produced the scene of Milly's death. Then I felt all was right – no one could doubt success was secured."

Letters, ix, 197–8[7]

NOTES

Charles Eliot Norton (1827–1908) was an American scholar and editor best known as a professor of the history of fine art at Harvard. For Benjamin Jowett, see 'Eton, Cambridge, and Oxford' in Part iv; other recollections by him appear in 'The Countryside' in Part iv and in Parts v–vii. Margaret Jean Holland, née Trevelyan (1835–1906), lived near the Heights, Witley, GE and GHL's country home.

1. An error for (Henry Wentworth) Acland, who invited GHL to the annual meeting, Acland presiding, 4–7 August 1868 (*Letters*, iv, 466 *n*. 6; 'The British Medical Association', *The Times*, 30 July 1868, p. 8).
2. Norton's quotation marks, repeated with each new line in the MS, have been regularized.
3. Not GE's, but GHL's – or rather those of his wife Agnes (Haight, p. 218).
4. GHL, who later protected GE from seeing reviews of her fiction, spoke often of her painful diffidence. 'A thousand eulogies would not give her the slightest confidence', he wrote in 1862, 'but one objection would increase her doubts' (*Letters*, iv, 58).
5. For 'Amos Barton' she got fifty guineas (Haight, p. 218). The *Blackwood's* essays GHL refers to are 'Metamorphoses: A Tale' in three parts, May–July 1856, and 'Sea-Side Studies', also in three parts, beginning in August.
6. Mrs Hackit, although not a widow; which scene is uncertain, but Mrs Hackit contributes lively dialogue, and in that sense dramatic texture, every time she appears.
7. In a rare error, Haight locates this MS in the Huntington Library. Its actual location has remained untraced.

Part IV
George Eliot 1859–78

A Few Good Friends

RICHARD AND MARIA CONGREVE

Frederic Harrison

How well I remember that New Year's day [1860] when I met Mr. and Mrs. Lewes at the dinner-table of Mr. and Mrs. Richard Congreve! She was then at the age of forty, in the first outburst of her fame as the author of *Adam Bede*, and was just finishing the second volume of the *Mill on the Floss*. She had no friends at Wandsworth except Mr. and Mrs. Richard Congreve, who had made her acquaintance the year before.[1] ...

I listened with lively interest to the words of one who was already famous, who from the first moment impressed every one with a sense of grave thought, high ideals, and scrupulous courtesy. She had not a grain of self-importance in her manner, and took quite a simple and modest part in the general talk, listening to the brilliant sallies of George Lewes with undisguised delight, respecting Congreve's views as those of a trained historian and scholar, and showing me the kindly welcome of a gracious woman to the friend of her friends. I remember an argument in which she engaged me, wherein I thought, as I still think, she was mistaken. She maintained, *apropos* of a review of troops she had lately seen, that "the pomp and circumstance of glorious war" was more conspicuous in our day than it was in the Middle Ages. Having some knowledge of mediæval art, Italian war-paintings, and illuminated Froissarts, I ventured to doubt. The company seemed to think me bold in venturing to differ from her opinion on a matter of local colour. But she did not think so herself; and nothing could be more graceful than the patience with which she listened to my points.

In the year 1860, at Wandsworth, she was working under severe pressure, having broken with her own family, retaining only one or two women friends, quite unknown to general society. Years afterwards, when she lived in London and at Witley, she had the cultured world at her feet; men and women of rank and reputation crowded her Sunday receptions, and she was surrounded by friends and reverential worshippers of her genius. But she remained still the same quiet, grave, reserved woman that she had been in her retreat and isolation at Wandsworth, always modest in her bearing, almost deferential towards any form of acknowledged reputation, almost morbidly distrustful of herself, and eager to purge out of her soul any germ of arrogance and pride that her fame and the court paid to her by men and women of mark could possibly tend to breed.[2]

'Reminiscences of George Eliot', in *Memories and Thoughts: Men – Books – Cities – Art* (London: Macmillan, 1906), pp. 143–60 (pp. 144–6); first publ. in *Harper's*, 103 (1901), 577–84

NOTES

Frederic Harrison (1821–1923, *ODNB*), a lawyer, journalist, social reformer, and positivist, later helped GE with legal matters in *Felix Holt, the Radical* and *Daniel Deronda*. He also asked her, to no avail, to write a positivist novel. Another recollection by him appears in 'Sunday Gatherings at the Priory', below. Maria Congreve, née Bury (1846–1915), was the daughter of the Coventry surgeon who attended GE's father in his last illness. In 1856 she married the positivist Richard Congreve (1818–99, *ODNB*), soon appointed by Comte to lead his British disciples.

1. Maria Bury first met GE *c*.1836 (see Frederic R. Evans's recollection, *n*. 1, in Part I); the Congreves were living in Wandsworth when GE and GHL moved there in 1859 (see Edith Simcox's recollection in Part III). GE considered Mrs Congreve 'the chief charm of the place' (*Journals*, p. 77).
2. Harrison made the same point later: 'She was, in 1860, nearly what she was in 1880 – reserved, earnest, dignified, speaking with deliberate force, and wholly free from pretension or exhilaration with her success' (*Autobiographic Memoirs*, 2 vols (London: Macmillan, 1911), I, 204).

BARBARA BODICHON

Matilda Betham-Edwards

I

There was one person, perhaps only one, privileged to invite herself to the two o'clock luncheon of George Eliot and George Lewes. This gifted friend and neighbour, Madame Bodichon, recounted to me how once she rang the gate-bell of the Priory a few minutes too soon, to be admitted, of course – the Grace and Amelia of those days understood their duty as gate-keepers – but on crossing the threshold, out rushed her hostess, pale, trembling, her locks disordered – veritable Sibyl, disturbed in the fine frenzy of inspiration.

"Oh, Barbara! Barbara!" she cried, extremely agitated, "what have you done?"

The ever-welcome guest had interrupted her friend in a scene of *Romola*.

"I felt ready to cry like a naughty child," said the narrator, "but from the opposite door rushed Mr. Lewes, who in the kindest manner put things right."[1]

'Madame Bodichon: A Reminiscence', *Fortnightly Review*, n.s. 51 (1892), 213–18 (p. 213)

II

The first thing Madame Bodichon did on her return from Algiers [in 1867 or 1868] was to call at the Priory, taking me with her. Being a privileged person, she used to call there at very unconventional hours, upon this occasion immediately after dinner.

"You stay outside," she said, "and if I obtain permission to introduce you I will call out."

So I waited in the road just behind the cloister-like gate, but only for a minute or two.

"You may come in," shouted Madame Bodichon from the hall door. Accordingly, in I went, receiving cordial welcome.

George Eliot was at this time about fifty, but looked years older. She wore, as she always did, a plain black silk dress, to-night having a white shawl about her shoulders and light gloves in her hand, being indeed dressed for the opera. Some people have talked and written of the ugliness of this great woman ... because, forsooth, she lacked dimpled cheeks, round eyes, and pretty mouth! If hers was ugliness, would we had more of it in the world! When in speaking, her large, usually solemn features lighted up, a positive light would flash from them, a luminosity irradiate, not her own person only, but her surroundings. A sovereign nature, an august intellect, had transported us into its own atmosphere.[2]

"I am very glad to see you, associated as you are so pleasantly with Barbara's letters from Spain," she said; then her friend took possession of her, and George Henry Lewes chatted with me on Spanish literature and the last new Spanish novel or play. This wonderful and most genial little man seemed to know everything, to be an encyclopaedia before, and not behind, his time, like Charles Lamb. As we talked the sound of carriage wheels was heard outside. Lewes started up.

"The overture to 'Fidelio,' my dear – we shall miss the overture! Our friends must excuse us," he cried.

They had seats at the opera, so we accompanied them to the door and saw them drive off, Lewes delighted as a schoolboy bound to the pantomime, George Eliot smiling gravely. "Fare thee well, dear," she said, waving her hand to Madame Bodichon, whom the minute before she had tenderly kissed.[3]

Reminiscences, new rev. edn (London: Unit Library, 1903), pp. 138–40

NOTES

Matilda Betham-Edwards (1836–1919, *ODNB*) was a novelist and writer on French life. Other recollections by her appear in 'Out and About in London' and in 'The Countryside', below. Barbara (Mme Eugène) Bodichon, née Smith (1827–91, *ODNB*), an artist and women's activist, first met GE in 1852. They became close friends, Bodichon feeling '"a kind of delight in her presence which could only be explained by a sonnet"' (Haight, p. 281). 'Amongst her intimate friends', Cross wrote to Bodichon after GE's death, 'I know there was none she valued more or who was more to her than yourself' (13 January 1881, Yale).

1. In a later version of this scene, Betham-Edwards says that GHL 'coaxed and soothed her as if she had been a child' (*Mid-Victorian Memories* (London: Murray, 1919), p. 61).
2. This scene too appears in *Mid-Victorian Memories*, where GE is 'a tall, prematurely old lady wearing black, with a majestic but appealing and wholly unforgettable face. A subdued yet penetrating light – I am tempted to say luminosity – shone from large dark eyes that looked all the darker on account of the white, marble-like complexion' (p. 39). Usually remembered as grey or blue, GE's eyes are also described as 'dark' by Sir George Leveson-Gower, *Years of Content: 1858–1886* (London: Murray, 1940), p. 68.
3. In *Mid-Victorian Memories*, Bodichon tells Betham-Edwards that GE congratulated her '"on possessing a friend who is without fringes." It is the only time', Betham-Edwards adds, 'that I have ever heard the word "fringes" used for "fads"' (p. 40). This version also adds an account of dinner the next evening, where the topic 'resolved itself into this problem: How and by what means would the world – that is to say, the terrestrial globe we inhabit – come to an end? By combustion, submergence, gradual decay, and so on. I seem to hear George Eliot's penetrating, pathetic voice: | "Yet, dear Barbara, might not this come about —" Or, "Suppose that —" | For myself, I was silent, over-awed as some alumnus when Pericles and Aspasia held their court' (p. 41).

GEORGIANA BURNE-JONES

One Sunday afternoon in February of this year [1868] we first saw George Eliot. It was at her own house, and from that day began our friendship with her and Mr. Lewes. She was very like Burton's portrait-drawing of her, but with more keenness of expression; the eyes especially, clear and grey, were piercing: I used to think they looked as if they had been washed by many waters. Her voice was a beautiful one, sometimes full and strong and at others as tender as a dove's. Greatly as Edward admired her early work, he was astonished by her intellectual power when he came to know her personally. "There is no one living better to talk to," he wrote the year before her death, "for she speaks carefully, so that nothing has to be taken back or qualified in any way. Her knowledge is really deep, and her heart one of the most sympathetic to me I ever knew." ... Occasionally we dined there [the Priory], or they drove over to the Grange on a weekday afternoon – they never dined out – and the general conversation that went on at such times, I am bound to own, was chiefly very funny, with much laughter and many anecdotes.

Memorials of Edward Burne-Jones, 2 vols (London: Macmillan, 1906), II, 4

NOTE

Georgiana Burne-Jones, née Macdonald (1840–1920, *ODNB*), was a friend for whom GE felt special tenderness, and the feeling was returned. '"Bless her"', she wrote to Cross after his *Life* appeared, 'that is what I begin and end with when I think of her' (10 April 1885, Yale). A recollection by her husband, Sir Edward Burne-Jones, appears in Part v.

HERBERT SPENCER

... My return from Scotland this year [1868] must have been the occasion for one of those witticisms which George Eliot sometimes uttered. I had, as commonly happened after an interval of absence, been giving an account of my doings; and, among other things, had laughingly described the dismay caused in two fishermen at Inveroran by the success of my hetero-dox flies. This led to an inquiry concerning the nature of my heterodoxy. I explained that I did not believe in the supposed critical powers of salmon and sea-trout, but held that if one of them, being hungry, saw something it took for a fly, it would rise;[1] and that consequently my aim was to make the best average representation of an insect buzzing on the surface of the water. "Yes," she said, "you have such a passion for generalizing, you even fish with a generalization."[2]

This reference to her good things reminds me of one which Lewes told me she had uttered at the expense of Dr. A —,[3] a friend of theirs who was remark-able for his tendency to dissent from whatever opinion another uttered. After a conversation in which he had repeatedly displayed this tendency, she said to him, "Dr. A — how is it that you always take your colour from your company?" "*I* take my colour from my company?" he exclaimed – "What *do* you mean?" "Yes," she replied, "the opposite colour."

Our talk, if not very often enlivened by witticisms, always contained a mixture of the gay with the grave: good stories and a little *badinage* [play-fulness] breaking our discussions, which were generally quite harmonious; for there were but few points on which we disagreed.[4] Then after luncheon came a walk, usually in Regent's Park, in which I joined: another hour of interesting conversation being the accompaniment.

Though they were partial adherents of M. Comte my friends did not display much respect for the object which he would have us worship. Reverence for humanity in the abstract seemed, in them, to go along with irreverence for it in the concrete. Few of these occasions I have described, passed without comment from them on the unintelligence daily displayed by men – now in maintaining so absurd a *curriculum* of education (which they reprobated just as much as I did),[5] now in the follies of legislation, which continually repeat, with but small differences, the follies of the past, now in the irrationalities of social habits.

An Autobiography, 2 vols (London: Williams and Norgate, 1904), II, 203–4

NOTES

For Herbert Spencer, see Part II.

1. A decade earlier it occurred to Spencer 'that considering how low is the nervous organization of fishes, it is unlikely that they should be able to discriminate so nicely as the current ideas respecting artificial flies imply – unlikely, too, that they should have such erratic fancies as to be taken by combinations of differently coloured feathers, like no living creature ever seen' (*Autobiography*, I, 485).

2. 'I went to Kew yesterday on a scientific expedition with Herbert Spencer', GE wrote in June 1852, 'who has all sorts of theories about plants – I should have said a *proof*-hunting expedition. Of course, if the flowers didn't correspond to the theories, we said, *"tant pis pour les fleurs"* [so much the worse for the flowers]' (*Letters*, II, 40).

3. Untraced. Two obvious alphabetical possibilities are physicians Thomas Clifford Allbutt and Neil Arnott.

4. In 1868 GE described Spencer's as 'a friendship which wears well, because of his truthfulness: that makes amends for <other> many deficits'; by 1877 she confessed that she and GHL had 'long given up vain expectations from him and can therefore enjoy our regard for him without disturbance by his negations. He comes and consults us about his own affairs, and that is his way of showing friendship. We never dream of telling him *our* affairs, which would certainly not interest him' (*Letters*, IV, 489; VI, 426).

5. GE gives a devastating picture of misaimed traditional education in 'School Time', Book Second of *The Mill on the Floss*. Both she and GHL liked Mark Pattison's 'Philosophy at Oxford', *Mind*, 1 (1876), 82–97, which argues that tutors teach to tests, gradually creating a system that 'carefully excludes thoroughness' and exalts '"smattering" into a method' (p. 89; see *Letters*, VI, 202). Spencer himself thought young minds 'overburdened with useless knowledge' (*Autobiography*, II, 263).

SARA HENNELL

Moncure Daniel Conway

I probably spoke to Sara Hennell of the possible bearing of the "Nemesis of Faith" – wherein a wife meeting one she loves regards her legitimate marriage as a sort of adultery – on George Eliot's union with Lewes. "We all regarded this union as a calamity," said Sara Hennell. "Mr. Bray regarded it as due to her defective self-esteem and self-reliance, and her sufferings from loneliness. She continued to suffer from loneliness, but came to love the characters in her books as if they were her children. She loved them even when they were wicked. Once when I was at her house in London [in February 1869], looking at some sketches from 'Romola,' we paused before 'Tito.' After a moment's silence George Eliot said softly, as if to herself: 'The dear fellow.' I exclaimed 'He's not a dear fellow at all, but a very bad fellow!' 'Ah,' she said, 'I was seeing him with the eyes of Romola.'"

Autobiography: Memories and Experiences, 2 vols (Boston and New York: Houghton, Mifflin, 1904), II, 415

NOTE

For Moncure Daniel Conway, see Part I. Another recollection by him appears in 'Out and About in London', below. Sara Sophia Hennell (1812–99, *ODNB*), a writer on religious subjects, first met GE at Rosehill in July 1842. By March 1843 GE was calling her 'dearest Friend' (*Letters*, I, 158). They shared a dozen years of frequent correspondence.

ALFRED TENNYSON

Hallam Tennyson

One [place Tennyson particularly liked] was "Waggoners' Wells" on Hindhead where he wrote his "Flower in the crannied wall," and of which "George Eliot" said to him, "What a good place for a murder in a novel!" ...

I read somewhere an account of a quarrel between "George Eliot" and A.T. carried on in loud tones with red faces and clenched fists, the subject being her want of belief in an after life.[1] I showed this to him, and he wrote down what actually happened. "I and she never had one moment of discussion, much less of quarrel. She called, and when she went away I pressed her hand kindly and sweetly and said, 'I wish you well with your molecules.' She replied as gently, 'I get on very well with my molecules.'"[2] Certainly A.T.'s voice never belied his feelings, nor do I suppose that "George Eliot's" did either.

I have the record of a later conversation between "George Eliot" and A.T. which took place at Aldworth.

They agreed as to "the Namby Pambyism of the age which hates a story to end in tragedy as if all the greatest moral lessons were not taught by tragedies." A.T. added "what the public do not understand is that the great tragedy is all balance throughout." "George Eliot" then objected to the many English writers who set up French literature against our own, for "is not ours," she said, "one of the greatest in the world"?

She wanted A.T. to make a poem of this story which she narrated as true and as having occurred in one of the midland counties. A drunkard boasted that "he would fight any bull ever born." He went out into the starlight and walked up to a well known ferocious bull and dealt him a blow on the forehead which felled both man and bull. By that shock the man became "undrunk" and never drank again, so great was the terror which seized on him while lying there, the bull nozzling him, those big eyes, head and horns between him and the sky. George Eliot thought that A.T. would make a fine analysis of what passed in the man's mind as he lay there under the starry heavens.

Materials for a Life of A.T., 4 vols ([n.p.]: [n. pub.], [1895?]),
III, 329, 340–1

NOTES

Hallam Tennyson (1852–1928, *ODNB*), 2nd baron, was his father's private secretary, and later governor-general of Australia. Poet Laureate Alfred Tennyson, 1st baron (1809–92, *ODNB*) – 'our beloved Tennyson', GE called him (*Letters*, VI, 431) – met her in 1858, but their friendship flourished later, when they were neighbours at Shottermill and then at Witley. She reread his *In Memoriam* (1850) after GHL's death, copying lines from it into her diary (*Journals*, pp. 156, 158–62).

1. Untraced. Less dramatic versions had appeared in C. Kegan Paul, 'George Eliot', *Harper's*, 62 (1881), 912–23 (p. 921), and in Blind, p. 190.

2. Tennyson also recounted the incident to A.D. Coleridge: 'George Eliot and I are said to have quarrelled angrily for two hours together, the truth being that we were sweet as summer – at parting I said: "Well, good luck to you and your molecules"' ('Notes of Conversations with Lord Tennyson 1888–1892', MS Tennyson Research Centre, fol. 4, reproduced with kind permission of the Tennyson Research Centre). To Wilfrid Ward he recalled 'at parting I shook her hand, and said very gently, "I hope you are happy with your molecules"' (*Problems and Persons* (London: Longmans, Green, 1903), p. 202). Based on what she heard at Shottermill, Grace Gilchrist Frend has yet another account of this parting: '"Well, good-bye, you and your molecules." She looked back, being already on her way down the hill, and rejoined in her deep contralto voice, which gained in depth as she became moved, "I am quite content with my molecules"' ('Great Victorians: Some Recollections of Tennyson, George Eliot and the Rossettis', *Bookman*, 77 (1929), 9–11 (p. 9)). On the matter of molecules, see Mary Ponsonby's recollection in 'Some Younger Women', below.

Some Younger Women

MARY E. HUDDY

One sad day I learned that I was to lose my playfellows the children of Mrs. Lewes, since neither they nor their mother were to be allowed to come to the house to visit Mrs. Willim that being the condition – as I was told afterwards – under which George Eliot would be introduced to her.[1] The old lady extended a welcome to her son's clever companion, but to the end of her life – which came suddenly as her hand lay in blessing on my head – she regretted the loss of her daughter-in-laws loving attentions. ...

While in my teens an accident to my hip obliged me to remain for nearly a year upon a mattress and during this time I saw much of George Eliot when she visited Mrs. Willim to whom she was much attached. At first when – as I gather from letters sent to Mrs. Gendle – when recovery seemed doubtful, she would speak with great earnestness on <religious> serious matters and when I remarked that the sound of the church bells especially in the calm of Sunday evenings invariably caused me to weep, though I did not do so at any other time, she said they always had a depressing effect upon her and made her sad. Another time she asked if I felt any fear of death and was relieved by my answer to the contrary.

Who could help loving such a tender-hearted lady who would sit some-times for hours at the bedside of a suffering girl?[2]

She would talk, or read aloud in measured tones or better still improvise<d> stories of prose or opera, holding me spell-bound under the fascination of the various emotions which her skilful rendering <awoke> called forth. Even now, <whenever> I never hear the "March of the Priests" from "Athalie" without calling to mind the wonderful manner in which she vividly pic-tured the scene in the Temple where the ambitious Queen beheld the Jewish prince whom she deemed had been slain with his royal brethren at her command.[3]

On Mrs. Willim's death, George Eliot still showed her kindly interest, asking me to lunch occasionally and encouraging my feeble attempts to write (?)[4] always urging reconstruction and constant correction of the penned matter. She would say "each time, Lizzie, you prune your manu-script it means the weeding of the garden in which you sow your thoughts" or words to that effect:

During the time I was teaching in the school at Hampstead of which the Unitarian preacher Dr. Sadler, who afterwards addressed the mourners at George Eliot's funeral, was Chairman I was several times invited to North Bank. On one occasion she spoke of the comfort <she had derived from> the sermons of Theodore Parker had been to her and to her dying father to whom she had read them aloud. She would question me about the children under my care and in inspiring words and solemn manner would speak of the immense influence wielded by a teacher in moulding the character of future citizens.

'Some Account of Mrs. Willim', 30 June 1926, Yale, fols 1, 3–4

NOTES

Mary Elizabeth (Mrs John) Huddy, née Lee, attended GHL's mother Mrs Willim (see *Letters*, v, 115). After her accident, GE may have employed her in some work or other, while GHL helped from 1873 to 1878 with cash payments (IV, 369; v, 109; VII, 73 *n.* 7). She was at one time Assistant Mistress of the Carlton Road Board School, Kentish Town, London.

1. I have not been able to verify this claim. Haight, p. 337, suggests that Mrs Willim met GE in January 1861, having refused to do so until she became famous. The Mrs Lewes here is Agnes, GHL's legal wife; the playfellows, her first three children by Thornton Hunt: Edmund Alfred, Rose Agnes, and Ethel Isabella Lewes, at this time around ten, nine, and seven years old respectively. (Incidentally, Huddy says that Charles Lewes, 'with a courage and determination which won the esteem and love of George Eliot, went openly and frequently to visit his mother' (fol. 2).)

2. Several years after GE's death the American journalist 'Halston' reported talking with a man who said that he came to know GE *c.*1860 in a London slum when she nursed a dying flower-girl named Maggie ('Some Hit and Miss Chat', *New York Times*, 12 July 1885, p. 3). I have found no evidence to support this story, which may be a distorted version of GE's charitable friendship with Mary Lee.

3. Association at work. This scene is not dramatized in the concert-hall version (1849) of Mendelssohn's 1845 incidental music (including the famous 'March') for Racine's play (1691). It is however dramatized in Handel's opera *Athalia* (completed 1756) and of course in Racine. GE may have been remembering either or both.

4. She later wrote 'This Is the Way We Eat Our Food', in *Prize Essays on Feeding School Children*, ed. by William Bousfield (London: Causton, 1890), pp. 189–251, and *Matilda, Countess of Tuscany* (1905), a biography.

OCTAVIA HILL

1 January 1865

My call at The Priory with Gertrude took place on Wednesday [28 December 1864].[1] We saw both Mr. and Mrs. Lewes, but I hardly spoke to Mr. Lewes, as Gertrude mainly talked to him. I am very glad that I went. Mrs. Lewes was very nice; a softened nature of great strength showed itself in all her words and looks. Best of all in her I liked a nervous intensity of expressive power in her hands, as she held mine for a second or two at parting. We spoke of Mme Bodichon.[2] It was a bond I know.

8 January 1865

We went to Hampstead to meet Mr. and Mrs. Lewes.[3] We plunged into great, wonderful, and beautiful subjects. They all love and reverence her, and I was afraid of usurping her, but naturally we came more together. Mr. Lewes was kindness itself. We had an argument about poetry; what it was; whether Thackeray possessed any. I quoted Ruskin and affirmed that if poetry be creative suggestion by the imagination of the noblest grounds for noble emotions,[4] then Thackeray, at moments, shows it in calling out our pity. This led to a quiet talk between Mrs. Lewes and myself about Dickens, and much did I enjoy it. Then we got into talk about Dissenters and the hold they had on the poor; its ground and tendency. You will know that she told me much that was interesting. Then we talked of Nottingham Place and the work here. I asked her what kind of help she had meant I was to ask her for. She told me that if I saw something she could do with money, and I could ask her more easily than anyone else, she should be so happy to give it.

To Mary Harris, in *Octavia Hill: Early Ideals, from Letters Edited by Emily S. Maurice* (London: Allen & Unwin, 1928), pp. 79–80

NOTES

Octavia Hill (1838–1912, *ODNB*), a social reformer, quickly earned GE's respect and support. When funds were solicited to free her from teaching so that she could devote herself full time to housing reform, GE and GHL contributed £200 (*Letters*, VI, 31 *n*. 11).

1. Gertrude Hill was Octavia's sister; she married Charles Lewes in March 1865.

2. In 1856 Octavia Hill had helped Barbara Bodichon in a campaign for a married women's property act.

3. Charles Lewes lived in Church Row (*Letters*, v, 258 *n.* 4a).
4. In *Modern Painters* III (1856) Ruskin defines poetry as 'the suggestion, by the imagination, of noble grounds for noble emotions', namely 'Love, Veneration, Admiration, and Joy' and their opposites, 'Hatred, Indignation (or Scorn), Horror, and Grief' (*Works of John Ruskin*, ed. by E.T. Cook and Alexander Wedderburn, 39 vols (London: Allen, 1903–12), v, 28).

EMILY DAVIES

I

I went to see Mrs. Lewes this afternoon, & tho' I did not stay very long, she said a great deal. We spoke of her health, which is such that she has scarcely ever had the feeling of being really well or can work without a sense of drag, but it does not come to an illness, & she is afraid she inherits from her father, longevity. The anxiety about Mr. Lewes's <sun> son[1] upsets her a good deal, "but one hates oneself for being perturbed." Then she remarked how easily we fall back into any little vice that belongs to us, after being disturbed in it, & spoke of the state of perturbation as entirely caused by not being sufficiently occupied with large interests. I referred to something in Felix Holt about Mr. Lyon's preoccupation which set him above small cares, & said what an enviable state it must be.[2] She said Yes, one only knew it by contrast, by the sense of the want of it. Somehow we got to talk of the Mill on the Floss. She said her sole purpose in writing it was to show the conflict which is going on everywhere <between> when the younger generation with its higher culture comes into collision with the older,[3] & in which, she said, so many young hearts make shipwreck far worse than Maggie. I asked if she had known actual people like the Dodsons & she said "Oh, so much worse." She thought those Dodsons very nice people & that we owe much to them for keeping up the sense of respectability, which was the only religion possible to the mass of the English people. Their want of education made a theoretic or dogmatic religion impossible, & since the Reformation, an imaginative religion had not been possible. It had all been drained away. She considers that in the Mill in the Floss, everything is softened, as compared with real life. Her own experience she said was worse. It was impossible for her to write an autobiography, but she wished that somebody else could do it, it might be useful – or, that she could do it herself. She could do it better than any one else, because she could do it impartially, judging herself, & showing how wrong *she* was. She spoke of having come into collision with her father & being on the brink of being turned out of his house.[4] And she dwelt a little on how much fault there is on the side of the young in such cases, of their ignorance of life, & the narrowness of their intellectual superiority.

Then we got to talk of fiction, & she was eager to explain the difference between prosaic & poetical fiction – that what is prosaic in ordinary novels is not the presence of the realistic element, without which the tragedy cannot be given ˢʰᵒʷⁿ – she herself is obliged to see and feel every minutest detail – but in the absence of anything suggesting the ideal, the higher life. She seems quite oppressed with the quantity of second rate art everywhere about. It gives her such a sense of nausea that it makes it almost impossible to her to write – "such a quantity of dialogue about everything, every hole and corner being ransacked, every possible incident seized upon." not *well* done, but done in such abundance that good art is discouraged & the higher standard works are thrust aside. She was anxious to impress upon me what she felt about the difference between prosaic & poetical work, because she thought I might disseminate it.[5] She said in an appealing tone – "Then when you talk to young people & teachers, you *will* advise against indiscriminate reading?" She thinks she has done very little, in quantity. She cannot write what she does not care about. She has not that kind of ability.

Whatever she has done, she has studied for. Before she began to write the Mill on the Floss, she <read> had it all in her mind, & read about the Trent to make sure that the physical conditions of <an> some English river were such as to make the inundation possible, & assured herself that the population in the neighbourhood was such as to justify her picture. It is still amazing to me, tho' she seemed only to feel how *little* she had done, how she has managed to get thro' so much work, actual hard labour, in the time. A great deal of it must have been very rapidly done. ...

Mrs. Lewes said a good deal besides what I have put down. She thinks people who write regularly for the Press are almost sure to be spoiled by it. There is much dishonesty, bad people's work being praised because they belong to the confederacy. She spoke very strongly about the wickedness of not paying one's debts. She thinks it worse than drunkenness, not in its consequences, but in the character itself.

> To Jane Crow, 21 August 1868, in *Emily Davies: Collected Letters, 1861–1875*, ed. by Ann B. Murphy and Deirdre Raftery (Charlottesville and London: University of Virginia Press, 2004), pp. 287–8 (editors' superscript words, indicating insertions) © 2004 by the Rector and Visitors of the University of Virginia. Reprinted by permission of the University of Virginia Press

II

I went late in the afternoon and found them at home. ... The talk was chiefly on Morals. It came in this way. Something being said about M. Thiers, Mr. Lewes repeated a bon mot of Royer Collard's – 'M. Guizot *sait* la morale; M. Thiers ne la connait pas.'[6] I threw out that really to know morals would be about the highest possible attainment. Mrs. L. did not agree. She thought people generally knew that there was a better and a worse thing to do. Then I told her of a controversy as to whether Morals should be taught as a lesson in schools, and that a friend of mine (Adelaide [Manning]) was going to do it.

She said at first that she thought it would be a most dangerous thing to do, but explained afterwards that she meant that, if it was as a set of dry maxims. Such lessons as Adelaide proposes she thinks may be very useful and interesting, and went into what they should be with zest. She spoke of truthfulness as *the* most important thing to teach – that it should be explained how important it is as the basis of mutual confidence. She said she thought she had succeeded 'with these servants, by talking to them,' in making them understand this, but it was the first time she had ever succeeded with any servants. Usually they only see the harm of falsity in the form of injury by backbiting. She would not admit the difficulty of deciding when truth ought to be spoken and when not. I instanced keeping secret the authorship of a book. She thought that might be done by refusing to answer questions, but Mr. L. agreed with me that often that is as good as telling, and maintained that denial in such a case was not lying. He said he had himself said No, flatly, when he had been asked about the authorship of her books. She said she did not know that he had, and did not support his view. She thought pains should be taken to avoid situations in which truth cannot be told, so as to keep up the habit of truthfulness. She thinks you are not bound to say all that you think, but would use as a test, whether your silence would lead to action being taken under a false impression. In teaching, she would ask the children to say for themselves *why* it is right to speak the truth, etc. She was anxious that my friend should impress upon them the wide, far-reaching consequences of every action, as a corrective of the common feeling that it does not signify what we do – and on the other hand how society reacts upon us, and how much we owe to it. People are always asking, *Why* should I do what is good for society? What is society to me? The answer is that if it were not for the accumulated result of social effort, we should be in the state of wild beasts. Something was said about 'Assuming life to be a blessing.' I asked if we were entitled to assume that, and she said, Certainly not, in talking to people who deny it, and she knew several people who think it a curse. But she says that so long as you don't commit suicide, you must admit that there is a better life, and a worse life, and may try for the better. Some deny even this, but when you come to such stupid scepticism as that it's no use talking to them. She hoped my friend would teach the girls not to think too much of political measures for improving society – as leading away from individual efforts to be good, I understood her to mean. I said I thought there was not much danger of that with girls. It is so much more inculcated upon them to be good and amiable than anything else. She said, was there not a great deal among girls of wanting to do some great thing and thinking it not worth while to do anything because they cannot do that? I said there might be, but I had not come across it. What I had met with more was not caring to do anything. She said, Yes, no doubt stupidity prevails more than anything. Then she hoped my friend would explain to the girls that the state of insensibility in which we are not alive

to high and generous emotions is stupidity, and spoke of the mistake of supposing that stupidity is only intellectual, not a thing of the character – and
of the consequent error of its being commonly assumed that goodness and
cleverness don't go together, cleverness being taken to mean only the power
of *knowing*. ...

To Jane Crow, 24 September 1876, in Barbara Stephen,
Emily Davies and Girton College (London: Constable, 1927), pp. 184–6

NOTES

Sarah Emily Davies (1830–1921, *ODNB*), an activist for women's rights, was instru-
mental in founding Girton College, Cambridge.

1. Thornton Lewes contracted tuberculosis of the spine in Natal, returned to England
   in May 1869, and died in October.
2. Lyon 'felt that serenity and elevation of mind which is infallibly brought
   by a preoccupation with the wider relations of things' (*Felix Holt, the Radical*,
   ed. by Fred C. Thomson (Oxford: Oxford University Press, 1988), p. 146
   (Chapter 15)).
3. In *The Mill on the Floss* GE writes of 'young natures in many generations, that in
   the onward tendency of human things have risen above the mental level of the
   generation before them, to which they have been nevertheless tied by the strongest fibres of their hearts' (ed. by Gordon S. Haight (Oxford: Oxford University
   Press, 1996), pp. 272–3 (Volume II, Book Fourth, Chapter 1)). GE's comments about
   respectability are also mirrored in this chapter.
4. In mid-January 1842, when she refused to go to church. See Mary Sibree Cash's
   first recollection in Part I.
5. She hoped that Davies would write a small book showing that 'the highest kind
   of work' can be done only by 'the few', and that education may lead women to
   recognize 'the great amount of social unproductive labour which needs to be done
   by women' (*Letters*, IV, 425).
6. 'M. Guizot knows morality; M. Thiers does not', contrasting the former's theoreti-
   cal sophistication to the latter's direct practicality; see Henry de Valori, *Petites pages
   d'histoire* (Paris: Téqui, 1881), pp. 100–1, where however the quotation ends with
   'Thiers l'ignore [Thiers ignores it]'.

ROSALIND HOWARD

G[eorge] & I walked to St. John's wood to call on Mrs. Lewis (George
Elliot) – I confess I was indisposed to go. G. had long been urging me to
come & I had felt unwilling partly because I was shy of going to see so
intellectual & powerful a woman – & partly because Mama opposed it on
moral grounds & partly because I did not wish to put myself under the
spell of her Positivist philosophy.[1] But when I had had an hour's talk with
her I was completely charmed & I felt that it was worth a great deal to
have had the privilege of knowing her – Such a gentle sympathetic feminine woman – not the least opinionative or alarming or self asserting,
so full of tenderness & charm – She talked on most interesting topics – She

said George had such a noble beautiful good nature that I must never allow him to worry himself with anxiety about doing some great work in his life & succeeding in being very great in his art, for she said the mere influence of his life especially in the high position he might some day have, would do good.[2] She said people were too restlessly anxious about doing some monumental work now – not content with living a perfect life & influencing others thereby. She said the influence of a person who has a living earnest experience of their own was so great, & yet she said pathetically, we cannot give the young our experience, they will not take it, there must be the actual friction of life the individual contact with sorrow to discipline the character – She spoke of affection as being the basis for all education because it quickened our sympathies with others & with all the outer world more than anything to have felt joy & love in ourselves – & that sympathy with the joys & sorrows of others was the most important quality to attain. She said as a child she always troubled herself about not feeling more intensely the joys & sorrows of others as if they were her own – & now, she said, through tender affection of her own she had reached that keenness of sympathy with others wch she used to desire so much. She said she was very pliant, too much so, that she did not like having to combat the opinions of others; but that moral wrongs roused her intense indignation – such things as Overend & Gurney made her very wrathful – She talked of my children & said "Now is it not a much higher idea that of looking forward to the future life of the race & the world in our own children than to expect an individual immortality." I dissented from this – She talked with enthusiasm about music – She is a woman who turns one inside out in a very short time – & gains all one's confidence – I had a walk with Lewis who said she had such a deeply philosophic mind she ought to write on it *but* that her mind was such a diffident one she could never write except in a dramatic form – & not in the first person – she was never sure in her own mind but saw the good on all sides of a thing – He seemed pleased that we liked the Spanish Gypsey. He says it was suggested by <the> Tintoret's picture of the Annunciation at San Rocco – how great a destiny Mary was called to fulfill – He seems to worship Mrs. Lewis. He says her power of entering into another person's pt of view is so great that if she is beside a woman praying to a winking virgin – she almost believes in that winking virgin. She was very cordial to me & hoped I should often come again – I hope so too – she is deeply interesting –

Diary, 7 February 1869, Castle Howard Archives
MS J23/102/15, reproduced with kind permission
of The Hon. Simon Howard; excerpts publ. in
Eeyan Hartley, 'A Country House Connection:
George Eliot and the Howards of Castle Howard',
GE-GHLS, 22–3 (1993), 17–21

NOTES

Rosalind Frances Howard, née Stanley (1845–1921, *ODNB*), later Countess of Carlisle, was an advocate of temperance reform and women's rights. Seven months after the visit described here, GE wrote to her: 'Short as our little interviews have been they have been delightful to me – as a little walk in a garden may be. One gets a great deal of good out of brief words & looks' (Hartley, p. 20).

1. One of Lord Acton's notes describes her fear: 'Mrs. G. Howard knew G Eliot very early at St. John's Wood. Many ladies ceased to see her when their girls grew up. She was very aggressive, and attacked young people's faith' (CUL, Add. MS 5019/1306, reproduced with kind permission of Lord Acton and the Syndics of Cambridge University Library).
2. A watercolourist, George Howard was the future 9th Earl of Carlisle.

JULIA WEDGWOOD

From one point of view, she appeared as the humblest of human beings. 'Do not, pray, think that I would dream of comparing myself to — ,' she once said, with unquestionable earnestness, mentioning an author whom most people would consider as infinitely her inferior. And the slow, careful articulation and low voice suggested, at times, something almost like diffidence. Nevertheless, mingled with this diffidence was a great consciousness of power, and one sometimes felt with her as if in the presence of royalty, while of course there were moments when one felt that exalted genius has some temptations in common with exalted rank. But they were only moments. How strong was the current of her sympathy in the direction of all humble effort, how reluctantly she checked presumption! Possibly she may sometimes have had to reproach herself with failing to check it. Surely the most ordinary and uninteresting of her friends must feel that had they known nothing of her but her rapid insight into and quick response to their inmost feelings she would still have been a memorable personality to them. This sympathy was extended to the sorrows most unlike anything she could ever by any possibility have known – the failures of life obtained as large a share of her compassion as its sorrows.

> 'The Moral Influence of George Eliot', in *Nineteenth Century Teachers and Other Essays* (London: Hodder and Stoughton, 1909), pp. 225–41 (pp. 233–4); first publ. in *Contemporary Review* 39 (1881), 45–60, signed 'One Who Knew Her'

NOTE

Frances Julia Wedgwood (1833–1913, *ODNB*) wrote two novels and, among other books and articles, *The Moral Ideal* (1888), a testament to the virtues of self-sacrifice.

ELIZABETH MALLESON

If I remember rightly, she always led the talk into channels of subjects dear to Barbara Bodichon and to me – the position of women, education, etc., and the impression given me was of her conservatism on many points that we held could only be treated with courageous reform. She seemed to me timid where we were bold. I always attributed this to her isolated hidden position. I remember well when 'Middlemarch' was coming out in 5s. volumes and we were all reading it, meeting George Eliot and Lewes arm in arm, the then fashion, in Regent Street, and we stopped in the busy street to talk – I to utter lamentations for Lydgate in his relation with Rosamund, she smilingly to insist upon the inexorable fate dramatically necessary for her story.

Elizabeth Malleson 1828–1916: Autobiographical Notes and Letters, with a Memoir by Hope Malleson ([n.p.]: [n.pub.], 1926), pp. 99–100

NOTE

Elizabeth (Mrs. Frank) Malleson, née Whitehead (1828–1916, *ODNB*), an educationist, first met GE in her *Westminster Review* days, and later pleased her greatly by sending her beautiful plants at Christmas. When Malleson established the College for Working Women, GE contributed annually, despite serious doubts, from 1872 to 1880 (*Letters*, VIII, 460).

ANNE THACKERAY RITCHIE

Scene — a cup of tea, George Eliot in a beautiful black satin dressing-gown by the fire, snow outside and German paper-books on the table, a green lamp and paper cutter.

The shrine was so serene and kind that this authoress felt like a wretch for having refused to worship there before.[1] She looked very noble and gentle, with two steady little eyes. You must go and see her.[2] I am sure she will be a friend just as I felt her yesterday, not a personal friend exactly, but a sort of good impulse, trying to see truly, not to be afraid, and to do good to other people.

She said it was much better in life to face the very worst, and build one's cottage in a valley so as not to fall away, and that the very worst was this, that people are living with a power of work and of help in them, which they scarcely estimate. That we know by ourselves how very much other people influence our happiness and feelings, and that we ought to remember that we have the same effect upon them. That we can remember in our own lives how different they might have been if others, even good people, had only conducted themselves differently.

This part I'm glad to say I couldn't follow, nor could I remember at the moment a single instance of any single person's misconduct. She said too we ought to be satisfied with immediate consequences, and respect our work. ...

To Richmond Ritchie [January or February 1873 or 1874], in *Thackeray and His Daughter: The Letters and Journals of Anne Thackeray Ritchie, with Many Letters of William Makepeace Thackeray*, ed. by Hester Thackeray Ritchie (New York and London: Harper, 1924), pp. 164–5 (editor's ellipses)

NOTES

Anne Isabella Thackeray (1837–1919, *ODNB*), later Mrs Richmond Ritchie, then Lady Ritchie, was William Makepeace Thackeray's eldest daughter and like her father, a novelist. Her *Story of Elizabeth*, serialized alongside *Romola* in the *Cornhill*, GE found 'charmingly written' (*Letters*, IV, 209). A similar account of the visit recalled here appears in *From the Porch* (London: Smith, Elder, 1913), pp. 11–12.

1. She had called at least twice before, the second time feeling 'overwhelmed by the importance of the situation, and therefore greatly in the way' (*From Friend to Friend*, ed. by Emily Ritchie (London: Murray, 1919), p. 65).
2. GE saw Richmond Ritchie at Cambridge in 1877, the year he and Anne Thackeray married. He was seventeen years younger than his wife. GE's comment at the time has since seemed pertinent to her own marriage to Cross: 'young men with even brilliant advantages will often choose as their life's companion a woman whose attractions are wholly of the spiritual order' (*Letters*, VI, 398).

MARY PONSONBY

When I was allowed to see her alone, which happened at last pretty often, I thought that to speak to her of all that was lying deepest in one's heart and mind without reserve, and to be received in the kindest and most sympathetic way, was a rare delight.[1] I felt compelled, if I had not felt inclined, to be perfectly true, to be not only veracious but true, and I was met in the same spirit. There was no feeling of egotism to disturb one, for there was very little personal confidence in the talk, except as far as opinions went. I mean any mental or moral struggle which I might in my life have gone through could only have been inferred by her from the result in my mind. She one day resented this, and traces of this mood can be seen in one of her letters to me because I objected to the dogmatic tone of some of her moral injunctions. I thought, and I think so still, more positively now, that she shrank from the pessimistic consequences which might be the result of logically carrying out her theories.[2]

'George Eliot', in *Mary Ponsonby: A Memoir, Some Letters and a Journal*, ed. by Magdalen Ponsonby (London: Murray, [1927]), pp. 89–104 (pp. 91–2)

NOTES

Mary Elizabeth (Mrs Henry Frederick) Ponsonby, née Bulteel (1832–1916, *ODNB*), a maid of honour to Queen Victoria, first wrote to GE in 1874 hoping for a way out of the 'hideous fatalism' (GE's words) of modern science. In what may be the letter referred to here, GE replied that 'molecular physics is not the direct ground of human love and moral action': 'One might as well hope to dissect one's own body and be merry in doing it, as take molecular physics (in which you must banish from your field of view what is specifically human) to be your dominant guide, your determiner of motives, in what is solely human' (*Letters*, VI, 99).

1. Previously Mary Ponsonby had put GE 'on such a towering pinnacle' that she deeply curtseyed when they first met, and then found her '*manierée* and stilted ...

as if each word must be considered in its effect and result' ('George Eliot', pp. 89, 91).
2. Probably a comment on GE's portrayal of the inexorable consequences of human actions, which may have seemed to Ponsonby implicitly fatalistic.

EUGÉNIE HAMERTON

In the afternoon [of 17 November 1876] we called upon George Eliot and Mr. Lewes, who were very friendly indeed. I was greatly struck by George Eliot's memory, for she remembered everything I had told her – seven years ago – about our rustic life, and her first question was — "Are your children well, and do you still drive them to college in a donkey-chaise?"[1] She was gravely sympathetic in alluding to the cause of our long absence from London,[2] and when I said how great was my husband's satisfaction in being there again, she seized both of my hands softly in hers, and asked in the low modulations of her rich voice — "Is there no gap?" ... "Thank God!" I answered, "there is none." Then she let go my hands, and smiling as if relieved she said — "Let us talk over the past years since you came" ...

Philip Gilbert Hamerton: An Autobiography 1834–1858 and a Memoir by His Wife 1858–1894 (London: Seeley, 1897), pp. 439–40 (first ellipsis author's)

NOTES

Eugénie Hamerton, née Gindriez (b.*c*.1839), the wife of artist Philip Gilbert Hamerton (1834–94, *ODNB*), first met GE *c*.1868. Her recollection of that occasion appears in 'Sunday Gatherings at the Priory', below.

1. In France, where her young sons' school was five kilometres from their home (p. 330).
2. The worsening of her husband's prolonged nervous disability, very like panic attacks: 'a terrible apprehension of something fearful – he did not know what' (p. 380). He was already suffering from this condition when GE first met him.

Publishers

JOHN BLACKWOOD

I

Her great difficulty seems to be that she, as she describes it, hears her characters talking, and there is a weight upon her mind as if Savonarola and friends ought to be speaking Italian instead of English. Her description of how she realised her characters was very marvellous. I never heard anything so good as her distinction between what is called the real and the imaginative. It amounted to this, That you could not have the former without the latter and greater quality. Any real observation of life and character must be limited,

and the imagination must fill in and give life to the picture. 'Silas Marner'
sprang from her childish recollection of a man with a stoop and expression
of face that led her to think that he was an alien from his fellows. The dialect
of Lisbeth in 'Adam Bede' arose from her occasionally hearing her father
when with his brothers revert to the dialect of his native district, Derbyshire.
She could not tell how the feeling and knowledge came to her, but when
Lisbeth was speaking she felt it was a real language which she heard.

To Julia Blackwood, his wife, 15 June 1861,
in *Letters*, III, 427

II

... I went to the Priory where I was rapturously received and remained for
about an hour and a half. She was looking a little worn and I think Lewes
fidgets her in his anxiety both about her and her work and himself. She
says she never reads any review, but she certainly hears plentifully all that
is said or written in London on the subject of Deronda. She remarked that
it was hard upon her that people should be angry with her for not doing
what they expected with her characters, and if people were no wiser in their
speculations about more serious subjects such as theories of creation and the
world than they were about the characters one poor woman was creating it
did not say much for human wisdom. These are not her exact words but the
meaning was how vain and foolish was the wisdom of the wise with their
dogmas about what they could not know.

To William Blackwood, his nephew, 18 May 1876,
in *Letters*, VI, 253–4

NOTE

John Blackwood (1818–79, *ODNB*), head of the Edinburgh publishing house of
William Blackwood and Sons, published *Scenes of Clerical Life* and all of GE's novels
except *Romola*. Tactful, patient, encouraging, and forgiving (see the next recollection),
Blackwood was for GE at the start of her career the 'best and most sympathizing of
editors', and at its end one who had been 'bound up with what I most cared for in
my life for more than twenty years' (*Letters*, II, 292; VII, 217).

GEORGE SMITH

It was always my policy to secure for 'the Cornhill Magazine' the best literary work available, and I naturally wished for a novel from George Eliot.
Talking with G.H. Lewes one day he mentioned to me that George Eliot
had in hand an Italian novel, and said that if I would come to their house
early one evening she would read me what she had written of it. I always
appreciated George Eliot's voice: a voice clear and sweet and soft. I have
always held with Shakespeare to be "an excellent thing in woman".[1] But till
I heard George Eliot read the first chapters of "Romola" I had not known

how deeply a woman's voice can charm. She had one of the softest and most agreeable voices that I have ever known; and those who have ever heard her will understand how the opening sentences of "Romola" charmed me as they fell from the author's lips.

The next day [13 May 1862] I wrote to Lewes offering £10,000 – a sum without precedent at that time – for the book for 'the Cornhill', with certain limited rights of publication afterwards, with a stipulation that the book should be of a certain length and extend through sixteen numbers of the magazine. ...

The story of how the £10,000 I originally offered for "Romola" shrank to £7,500 is curious. In her journal George Eliot makes no explanation;[2] but the explanation is so honourable to her artistic temperament that I give it in detail.

When the work was almost completed and its publication about to begin George Eliot said to me: "I find I cannot properly divide the book into sixteen parts. It doesn't lend itself to this division. It must be published in twelve parts." This somewhat disturbed me, and I argued against her decision. But George Eliot was firm. She would not inflict what she thought would be an artistic injury upon her book by breaking it up into sixteen parts.

I said at last "I daresay this has not occurred to you, that this change would make a serious difference to me. For one thing, under the division into twelve parts each part will occupy more pages in 'the Cornhill' than we should care to give to one novel. This, perhaps, is not an insuperable difficulty; but there remains a consideration of another kind. I have to consider what 'the Cornhill' can afford to pay for its contributions. If I divide £10,000 by sixteen I get one amount; but you will see that if I have to divide £10,000 by twelve I get a much larger sum, and the cost falls much more heavily on each number of the magazine. Under the original arrangement, dividing the novel by sixteen, I should pay £625 for each instalment; but dividing it by twelve the cost to me for each is a little over £833." "Yes," George Eliot replied: "that *has* occurred to me; but I thought it would be a simple calculation to see how much less I should receive for the book if published in twelve parts instead of sixteen." "The calculation," I said, "is simple enough; but it means a substantial reduction in the amount you would receive. You will get £7,500 instead of £10,000;" and I begged her to reconsider the question. I reminded her that the magazine form of the story was temporary; the book would afterwards appear in a complete form, and any artistic injury the work might be supposed to suffer owing to its being broken up into sixteen parts would be temporary.

But George Eliot was firm. She was cheerfully content to accept the smaller sum for the sake of an artistic division of her novel. Lewes himself by no means shared George Eliot's artistic scruples. He seconded me heart and soul; for he was not so indifferent to money considerations as the woman of genius.[3] But George Eliot was immovable; and, much to Lewes's disgust, instead of paying £10,000 for "Romola", I paid her £7,500. Its author threw away £2,500 on what many people would think a literary caprice, but what she regarded as an act of loyalty to her canons of art.

George Eliot was nobly free from any undue love of gain and capable of fine acts of generosity. She once sent me for 'the Cornhill' a very remarkable story entitled "Cousin Jacob". When I met Lewes I said, "I really don't know what kind of a cheque I must send to Mrs. Lewes for that beautiful story." "You had better not send her any cheque at all," he replied; "she intends that as a present." I found this to be the case. She told me she had long wanted to "make me a little present", and insisted with great obstinacy that I should accept "Cousin Jacob" in that light.

'Recollections of a long and busy life', NLS, MS 23191, fols 211–15, reproduced with kind permission of the Trustees of the National Library of Scotland

NOTES

George Murray Smith (1824–1901, *ODNB*), founder of the *Dictionary of National Biography*, was one of the most distinguished and prosperous publishers of his time. An old friend of GHL's, in 1848 he brought out GHL's novel *Rose, Blanche, and Violet*, and from 1860 to 1865 published essays by him in the *Cornhill*. Smith also did a de luxe edition of *Romola* in 1880. Another recollection by him appears in 'Other Personal Meetings', below.

1. Lear's description of Cordelia: 'Her voice was ever soft, | Gentle, and low, an excellent thing in woman' (*King Lear*, v, iii). Smith's sentence is incomplete in the original.

2. In the passage omitted here (fol. 212), Smith copied from Cross's *Life* GE's diary entries of 23 January, 27 February and 23 May 1862 (II, 332, 337, 339), where she recorded ('not with exact accuracy', he notes) that Smith's £10,000 offer was reduced to £7,000 rather than £7,500. But his published version of this reminiscence also presents the amount as £7,000 ('Our Birth and Parentage', *Cornhill Magazine*, n.s. 10 (1901), 4–17 (p. 10)). The difference probably reflects his attempt to ease the increased financial pressure on each number – with undecided results, since he never knew 'if "Romola" "paid" "the Cornhill". Certainly the sale of the magazine did not improve during its appearance' (fols 223–4). GE offered Smith her next novel, *Felix Holt*, expecting £5,000. When he declined, she returned to Blackwood.

3. In her diary GE wrote that Smith's offer 'made me think about money – but it is better for me not to be rich' (*Journals*, p. 108).

MARY BLACKWOOD PORTER

On one occasion when we were calling on her that summer [1875] she said she was very anxious about the safety of the MS. of 'Deronda,' and wanted to have it back, but dared not trust it to the post-office.[1] My father said he could not bring it himself next day, but could send it by a trusty messenger (the footman). At this she quailed. "Oh, he might stop at a public-house and forget it." We assured her such a lapse had never been known to occur. "Then might he not, if he were the sort of high-minded Bayard we described, be very likely to stop and help at a fire?" This was a contingency we had never contemplated, and finally, after much laughter, we promised her that some member of the family should place the MS. in her hands, and as a matter of fact I think my mother drove over with it to her the next morning. On this, as on all occasions when I saw her, the impression was that of a person beyond all things kindly and sympathetic, ever ready to be amused and interested in all that concerned her friends. Her sense of humour, too, was extremely keen, and my father, I remember, always made her laugh.

> Margaret Oliphant, *Annals of a Publishing House: William Blackwood and His Sons, Their Magazine and Friends*, 3rd edn, 3 vols (Edinburgh and London: Blackwood, 1897–98), III: *John Blackwood, by His Daughter Mrs. Gerald Porter* (1898), pp. 388–9

NOTE

Mary Blackwood (Mrs Gerald) Porter (1855–1939) was the daughter of John and Julia Blackwood. Another recollection by her appears in 'Sunday Gatherings at the Priory', below.

1. When William Blackwood called in April and proposed taking Volume I to his uncle John, GE reacted with 'horror and fright and meek expression': 'It was one of the most striking scenes I have ever seen', he wrote, 'and for a minute or two she would not speak. She seemed just to tremble at the idea of the M.S. being taken from her as if it were her baby ...' (*Letters*, VI, 136).

ALEXANDER MACMILLAN

I have just come back from a very pleasant interview with George Eliot. She did not say *no*, and promised to think it over and write to us.[1] She repeated what Lewes told us was her feeling, that she has a dread of coming forward in her own person and passing judgment on authors, and spoke as you, or even I, might speak with aversion of the habit of mind that leads people to pass off as sort of *final utterances* the feelings and thoughts which come to you in reading an author. She quoted a passage from Ste. Beuve which she thought should be the motto of such a series as we propose. I cannot give you the French – she is to send it – but the effect of it was that the business of a true critic was to appreciate, not *fix the doom* of an author. When you see it you will, I have no doubt, at once adopt it – if we can't get her to contribute a book it will be something at least to have a motto from her.[2]

> To John Morley, 9 November 1877, in Charles L. Graves, *Life and Letters of Alexander Macmillan* (London: Macmillan, 1910), p. 343

NOTES

The son of a Scottish farmer, Alexander Macmillan (1818–96, *ODNB*) began publishing in London with his brother in 1843. After years of distinguished work in Cambridge, he founded *Macmillan's Magazine* in 1859 and, moving Macmillan & Co. back to London, built one of the most esteemed lists in English publishing history.

1. Macmillan asked her to write the volume on Shakespeare in what became the English Men of Letters series (originally Short Books on Great Writers), edited by John Morley, who conceived the idea. Macmillan's letter has a further remark omitted by Graves: 'It is clear that our *Prima Donna* must be paid on a different scale from the others – whether 3 or 5 times we must consider and consult' (Charles Morgan, *The House of Macmillan (1843–1943)* (London: Macmillan, 1944), p. 117).
2. GE declined the offer but sent the motto (*Letters*, VI, 416): 'La critique pour moi (comme pour M. Joubert), c'est le plaisir de connaître les esprits, non de les régenter [Criticism for me (as for M. Joubert), is the pleasure of knowing minds, not ruling over them]' (*Les cahiers de Sainte-Beuve* (Paris: Lemerre, 1876), p. 11). I have not found that Morley adopted it. Matilda Betham-Edwards remarks of GE and GHL's evening reading that the two discovered the best in a book, 'instead of the faults being held up to scorn' ('A Week with George Eliot', *Temple Bar*, 73 (1885), 226–32 (p. 230).)

Other Personal Meetings

'NOT GIFTED, BUT ENTHUSIASTIC'

Frederick Lehmann

Through [G.H. Lewes] I became acquainted with George Eliot, and at one time saw a great deal of her. What first struck one about her was the strange contrast between the large head, the masculine, Dantesque features, and the soft melodious voice, which always cast a spell over me.[1] One might almost have forgotten that she was a woman, so profound was her insight; but I, at least, could never forget while in her company that I was with an exceptional being.

In the winter of 1866 my wife and family were at Pau, while I was alone in London. George Eliot was a very fair pianist, not gifted, but enthusiastic, and extremely painstaking. During a great part of that winter I used to go to her every Monday evening at her house in North Bank, Regent's Park, always taking my violin with me. We played together every piano and violin sonata of Mozart and Beethoven. I knew the traditions of the best players, and was able to give her some hints, which she always received eagerly and thankfully. Our audience consisted of George Lewes only, and he used to groan with delight whenever we were rather successful in playing some beautiful passage. Now that both he and George Eliot are no more, the scene is to me a strange, sad, and quite unique memory.

Memories of Half a Century, ed. by R.C. Lehmann
(London: Smith, Elder, 1908), pp. 131–2

NOTE

A wealthy businessman and art collector, Frederick Lehmann (1826–91) met GE in 1864 at Covent Garden, when she and GHL happened to sit next to him and his wife Nina, who had known GHL years earlier. (Her recollection appears in 'The Continent', below.) As John Rignall points out, GE's friendship with the Lehmanns and their circle marked the social acceptance that finally came to her from her literary success (*Companion*, p. 197).

1. '"She speaks always in a very low voice"', Lehmann wrote to his wife of a dinner with GE and GHL, '"and somehow everybody is on his best behaviour and tries for his best mental posture in the presence of these two extraordinary mortals"' (John Lehmann, *Ancestors and Friends* (London: Eyre & Spottiswoode, 1962), p. 171).

CLOSE, LOW, AND EAGER

Charles Eliot Norton

We met Lewes at Oxford last summer [1868], & as soon as we came to London he came to see us, & asked us to come to see his wife, saying that she <was> never made calls herself, but was always at home on Sunday afternoons. She is an object of great interest and great curiosity to society here. She is not received in general society, and the women who visit her are either so emancipée as not to mind what the world says about them, or <are people who> have no social position to maintain. Lewes dines out a good deal, & some of the men with whom he dines go without their wives to his house on Sundays. No one whom I have heard speak, speaks in other than terms of respect of Mrs. Lewes, but the common feeling is that it will not do for society to condone so flagrant a breach as hers of a convention & a sentiment (to use no stronger terms) on which morality greatly relies for support. I suspect society is right in this; – at least since I have been here I have heard of one sad case in which a poor weak woman defended her own wretched course, which had destroyed her own happiness & that of other persons also, by the example of Mrs. Lewes. I do not believe that many people think that Mrs. Lewes violated her own moral sense, or is other than a good woman in her present life, – but they think her example pernicious, & that she cut herself off by her own act from the society of the women who feel themselves responsible for the tone of social morals in England.[1]

After a while, as Susan did not call, an invitation came for her & me to lunch, and this we very readily accepted. The Leweses live in the St. John's Wood district, not far from Regent's Park. Their house, called "The Priory" is a little square two story dwelling standing in a half yard, half garden, surrounded with one of those high brick walls of which one grows so impatient in England. Lewes received us at the door with characteristic animation; – he looks & moves like an old fashioned French barber or dancing master, very ugly, very vivacious, very entertaining. You expect to see him take up his fiddle & begin to play. His talk is much more French than English in its liveliness, & in the grimace & gesture with which it is accompanied, – all the action of his mind is rapid, & <he is so very sure with> it is so full that it seems to be running over. "Oh!, if you like to hear stories" he said one day. "I can tell you stories for twelve hours on end," – it is just the same if you like to hear science, or philosophy. His acquirements are very wide, wider, perhaps, than deep, but the men who know most on special subjects speak with respect of his attainments. I have heard both Darwin & Sir Charles Lyell speak very highly of the thoroughness of his knowledge in their departments. In fact his talents seem equal to anything. But he is not a man who wins more than a moderate liking from you. He has the vanity of a Frenchman, his <social> moral perceptions are not acute & he consequently often fails in social tact & taste. He has what it is hard to call a vulgar air, but at least there is something in his air which reminds you of vulgarity.

He took us into the pleasant, cheerful drawing rooms which occupy one side of the lower floor of the house, where Mrs. Lewes received us very pleasantly, – and we soon had lunch, the only other person present being his eldest, and married, son [Charles]. Lunch was set in the study, a cheerful room like the others, lined with well filled bookshelves, save over the fireplace where hung a staring likeness and odious, vulgarizing portrait of Mrs. Lewes.[2] Indeed all the works of art in the house bore witness to the want of delicate artistic feeling, or good culture on the part of the occupants, with the single exception so far as I observed of the common lithograph of Titian's Christ of the Tribute Money. The walls of the drawing room in which we sat after lunch were adorned with proof impressions (possibly the original drawings, I am not sure) of the illustrations to "Romola."[3] The portrait of Mrs. Lewes reminded me, <of> not by its own merit, of Couture's drawing of George Sand, – & there is a strong likeness to this drawing in her own face. The head & face are hardly as noble as George Sand's, but the lines are almost as strong & masculine; the cheeks are almost as heavy, & the hair is dressed in a similar style, but the eyes are not so deep, & there is less suggestion of possible beauty & possible sensuality in the general contour & in the expression. Indeed one rarely sees a plainer woman; dull complexion, dull eyes, heavy features. For the greater part of two or three hours she & I talked together with little intermission. Her talk was by no means brilliant. She said not one memorable thing, but it was the talk of a person of strong mind who had thought much & who felt deeply, & consequently it was more than commonly interesting. Her manner was too intense, she leans over to you till her face is close to yours & speaks in very low & eager tones; nor is her manner perfectly simple, it is a little that, or it suggests that, of a woman who feels herself to be of mark & is accustomed, as she is, to the adoring flattery of a coterie of not undistinguished admirers.

In the course of the afternoon three or four men came in, – the only one whom I knew was Professor Beesly. We came away just before sunset. As the gate shut behind us I said, "Well, Sue, do you want to go there again." "No" said she, "I don't care much about it."[4]

Everyone who knows Mrs. Lewes well seems to be attached to her, & those who know speak in the warmest terms of her relations to her husband & his family, – of her good <ceaseless [?]> sense & her goodness.

> Letter to George W. Curtis, 29 January 1869, Houghton Library, Harvard University, bMS Am 1088.2, fols 2^r–5^r, reproduced with kind permission of the Houghton Library; publ. with alterations and omissions in *Letters of Charles Eliot Norton*, I, 316–19, the source for *Letters*, V, 7–9

NOTES

For Charles Eliot Norton, see Part III.

1. Another American, Louisa May Alcott, gathered a different impression: 'All whom I saw loved, respected, and defended her; some upon the plea that, if genius, like charity, covers a multitude of sins in men, why not in women? Others, that outsiders know so little of the sorrowful story that they cannot judge the case; and, though they may condemn the act, they can pity the actors, and heartily admire all that is admirable in the life and labor of either' ('Glimpses of Eminent Persons', *Independent*, 1 November 1866, p. 1). (GE was too ill to see Alcott when she called in June 1866.)
2. By Frederic Burton, widely reproduced; GE's friends, she wrote, considered it 'a remarkably fine portrait' (*Letters*, IV, 212).
3. By Frederic Leighton, either the original drawings or the woodcuts (Leonée Ormond, *Companion*, pp. 197–8).
4. In this letter to a friend back home, Norton screens his wife by presenting her first as not calling on GE and then as not caring to visit again. In fact, she returned more than once, and on 8 February took her two daughters to the Priory for lunch (*Letters*, V, 10 *n*. 3a).

'BEHOLD ME LITERALLY IN LOVE'

Henry James

The one marvel as yet, of my stay, is having finally seen Mrs. Lewes ... I was immensely impressed, interested and pleased. To begin with she is magnificently ugly – deliciously hideous. She has a low forehead, a dull grey eye, a vast pendulous nose, a huge mouth, full of uneven teeth and a chin and jaw-bone *qui n'en finissent pas* [which never end]. ... Now in this vast ugliness resides a most powerful beauty which, in a very few minutes steals forth and charms the mind, so that you end as I ended, in falling in love with her. Yes behold me literally in love with this great horse-faced blue-stocking. I don't know in what the charm lies, but it is thoroughly potent. An admirable physiognomy – a delightful expression, a voice soft and rich as that of a counselling angel – a mingled sagacity and sweetness – a broad hint of a great underlying world of reserve, knowledge, pride and power – a great feminine dignity and character in these massively plain features – a hundred conflicting shades of consciousness and simpleness – shyness and frankness – graciousness and remote indifference – these are some of the more definite elements of her personality.[1] Her manner is extremely good tho' rather too intense and her speech, in the way of accent and syntax peculiarly agreeable. Altogether, she has a larger circumference than any woman I have ever seen.[2]

To Henry James, his father, 10 May 1869, in *Henry James Letters*, ed. by Leon Edel, 4 vols (Cambridge, Mass.: Belknap Press of Harvard University Press, 1974–84), I, 116–17

NOTES

The novelist Henry James (1843–1916, *ODNB*), born in New York City and naturalized in 1915, was twenty-six years old at the time of this meeting. Almost a decade later, he attended her Sunday gatherings, still finding her 'both sweet and superior', her only fault 'a tendency to *aborder* [broach] only the highest themes' (II, 172). He also visited her at Witley, where she was 'bland, benign, commiserating ... beside the fire in a chill desert of a room' (*The Middle Years* (New York: Scribner, 1917), p. 82). Elizabeth Deeds Ermarth surveys James's reviews of GE's fiction in *Companion*, pp. 176–7; selections from them are in *Critical Heritage*, pp. 273–7, 353–9, 362–3, 417–33. Another recollection by James appears in Part VI.

1. In 1914, seventy-one years old, James dictated from memory a much longer narrative of this meeting, later published in *The Middle Years*, pp. 61–70. There he replaces the present description with: 'It infinitely moved me to see so great a celebrity quite humanly and familiarly agitated – even with something clear and noble in it too, to which, as well as to the extraordinarily interesting dignity of her whole odd personal conformation, I remember thinking her black silk dress and the lace mantilla attached to her head and keeping company on either side with the low-falling thickness of her dark hair effectively contributed. I have found myself, my life long, attaching value to every noted thing in respect to a great person – and George Eliot struck me on the spot as somehow *illustratively* great ...' (pp. 65–6). She was agitated because GHL's son Thornie was writhing on the floor in agony from spinal pain.
2. In the *Middle Years* recollection, GE tells James of her recent holiday in the south of France, and he is struck by 'the moral interest, the absence of the *banal*' in her account, especially her mentioning 'the frequency in all those parts of "evil faces: oh the evil faces!" *That* recorded source of suffering enormously affected me – I felt it as beautifully characteristic: I had never heard an *impression de voyage* so little tainted with the superficial or the vulgar' (p. 67).

THE IMAGINED AND THE REAL

Soph'ia V. Kovalevskaia

However imperceptibly, I had composed a very definite and distinct image of the ideal George Eliot in my own imagination. Alas, it was suddenly clear that the image in no way resembled the reality. A small lean figure with a disproportionately large, heavy head, a mouth with huge protrud-ing "English" teeth, a nose which, though straight and beautifully out-lined, was too massive for a feminine face, some kind of old-fashioned strange coiffure, a black dress of light sheer cloth exposing the thinness and boniness of her neck which even more sharply underlined the sickly, yellowish tinge of the lace – this is what, to my horror, appeared in that first minute. I was still overcome by confusion when George Eliot came towards me and spoke in her soft, beautiful, velvety voice. The first sounds of this voice reconciled me to reality and returned to me my George Eliot, the one who lived in my imagination. Never in my life have I heard a softer, more "enchanting" voice. When I read the famous words of Othello about Desdemona's voice,[1] I can't help remembering George Eliot's.

She seated me on a small sofa next to her and immediately a sincere, easy conversation started as if we had been acquainted for a long time. I cannot now recall what we talked about at our first meeting; I cannot say whether what she said was clever or original, but I know that within a half hour I was completely captivated by her charm, felt that I loved her very much, and was convinced that the real George Eliot was ten times better and more beautiful than the imagined one.

I am absolutely incapable of describing or explaining the special, indis-putable quality which captivated everyone who approached her. It would be impossible to convey it to someone who had not experienced it; but, truly, anyone who has known George Eliot closely would confirm my words. Turgenev, who, as we know, was a great admirer and connoisseur of female beauty once said to me about George Eliot: "I know that she is not attractive, but when I am with her I do not see this." He also said that George Eliot was the first woman who made him understand that it was possible to fall madly in love with a woman who was decidedly not pretty. As for myself, whenever I saw her after some time, I was invariably struck by her appearance and said to myself, "No, she is ugly, indeed," but within a half hour I would be once more amazed that I could have found her so.

'A Memoir of George Eliot', trans. and introd. by Miriam Haskell Berlin, *Yale Review*, 73 (1984), 533–50 (pp. 537–8) © 1984 by The Yale Review; reproduced with permission of Blackwell Publishing Ltd

NOTE

Only nineteen years old at the time of this meeting, 3 October 1869, Soph'ia V. Kovalevskaia (1850–91) would become a professor of mathematics at the University of Stockholm, making her 'the first woman to hold such a position in Europe' (Berlin, p. 533). These recollections were published in 1885, in the wake of Cross's *Life*, which Kovalevskaia read when it appeared (p. 536). GE found her 'a pretty creature with charming modest voice and speech' (*Journals*, p. 138). Other recollections by her appear in 'Sunday Gatherings at the Priory', below, and in Part VI.

1. A confusion; see George Smith's recollection, *n.* 1, in 'Publishers' above.

'A LIBERAL EDUCATION'

George Smith

George Eliot is the only woman I have known who gave me a glimpse of the truth of Steele's well-known saying that to have known her was an "equivalent to a liberal education".[1] She had a curious faculty – which was very agreeable to one's vanity – of making her interlocutor pleased with himself. I seldom left her presence without having a less modest estimate of my intellectual faculties than I had when I entered it! Perhaps her genius acted as a stimulus to an ordinary brain: or, perhaps, it was her gift of seizing upon a commonplace remark as it fell from your lips, translating it into philosophical terms, clothing it in the choicest words, and giving it back to you with the subtle suggestion that *you* had uttered some profoundly wise observation!

My experience at this point was not unique. I said to George Du Maurier on one occasion, as we left the house to walk home together, "How very strange it is that I never leave that house without thinking myself a cleverer fellow than when I entered it!" "Well," Du Maurier replied, "I can tell you something still stranger. I have exactly the same sensation!"[2] ...

George Eliot's personal appearance, judged artistically, was not attractive. Her face was large; the under-jaw was of masculine heaviness. She sometimes impressed strangers as a harsh and masculine woman. She came of peasant parents, and there survived perhaps a peasant strain in her. She did not dress well. Her dress was rich and handsome, and not exactly in bad taste: but its style would not have satisfied a French milliner. It was a put-your-things-on-anyway sort of dress.[3] But you lost the impression her appearance first made as you listened to George Eliot speaking. She was undoubtedly a sad woman, and she excited one's sympathy; it would scarcely be an exaggeration indeed, to describe her as unhappy. There was much that was painful in her position. She had a genuine affection for Lewes, who gave her what she wanted – a constant atmosphere of appreciation and shrewd practical assistance in her affairs, and she was unconscious of moral wrong in her relationship with him. But the relationship cost her much. Lord Acton says that for the happiness that her unwedded life with Lewes gave her she paid the price of "liberty of speech, the foremost rank amongst the women of her time, and a tomb in Westminster Abbey".[4] Sometimes perhaps she was uneasily conscious of the price she paid;[5] certainly her friends had that consciousness. It was peculiarly painful to me when she asked about my wife and children; for I did not introduce them to her. She insisted on my describing them to her; she knew all about them, even to the pet names of the children in the household circle.[6] But though I wished my wife to know her, and my wife shared that wish, social considerations somehow rendered that impossible. Our daughters were growing up; we were living at

Hampstead, the favourite abode of "Mrs. Grundy". George Eliot was more or less a public character: her actual position was perfectly well known, and unpleasant social results might have followed if young girls had been known as her visitors. I took my eldest son to see George Eliot, and the visit gave her the greatest pleasure. On one occasion, too, I had taken my eldest daughter to the theatre, and found we were sitting in the next stalls to Lewes and George Eliot. When I made the necessary introduction Mrs. Lewes turned round and said "And *this* is Dolly!" My daughter was struck dumb with the discovery that her household name was thus familiar.

'Recollections', fols 210–11, 215–17

NOTES

For George Smith, see 'Publishers', above.

1. *Tatler* 49 (2 August 1709), of Lady Betty (Elizabeth Hastings): 'to behold her is an immediate check to loose behaviour, and to love her is a liberal education' (*The Tatler and the Guardian* (Edinburgh: Nimmo, 1880), p. 113).

2. Compare Soph'ia V. Kovalevskaia: '"I never feel myself so clever and profound as when I am talking with George Eliot," one of our common friends once said to me, and I must acknowledge experiencing the same thing frequently' (p. 539). Not everyone was comfortable with this particular feature of her conversation. Frederic Wedmore found GE 'curiously deferential in her reception of crude things said to her by crude young people like myself: one would almost have thought it an affectation – so marked was it; but I think it was part of the character; I think it was sincere, though undeserved' (*Memories* (London: Methuen, 1912), p. 83). In a slightly different context, Mary Ponsonby remarks that 'the desire that any good things said by others should be appreciated gave one a feeling of discomfort if it so happened that a remark of one's own was being made to sound better than it deserved' ('George Eliot', p. 91).

3. Charles Lewes's schoolmate John Payne recalled GE as '"the most untidy woman he ever knew"', her stockings at her heels (Thomas Wright, *The Life of John Payne* (London: Unwin, 1919), p. 16).

4. 'George Eliot's Life', *Nineteenth Century* (1885), repr. in *Historical Essays and Studies*, ed. by John Neville Figgis and Reginald Vere Laurence (London: Macmillan, 1907), pp. 273–304 (p. 291). Earlier Acton wrote that 'looking to the long period of isolation, to the consequent excessive importance of Lewes in her social horizon, to the loss of much useful contact and the exclusion of some kinds of influence and experience, I must think that too much was sacrificed to Lewes and that it is apparent that, in 1853, she immeasurably underestimated herself, to say nothing of her estimate of him and of some of the literary and social consequences' (letter to J.W. Cross, 21 December [1883?], Yale).

5. Two other persons second this observation. Elizabeth Rundle Charles remarked of GE's marriage to Cross that 'perhaps to her the name of *wife* may have seemed a refuge from all the agony of years. She told me she used to *tremble* when she met anyone. She felt it all so bitterly. She had given up everything, good position and respectability for Mr. Lewes' (Hester Thackeray Fuller and Violet Hammersley, *Thackeray's Daughter: Some Recollections of Anne Thackeray Ritchie* (Dublin: Euphorion, 1951), p. 154). In December 1894 Frederic Burton said that GE 'had no religious

scruples' over living with GHL unmarried, 'but felt in the long run very bitterly the having cut herself away from social life' (*Lady Gregory's Diaries, 1892–1902*, ed. by James Pethica (New York: Oxford University Press, 1996), p. 58).
6. When Arthur Hugh Clough's widow Blanche called one Sunday with her son, GE's 'first question was a pathetic, "What is his name?" She always liked to call children by their names, she added' (Betham-Edwards, *Mid-Victorian Memories*, p. 55).

ON NOT READING CRITICISM

Lewis Wingfield

The lamented George Eliot told me once [*c*.1871–72], in the course of a friendly chat, that she carefully avoided the sight of newspaper critiques on her works, not on account of a sense of superior loftiness and incapacity of improvement, but because:

1. A novelist who is at all successful in his extremely difficult craft is usually the equal, at least, in intellect of his anonymous professional critic.

2. The intelligent person who has made a careful and conscientious study of a period, during years perhaps, is likely to know more about it than an individual who, having many other matters to attend to, has not given special care and attention to one subject.

3. It is easier to pick holes than to do a thing yourself; very easy indeed to point to minute variations from strict historical accuracy as due to ignorance, which slight changes are made deliberately for a set purpose. We all know that by exposing apparent ignorance in others we exalt our own wisdom.

4. It is not unusual for keen but maiden swords to be fleshed, brightened, and sharpened in the field of professional criticism – a state of things productive of unnecessary vexation to the victim, rather than improvement in art.

'L'Envoi', *Barbara Philpot: A Study of Manners and Morals*, 3 vols
(London: Bentley, 1885), I, p. xi

NOTE

An artist and actor born in Ireland, the Hon. Lewis Strange Wingfield (1842–91, *ODNB*) was a neighbour of GE's from 1871 and saw much of her the following year. At this time Wingfield was exhibiting occasionally at the Royal Academy.

'THE PRINCESS AND THE DRAGON'

Steele MacKaye

I was ushered into a room furnished richly but unpretentiously and in exquisite taste. 'Mrs. Lewes would see me directly.' She received me with dignity, took my letter, read it deliberately, and then for the first time looked intently at my face, at the same time extending her hand to me with charming frankness. In another moment I was perfectly at home and forgot everything in the presence of this charming woman, for she is the most fascinating and the ugliest woman that I ever saw in my life.

Her husband, Lewes, was there, and it was not long before I found myself comparing the couple to the Princess and the Dragon. Mr. Lewes sat glowering at me all the time I was there, but after a while I succeeded in forgetting his presence and that he was, as far as could be, the husband of George Eliot, in intellect and genius the queen of all England. ... I told her of the changes I had made in her story, particularly in the conclusion, which I had found necessary to alter wholly.[1] The denouement, as I left it, made a really strong dramatic effect, and the author of *Silas Marner* acknowledged the improvement and regretted, so she said, that she had not thought of it herself. ... I talked with her three hours and I was amazed, when I rose to go, to see how the time had flown. I was to call again the next day to read her my play, in which she seemed to have taken a real interest, but on that very day I received a note from 'the Dragon' saying that 'Mrs. Lewes had, upon mature deliberation, decided not to have her story dramatised.'[2] Of course the play was never produced, and it now lies with scores of other manuscripts of mine, which may some day see the light.

Percy MacKaye, *Epoch: The Life of Steele MacKaye*, 2 vols
(New York: Boni & Liveright, 1927), I, 187–8
(author's ellipses)

NOTES

Steele MacKaye (1842–94) was an American actor, playwright, and director. He called on 16 January 1873 to propose an adaptation of *Silas Marner* for the stage (see *Letters*, V, 368).

1. In MacKaye's version, William Dane reappears, confesses his treachery, and is pardoned: 'Ah!' Silas says, 'We can forgive anything to errin' man. 'Tis only God it's hard to doubt.' The curtain falls after Silas agrees to join Nancy and Godfrey in their house, along with Eppie and Aaron, where he will 'play grand'ther' to them all ('Silas Marner: A Play in Four Acts Based on George Eliot's Novel by Steele MacKaye (1873)', fols 85–6, TS, New York Public Library). MacKaye retains from the novel Eppie's refusal to leave Silas, but joins everyone in a final embrace. In the play, apology and pardon allow reunion with the past; only after all-round forgiveness can Godfrey and Nancy have a genuine home. (The MS of the play, slightly revised in the TS, is in Papers of the MacKaye Family, Rauner Special Collections Library, Dartmouth College.)

2. For the rejection MacKaye blamed GHL, 'outrageously egotistical, and so void of good taste as to even bully the woman – who has sacrificed everything for him – before me' (*Epoch*, I, 187). Percy MacKaye prints GHL's letter, which has remained uncollected: 'Dear Sir: After fuller consideration, we find ourselves compelled to forego the pleasure of hearing you read *Silas Marner*. The fact is that the idea of having her novels produced on the stage has always been extremely distasteful to Mrs. Lewes, and indeed the structure of the two forms of art is so essentially

different that every author sensitive about his work cannot but be pained at the deformations and transformations necessary to convert a novel into a drama. | This being the case, she must continue – as heretofore – to hold herself entirely aloof from any contemplated adaptation of her works. She begs me to express her regret at the possible disappointment she is thus forced to entail upon you. | I remain, dear Sir, Yours truly, *G.H. Lewes'* (I, 188). Later Sir W.S. Gilbert was granted permission and came up with *Dan'l Druce, Blacksmith* (1876), which GHL thought 'wretched stuff, poorly acted' (*Letters*, V, 368 *n*. 9).

KRASINSKI AND HENGLER'S

Richard Davey

I had the honor of being received by Mrs. Lewes some two years ago [*c*.1878]. She lived, as all the world knows, in St. John's wood, in a very beautiful villa, brim full of artistic gems – at least so I have been told. When I arrived it was twilight and I saw only dim outlines – a very dim one of the illustrious lady herself; so dim, that, although in the room for over an hour, I fear I could not have recognized her afterwards. I am told she loved the soft light which follows the set of sun,[1] and also she was passionately fond of sitting in the fire glow of an evening. ... I had sent Mrs. Lewes a copy of Mrs. Cook's "Krasinski's Undivine Comedy," and she begged me to call upon her to receive her thanks. She pronounced it, in her beautiful rich voice, a most noble and affecting book, admirably translated, and praised it as full of generous thought and profound learning. ... "I envy you," said George Eliot, "the friendship of this lady. I would like to have known her. She must have possessed an unusual mind and a grand nature. American women are certainly enthusiastic, more so, I think, than the English. We are cold and formal, but they are expansive, like the French. Still, human nature is pretty nearly the same all the world over."

Singular to relate, the next time I saw George Eliot was at Hengler's Circus with Mr. Lewes and also with Mr. Cross, his speedy successor. They appeared to enjoy the performance, although, I must say, a circus was about the last place I ever expected to see George Eliot in.

'Our London Letter', *Evening Mail*,
18 November 1881, p. 1

NOTE

An English journalist based for ten years in New York, Richard Davey (1848–1911) returned to England to work on the *Morning Post* and the *Saturday Review*. He also wrote historical fiction.

1. 'The light in this quarter of London and at Hampstead falls earlier upon the many north windows constructed to receive it, and dwells longer in its gentle merging into night ...' (Joseph Hatton, 'Some Glimpses of Artistic London', *Harper's*, 67 (1883), 828–50 (p. 844)).

WITH A GOVERNESS

Arthur Paterson

A former nursery governess to Mr. Lewes's grandchildren has a vivid remembrance of an unexpected visit [*c.*1878] paid them by George Eliot:

"I was quite alone," she writes, "when the carriage drove up, and George Eliot came down the garden walk. I felt quite inadequate to the occasion, and dreadfully nervous, but she put me at my ease at once by asking where I had bought the frilling I had in my frock, as she would like her maid to buy some for her like it. Imagine my feelings! She had descended to earth, and put herself on a sort of footing with me! From that moment I felt I could talk and entertain her. She asked to see my paintings, which, alas! I know now must have been very feeble attempts at art – but her sympathy cheered me, I remember, and made me aim at higher things."

George Eliot's Family Life and Letters (London: Selwyn & Blount, 1928), p. 251

NOTE

Arthur Paterson (1862–1928) was a biographer and novelist, the brother of GE's friend Helen Allingham. The governess has remained untraced.

Sunday Gatherings at the Priory

'A TRUE "SALON"'

Frederic Harrison

At their Sunday afternoon receptions, sometimes preceded by a small and early dinner with chosen friends, there was a continuous flow of varied company.[1] One listened to the measured *ipse dixit*[2] of Herbert Spencer, who once fell into a passion with me when I said that in its evolution language became more simple, not more complex, and so far contradicted his rule of universal evolution accentuating differences. One met the rare learning of Emanuel Deutsch (d. 1873), who used to maintain that in the first century A.D. there were plenty of young enthusiasts besides Jesus preaching a similar Gospel; so that the New Testament was the common evangel of a school of Syrian moralists such as that of Hillel, many of whom were quite equal to the preacher of Nazareth. At times George Eliot would play Beethoven with fine power and taste, or George Du Maurier would sing one of his exquisitely comic French songs, or G. Lewes and Edward Pigott would act an impromptu charade, with witty dialogue invented on the spur of the moment. The superb Frederic Leighton would drop in, who had made fine illustrations for *Romola*; or the hearty Robert Browning, with endless anecdotes and happy *mots*; George Meredith, the inexhaustible and the *mitis sapientia*[3] of Lecky; the first Lord Acton, the omnivorous student, the gentle irony of Charles Bowen, and the second Lord Lytton, the cosmopolitan courtier; the jolly rattle of Anthony Trollope; the ever-welcome and genial Lord Houghton; Lord and Lady Amberley, in spite of her mother's frowns; that most thoughtful of painters, Frederick Burton; and that gentle, modest, and cultured poet, Leicester Warren, last Lord de Tabley.

Nor were "illustrations" from abroad wanting – Ministers from United States, Lowell and Motley; Emerson, the unfathomable prophet "of the eternal silences"[4] – for I never could hear him make a remark beyond monosyllables; Longfellow, whose features might be the model to serve for a Greek philosopher, whose poetry, I thought, might serve for a lady's album. I have seen there, too, Richard Wagner, looking like one of the heroes of the Nibelungen, with his beautiful wife; and Tourgenieff, with a head and frame that might fit Zeus, the father of gods and men. The gatherings at the Priory were a true "salon" in the French sense of the word, except that there was no pretence of "esprit," and their vogue was maintained by the social manysidedness of G.H. Lewes and by George Eliot's own sincerity and devotion to the best in thought and in art.

Autobiographic Memoirs, 2 vols (London: Macmillan, 1911), II, 109–10

NOTES

For Frederic Harrison, see 'A Few Good Friends', above.

1. David Hunter Blair remarks upon how numerous were Sunday receptions, as a form of 'quiet entertaining', in the London of the 1870s (*In Victorian Days and Other Papers* (London: Longmans, Green, 1939), p. 47).
2. 'The master himself has pronounced it (an expression of the Pythagoreans)' (C.D. Yonge, *A Phraseological Latin-English Dictionary* (London: Bentley, 1856), p. 275).
3. 'Gentleness and wisdom.' Horace, from Satire I of Book II, but surely not ironic here: Harrison later used it explicitly to praise Gibbon's letters (Royal Historical Society, *Proceedings of the Gibbon Commemoration 1794–1894* (London: Longmans, Green, 1895), p. 24).
4. 'Not for Him our violence | Storming at the gates of sense, | His the primal language, his | The eternal silences!' (John Greenleaf Whittier, 'The Prayer of Agassiz', ll. 51–4).

'SERIOUSNESS AND SOLID SENSE'

Julia Clara Byrne

"The Priory" [in 1865–70] was a quiet, simple, unpretending, yet elegant, villa, where one seemed to breathe an atmosphere of literature.

The almost classic drawing-room, half library, had a pleasant look-out into the garden,[1] and ... [the] Sunday "at homes," though certainly not always lively, were necessarily interesting; ... still, as it was always a chance gathering, there was much uncertainty as to the materials of which it would consist; these *réunions* therefore varied considerably in brilliancy and attractiveness. George Eliot was by no means sparkling in conversation, indeed, her social attributes were rather of the heavier, almost Johnsonian, order, and her remarks were often sententious, though apparently not designedly so, for there was obviously no intentional arrogation of superiority, though perhaps an almost imperceptible evidence of self-consciousness. The impression she left was that of seriousness and solid sense, untempered by any ray of humour,[2] scarcely of cheerfulness; she spoke in a measured, thoughtful tone which imparted a certain importance to her words, but her speech was marked rather by reticence than volubility: now and then she would give out an epigrammatic phrase which seemed almost offered as a theme for discussion, or as a trait of originality to be perhaps recorded by her chroniclers.[3] I remember, among many remarks of this kind, her once saying in a reflective tone, "Many suicides have greatly surprised me; I find life so very interesting." Lewes, on the other hand, was really witty, interspersing his conversation with natural flashes of humour, quite spontaneous in character, which would continually light up his talk: even when he said bitter things he had a way of putting them amusingly.

Gossip of the Century: Personal and Traditional Memories – Social Literary Artistic Etc., new edn, 4 vols (London: Downey, 1899), I, 213–14

NOTES

Known for her lively conversation at her own receptions, Julia Clara (Mrs William Pitt) Byrne, née Busk (1819–94, *ODNB*), wrote books on travel and on contemporary social conditions. Another recollection by her appears in 'Out and About in London', below.

1. As did GE's writing-room upstairs, which also faced south (A.M.W. Stirling, *Victorian Sidelights: From the Papers of the Late Mrs. Adams-Acton* (London: Benn, 1954), p. 164).
2. Henry Sidgwick too found 'comparatively little humour' in GE's conversation (A[rthur] S[idgwick] and E[linor] M[ildred] S[idgwick], *Henry Sidgwick: A Memoir* (London: Macmillan, 1906), p. 270), as did Oscar Browning: 'Her conversation was deeply sympathetic, but grave and solemn, illumined by happy phrases and by thrilling tenderness, but not by humour' (Browning, p. 89; for Browning's recollection of the Sunday gatherings, see pp. 89–90).
3. Compare Marie Souvestre, who met GE in 1873: 'Elle parle à merveille – mais elle s'écoute quand elle parle! [She speaks marvellously – but she listens to herself when she speaks!]' (quoted in Martha S. Vogeler, 'George Eliot and the Positivists', *Nineteenth-Century Fiction*, 35 (1980), 406–31 (p. 416)).

TO THE RESCUE

Charles Walston

I shall always hold in pious memory the days of my early youth, when (more than forty years ago [*c.* October 1865]) in the distinguished circle of intellectual luminaries at George Henry Lewes' house "The Priory" in London, George Eliot gave the most vital illustration of the qualities of the true conversationalist in support of my own weakness. I had come to England as a very young man from a continuous stay of over three years at several German universities, speaking and reading nothing but German and dwelling exclusively in an atmosphere of German thought, and had seriously impaired the spontaneity of expression in my native tongue. I shall never forget, how, when in this disconcerting position among my elders and intellectual superiors, I ventured haltingly and blunderingly to express my own opinions, she would then come to my rescue, and, with delicate tact, suffused with kindliness and with penetrative intellectual sympathy, and with her mellow voice and mellifluous though precise diction, would give perfect, lucid form to my own involved thoughts – leaving me with increased self-confidence, almost proud of the pertinence and importance of my own remarks. How grateful I was to her, how I loved her – and how much she contributed, by her unselfish intellectualism and passion for Truth, to the flow and elevation of the conversation itself!

Truth: An Essay in Moral Reconstruction (Cambridge: University Press; New York: Putnam, 1919), pp. 75–6

NOTE

Sir Charles Walston, formerly Waldstein (1856–1927, *ODNB*), a classical archaeologist, also published an earlier recollection of his Priory visits, where he adds: 'No wonder that one often saw and heard of a great number of people, young girls or young men, who by letter or in person sought help and spiritual guidance from her, and went away strengthened by her sympathy and advice' ('George Eliot', *Library of the World's Best Literature*, ed. by Charles Dudley Warner, 46 vols (New York: International, 1896–98), XIII, 5359–75 (p. 5364)). Other recollections by him appear in Part V.

BROKEN CONVERSATIONS

Sidney Colvin

The Sunday afternoon receptions at The Priory [in the early 1870s] were not always quite free from stiffness, the presiding genius allowing herself – so at least some of us thought – to be treated a little too markedly and formally as such. Perhaps, however, the secret was that she by nature lacked the lightness of human touch by which a hostess can diffuse among a mixed company of guests an atmosphere of social ease.[1] Humour in abundance she had, but not of the light, glancing kind: it was a rich, deliberate humour springing from deep sources and corresponding with the general depth and power of her being. The signs of such depth and power were strongly impressed upon her countenance. I have known scarce any one in life whose looks in their own way more strongly drew and held one. She had of course no regular beauty (who was it that asked the question, "Have you seen a horse, sir? Then you have seen George Eliot"?): but the expression of her long, strong, deeply ploughed features, was one not only of habitual brooding thought and intellectual travail but of intense and yearning human sympathy and tenderness. There could hardly be a truer record of her looks than that conveyed in the well-known etching by Rajon after the life-sized drawing by F.W. Burton. If it had been her nature to seek equality of regard and companionship from those visitors who came about her, Lewes, I think, would have hardly made it possible. His own attitude was always that of the tenderest, most solicitous adoration; and adoration, homage, was what he seemed to expect for her from all who came about them. He never encouraged the conversation among the Sunday guests in the room to become equal or general, or allowed one of them to absorb her attention for very long, but would bring up one after another to have his or her share of it in turn, so that if any of us began to feel that talk with her was taking an easier and closer turn than usual, the next thing was that it was sure to be interrupted.[2] I recall the beginnings of several conversations which were thus broken before I had succeeded in getting more from her than sympathetic enquiries about my own work and studies, or perhaps about the places I had last been visiting in France or Italy. Naturally I valued such enquiries, but was not at all seeking them: what I wanted was not to be drawn out myself but to draw out my hostess and feel her powers playing – the spell of her mind and character acting – upon me and upon the company generally.

Lewes, when he had cut into the talk and carried one off as I have said, would entertain one genially and kindly in his own way in another part of the room, among some group of guests either fresh from or awaiting similar treatment. If George Eliot's countenance was of the equine type, his was not less distinctly of the simian, but having its ugliness redeemed by winning smiles both of humour and affection. Besides entertaining the day's guests, or helping them to entertain each other, in groups, Lewes liked sometimes to get a few minutes' chat apart with a single one coming or going; but the subject was almost always connected in some way with George Eliot's work and fame. During the serial publication of *Middlemarch* I particularly remember his taking me apart one day as I came in, and holding me by the button as he announced to me in confidence concerning one of its chief characters, "Celia is going to have a baby!" This with an air at once gratified and mysterious, like that of some female gossip of a young bride in real life.

Memories & Notes of Persons & Places 1852–1912
(London: Arnold, 1921), pp. 90–2

NOTES

A young man in his late twenties at the time of the receptions described here, Sir Sidney Colvin (1845–1927, *ODNB*) later became Slade Professor of Fine Art at Cambridge and Keeper of the Department of Prints and Drawings at the British Museum. He reviewed several of GE's novels in the *Fortnightly*, including *Middlemarch* (repr. in *Critical Heritage*, pp. 331–8).

1. Cross remarks that GE 'was eminently *not* a typical mistress of a *salon*. It was difficult for her, mentally, to move from one person to another. Playing around many disconnected subjects, in talk, neither interested her nor amused her much. She took things too seriously, and seldom found the effort of entertaining compensated by the gain' (*Life*, III, 335). Not everyone saw it that way; Sir Mountstuart E. Grant Duff, calling several times in 1870, thought that she had 'a good deal of skill in managing a *salon*' (*Notes from a Diary 1851–1872*, 2 vols (London: Murray, 1897), II, 139).

2. Sir Frederick Pollock too traced the one-at-a-time rule to GHL's protectiveness, believing it spoiled GE's talk (*For My Grandson: Remembrances of an Ancient Victorian* (London: Murray, 1933), p. 67).

'UNE SINGULIÈRE PUISSANCE'

Philip Gilbert Hamerton

Son salon est un modèle de gôut et d'élégance, et toute sa maison est aussi bien tenue que celle de Millais, par exemple. Nous avons causé de beaucoup de choses, entre autres précisément de cette curieuse question de prière selon Comte. Elle soutient que c'est raisonnable dans le sens d'expression de vif désir, de concentration de l'esprit vers son but. Son argument était bien fortement soutenu par sa manière énergique de raisonner, mais je lui ai tenu tête avec beaucoup d'obstination, et nous avons eu une véritable lutte. Elle a une singulière puissance, quelque chose qui ne se trouve jamais que chez les personnes d'un génie extraordinaire. Quand elle a voulu me convaincre, elle y mettait tant de persuasion et de volonté qu'il me fallait un certain effort pour garder la clarté de mes propres-idées. [Her salon is a model of taste and elegance, and all her house is as well kept as Millais's, for instance. We talked about many things,[1] among which precisely this curious prayer question according to Comte.[2] She maintains that it is reasonable as an expression of vivid desire, of concentration of the mind towards its goal. Her argument was quite strongly supported by her energetic way of reasoning, but I stood up to her with much stubbornness, and we had a real struggle. She has a singular power, something which can ever be found only in persons of extraordinary genius. When she wanted to convince me, she put so much persuasion and so much will in her argument that it took a certain effort in order for me to retain the clarity of my own ideas.]

Letter to Eugénie Hamerton, his wife, in *Philip Gilbert Hamerton*, pp. 323–4; translated by Véronique Maisier

NOTES

By the time of the meeting described here, January 1866, the artist and writer Philip Gilbert Hamerton (1834–1894, *ODNB*) had contributed several pieces to GHL's *Fortnightly Review*. When his *Modern Frenchmen* appeared in 1878, GE read it aloud and liked it; she found him personally unaffected and plain (*Letters*, IX, 234; VIII, 359).

1. He says that on a later visit GE told him 'que personne n'avait eu plus d'inquiétudes et de souffrances dans le travail qu'elle, et que le peu qu'elle fait lui coûte énormément [that no one had had more worries and suffering in their work than she has, and that the little she produces costs her enormously]' (*Philip Gilbert Hamerton*, p. 345).
2. In worship of wife, mother, and daughter, Comte prayed three times daily (an hour upon arising, thirty minutes before retiring, fifteen minutes at midday), recommending this practice to his followers (*System of Positive Polity*, trans. by J.H. Bridges and others, 4 vols (London: Longmans, Green, 1875–77), IV: *Theory of the Future of Man*, trans. by Richard Congreve (1877), p. 103).

'MOBBED LIKE A QUEEN'

Eugénie Hamerton

The person who sat next to George Eliot seemed determined to monopolize her attention; but as a new-comer was announced she came forward to meet him, and kindly taking me by the hand, made me sit in the chair she had herself occupied, and motioned to my husband to come also.[1] He remained standing inside the circle, whilst the Monopolizer had, at once, to yield his seat to the mistress of the house, as well as a share of her conversation to others than himself.

I immediately recognized the description given of her by my husband; her face expressed at the same time great mental power and a sort of melancholy human sympathy; her voice was full-toned, though low, and wonderfully modulated. We were frequently interrupted by people just coming in, and with each and all she exchanged a few phrases appropriate to the position, pursuit, or character of her interlocutor, immediately to revert to the subject of our conversation with the utmost apparent ease and pleasure.

Mr. Lewes offered tea himself, because the worshippers surrounded the Idol so closely that they kept her a prisoner within a double circle, and they were so eager for a few words from her lips, that as soon as she moved a step or two they crowded about her in a way to make me think that, in a small way and in her own drawing-room, she was mobbed like a queen at some public ceremony.

The next time we called upon George Eliot she had heard of our meeting with Mr. Tennyson, and said –

"So you have seen the great man – and did he talk?"

"Talk?" answered my husband; "he talked the whole time, and was in high spirits."

"Then you were most fortunate."

We understood what was implied, for Mr. Tennyson had the reputation of not being always gracious. However, we had learned from himself that nothing short of rudeness could keep his intrusive admirers at a distance, so as to allow him some privacy.

Philip Gilbert Hamerton, pp. 369–70

NOTE

For Eugénie Hamerton, see 'Some Younger Women', above.

1. 'It became, later, an acknowledged custom that when you entered the room anyone who was sitting in the chair beside George Eliot moved away, either at once or within a very few minutes; you took his or her place beside the hostess and, in turn, moved away when the next visitor arrived. Each visitor in succession thus had a brief talk with the hostess' (George Smith, 'Recollections', fol. 210).

'THE SOCIAL DEPENDENCE OF WOMEN'

Katharine Louisa Russell

Mrs. Lewes sat on the sofa by me and talked to me only in a low sweet voice; her face is repulsively ugly fr. the immense size of the chin but when she smiles it lights up amazingly and she looks both good and loving and gentle.

We talked about the book of the Social Dependence of Women which she attributed [wrongly] to Miss Taylor.[1] Mrs. Lewes wd. not allow it was coarse. I only know what I saw in the review of it in the "Pall Mall" yesterday which quoted amongst other things "that a man ought to be able to be punished for a rape on his wife"![2] Mr. Sanderson came in during our visit to meet us there and he told me afterwards that he liked Mrs. Lewes, that there was something powerful and interesting about her which interested him and that he wd. like to see her again. We all talked about Browning's Poems, Mr. Lewes told me that "Caliban" and "The Death in the Desert" were the 2 finest and that I shd. be sure to admire those. They told us that Mrs. Browning's love Poems were the finest expressions of love in the language –

The Amberley Papers: Bertrand Russell's Family Background,
ed. by Bertrand Russell and Patricia Russell, 2 vols (London: Hogarth
Press, 1937; repr. London: Allen & Unwin, 1966), ii, 38

NOTES

Katharine Louisa Russell, née Stanley, Viscountess Amberley (1842–74, *ODNB*), an activist for women's rights, met GE ('an ugly large woman') at a lecture on Positivism (ii, 33). Three weeks later, on 26 May 1867, she paid her first call at the Priory, described here. GE approved of her lecture on 'The Claims of Women' (May 1870), in which she advocated suffrage, equality in education and employment, and property rights for married women (*Letters*, viii, 477).

1. The bracketed correction is in the source. Published anonymously, *The Social and Political Dependence of Women* (1867) is by Charles Anthony, not Helen Taylor.
2. 'Dependent Woman', *Pall Mall Gazette*, 24 May 1867, pp. 10–11, where Taylor is suggested as the author. The reviewer too finds the idea of conjugal rape shocking: 'Think of that as a good and practicable subject for legislation!' (p. 11).

'A SINGULAR EARNESTNESS'

Henriette Field

She lives in London, near Regent's Park, on what is called the "North bank," where the great city verges away into the country; and, spreading out in all directions, the houses are no longer crowded together in solid masses, each square looking like a huge factory, but stand apart, surrounded by grass and flowers. Such a position has all the convenience of the city, with rural retirement. The roar of London, which never ceases day nor night, here sinks into a faint murmur as if dying away in the distance. All is silence, comfort, and repose. In this beautiful suburb, hidden by a wall which shuts out all jarring sights and sounds, stands the home of the author of Adam Bede. Enter the gate, and you see a square house of two stories, with no architectural pretensions, but which yet has about it an air of taste which is very attractive. ... The interior has the same character of refined simplicity. There is nothing pretentious. The furniture is simple and modest; yet there is a harmony of color which pleases the eye. White draperies soften, without intercepting, the rays of the sun, which play among the flowers in the window, the smell of which fills the room. All this the eye takes in at a glance, before it rests on the mistress of this charming English home.

... No one who had ever seen her could mistake the large head (her brain must be heavier than most men's) covered with a mass of rich auburn hair. At first I thought her tall; for one could not think that such a head could rest on an ordinary woman's shoulders. But, as she rose up, her figure appeared of but medium height. She received us very kindly. In seeing, for the first time, one to whom we owed so many happy hours, it was impossible to feel towards her as a stranger. All distance was removed by her courtesy. Her manners are very sweet, because very simple, and free from affectation. To me her welcome was the more grateful as that of one woman to another. There is a sort of free-masonry among women, by which they understand at once those with whom they have any intellectual sympathy. A few words, and all reserve was gone. "Come, sit by me on this sofa," she said; and instantly, seated side by side, we were deep in conversation. It is in such intimacy one feels the magnetism of a large mind informed by a true woman's heart; then, as the soul shines through the face, one perceives its intellectual beauty. No portrait can give the full expression of the eye, any more than of the voice. Looking into that clear, calm eye, one sees a transparent nature, a soul of goodness and truth, an impression which is deepened as you listen to her soft and gentle tones. A low voice is said to be an excellent thing in woman.[1] It is a special charm of the most finely cultured English ladies. But never did a sweeter voice fascinate a listener, – so soft and low, that one must almost bend to hear. You can imagine what a pleasure it was thus to sit for an hour beside this gifted woman, and hear her talk of questions interesting to the women of England and America.

But I should do her great injustice, if I gave the impression that there was in her conversation any attempt at display. There is no wish to 'shine.' She is above that affectation of brilliancy which is often mere flippancy. Nor does she seek to attract homage and admiration. On the contrary, she is very averse to speak of herself, or even to hear the heartfelt praise of others. She does not engross the conversation, but is more eager to listen than to talk. She has that delicate tact – which is one of the fine arts among women – to make others talk, suggesting topics the most rich and fruitful, and by a word drawing the conversation into a channel where it may flow with a broad, free current. Thus she makes you forget the celebrated author, and think only of the refined and highly-cultivated woman. You do not feel awed by her genius, but only quickened by it, as something that calls out all that is better and truer. While there is no attempt to impress you with her intellectual superiority, you feel naturally elevated into a higher sphere. The conversation of itself floats upward into a region above the common-place. The small-talk of ordinary society would seem an impertinence. There is a singular earnestness about her, as if those mild eyes looked deep into the great, sad, awful truths of existence. To her, life is a serious reality, and the gift of genius a grave responsibility.

'The Author of Adam Bede in Her Own Home',
in *Home Sketches in France, and Other Papers*
(New York: Putnam, 1875), pp. 208–18 (pp. 211–14)

NOTE

Born in Paris, Henriette (Mrs Henry Martyn) Field, née Desportes (1813–75), had been a governess in England and then in France, where she was wrongly accused as an accessory to murder. In the United States she married a Congregational minister and became a society hostess in New York City, where she also headed the School of Design for Women. The visit described here seems to have been sometime in 1868.

1. See George Smith's recollection, *n.* 1, in 'Publishers', above.

SOME WORDS ON SHELLEY

William Michael Rossetti

Sunday, 7 February [1869]. – ... I was introduced to Mrs L[ewes], whom I had seen, but never been made known to before. Her face, manner, and conversation, show great intellectual sensibility.[1] She spoke with much enthusiasm of the *Prometheus Unbound* and *The Cenci*: objects however to the subject of the latter, and demurs to my saying that *Prometheus* is the greatest English poem since Milton – interruptions prevented my ascertaining what she would prefer to it. She exalts Shelley above Byron, and his blank verse above Tennyson's. Some talk about spiritualism, which Lewes, and also evidently Mrs L[ewes], repudiate.[2] ... Lewes (so Mrs L[ewes] informs me) knew Mrs Shelley, and thought her a somewhat conventional person, by no means capable of responding to the innermost feelings of Shelley.

Rossetti Papers: 1862 to 1870 (London: Sands, 1903), pp. 382–3
(Rossetti's brackets identifying 'Mrs L')

NOTES

William Michael Rossetti (1829–1919, *ODNB*) was an art and literary critic, editor, and memoirist, and the brother of poet Christina Rossetti and poet and painter Dante Gabriel Rossetti.

1. 'It is well known', Rossetti wrote later, 'that Mrs. Lewes was a woman with next to no feminine beauty or charm of countenance or person: she was, in fact, plain to the extent of being ugly. Her conversation was able and spirited: and in talking her face lit up in a degree which impressed me, and which almost effaced her natural uncomeliness' (*Some Reminiscences of William Michael Rossetti*, 2 vols (London: Brown Langham, 1906), II, 338–9).

2. Henrietta Litchfield, Charles Darwin's daughter, describes a seance at the home of Erasmus Darwin, her uncle, in January 1874 where GHL 'was troublesome and inclined to make jokes and not play the game fairly and sit in the dark in silence' (*Emma Darwin: A Century of Family Letters 1792–1896*, ed. by Henrietta Litchfield, 2 vols (London: Murray, 1915), II, 216). He noted afterwards that 'as complete darkness was insisted on we left in disgust' (*Letters*, VI, 6 *n.* 3).

'A SENSE OF PERFECTNESS'

Annie Fields

It was my good fortune to pass a month or more during the early summer of 1869 in London, at a hotel opposite St. George's Church, Hanover Square. It was a small, old-fashioned hotel kept by two ladies, and our parlor wore the air, as Dickens used to say when he came into it, "of a stage drawing-room." The vases and artificial flowers and small mirrors and unnecessary tables were all there, and were often in strange contrast to the simple tastes of its temporary occupants and their guests; although it could not be denied that the lightness and cheer and fancifulness had a real charm for us in the somewhat dark world of London. It was here that Mr. Lewes found us one afternoon (by great good fortune we had just returned from rambling about, sight-seeing), and while he explained that Mrs. Lewes was never able to make visits, stayed himself, and talked freely about George Eliot and literary affairs.[1] He was not a very prepossessing person in his appearance, but his mercurial temperament and his large intelligence made him gay and interesting in conversation. He lingered, full of agreeable subjects of talk, until we knew something of each other, and he had obtained a promise that we would go on the following Sunday [16 May? 1869], in the afternoon, to see his wife.

We found them at the time appointed in a pleasant house somewhat retired from the road, with trees and shrubbery outside, and plenty of books inside. A small company of ladies and gentlemen were already assembled, and there was much conversation. Presently, however, George Eliot disengaged herself from the general talk, and, allowing the company to break up into groups, came and seated herself by my side for a more intimate acquaintance. I recall the glow which overspread her face when she discovered that we had a common friend in Harriet Beecher Stowe. The affectionate generosity with which she poured out her unbounded admiration for Mrs. Stowe, and her love for her work, is never to be forgotten. She seemed to understand the rapt intensity of Mrs. Stowe's nature as few of her contemporaries have done, and to rejoice in the inspiration which prompted her great book. Nor did she stop there. She had read and appreciated her later books as well, and she loved and reverenced the woman.[2]

After this first visit to "The Priory," the doors were kindly open to us on Sundays during our stay in London. Unhappily, I have no notes of those visits, nor of George Eliot's conversation, but I must always remember how the beauty of her voice impressed me. I also remarked the same quality I have mentioned in speaking of her letters – a sense of perfectness in her presentation of any scene or subject. I recall this impression especially in connection with a description she gave one afternoon of a late visit to Germany, portraying the charm of living in one of the places (was it Ilmenau?) made classic to us by association with Goethe. The whole was so clearly yet simply and vigorously said, that any listener, ignorant of her fame, must have felt her unusual qualities both of mind and heart. On another occasion, in speaking of music, the name of Pauline Viardot was mentioned, and her last appearance in Paris; also Charles Dickens's appreciation of Viardot, who was accustomed to say that she did him the honor to journey from Geneva to Paris when it was known he was to read there. "And she was audience enough!" he would add gaily.

George Eliot was a great admirer of the genius of Viardot. "Think of it!" she said, with a sense of irreparable loss. "We lived for six weeks under the same roof once in Germany, and never found each other out. We were both in search of rest and retirement; but what a lifelong pleasure if we could have passed some of our quiet hours in each other's society!"[3] Before we left the house Mr. Lewes invited us into his private room on the lower floor, where his wife's portrait by Sir Frederic Burton, which he preferred at that time to any other, hung over the fireplace. In one corner of this room were shelves, carefully covered by a curtain, where the bound manuscripts of her books stood – the volumes containing the touching dedications to himself which have since their death been published.[4] She was his chief topic of conversation, the pride and joy of his life, and it was quite evident that she returned his ardent devotion with a true love.

'George Eliot', *Century*, 58 (1899), 442–7 (pp. 443–4)

NOTES

Annie Fields, née Adams (1834–1915), was an American literary hostess, writer, and social reformer.

1. Fields's husband, James Thomas Fields of Ticknor and Fields, the American publishing house, was proposing a uniform edition of GE's works, and also offered £300 for 'Agatha' for the *Atlantic* (*Letters*, v, 34; viii, 451–2). See Charles Dickens's recollection in 'Vignettes' below.
2. GE read Stowe's 'great book' *Uncle Tom's Cabin* (1852) when it appeared, later praising it and *Dred* (1856) ('Belles Lettres', *Westminster Review* (1856), repr. in *Essays*, pp. 379–81). Stowe had written to GE shortly before Fields's visit, beginning a long and intimate correspondence, although they never met.
3. In late May and early June 1868, for only nine days, GE was in Baden-Baden, where Pauline Viardot resided; evidently, however, they were not under the same roof (*Letters*, iv, 449 n. 3). On 23 April 1871 Viardot sang 'divinely' at the Priory, GHL wrote, 'and entranced every one, some of them to positive tears' (v, 143–4).
4. In *Life*, ii, 71, 159, 354, 430; iii, 51, 167, 284.

A SUNDAY DUEL

Soph'ia V. Kovalevskaia

The contrasting characters of George Eliot and Lewes were sharply evident when they were receiving guests. Lewes paced the floor the whole time, going from one guest to another, gesticulating, speaking with pleasure and interest to each one, his whole face radiating delight when he saw that conversation flowed vividly and the guests were enjoying themselves. George Eliot never abandoned her customary composure. In her usual place, lost in the large Voltaire armchair, protected from the light by a dark lampshade, she usually devoted herself to one guest at a time, as if oblivious to the fact that she was hostess of the salon. If the conversation interested her she was unaware of the coming of new guests, and suddenly would be surprised when her glance fell on some new face which had already greeted her half an hour before. ...

I had already been there some time when an elderly man with grey whiskers and a typical English face entered. No one spoke his name, but George Eliot went to him immediately saying, "How glad I am that you have come today. I can present to you the living refutation of your theory – a woman mathematician. Permit me to present my friend. I must warn you," she said to me, still not uttering his name, "that he denies the very possibility of the existence of a woman mathematician. He admits that from time to time a woman might appear who equals the average level of men in intellectual capacity, but he argues that an equal woman always directs her intellect and insight to the analysis of her friends' lives and never would chain herself to pure abstraction.[1] Try to dissuade him."

The old gentleman sat next to me, looking at me with some curiosity. I had no idea who he was; nothing in his manner was imposing. The conversation turned to the eternally changeless theme of the rights and capacities of women, and whether it would be harmful or useful for mankind if a large number of women were to study science. He made some half-ironical observations, chiefly to stimulate my objections. At that time I was not yet twenty years old and had spent the few years which separated me from childhood in continuous battle with my family, defending my right to devote myself to my beloved studies. Small wonder that I argued the "woman's question" with the enthusiastic fervor of a neophyte, abandoning all timidity to break a lance in a just cause. I had no idea with whom I was arguing, and George Eliot did all in her power to incite me in the discussion. Carried away, I quickly forgot the surroundings and did not even notice that the rest of the company gradually fell silent, listening with curiosity to our conversation, which became more and more lively.

Our duel went on for three-quarters of an hour until George Eliot decided to put an end to it. "You have defended our common concern with such courage," she said to me, "and if my friend Herbert Spencer is not yet persuaded, then I am afraid that he must be judged incorrigible." Only then did I realize who my antagonist had been. I was amazed at my daring.

'A Memoir of George Eliot', pp. 544–5 © 1984 by The Yale Review; reproduced with permission of Blackwell Publishing Ltd

NOTE

For Soph'ia Kovalevskaia, see 'Other Personal Meetings', above. The incident described here may have been early in 1870.

1. Spencer argued that the reproductive function in women had produced in comparison to men of the same society and time 'a perceptible falling short in those two faculties, intellectual and emotional, which are the latest products of human evolution – the power of abstract reason and that most abstract of the emotions, the sentiment of justice – the sentiment which regulates conduct irrespective of personal attachments and the likes or dislikes felt for individuals' (*The Study of Sociology* (London: King, 1873), p. 374). Nancy L. Paxton traces this idea in Spencer's thought in *George Eliot and Herbert Spencer: Feminism, Evolutionism, and the Reconstruction of Gender* (Princeton: Princeton University Press, 1991), esp. pp. 117–21, 171–2.

NOTE-TAKING

Charles Godfrey Leland

[In 1870] Mrs. Lewes ... left on me the marked impression, which she did on all, of being a woman of genius, though I cannot recall anything remarkable which I ever heard from her.[1] I note this because there were most extraordinary reports of her utterances among her admirers. A young American lady once seriously asked me if it were true that at the Sunday-afternoon receptions in South Bank [*sic*], one could always see rows of twenty, or thirty of the greatest men in England, such as Carlyle, Froude, and Herbert Spencer, all sitting with their note-books silently taking down from her lips the ideas which they subsequently used in their writings! There seemed, indeed, to be afloat in America among certain folk an idea that something enormous, marvellous, and inspired went on at these receptions, and that George Eliot posed as a Pythia or Sibyl, as the great leading mind of England, and lectured while we listened.[2] There is no good portrait, I believe, of her. She had long features, and would have been called plain but for her solemn earnest eyes, which had an expression quite in keeping with her voice, which was one not easily forgotten. I never detected in her any trace of genial humour, though I doubt not that it was latent in her; and I thought her a person who had drawn her ideas far more from books and an acquaintance with certain types of humanity whom she had set herself deliberately to study – albeit with rare perception – than from an easy intuitive familiarity with all sorts and conditions of men.[3] But she worked out *thoroughly* what she knew by the intuition of genius, though in this she was very far inferior to Scott. Thus she wrote the "Spanish Gypsy," having only seen such gypsies two or three times.[4] One day she told me that in order to write "Daniel Deronda," she had read through two hundred books. I longed to tell her that she had better have learned Yiddish and talked with two hundred Jews. ...

Memoirs, 2nd edn (London: Heinemann, 1894), pp. 389–90

NOTES

Charles Godfrey Leland (1824–1903) was an American humorist and folklorist best known for his dialect poems. He wrote over fifty books on various subjects and considered himself an expert on gypsies.

1. See Bessie Rayner Parkes's recollection, *n.* 4, in Part I.
2. Not only in America. GE's acquaintance Rudolf Lehmann pictures her 'surrounded by a circle of men, listening like a congregation to her utterances ... Is it a Pythoness on a tripod, delivering oracles?' (*An Artist's Reminiscences* (London: Smith, Elder, 1894), p. 234).
3. Still, in *The Art of Conversation, with Directions for Self Education* (New York: Carleton, 1864), pp. 145–96, Leland has eight chapters stocked with recommended readings.
4. When Leland first met GHL and GE, she 'turned the conversation almost at once to gypsies. They spoke of having visited the Zincali in Spain, and of several very

curious meetings with the *Chabos*. Mr. Lewes, in fact, seldom met me – and we met very often about town, and at many places, especially at the Trübners' – without conversing on the Romanys. The subject evidently had for him a special fascination' (*The Gypsies* (Boston: Houghton, Mifflin, 1882), p. 181).

'AS IF THE TIDES HAD ALL COME IN'

Charles Warren Stoddard

On one side of the gate, in small letters, was this legend: "The Priory;" on the other side the two bell-pulls for visitors and servants. Above the wall the upper half of the top windows of the Priory were just visible. I rang the visitors' bell and waited. The gate was unlocked mysteriously. I heard no footstep upon the gravel walk within, but the bolt slid back and the gate swung partly open through some invisible agency. ...

Somewhat to my surprise, I found her intensely feminine. Her slight figure, – it might almost be called diminutive, – her gentle, persuasive air, her constrained gesticulation, the low, sweet voice, – all were as far removed from the repulsive phenomenon, the "man-woman," as it is possible to conceive. The brow alone seemed to betray her intellectual superiority. Her face reminded me somewhat of the portrait of Charlotte Brontë, with which every one is familiar.[1] Yet there was no striking similarity; I should rather say, the types of face and head are the same. When she crossed the room to call attention to a volume under discussion, she seemed almost like an invalid, and evidenced also an invalid's indifference to fashion and frivolity in dress. ... The conversation which I had interrupted was soon renewed, and it was better than a thousand books to hear the riches that these three souls lavished upon one another.[2] Art, philosophy, the music of Wagner; Rome ancient and Rome modern; Florence – how they all love Florence, and how they detest modern Rome! ... Professor Lewes was the life of the circle, which increased as the reception hours drew to a close. Mrs. Lewes was always the same placid, self-poised, kind-hearted, womanly soul, who suffered no one present to feel neglected; for she took care to call the forlorn ones to her and distinguish them for a moment at least. ...

I shall never forget the absolute repose of Mrs. Lewes, the deliberation with which she discussed the affairs of life, speaking always as if she were revealing only about a tenth part of her knowledge upon the subject in question. With her it seemed as if the tides had all come in; as if she had weathered the ultimate storm; as if the circumstance and not desire had swept her apart from her kind and left her isolated, the unrivalled mistress of all passionless experience.

'George Eliot', in *Exits and Entrances: A Book of Essays and Sketches* (Boston: Lothrop, 1903), pp. 137–47 (pp. 142–5, 146–7); first publ. in *San Francisco Sunday Chronicle*, 14 July 1878, pp. 1–2

NOTES

Charles Warren Stoddard (1843–1909), an American poet, travel writer, and educator, called at the Priory on 16 November 1873 (*Letters*, IX, 105–6 *n*. 8). He had sent GE his *Poems* from San Francisco, and in reply she said that she imagined him 'an almost solitary singer in a remote corner of the earth' inspired only by nature, 'the best of all inspirations' (pp. 137–8).

1. By George Richmond (1850), in the National Portrait Gallery (NPG 1452).
2. GE, GHL, and Sir Edward Burne-Jones, 'who sat careless, cross-wise in his chair' in 'a blue merino shirt, collar and cuffs as blue as indigo, artist jacket, and a general every-day air that bordered on affectation' (pp. 144–5).

HOMER AND FLAT-IRONS

John Fiske

Well, what do I think of her? She is not a "fright" by any means. She is a plain-looking woman, but I think not especially homely. I see no reason why her photograph should not be circulated about. She is *much* better looking than George Sand. She isn't a blooming beauty, of course; you don't expect that at fifty-two;[1] but her features are regular, her nose is very good, her eyes are a rich blue and very expressive, her mouth is very large, but it is pleasant in expression. Her hair is light and profuse, and she wears a lovely lace cap over it – and looks simple, frank, cordial, and matronly, and seems ever so proud of Lewes, and ever so fond of him. I call her a good, honest, genuine, motherly woman with no nonsense about her. She seemed glad to see me. She said when my Myth-book came to her – I sent her a copy last summer, as you know – she was sitting on the floor fixing a rug, or something of the sort, and she got so absorbed in my book that she sat on the *floor* all the afternoon, till Lewes came in and routed her up![2] She thought it was "a beautiful book"; but she had known me ages ago, when I first wrote to Lewes and sent things to the "Fortnightly". But she disagreed with me as to the unity of the Homeric poems. I found she was a strong Wolfian! Well we had a hard battle over it – she and I. I never saw such a woman. There is nothing a bit masculine about her; she is thoroughly feminine and looks and acts as if she were made for nothing but to mother babies. But she has a power of *stating* an argument equal to any man; equal to any man do I say? I have never seen any man, except Herbert Spencer, who could state a case equal to her. I found her thoroughly acquainted with the whole literature of the Homeric question; and she seems to have read all of Homer in Greek, too, and could meet me everywhere. She didn't talk like a bluestocking – as if she were aware she had got hold of a big topic – but like a plain woman, who talked of Homer as simply as she would of flat-irons. She showed an amazing knowledge of the subject. But, you see, I am not a fool on the Homer question. I know every bit of the "Iliad" and "Odyssey" as well as I know the "Pickwick Papers", and so I was a little too much for her. On the whole, she was inclined to beat a retreat before we got through, and said she was glad of some new considerations that I had presented on the subject – though, on the whole, I don't think I converted her.

I never before saw such a clear-headed woman. She thinks just like a man, and can put her thoughts into clear and forcible language at a moment's notice.[3] And her knowledge is quite amazing. I have often *heard* of learned women, whose learning, I have usually found, is a mighty flimsy affair. But to meet a woman who can meet you like a man, on such a question as that of Homer's poems, knowing the ins and outs of the question, and not *putting on any airs*, but talking sincerely of the thing as a subject which has deeply interested her – this is, indeed, quite a new experience.

On the whole, I enjoyed Mr. and Mrs. Lewes immensely today; and I think Lewes a happy man in having such a simple-hearted, honest, and keenly sympathetic wife. I call them a wonderful couple. Spencer thinks she is the greatest woman that has lived on the earth – the female Shakespeare, so to speak; and I imagine he is not *far* from right. My only sorrow is that the afternoon was not quite long enough; but I shall go there again.

> To Abby Fiske, his wife, 23 November 1873, in *The Letters of John Fiske*, ed. by Ethel F. Fisk (New York: Macmillan, 1940), pp. 277–9

NOTES

John Fiske (1842–1901), an American historian and follower of Herbert Spencer, had been in contact with GHL several years before this visit, when he published essays in the *Fortnightly*. GE found him 'altogether rather in the heavy style. Yet he is not at all a heavy writer' (*Letters*, VI, 119).

1. She turned fifty-four on 22 November 1873, the day before Fiske's visit.
2. This scene was later decorated by Laurence Hutton, who said that Fiske, invited to the Priory for tea, 'found George Eliot sitting on the floor – of all things – with hammer in hand and a mouth full of tacks, putting down the dining-room carpet' (Isabel Moore, *Talks in a Library with Laurence Hutton* (New York and London: Putnam, 1905), p. 303). Hutton's version was widely reprinted for its purported disclosure of GE's practical domesticity. The book Fiske had sent was his *Myths and Myth-Makers* (1873); see *Letters*, V, 464 n. 5.
3. A complementary perspective comes from Fiske's friend Jeremiah Curtin: 'I had been told that Mrs. Lewes was a reserved and taciturn woman. I found her quite the reverse; she was affable and social, but eccentric – a woman who fully and frankly appreciated her own remarkable gift of narrative' (*Memoirs of Jeremiah Curtin*, ed. by Joseph Schafer, Wisconsin Historical Publications, Biography Series, 2 (Madison: State Historical Society of Wisconsin, 1940), p. 243). Politeness obliged GHL to invite Curtin to the Priory because he was with Fiske when GHL met him (*Letters*, V, 453).

'IN A KIND OF DREAM'

Annie Sawyer Downs

Mr. Lewes led me forward and presented me to his wife. A slender, tallish woman, with an oval face, abundant hair, doubtless once fair, now almost gray, and questioning light eyes. This at first, but when she put out her hand and smiled, her face became so illumined that it was like an alabaster vase with a light behind it. And she had been described to me as plain and entirely unprepossessing! ...

They gave me a seat beside her, and she introduced me to some people near, who all seemed to stop talking to listen to her. I was in a kind of dream which quickened all my faculties so that I heard and saw everything, although at the time I was conscious only of Mrs. Lewes. Her talk was most charming.[1] Without a trace of exaggeration, with a clear and wonderfully swift discernment of every point involved, and when you least looked for it, an odd, quaint turn, that produced the effect of wit.[2] While her opinions on all the subjects they spoke of were definite and decided, there was at the same time such a sincere deference to those of others, that you were drawn to talk in spite of yourself. I could have bitten out my own tongue when I found I was using it, but somehow she would make you give long answers involving individual opinion. Although the company seemed very miscellaneous, so large a proportion of it was English that the ordinary conversation of the hunting season kept coming to the surface. Mrs. Lewes objected to the sport in all its phases, and her defense of the hunted as well as her vigorous presentation of the effect of unnecessary cruelty on the character of the hunter, all said in the most natural way, as if it was the only thing one could say, and in that marvelous, delicious voice, had a startling effect. She owned herself ignorant of America, and when I smiled a little at some of her eager questions, confessed that it puzzled her to understand much about us.

As the room was rapidly filling I had more opportunity to look at her. I noticed her high-bodied black velvet dress, its simple sleeve falling back a little from the graceful hand. ...

In these simple sleeves and at her throat was some beautiful lace, the latter, I remember, fastened by an exquisite cameo surrounded by pearls. Her hair, worn very low on the broad forehead, was brought down around the ears (as I have seen it in portraits half a century old), and coiled at the back. Just on the top of the head a bit of lace was pinned, matching that at the throat and sleeves. She seemed to prefer standing as she talked, and moved her head as well as her hands far more than is common with English women.[3] The room was beautiful enough to make a suitable frame for the lovely picture she made through the whole interview. An open grand piano (Mrs. Lewes told me she loved music passionately) covered with music, stood at the remote end of the room, over which hung an engraving of Guido's Aurora, while water colors of brilliant flowers gleamed from corners of the wall. Books were numerous, while small tables standing on warm-hued Persian rugs, held easel pictures, exquisite vases of still more exquisite flowers, and small casts of antique statues.[4] And as it comes back to me, the pleasantest remembrance of all, pleasanter even than that of the almost reverential homage with which the many justly celebrated men and women there assembled regarded her, was the proud, loving, yet natural and easy manner in which her husband, himself a man of genius and a most brilliant, gifted talker, would pause and draw closer to her so as not to lose one of her words.[5]

'George Eliot. One of Her Receptions. – Face – Figure – Manner – Voice – Dress', *New-York Tribune*, 25 March 1876, p. 7

NOTES

Annie Sawyer Downs (*c*.1836–1901) was from Andover, Massachusetts, where she occasionally lectured on art and literature at the Abbot Female Academy. She arrived in London with an introduction from Ralph Waldo Emerson, so it was necessary to invite her, and she called at the Priory on 4 January 1874 (*Letters*, IX, 113). She published a later account of the occasion in 'A Visit to George Eliot', *Congregationalist*, 28 May 1879, p. 3. Her writing up the visit for the newspapers was exactly what GE dreaded when strangers, especially American strangers, came into her circle.

1. In the *Congregationalist* Downs says: 'She talked of Agassiz, of his museum at Cambridge, of the great natural history collections at Naples, of Sir Edwin Landseer's pictures, and with enthusiasm of Mr. Furnival's Shakespeare and Chaucer classes at the Working Men's College. Appealing to Mr. Lewes to direct me, a stranger, to Red Lion Square, as a landmark for the College, she said she never could get that part of London clearly into her mind.' The quotations in the following notes come from this later version.

2. 'She had quaint etchings of some of the monkeys in the Zoological Gardens, and told me she was more interested in them than any of the other animals, they exhibited traits so distinctively human. She declared, while her husband and friends laughingly teased her for the assertion, that she had seen a sick monkey, parched with fever, absolutely refuse the water he longed for, until the keeper had handed it to a friend who was suffering more than he. As an illustration of their quickness, she told me, in a very dramatic manner, of a nurse who shook two of her little charges for some childish misdemeanor while in the monkey house. No one noticed the monkeys looking at her, but pretty soon every old monkey in the house began shaking her children, and kept up the process until the little monkeys had to be removed for fear their heads would be shaken off. I felt no incongruity between her conversation and her books. She talked as she wrote; in descriptive passages, with the same sort of humor, and the same manner of linking events by analogy and inference.'

3. 'Both Mr. and Mrs. Lewes spoke English as Americans do, without the rising inflection, and with remarkable distinctness.' GE may have stood to terminate the interview (Haight, p. 461).

4. 'The walls were covered with pictures. I remember Guido's Aurora, Michael Angelo's Prophets, and Raphael's Sybils, while all about were sketches, landscapes and crayon drawings, gifts from the most famous living painters, many of whom are friends of the house. ... If she disposed the flowers, on shelves, tables and in shady corners, she had great discernment in arranging as well as understanding of their individualities. A cluster of laurestinus and a spray of holly with its shining leaves and glowing berries haunted me for days with its perfection.'

5. GHL 'had a very charming way of stopping as if to listen, and once I heard him say: "Mrs. Lewes is speaking of Holman Hunt's Shadow of the Cross; let us hear."'

'A CLAIRVOYANT INSIGHT INTO MIND AND CHARACTER'

James Sully

In the Priory she was hidden away from public gaze as in a nunnery. In response to the bell the entrance gate opened, yet so slowly and suspiciously as to give me for a moment a throb of trepidation. Whilst passing from the gate to the front door I had an awful glimpse through a bay window of a lady in a lace cap, who fortunately was not facing me. In the long drawing-room, to which I was conducted by a quiet middle-aged woman, were a number of persons – mostly men, I think – sitting round the fire, in a semi-oval arrangement. I was taken up by Lewes to the farther end of the oval and presented to George Eliot, the lady I had glimpsed through the window. She looked elderly and a little worn as she sat on a low chair. Her strong face, with its prominent cheek-bones and its unusual length from mouth to chin, is known to everybody. What is less well known is the marvellous transformation of the heavy features when expression gave the alchemist's touch. As she extended a long, thin hand to me and smiled, the grey eyes seemed to light up, while the ripples of the smile broke up the heavy facial masses with sweet and gracious lines. It was, I think, this metamorphosis of a face, looking in repose decidedly heavy, which led one well qualified to judge of faces to speak of it as the plainest and the most fascinating he had ever seen.[1] The captivating effect of the smile was supported by the charm of the low-pitched voice, which had a rich timbre and was finely modulated.

In my time [1874–78] the Sunday afternoon gatherings lasted from about 3.30 to 6. The talk would sometimes be general, but when the number of guests was large it tended to split up. George Eliot had her own quiet chats with one or two of the visitors at a time. Lewes would now and then bring up a guest, and generally would keep his eye on her so far as to see that she was not wearied. The other end of the elliptical curve was his special domain. Here he could entertain the men at the tea-table after he and his son Charles had taken cups to the ladies. I saw nothing of "the mercurial little showman" of whom George Meredith writes, indulging, I suspect, his most merciless vein of caricature.[2] Lewes was much too occupied with his half of the company, from which he got a good deal of entertainment, to make a proper show man. He and I used to talk "shop," exchanging our views, often unflattering enough, of the philosophers of the hour and their productions. He was an excellent story-teller, and would throw himself into what I guessed was an oft-repeated jest with wonderful elan, accompanying his recitals with a good deal of gesticulation and mimetic action. The son of a comedian, and himself a connoisseur of the stage, it might seem to any one listening to his stories that he was more than half acting the incident narrated.[3] ...

If Lewes amused his company by his jocosities, George Eliot enfolded her auditors in an atmosphere of discriminative sympathy. She had a clairvoyant insight into mind and character, which enabled her to get at once into spiritual touch with a stranger, fitting her talk to his special tastes and needs, and drawing out what was best in him. Her conversation ranged over a large area of subject, touching not only English, but French, German, and Italian literature, and passing easily from homely everyday topics up to art and philosophy. She had read Schopenhauer, and spoke warmly, almost indignantly, of his conception of human life. She could not understand, she said, how any one who had the ability and the opportunity to better the lot of others could sink into pessimism. She herself, she added, held a view midway between those of the optimist and the pessimist, to which she gave the name of Meliorism; and when I was about to bring out my book on Pessimism she allowed me to quote her words, if I "found it useful for the doctrine of Meliorism to cite one unfashionable confessor of it, in the face of the fashionable extremes."[4] Among writers of fiction she spoke highly of Turgeniev, urging me to read him.

'George Eliot in the Seventies', in *My Life & Friends: A Psychologist's Memories* (London: Unwin, 1918), pp. 259–66 (pp. 259–61, 263–4)

NOTES

A psychologist and philosopher, James Sully (1842–1923, *ODNB*) helped GE prepare the third series of *Problems of Life and Mind* for publication after GHL's death. Another recollection by him appears in Part v.

1. Perhaps the artist George du Maurier, whom Sully met at the Priory.
2. See Meredith's recollection in 'Vignettes', below.
3. Not GHL's father but his grandfather, Charles Lee Lewes, was a comic actor (Rosemary Ashton, *G.H. Lewes: A Life* (Oxford: Clarendon Press, 1991), pp. 6–10).
4. Quoted from one of GE's letters to Sully, 19 January 1877 (*Letters*, vi, 333). In *Pessimism: A History and a Criticism* (London: King, 1877) he defines meliorism as 'the faith which affirms not merely our power of lessening evil – this nobody questions – but also our ability to increase the amount of positive good'; while pessimism paralyzes effort, and optimism tends to enfeeble it, meliorism 'can really stimulate and sustain human endeavour' (p. 300).

'ALL THAT SHE SAID WAS WORTH HEARING'

C. Kegan Paul

In the group of which George Eliot was one there is the same straight wall of brow; the droop of the powerful nose; mobile lips, touched with strong passion kept resolutely under control;[1] a square jaw, which would make the face stern were it not counteracted by the sweet smile of lips and eye. ... The two or three portraits that exist, though valuable, give but a very imperfect presentment. The mere shape of the head would be the despair of any painter.

It was so grand and massive that it would scarcely be possible to represent it without giving the idea of disproportion to the frame, of which no one ever thought for a moment when they saw her, although it was a surprise, when she stood up, to see that, after all, she was but a little fragile woman who bore this weight of brow and brain.

... When London was full, the little drawing-room in St John's Wood was now and then crowded to overflowing with those who were glad to give their best of conversation, of information, and sometimes of music, always to listen with eager attention to whatever their hostess might say, when all that she said was worth hearing. Without a trace of pedantry, she led the conversation to some great and lofty strain. Of herself and her works she never spoke; of the works and thoughts of others she spoke with reverence, and sometimes even too great tolerance. But those afternoons had the highest pleasure when London was empty or the day wet, and only a few friends were present, so that her conversation assumed a more sustained tone than was possible when the rooms were full of shifting groups. Those who knew her carried away from her presence the remembrance of a charm even greater than any which lay in her writings; of a low sweet voice vibrating with emotion; of language in which, without the faintest tinge of pedantry, every sentence was as complete, as fully formed, as though written in her own published works; of a knowledge and a breadth of thought which, had we not found them in her, the pride of the male intellect would have designated masculine; of a sympathy which never failed, a toleration almost excessive, and of a nature which, with all this weight of learning and greatness, was feminine and tender.[2]

> 'George Eliot', in *Biographical Sketches* (London: Paul, Trench, 1883), pp. 141–70 (pp. 162–4); first publ. in *Harper's*, 62 (1881), 912–23

NOTES

Charles Kegan Paul (1828–1902, *ODNB*) was a chaplain at Eton and writer of religious works before leaving the Church and taking over the publishing firm that would bear his name. He came to London in 1874, meeting GE and GHL shortly afterwards.

1. Compare Sir Walter Besant, who said that 'no woman's face had ever struck him as more sensual' (Douglas Sladen, *Twenty Years of My Life* (London: Constable, 1914), p. 251). T.A. Trollope too found her lips and mouth 'distinctly sensuous in form and fulness' (*What I Remember*, 3 vols (London: Bentley, 1887–89), II, 296). The 'group' Paul mentions is a facial group including Dante, Savonarola, and John Henry Newman.

2. At first Paul visited GE without his wife, but desisted because she would not go with him. Then she went, 'and when walking home, she said, "I am convinced that she is a good and pure woman, and I will go whenever you like"' (*Memories* (London: Paul, Trench, 1899), p. 335). *Memories* also includes this striking recollection: 'I was on one occasion at their house when no one was present but Mr. and Mrs. Lewes and myself, and we were talking of social proprieties. "You know," said

Lewes to her, "how completely we have set these at defiance, and how often we have doubted whether we were wise in doing so"' (p. 336).

THEIR QUIETUS MADE

Mary Blackwood Porter

The ponderosity of her conversation and the difficulty of making any way with her, of which some visitors have complained, must, we think, have been caused by their selecting topics not really congenial to themselves simply because they were talking to George Eliot, scaling heights that were beyond them, and as a result getting crushed by a solid avalanche of learning. But if one talked with her upon music, which she loved, pictures, the play, a flower-show, or equally a horse-show, she was with you – we were all talking upon what we equally understood. But the views of the novice on the latest metaphysical puzzles of the day, or an uncertain dive into scientific research, might have involved disaster. A mind so quick as hers could not fail to see when her companion was out of his depth, and then no doubt she felt contempt for what was mere pretension. Large numbers of people used to invade her Sunday receptions who had often small claim upon her forbearance. We remember one ridiculous incident [in summer 1875] of two enterprising young men who sat down opposite her with the intention of eliciting her opinions on the Turko-Russian war. They were nothing if not simple and direct, and without any preamble whatever they fired off their first shot at their gentle-mannered hostess, startling the whole room with, "Are you a Russian or a Turk?" "Neither," came the grave reply in that deep musical voice, which we may well imagine gave them their quietus for the rest of the afternoon.

John Blackwood, pp. 389–90

NOTE

For Mary Blackwood Porter, see 'Publishers', above.

THE BIBLE VERSION

Ethel Romanes

One afternoon, when there were very few people at the Priory, the conversation drifted on to the Bible, and George Eliot and Mr. Romanes began a discussion on the merits of the two translations of the Psalms best known to English people – the Bible and the Prayer Book version. They 'quoted' at each other for a short time, and then Lewes, who had not his Bible at his finger ends to the extent the other two had, exclaimed impatiently, 'Come,

we've had enough of this; we might as well be in a Sunday school.' Both
George Eliot and Mr. Romanes, by the way, preferred the Bible version.
The Life and Letters of George John Romanes, new edn
(London: Longmans, Green, 1896),
p. 50

NOTE

Ethel Romanes, née Duncan (1856–1927, *ODNB*), was a writer and religious activist.
Her husband, George John Romanes (1848–94, *ODNB*), was a Canadian evolutionary
biologist whose *Candid Examination of Theism* (London: Trübner, 1878) GE read in
January 1880. It argues that there is no scientific or rational evidence for the existence of God, 'yet we have no right on this account to conclude that there is no God'
(p. 107). The occasion recalled here was probably in late 1875 or early 1876.

TWO DESCRIPTIONS OF TWO HOURS

Edward Dowden

I

Then I went on, and stayed from 4 to 6 with Mr and Mrs Lewes – a house
of great beauty and refinement, without ostentation – only quite a few
guests. Millais, Paul (of King & Co), Lord and Lady Lindsey, and one or
two others. Mrs L. is really very like Dante, with a large, mobile mouth,
sweet penetrating eyes, and a delicate feminine voice. Her perfect refined
feminine personality was what impressed me most. She was not in her best
talking vein, but everything she said was exactly right and accurate, and
beautiful in manner. I sat next her for some time and had some *tête-à-tête*
talk, but she prefers to get the circle into talk. Lewes was friendly, clever,
and pleasant, and Millais said much that was interesting about his work
as a painter.[1]
    To Hester Dowden, his daughter, 9 April 1876, in *Letters of Edward
Dowden and His Correspondents* (London: Dent, 1914), p. 96

II

From my two hours with G. Eliot, I cannot report any great sayings of
hers – only each thing she said was the most right and best thing (best from
an intellectual and spiritual point of view), the occasion suggested, and was
said in the most perfect words. Millais and G.H. Lewes were the chief talkers,
and Millais said much that was interesting about his work. Mr Lewes is vivacious, clever, like a Frenchman, and I can believe that G. Eliot's superiority
is not squandered on one who cannot give back intelligence and versatile
gifts and loyalty to one known to be above him.[2] I liked him, and he was
very friendly with me (but that I fancy is his way). She was very kind, and

if the word had no soft or saccharine suggestion about it, I should say very *sweet*, gracious and beautiful in manner.

To Elizabeth Dickinson West, later his wife, 20 April 1876,
in *Fragments from Old Letters: E.D. to E.D.W. 1869–1892*,
2 vols (London: Dent, 1914), II, 114

NOTES

Born in Ireland, the poet and scholar Edward Dowden (1843–1913, *ODNB*) was the first Professor of English Literature at Trinity College, Dublin. In 1872 and 1877 he published two essays on GE in the *Contemporary Review* (repr. in his *Studies in Literature 1789–1877* (London: Paul, 1878), pp. 240–72, 273–310, with extracts in *Critical Heritage*, pp. 320–2, 439–47). Both pieces gratified GHL and GE (*Letters*, V, 300; VI, 336). At the time of the visit described here, Dowden was planning a book on GE, never carried out.

1. According to Walter Sichel, Sir John Everett Millais attended GE's Sunday parties until he noticed a change in her: 'She discoursed heavily of German philosophy. She played Beethoven with an elephantine touch. It was too much for him and reluctantly he made his exit. The people were new, the talk was tall. "It was too much for an ignoramus like me," he murmured' (*The Sands of Time: Recollections and Reflections* (London: Hutchinson, 1923), p. 47). They still remained friends. Similarly, to Thomas Armstrong GE's gatherings were so solemn that 'one felt as if one must not speak above a whisper' – although on one occasion things got interesting because a pretty young woman (probably Lady Olivia Sebright) 'did not seem to recognise the sanctity of the place', 'talked freely and gaily', and 'put the men on their mettle' (*Thomas Armstrong, C.B.: A Memoir 1832–1911* [ed. by L.M. Lamont] (London: Secker, 1912), p. 28).

2. Dowden later said of GHL: 'The best word he ever wrote is in a letter to me, where he (on his death-bed, I think), speaks of George Eliot as *"dearer to me than life itself"*' (*Letters of Edward Dowden*, p. 336).

SUTTEE AND JUGGERNAUT

Alfred Austin

We took the first opportunity of going to call on her at her request in St. John's Wood. But there I found pervading her house an attitude of adoration, not to say an atmosphere almost of awe, thoroughly alien to my idea that persons of Genius, save in their works, should resemble other people as much as possible, and not allow any special "fuss" to be made about them.[1] I do not say the fault lay with her. I am pretty sure the blame lay with others. But, in addition to this drawback, she rather astonished me by saying, incidentally, that the British Government in India had no right to prevent widows from immolating themselves on the death of their husbands, or to interfere with the Car of Juggernaut.[2] When we got into the open air, I said to my wife, "In politics, and all practical affairs, 'that way madness lies.'" She heartily agreed with me.[3]

The Autobiography of Alfred Austin: Poet Laureate 1835–1910, 2 vols
(London: Macmillan, 1911), ii, 197

NOTES

Poet Laureate from 1896, Alfred Austin (1835–1913, *ODNB*) published in the
Fortnightly when it was edited by GHL, but did not meet him and GE until some ten
years later. The gathering described here was some time between 1876 and 1879,
although Austin and his wife also called at the Priory in January 1880 (*Journals*,
p. 196).

1. Austin's elegy 'George Eliot' (beginning 'Dead! Is she dead? | And all that light
   extinguished?') appeared in *Soliloquies in Song* (London: Macmillan, 1882),
   pp. 100–3. Margaret Harris comments on this poem and ten other tributes in
   'George Eliot: Elegies and Eulogies', *George Eliot Review*, 34 (2003), 28–42.
2. Recent studies, with *Daniel Deronda* at centre, have argued both for and against
   GE's complicity in colonial expansion; for a comprehensive historical treatment
   of the question, see Nancy Henry, *George Eliot and the British Empire*, Cambridge
   Studies in Nineteenth-Century Literature and Culture, 34 (Cambridge: Cambridge
   University Press, 2002), esp. pp. 113–27.
3. When Austin first met GE *c*.1876 he was placed next to her at dinner; she immediately asked if a certain woman across the table were his wife, 'and on my saying
   "Yes," she added, "I thought so; a poet's ideal wife"' (*Autobiography*, ii, 197; also
   related in i, 205).

'ALMOST OLD-MAIDENISH REFINEMENT'

Joseph Jacobs

I can still recall the feelings of ardent reverence with which I approached
the Priory, North Bank, one Sunday afternoon in [February] 1877. I had written an enthusiastic – I fear I must add gushing – defence of *Daniel Deronda*,
from a Jewish point of view, in the June number of *Macmillan's Magazine* of
that year,[1] and George Henry Lewes had expressed a wish that I should call
upon them. I went with all the feelings of the neophyte at the shrine for
the first time. Need I say that I was disappointed? Authors give of their best
in their works under the consciousness of addressing the whole world. We
ought not to expect them to live up to that best at all times and before all
onlookers: but we do.

I have few Boswellisms to offer. I remember being struck even at that
early stage of my social discernment by the contrast between the boisterous
Bohemian *bonhomie* of George Lewes and the almost old-maidenish refinement of his life's companion. I had tried to lead her talk to my own criticism,
but was met by the quiet parry, 'I never read criticisms of my own works.'
I could not help thinking at the time *'que fais-je donc dans cette galère?'*[2] but
she was obviously in the right. Others were present and the topics had to
be general. We got upon songs for singing, and I was attempting to contend

that the sweetest songs for vocal purposes were nowadays not those of the poets of the day. She pointed out that even Tennyson's in the *Princess* were unsuitable for that purpose, whereas the Elizabethans produced songs that were gems of literary art, yet trilled forth as naturally as a bird's carol.

Literary Studies (London: Nutt, 1895), pp. xv–xvi; first publ. 1891

NOTES

Born in New South Wales, Joseph Jacobs (1854–1916, *ODNB*) was a folklorist and historian known for his demographic studies of English and Spanish Jews as well as for his collections of English, Celtic, and Indian fairy tales. Another recollection by him appears in Part v.

1. 'Mordecai: A Protest against the Critics, by a Jew', vol. 36, pp. 101–11, Jacob's first published literary essay, explores 'the wonderful completeness and accuracy with which George Eliot has portrayed the Jewish nature' (p. 102), but also notes some errors in her presentation of rituals. For Jacobs 'the adverse criticism' of the Jewish part of *Deronda* stems from critics' 'lack of sympathy and want of knowledge': 'If a young lady refuses to see any pathos in Othello's fate because she dislikes dark complexions, we blame the young lady, not Shakspeare ...' (p. 111).

2. 'Then what am I doing here?': '*Mais que diable allait-il faire dans cette galère*, (this phrase, taken from the eleventh scene of the second act of *Molière's* Fourberies de Scapin, has become proverbial), But what the deuce had he to do in that galley – i.e. – what business had he to go there?' (J[ohn] Ch[arles] Tarver, *The Royal Phraseological English-French, French-English Dictionary*, 5th edn (London: Dulau, 1879), pp. 392–3).

FROM THE MOUTHS OF CHILDREN

Justin McCarthy

George Eliot had a sweet sympathetic voice, with a certain melancholy in its cadence which rested like music on the ear. Her object, apparently, in her Sunday gatherings, was to get all her guests to talk and to relieve the newer visitors from the awkwardness of a silent shyness. She did not do much of the talking herself, but she always listened with the closest attention, and gently intervened whenever any pause took place, either for the sake of carrying on the old conversation, or of taking care that some new subject should be presented to the group. It seemed to be no part of her desire that the talk should be exclusively, or even mainly, about philosophy, or science, or letters, for everything that was going on in the world around appeared to have interest for her, and the most modest among her company was encouraged to offer an opinion, or to tell of an experience. As might naturally be expected, there was a certain quality of fine humour in her way of looking at things and setting them up for observation. ... I can well remember that on more than one occasion she made me talk with a fluency which rather surprised myself. I recollect, for example, that on one of her Sundays, having heard that I had made some little personal study of the conditions of Mormon life in Salt Lake City, she drew me out upon the subject, until I found myself discoursing to a group of really famous persons as if I had something new and valuable to tell.

I have often heard it said, too, and read it in magazine sketches, that George Eliot was very unwilling to have any of her books talked about, and was inclined rather to resent the pushfulness of any unlucky person who ventured on such an intrusion. ... But I must say that I have heard George Eliot enter courteously and gracefully into talk on one of her own novels, or a character or a passage in one of her own novels, where the talk was justified by something in the occasion, and was suggested by intelligent interest and sympathy. I took my son and daughter [Justin Huntly and Charlotte], who were then but children, to see George Eliot, and I told them to be sure to remember all about the visits, for that the time would certainly come when they, as grown-up persons, would be proud to remember that George Eliot had received and had spoken to them. The little girl, with the unconscious audacity of childhood, bluntly asked the great authoress which of her novels she herself liked best; and George Eliot sweetly told her that she liked 'Silas Marner' best. And then some grown person struck in to the conversation and we talked about 'Silas Marner,' and George Eliot showed no desire to stop our talk, but good-naturedly joined in and had her say too.

Reminiscences, 2 vols (New York and London: Harper, 1900), I, 299–302

NOTE

The Irish historian Justin McCarthy (1830–1912, *ODNB*) came to London in 1860 as a journalist. By 1868 he was having some success writing fiction, and in 1879 he was elected to Parliament. McCarthy met GE through GHL, to whom he gives a loving tribute in *Reminiscences*, I, 303–9. He also wrote an admiring article on GE and GHL in *Galaxy* (1869), reprinted in *Modern Leaders: Being a Series of Biographical Sketches* (New York: Sheldon, 1872), pp. 136–44.

'A PECULIAR PATHETIC CHARM'

Leslie Stephen

It was a rather awful moment for the neophyte when he was presented to the quiet and dignified lady seated in her armchair, to stammer out the appropriate remarks which sometimes failed to present themselves before he had to make room for a new comer; and if the company was numerous, any general conversation was impossible. George Eliot's gentle voice was not calculated, if she had desired such a result, to hold the attention of a roomful of receptive admirers. But if rainy weather had limited the audience, and the tentative sparks of conversation had been fanned into life, she could be as charming as any admirer could desire. Her personal appearance was intellectually attractive, and had a peculiar pathetic charm. She looked fragile, overweighted perhaps by thought, and with traces of the depression of which she so often complains in her letters. ... If her talk might be at times a little too solemn for the frivolous, she could brighten into genuine playfulness, and, on occasion, into flashes of hearty scorn directed against the unlucky cynic. If the incense offered was not always of the finest quality, there was no want either of dignity or gentleness in the recipient.[1] And nobody could watch Lewes on such occasions without being struck by the cordial and generous devotion of a man not too much given to an excess of veneration. Her belief in him was equally visible in her manner and every allusion to his work.

George Eliot (London: Macmillan, 1902),

pp. 144, 145

NOTE

Sir Leslie Stephen (1832–1904, *ODNB*), man of letters and the first editor of the *Dictionary of National Biography*, helped GE with *Daniel Deronda* in 1875 on details of Cambridge life. By the time he met her, he had become editor of *Cornhill Magazine*, for which he wrote her obituary.

1. In 1876 Stephen remarked that GE was 'really a very noble sort of person, and as little spoilt as a prophetess can well be in these days. I always like to talk to her' (Frederic William Maitland, *The Life and Letters of Leslie Stephen* (London: Duckworth, 1906), p. 294).

'THE GODDESS ON HER PEDESTAL'

Eliza Lynn Linton

Not a line of spontaneity was left in her; not an impulse beyond the reach of self-conscious philosophy; not an unguarded tract of mental or moral territory where a little untrained folly might luxuriate.[1] She was always the goddess on her pedestal – gracious in her condescension – with sweet strains of sympathetic recognition for all who came to her – ever ready to listen to her worshippers – ever ready to reply, to encourage, to clear from confusion minds befogged by unassimilated learning, and generous in imparting her own. But never for one instant did she forget her self-created Self – never did she throw aside the trappings or the airs of the benign Sibyl. Her soft, low voice was pitched in one level and monotonous key, and her deliberation of speech was a trifle irritating to the eager whose flint was already fired. Her gestures were as measured as her words; her attitudes as restrained as her tones. She was so consciously "George Eliot" – so interpenetrated head and heel, inside and out, with the sense of her importance as the great novelist

and profound thinker of her generation, as to make her society a little overwhelming, leaving on baser creatures the impression of having been rolled
very flat indeed.[2] ...

With all her studied restraint of manner, George Eliot had a large amount
of what the French call temperament. As a lover she was both jealous and
exacting, and the "farfallone amoroso [amorous butterfly]"[3] whom she had
captured was brought pretty tautly to his bearings. If even he went so far
as Birmingham to lecture, he had to return home that night – as she quite
gravely said to a lady in my presence:

"I should not think of allowing George to stay away a night from me."

'A First Meeting with George Eliot', in *My Literary Life*
(London: Hodder and Stoughton, 1899), pp. 98–100

NOTES

For Eliza Lynn Linton, see Part ɪɪ. Another recollection by her appears in Part ɪɪɪ.

1. Among those who agreed with Linton's description of GE as 'artificial, *posée*,
   pretentious, unreal' (p. 92) was Theodore Watts-Dunton, with whom his biog-
   raphers contrast 'a whole-hearted admirer like Mr. Buxton Forman, who knew
   George Eliot very intimately, and found her one of the most inspiring personalities that he had ever met in his long and varied life, with a soul as great as
   her mind' (Thomas Hake and Arthur Compton-Rickett, *The Life and Letters of
   Theodore Watts-Dunton*, 2 vols (London: Jack; New York: Putnam, 1916), ɪ, 161).
2. Linton is usually said to have been jealous of GE's success, but her friend Edward
   Clodd insisted that she simply hated 'shams and snobbery', and 'was angry with
   the "Society" crowd that fawned at the feet of a woman living with a married man
   because of her eminence in literature' (*Memories*, 3rd edn (London: Chapman and
   Hall, 1916), pp. 268–9).
3. From Figaro's closing Act I aria in Mozart's *Nozze di Figaro*, libretto by Lorenzo Da
   Ponte: 'Non più andrai, farfallone amoroso, | Notte e giorno d'intorno girando [No
   more, you amorous butterfly, | Will you go fluttering round by night and day]'
   (trans. by Lionel Salter, Archiv CD 439 871–2).

FROM THE OUTER CIRCLE

T.H.S. Escott

I

The function was more like a religious ceremonial than a social reunion, and
Mr. Lewes played to perfection the part of Hierophant.[1] The gifted lady ...
sat in the centre of a little crowd of worshippers, of whom some were permitted to hold personal converse with her. But the majority gazed at her
reverently and mutely from afar, as if they were looking upon the beatific
vision. If any one spoke in too loud a tone, or spoke at all, when George
Eliot happened to be speaking herself, he was at once met with a "hush"
of reprehension by Mr. Lewes, and made to feel that he had perpetrated a

sort of iniquity. George Eliot had unquestionably immeasurable charm of mind, manner, and conversation for those who knew her well. But ... I must say that I never advanced beyond the outer circle of worshippers, and that I always felt myself one of the Levites at the gate.

Politics and Letters (London: Chapman and Hall, 1886), pp. 26–7

II

The etiquette dominating the premises sacred to her who wrote *Adam Bede*, and to him who tried to popularise Comte, was overpoweringly severe. The Positivist himself, with an air of worshipping proprietorship, met his guests on the threshold, and with something between a nod and a sigh signified that here a hat might be left, there an umbrella deposited; or that yonder was a vase for receiving the votive flowers sacred to the goddess, which visitors often brought. Inside the chamber wherein SHE sat, a space was marked off, behind which the neophytes were not permitted to go. Initiated bystanders informed those resorting for the first time to the shrine, that only after probationary years could the rite of presentation, if ever, arrive. ... To a per centage of candidates it never came at all. Though they had seen the Sibyl in her splendour, they were not permitted by her possessor to touch her garment's hem.[2]

Platform, Press, Politics & Play: Being Pen and Ink Sketches of Contemporary Celebrities from the Tone to the Thames, Viâ Avon and Isis (London: Simpkin, Marshall, Hamilton, Kent [1895]), pp. 258–9

NOTES

Thomas Hay Sweet Escott (1844–1924, *ODNB*) lectured in logic and classics in King's College, London, from 1866 to 1873 and wrote for the *Standard*, the *World*, and the *Fortnightly*, which he also edited. Another recollection by him appears in 'Out and About in London', below.

1. Edmund Yates, whose recollection appears in 'Vignettes', below, says of GHL that 'in treating of Miss Evans to outsiders he used to speak in terms of hyperbolical mystery, which would have well suited a priest of the Grand Llama of Thibet' (*Edmund Yates: His Recollections and Experiences*, 4th edn (London: Bentley, 1885), p. 351; first publ. in 'Meditations of a Recluse: No. II', *World*, 4 February 1885, p. 10).
2. The only claim I have encountered that some Priory callers never met their hostess.

'A GREAT ACHIEVEMENT IN YOUR LIFE'

Lucy Clifford

To go even to one of the Sunday afternoons was felt to be an honour, an evidence that there might be unsuspected possibilities in the new-comer;

though, with one or two exceptions, everyone who arrived was already an intellectual big-wig. To this rule, of course, I was an exception – my sole claim was through my husband, and that it covered me I felt to be yet another proof of his genius; but this did not help to set me at ease on my first visit.[1] It was the most frightening one I ever paid. When we arrived outside, and had pulled at the jingling bell-wire, the wooden gate automatically unlatched; beyond it a paved or brick-laid path led up to the front door: and walking even those few steps was a blessed respite. Through a low window on the left I could see a head with some white lace on it – a first glimpse of George Eliot. The front door opened upon a comfortable little square hall, with rugs on the floor and books on the wall.[2] The well-trained middle-aged woman servant looked at my husband with tolerant recognition, at me with something that was probably a tolerant shrug; then showed us into a small double drawing-room on the ground floor – booky, comfortable-looking rooms, with more than a suggestion of Morris colouring. ... On the left, as you faced the fire, but some little distance from it, with her back to the window, sat George Eliot. Beside her, on the left, between her and the fire, was a chair, often vacant; it was rush-bottomed, I think, rather low and of ebonised wood. This fearful chair most people had sat upon once; it was kept for the first-time visitor – for the greatest stranger, or for some illustrious person who, having conquered the difficulties, was permitted to appear.[3] ... I remember a certain great lady once occupying the stranger's chair. With the faintest touch of triumph (only years later did I grasp the meaning of it: at the time her carefully repressed and yet evident pleasure in the visit repelled one just a little) George Eliot told me that she was – I suppress the name – someone in close attendance on the Queen (Victoria) who had been sent to inquire if Mrs. Lewes had recovered from a recent illness.[4] ...

... [Each guest] spoke in turn and was listened to by the rest. It was a terrible ordeal for the average intelligence, if by a freak it strayed there, for inevitably at last, or at some time, eyes gravitated towards you, and you simply had to say something.[5] If you happened to be frightened out of your wits (as I was), you felt a choking sensation in your throat, and made a sound that conveyed nothing: whereupon some earnest thinker, or one of the geniuses seated round, would lean forward and ask, while all the eyes stared at you, 'What did you say? Won't you repeat your remark?' Then perhaps you managed to get out, in a squeaky voice, 'I merely said that I thought so too,' or something to that effect, and the intense ones would draw back a little, almost obviously thinking 'Who is this idiot, and how did it get here?'

But Mrs. Lewes probably helped you through, and looked at you with a kindly expression on her wonderful face. Wonderful? Yes, and like a horse's. Her likeness to Savonarola has often been mentioned: you were sensible of it the moment you saw her first; but you were also immediately reminded of a horse, a strange variety of horse that was full of knowledge, and beauty of thought, and mysteries of which the ordinary human being had no conception. It was another form of humanity, of individuality, added to her own. And her fascination, her magnetism, the exquisite thrill that went through you at the sound of her low measured voice, at the sight of her little generally undeveloped smile, like a fitful gleam of pale sunshine, was beyond all description, and had the effect of making you feel that there was nothing in this world you would not do for her; and that to be with her, even on one of those rather terrible Sunday afternoons, for a single hour, was a great achievement in your life.

At five o'clock tea was brought in and put on a side-table just inside the further room. Mr. Lewes poured out the tea; there was a little movement among the men. Mrs. Lewes was reverently served, and we all sat solemnly down again with our cups in our hands and bits of doubled thin bread and butter in our saucers. Then talk was resumed. It was about everything, literature, philosophy – a great deal of philosophy – painting, and occasionally, not often, music: she loved music – no one could see her at the Saturday concerts and not feel that. I have heard that to a privileged few she sometimes played, Chopin and Beethoven mostly; and one or two great musicians were among her friends. The talk was a little sententious, a little too good, so that it seldom had an air of spontaneity; the best things at any of the discussions were generally said by George Eliot herself: they might have been printed right off and no proofs corrected; but, though they were spoken with an air of soft appealing finality, she seemed quite unaware of their value or wisdom. In an argument that greatly interested her, now and then her beautiful hands contributed something to the scene it otherwise lacked, something natural, a suggestion even of poetry, or of passion; not often, for it was an astonishingly well-balanced, dignified group.

When the clock struck six, she made a little movement, and those who had remained to the end and not softly stolen away, took the hint and made their adieux; George Henry Lewes generally followed them to the door. Once – it was about our fourth visit, I think – she looked at me rather oftener than usual; perhaps she knew that I had felt like a scared hare, taken there on the kind but firm lead of a husband, for she made a sign, when gradually the other visitors were going, to delay us for a minute or two; and, while my husband retreated to talk over some matters with George Henry Lewes, she asked me about our house and its furnishing, and told me how, in early days – but I don't know precisely to what period she referred – she used to buy things and call them after the stories or books that had provided the money. I remember her saying: 'We have still some tablecloths that Maggie Tulliver gave us.' The remark is interesting, for it shows that she thought of the book by the name of its heroine – it was originally to have been called *Sister Maggie*. But no allusion to her work was ever made on Sunday afternoons by her visitors, nor by herself. There was one exception to this rule, when an adventurous spirit that had come for the first or second time, and was presumably unfamiliar with the ways of the circle, began: – 'But, Mrs. Lewes, I remember that in *Silas Marner* —' She looked up at him and said coldly in a firm, low voice, 'The works by the author of *Silas Marner* are never mentioned here.' And the adventurous spirit – it was young – collapsed.

On one other occasion we stayed behind again for a little while. My husband had been ill; we were going abroad in a few days, and not likely to see her soon again. When we four were alone – the Leweses and ourselves – and stood in a group, she took my hand and held it tightly while she talked to my husband; and, when at last we were going, she kissed my cheek and said 'God bless you, dear,' with something in her voice that made my heart bound and tears come to my eyes.[6] Perhaps she divined, though we did not, that it was the last time *we* should ever go there – or see them together. A few days afterwards she and George Henry Lewes came to see us, but unhappily we were out; we never quite got over it – and they never came again: it was never possible.[7]

'A Remembrance of George Eliot', *Nineteenth Century*, 74 (1913), 109–18 (pp. 112–13, 114–16)

NOTES

Born in the West Indies, Sophia Lucy Clifford, née Lane (1853–1929, *ODNB*), had married the well-known Cambridge mathematician and philosopher William Kingdon Clifford (1845–79, *ODNB*) in 1875, two years before meeting GE. When her husband died, leaving her with two children to support, friends established a fund to which GE contributed. (Her letter of condolence is in Blind, p. 215, and *Letters*, VII, 123.) Later Lucy Clifford became known for her novels, stories, and plays. Later still she wrote 'George Eliot: Some Personal Recollections', *Bookman*, 73 (October 1927), 1–3. Other recollections by her appear in 'Out and About in London', below, and in Part V.

1. Clifford notes that GE 'never invited a woman'; at first her husband had attended the receptions alone, expecting his wife to be asked, and then, feelings hurt because she wasn't, he stayed away until a friend told him to '"ask to be allowed to take her, and show that you would consider it a great honour"' ('Remembrance', p. 110, 111).
2. As with her writing room upstairs, which had 'bookshelves all round from floor to ceiling' (Stirling, *Victorian Sidelights*, p. 164).
3. 'I remember so well her first greeting', Clifford says in *Bookman*. 'She got up, though I was only a girl, from a chair on the left of the fire-place, and taking both my hands looked at me with a little smile, then nodded to my husband as much as to say that she accepted me' (p. 2).
4. Perhaps Mary Ponsonby (see 'Some Younger Women', above). Matilda Betham-Edwards remarks that eventually the Sunday gatherings acquired 'a fashionable, even frivolous element. Handsome equipages, powdered footmen, and elegantly dressed ladies now animated those sober precincts, greatly to the delight of Grace

and Amelia', the servants, who 'firmly believed that some fine day the Queen herself would call upon their mistress, but the hope and the dream were never realised' (*Reminiscences*, p. 144).

5. 'Those "Sunday afternoons" were somewhat terrible ordeals for shy people. We sat in a semicircle round the fireplace, and it was startling in the midst of a pause to be suddenly asked by the hostess from the opposite side of the circle: "Mr. Sayce, what is your view of the article on the immortality of the soul in the last number of the ... Review?"' (A.H. Sayce, *Reminiscences* (London: Macmillan, 1923), p. 143; his ellipses).

6. One of a number of recorded instances of GE's open physical affection. Of a visit in February 1868 Lucy Smith reports, 'In going away, I saw in her dear eyes that I might kiss her, and I can't tell you how kindly she put her arms about me' (*The Story of William and Lucy Smith*, ed. by George S. Merriam (Edinburgh and London: Blackwood, 1889), p. 360). Edith Simcox recalls that after greeting her GE 'reflected she had not returned my kiss, and did so – she thought it such a horrid habit of people to put their cheek and make no return' (*Shirtmaker*, p. 108).

7. GHL died on 30 November 1878.

Out and About in London

WINDOW-SHOPPING

Matilda Betham-Edwards

The two great friends would sometimes stroll along the streets together and look at the shops like other womenkind.

One morning as they sauntered down Bond Street, pausing before each glittering display, George Eliot said: "How happy are we both, dear Barbara, that we want nothing we see here!"

Mid-Victorian Memories, p. 56

NOTE

For Matilda Betham-Edwards, see 'A Few Good Friends', above. The friend here is Barbara Bodichon. Another recollection by Betham-Edwards appears in 'The Countryside', below.

THE PRINCESS'S THEATRE

Jane Welsh Carlyle

I went to see Fechter [in *Hamlet*] the other night [26 July 1861] and found myself between Lewes and Miss Evans! – by Destiny and *not* by my own Deserving. At least Destiny in the shape of Frederick Chapman who arranged the thing. Poor soul! there never was a more absurd miscalculation than *her* constituting herself an improper *woman*. She looks Propriety personified![1] Oh so *slow!*

Letter to Alexander Gilchrist, 31 July 1861, in *Anne Gilchrist: Her Life and Writings*, ed. by Herbert Harlakenden Gilchrist (London: Unwin, 1887), p. 86

NOTE

Equally famous for her sharp letters and sharp conversation, Jane Baillie Welsh Carlyle (1801–66, *ODNB*), literary hostess and Thomas Carlyle's wife, was one of the few persons to whom GE had copies sent of *Scenes of Clerical Life* and *Adam Bede*. She proved a sympathetic and encouraging reader, but evidently the two met no more after the occasion described here.

1. According to Margaret Oliphant, Jane Welsh Carlyle said that "'Mrs Lewes' has mistaken her *rôle* – that nature intended her to be the properest of women, and that her present equivocal position is the most extraordinary blunder and contradiction possible' (*The Autobiography and Letters of Mrs M.O.W. Oliphant*, ed. by Mrs Harry Coghill, 2nd edn (Edinburgh and London: Blackwood, 1899), p. 180).

THE NATIONAL GALLERY

Julia Clara Byrne

One day, just after the picture of *The Dead Warrior*, "attributed to Velasquez" had been bought for the National Gallery [in 1865], I went with Lewes and George Eliot to see it. Various interpretations of the meaning of the subject had been circulated, and none had been universally accepted. Anthony Trollope had joined us and each started a different supposition, no one appearing willing to accept the version hazarded in the catalogue.[1] If, as supposed there, "the Dead Warrior" be Orlando, *alias* Rolando, he must have been "squeezed to death," that hero having been represented as "invulnerable by the sword," and certainly the figure as there painted does not bear out that theory; nevertheless it is catalogued as the "body of the peerless Paladin Orlando" who fought at Roncesvalles by the side of Charlemagne. No attempt has been made to account for the surroundings and accessories; the cavern in which he lies, the armour he still wears, the extinguished lamp suspended over his feet, and the skulls and bones scattered about, add to the mysterious suggestiveness, and, no doubt, all these details had a meaning. We looked at it a long time, and came away without solving the enigma which, George Eliot remarked, "left much room for the play of imagination."

"Ah!" said I, "if I had your powers I would take it as the text of a romance."

"Who knows but I may?" she answered.[2]

Gossip of the Century, I, 215

NOTES

For Julia Clara Byrne, see 'Sunday Gatherings at the Priory', above.

1. 'No. 741. A DEAD WARRIOR, known as "EL ORLANDO MUERTO" or Roland dead. The Paladin Orlando was killed at the Battle of Roncesvalles; invulnerable to the sword he was squeezed to death by Bernardo del Carpio ...' (Ralph Nicholson Wornum, *Descriptive and Historical Catalogue of the Pictures in the National Gallery: With Biographical Notices of the Painters. Foreign Schools*, 42nd edn (London: HMSO, 1865), p. 272). Now called 'A Dead Soldier', it has since been classified as probably seventeenth-century Italian.
2. GE records seeing the picture with Barbara Bodichon on 21 July 1865 and again the next day (*Journals*, p. 125).

THE ROYAL ACADEMY

T.H.S. Escott

Towards the sixties' close or the seventies' beginning, I can recall at the Royal Academy, not the so-called "private view" day, but that which has of late become much what the private view used to be – the first of the critics' or press inspections. In the portion of the room where I chanced to be, the objects of universal and reverent gaze were no *chef d'oeuvre* by Millais or Leighton; only a gentleman and lady, neither of them longer young, both, I think, wearing glasses, each showing in their expression something of the facial similarity that years of mutual admiration are said to produce on human features. The lady's countenance, like her companion's, was unusually elongated, with the same intellectual brow which he possessed. If, with all respect to an illustrious memory, it may be said, the lady, as she stalked to and fro where the crowd was thinnest, might have reminded one of the Cumaean Sibyl; while the visage's length almost suggested the head of an Arab steed advanced in years. Royal personages would not have been received with the respect that from the spectacled spinsters, simpering curates, and double eye-glassed savants, of which the company on these occasions is chiefly composed, followed or preceded this remarkable couple, wherever they went. The lady dropped a fragment of paper that may, I imagine, at one time have contained a sandwich. Quick as thought a Cambridge don, smooth shaven, ashen hued, darted forward, snatched up the precious relic, placed it in his pocket-book, pressed it adoringly to that part of his person where his heart may have been.

At a respectful distance there came behind, a short, sturdy, middle-aged beau, whom long after this I knew as Robert Browning. The poet stopped short, and in tones of confidential devotion said to a great painter by his side, "She" (meaning the lady) "has the nose of Dante, the mouth of Savonarola, and the mind of Plato." Awe-stricken, the painter reprovingly rejoined, "Hush! She speaks!"

Platform, Press, Politics & Play, pp. 256–7

NOTE
For Thomas Hay Sweet Escott, see 'Sunday Gatherings at the Priory', above.

DINNER AT THE LYTTONS'

Wilfrid Scawen Blunt

1875

April 8. Again at the Lyttons' – a delightful dinner. Lewes and his wife [George Eliot], Miss Mary Boyle, Hamilton Aidë and ourselves.[1] I took Mrs. Lewes in to dinner. She is a remarkable looking woman, with a large rugged face, pale and calm, without pretension to good looks or other grace than that of manner – a pleasant soft voice, however, for the utterance of excellent English. She talks as she writes (a nominative case, a verb, a preposition and all the other parts of speech in regular order), listens to what others have to say, and thinks before she answers – a woman of mind with sense enough to sink her intellect. You might take her at first sight for a very superior governess, the type of decorum and respectable feminine virtues. Her conversation pleased me, though it turned mostly on subjects not my own, the stage, modern novelists, the machinery of literature. Lewes took the lead in the conversation, which was a general one. He is a striking contrast to his wife, an obtrusively ugly man, redeemed in some measure by a pair of piercing dark eyes, – by nature, I should think, an actor, but too ugly for the stage, a brilliant dramatic talker, knowing how to catch the ear of his audience and expecting applause. This we were all ready enough to give. After dinner, Lytton read us his father's unfinished play, the one we had heard in Paris.[2] It was agreed something should be made of it. "Lady Juliet" should have her character defined. She ought to fall, if not quite on her back, enough to give a reason for her repentance. The seducer should be given a backbone etc. etc. We sat discussing these matters till past 1.

'Alms to Oblivion Vol. 4', Fitzwilliam Museum, Cambridge University, MS 43-1975, fol. 63, reproduced by permission of the Syndics of the Fitzwilliam Museum to whom rights in this publication are assigned; quoted from an earlier notebook also entitled 'Alms to Oblivion', MS 318-1975, fol. 13

NOTES

The poet Wilfrid Scawen Blunt (1840–1922, *ODNB*) met GE and GHL through their good friend Lord Lytton (1831–91, *ODNB*), the son of Sir Edward Bulwer Lytton (1803–73, *ODNB*), who himself had called on her in 1860 (*Letters*, iii, 264). Shortly after the dinner recounted here, GHL assisted Blunt in the publication of his *Sonnets and Songs by Proteus* (ix, 150).

1. His wife Anne accompanied him, as she had to luncheon with the Lyttons the day before. The bracketed insertion is Blunt's.
2. *Darnley*, a historical drama read aloud by Lytton on 15 February, when they 'sat up till 2 discussing it' (fol. 27). With a fifth act by Charles Coghlan, it was first performed on 6 October 1877 (*The Works of Edward Bulwer Lytton (Lord Lytton)*, 9 vols (New York: Collier, [1850?–1892?]), ix: *The Dramatic Works* (1892), p. 361).

In an 1882 preface and note, Lytton found Coghlan's addition incongruous and countered it by printing fragments of scenes his father had written for the fifth act (pp. 359–60, 394–9). In the play Lady Juliet Darnley is fooled into believing that her husband has a mistress, and then is herself compromised by her jealousy.

LUNCHEON AT 'THE T — 'S'

A Lady

I lunched with the T — 's the other day, and amongst their guests was George Eliot, or rather Mrs. Lewes. She is by no means handsome or agreeable. She looks like the picture of Lorenzo de Medici, with very large, thin features, and possessing penetrating eyes. She dresses plainly, but well, neither in nor out of fashion. Her manner is not at all pleasing; it is abrupt and harsh; and, indeed, I was altogether so little agreeably impressed by her, that, admiring her works as I do, I took quite a dislike to her, and was sorry I ever met her. The disillusion was too great.

'Literary Table-Talk', *Literary World* (London), 28 May 1875, p. 351

NOTE

This anonymous recollection is quoted from 'a private letter addressed to a friend in New York'.

DRIVING HOMEWARDS

Edmund Gosse

In and after 1876, when I was in the habit of walking from the north-west of London towards Whitehall, I met several times, driven slowly homewards, a victoria which contained a strange pair in whose appearance I took a violent interest. The man, prematurely ageing, was hirsute, rugged, satyr-like, gazing vivaciously to left and right; this was George Henry Lewes. His companion was a large, thickset sybil, dreamy and immobile, whose massive features, somewhat grim when seen in profile, were incongruously bordered by a hat, always in the height of the Paris fashion, which in those days commonly included an immense ostrich feather; this was George Eliot.[1] The contrast between the solemnity of the face and the frivolity of the headgear had something pathetic and provincial about it.

Aspects and Impressions (London: Cassell, 1922), p. 1

NOTE

Sir Edmund William Gosse (1849–1928, *ODNB*) – poet, literary critic, editor, and biographer – was best known for his autobiographical *Father and Son* (1907). He is not the most reliable of witnesses. Alfred Noyes notes Gosse's 'very amusing additions to literary history', which Noyes illustrates by concocting a recollection, as he thinks Gosse would have written it, of GE and Herbert Spencer sitting on a park bench discussing '"the theories of G.H. Lewes on marriage"' (*Two Worlds for Memory* (London and New York: Sheed and Ward, 1953), p. 58).

1. GE's interest in fashion appears in a number of her letters – for example, when she thanks Frances Eleanor Trollope for the gift of 'the impossible Hat' she evidently had mentioned wanting (*Letters*, IX, 237) – and it became part of the friendly gossip about her. William Butler Yeats, all of fifteen years old when GE died, confidently informed Katharine Tynan that she 'liked nothing so much as a talk about dress' (*Collected Letters of W.B. Yeats*, ed. by John Kelly (Oxford: Clarendon Press, 1986–), I (1986), p. 73).

AT THE LEHMANNS', RUBINSTEIN PERFORMING

Lucy B. Walford

That it cast a spell over her was obvious. Her massive brow unbent, and a softened expression stole over her heavy features. She did not look the same woman as when last I saw her.[1]

Music, it was said, always had on her a great effect. "Indeed, she is a real lover of it," said Mr. Lehmann, sitting down beside us in an interval. "The pity is, that she rather prides herself on being a performer too, as I know to my cost. I play duets with her sometimes. Well, they are odd performances, those duets. She has feeling, certainly she has feeling – but her execution is – erratic;" – and he laughed a little. "However," he continued, "it gives pleasure to one auditor at any rate, for whenever we get through a whole page without a breakdown, Lewis claps his hands and cries 'Exquisite!'"[2] ...

As far as I remember, it [her gown] was a rich silk of pale heliotrope colour, made high – (though bare necks were even then *de rigueur*) – and a quantity of soft old lace was disposed upon the bodice and sleeves. A cap of the same old lace – probably Mechlin – had strips of heliotrope ribbon artfully inserted to take off the *cappy* look, – and in short, the whole get-up was effective and becoming. Having studied it, we came to the conclusion that its wearer was an imposing and majestic, if not precisely a handsome woman. The resemblance to a *horse* was still there, but modified.

> *Memories of Victorian London* (New York: Longmans, Green;
> London: Arnold, 1912), pp. 142, 143

NOTES

Born in Edinburgh, Lucy Bethia (Mrs Alfred Saunders) Walford, née Colquhoun (1845–1915, *ODNB*), had some success as a painter before coming to London in 1869 and later publishing her popular novel *Mr Smith: A Part of His Life* (1874). Around the time of the occasion recalled here, May 1876, she was presented to Queen Victoria.

1. At a dinner party hosted by John Blackwood, who published *Mr Smith* and wanted Walford to meet GE. It 'proved barren of any real enjoyment', Walford says;

although GE 'had meant to be civil and kind ... how heavily drave the wheels of her chariot! How interminably dragged that interview!' (p. 140). In another description of this dinner, she remarks that GE was 'destitute of personal charm', at least in public (*Recollections of a Scottish Novelist* (New York: Longmans, Green; London: Williams and Norgate, 1910), p. 257).

2. Compare Lehmann's report to his wife on GE's pianism in 'Other Personal Meetings', above.

ST JAMES'S HALL

I
Ethel Smyth

From my place I used to watch [in 1876–77] George Eliot and her husband sitting together in the stalls like two elderly love-birds, and was irritated by Lewes's habit of beating time on her arm with his *pince-nez*. There is a well-known syncopated passage in Beethoven's Quartett, Op. 132,[1] and I noted with scornful amusement how the eyeglass, after a moment of hesitation, would begin marking the wrong beat, again hover uncertainly, and presently resume the right one with triumphant emphasis as if nothing had happened. All this George Eliot took as calmly as if she were the Sphinx, and Lewes an Arab brushing flies off her massive flanks.

Impressions that Remained: Memoirs, 2nd edn, 2 vols
(London: Longmans, Green, 1919), I, 124–5

II
Alexander Ewing

Lewes is a very repulsive creature – and two ladies (with brains) who were with me [on 23 March 1877] shrieked at him worse than I. He 'nodded his empty head' (I don't forget your hits!) wherever the music was lightest and shallowest. During a scherzo, for instance, it went like a mandarin's in a tea-shop window. I am far from meaning that it is empty except as regards music, for I think some of his writing most able – but the head that noddles at a scherzo must be empty of that. G. Eliot sits and gazes, as if afar, with a great rough powerful face.[2] She goes to all these St. J. Hall Concerts, and I should think, and hope, 'twas a real comfort to her great soul (for a Lewes cannot be, that I am sure of) and she is worked harder than any carthorse.

Letter to Ethel Smyth, in her *Impressions that Remained*, I, 140

III
Lucy Clifford

It was always an arresting thing to see them come in; he happy and alert, a little way ahead of her as they went along the gangway; she in black or soft grey, with a lace veil hanging low in front of her bonnet or thrown back and making a sort of halo about her head, walking slowly, bending a little forward, looking a little preoccupied, but with the dawn of a smile, as of expected enjoyment, on her long pale face.

'A Remembrance of George Eliot', p. 111

NOTES

The composer Dame Ethel Mary Smyth (1858–1944, *ODNB*) was only eighteen or nineteen years old at the time of the occasions recalled here. Her Scottish friend Alexander Ewing (1830–95) was an amateur composer known for his hymn-tune 'Jerusalem the Golden'. For Lucy Clifford, see 'Sunday Gatherings at the Priory', above. Another recollection by her appears in Part v.

1. Uncertain, but probably measures 63–75 or 144–59 in the fourth movement.
2. Compare Kegan Paul: 'There, in a front row, in rapt attention, were always to be seen Mr. and Mrs. Lewes, and none who saw that face ever forgot its power and spiritual beauty' (*Biographical Sketches*, p. 161). Eugenie Schumann confirms the front row stalls as their usual places (*The Schumanns and Johannes Brahms: The Memoirs of Eugenie Schumann*, trans. by Marie Busch (London: Heinemann, 1927), p. 139). This was in the 1870s; ten years earlier they sat in the cheap seats, hearing 'to perfection for a shilling!' (*Letters*, iii, 364).

DINNER AT THE MILLAISES', AND ALBERT HALL

Jane Croly

He [an unnamed gentleman] said the first time he met her was at an entertainment [*c*.1877?] given by Millais, the artist, and delighted to find himself in company so distinguished, he requested an introduction of a friend, who was on speaking terms with her. "That," he replied, "is a liberty I should not dare to take; George Eliot never allows any one to be introduced to her at a gathering of this kind; if she wishes to do so, she will speak to you without being introduced."

At the table the gentleman found himself placed between George Eliot and the young lady to whom he had been directed to act as escort, and afraid to address the lion personally, he "laid himself out" to attract her attention by much that he said. She did not speak to him, however, and he felt greatly disappointed.

Shortly afterwards he attended a popular concert at the Royal Albert Music Hall, and again found himself seated beside the famous author. This time she addressed him, asking him if she had not met him at Mr. Millais' house, and an animated, and to him delightful, conversation ended in the extension of an invitation to her "Monday Evenings" [*sic*] an opportunity he was only too happy to avail himself of, and which gave him the most valued and charming of his London recollections.

'Jennie June', *Baltimore American*, 13 June 1880, p. 2

NOTE

Born in England, Jane (Mrs David G.) Croly, née Cunningham (1829–1901), later moved to the United States, where as 'Jennie June' she was a journalist and magazine editor.

A LITERARY DINNER PARTY

'An English Gentleman'

Col. Thomas W. Knox, now on his way around the world, was told this story by an English gentleman in Tokio, Japan: The latter had attended, not long before, a dinner party in London, at which George Eliot was present, among other noted *littérateurs*. The conversation naturally turned upon the shop, and, referring to American authors, she pronounced John Hay's "Jim Bludso" one of the finest gems in the English language.[1] At the general request of the company she arose and recited the poem, the tears flowing from her eyes as she spoke the closing lines.[2]

The Complete Poetical Works of John Hay, intro. by Clarence L. Hay (Boston: Houghton Mifflin, 1917), p. xi

NOTES

This anecdote, quoted from a newspaper item, appears in Hay's introduction to his father's poems. The item dates this rather doubtful occasion *c*.1877.

1. Joaquin Miller reports of Bret Harte's 1880 London visit that '"George Eliot" asked after John Hay, and told Bret Harte that one of his poems was the finest thing in our language' (T. Edgar Pemberton, *The Life of Bret Harte* (London: Pearson, 1903), p. 165). The ballad 'Jim Bludso of the Prairie Belle' tells the story of an honest Mississippi River engineer (he does, however, have two wives) who perishes on his burning boat in saving his crew.
2. 'He were n't no saint, – but at jedgment | I'd run my chance with Jim, | 'Longside of some pious gentlemen | That would n't shook hands with him. | He seen his duty, a dead-sure thing, – | And went for it thar and then; | And Christ ain't a-going to be too hard | On a man that died for men' (ll. 49–56; *Complete Poetical Works*, p. 5).

MUSIC AT HENSCHEL'S

Lucy C. Lillie

Only a few people were present.[1] The large, quaintly furnished room seemed half empty as I entered, and took my place near one or two musical friends; but, almost at once, I was struck by the appearance, manner, and voice of a lady sitting close beside me, – a large woman, apparently about forty-five years of age, with wonderfully sweet eyes, a massive brow, soft chestnut hair, and features irregular and somewhat masculine, but fairly illumined by an expression of intelligence and peculiarly sympathetic sweetness.

She was richly dressed, with some disregard to the detail of fashion, but with an air of dignified splendor in the materials, as well as in the cut of her gown and cloak, in the fashion of her hat, and even in the exquisite and rare old lace which fell about her neck and wrists.

Looking at her impressive face and figure, I thought her the most striking person I had ever seen. Yet no picture, no pen-portrait, could do her justice; for who could describe that inspired look when she spoke, or give the peculiar charm of her deep, melancholy eyes, in which sometimes her rare, sweet smile lingered, deepening the kindly look, yet never banishing that curious pathetic expression, which was as of one who had looked into the very depths of human sadness, and come back to the lighter visions of the world with a melancholy never to be cast aside?

I could not keep away from the fascination of this strange, dignified lady, who sat for some time a little apart, but with her eyes often eagerly upon the musicians. Presently, a chance phrase led us into conversation.

I felt myself eager to catch every syllable this unknown lady spoke, for the charm of her rich, sweet voice warmed the most insignificant phrases of our conversation. When something peculiarly fine occurred in the first music performed, I remember her turning, flashing that rare, soft smile upon me;[2] and from that sympathetic moment, we talked freely of the music about us, and also the music of the then melodious London season.

It has been my good fortune to meet many amateurs whose musical instincts were as keen as their knowledge was fine; but I have never met any person, who, in a few words, could say what she did of the very fibre of the musician's art. As she talked, with the utmost simplicity, but showing, not only absolute technical knowledge, but the daintiest appreciations, I listened, wondering and debating in my mind who she could be. Surely, I said to myself, it must be some famous *artiste*, with whose face and voice I am unfamiliar. Almost at that moment, the voice of a young friend, just behind me, whispered, –

"Do you know you are talking to George Eliot?"

I then realized why it was I had been involuntarily paying such homage to the woman's presence. Though I saw her often later, the abiding association in my mind will be of the "George Eliot" of that tuneful day, – the brilliant, quiet, magnetic woman, whose face reflected her feelings with half shadows, half lights, yet who seemed so strong in her personality that it was impossible for a moment to forget the woman in the genius.

'A Meeting with George Eliot', in *Some Noted Princes, Authors, and Statesmen of Our Time: By Canon Farrar, James T. Fields, Archibald Forbes, E. P. Whipple, James Parton, Louise Chandler Moulton, and Others,* ed. by James Parton (New York: Crowell, 1885), pp. 62–5 (pp. 62–4)

NOTES

An American, Lucy Cecil (Mrs John) Lillie, née White (1855–1910?), was a prolific writer of fiction for young readers.

1. In 'Music and Musicians in England', *Harper's*, 60 (1880), 827–44, Lillie identifies what is almost certainly this event as taking place at Sir George Henschel's, probably in 1877, where a quintet read a Moscheles piano concerto (p. 840). Henschel himself provides a richly detailed account of London musical life in 1877 in *Musings and Memories of a Musician* (London: Macmillan, 1918), pp. 141–76 – and a charming picture of GHL, 'standing with his back to the fireplace, his hands in his trouser pockets and the tails of his coat flung over his arms', making Henschel sing song after song while 'excitedly shouting, "I know it's cruel, but go on!"' (p. 220).

2. Emphasized by the drawing on p. 63, which portrays only three persons: GE standing and slightly smiling upon a seated woman, with Henschel at a piano in the background.

'MUSICAL MATTERS'

George Grove

The writer knew her, and has sat next her at more than one performance of chamber music. She listened absolutely with the air of knowing everything beforehand; but it was evident from her remarks afterwards that she looked on music, not as a pleasure in itself but, as a branch of knowledge interesting from its effect on the human mind. It was one of the minor defects of both this remarkable woman and her husband, that they were too fond of meddling with what they did not understand.[1] In musical matters this often led to ludicrous scenes. Some one besides the writer may recollect Lewes's behaviour at the first rehearsal of Brahms's C minor Symphony in London [on 5 March 1877], at the Academy concert-room – Joachim conducting. To look at him a stranger would have thought him a real professional musician, in easy and almost boisterous enjoyment of that new and complicated work; and it was not till he ostentatiously beat time utterly wrong that that idea was dispelled, and he was proved to be only a very busy member of the great army of amateurs.

A Correspondent, 'Occasional Notes', *Musical World*, 64 (1886), 711, with Grove identified as 'the writer' in Charles L. Graves, *The Life and Letters of Sir George Grove, C.B.* (London: Macmillan, 1903), p. 318

NOTE

Sir George Grove (1820–1900, *ODNB*) edited the *Dictionary of Music and Musicians* as well as *Macmillan's Magazine*, and later directed the Royal College of Music. An appreciative letter to GE in 1876 earned him her thanks for being 'a sympathetic reader' of *Daniel Deronda* (*Letters*, IX, 173).

1. Earlier in this note Grove accuses GE of a 'false air of learning' in the 'descending thirds and fifths' passage of *The Mill on the Floss* (p. 368 (Book Sixth,

Chapter 1)). He was quarrelling with Frederick Niecks, who had just written that GE treats music 'unpretentiously, and in a way which proves that she had a right to speak on the subject' ('George Eliot as a Musician', *Monthly Musical Record*, 16 (1886), 219–22, 244–6 (p. 219)).

THE GROSVENOR GALLERY

Marion Adams-Acton

All the world was – bewilderingly – there! To my husband it seemed the bringing in of a new party among the old stagers of the art world. I remember being impressed by their long hair, and bushy faces, and short jackets – for many were not in morning clothes. There was one enormous picture covering a great space at one end of the room, and in the foreground a gigantic cabbage with other specimens of agriculture next it, and a great crowd blocked it up and talked about the "realism of the cabbage"![1] Lady Lindsay was extremely kind, gushing and amiable, and all over everywhere at once. Every now and then there was another rush through the crowd, and it was Lady Lindsay again, seeing some interesting person enter, and flying to greet them; and everyone arrived with an expression of having come to see something SPECIAL and hoping it wouldn't be very AWFUL!

It was a most exciting day [30 April 1877], both for her and Sir Coutts, for they certainly had embarked on a big undertaking. It had long been felt that another exhibition was required besides the Academy, to give other artists wall-space for their work; but none were so anxious as the Academicians to be represented in the new show!

We soon picked out our friend Robert Browning, with his white beard and pale face. His greeting, as was often the case, was somewhat *distrait* [absent-minded] and formal; and he let us do all the talking. Then, all of a sudden, his mood changed, he seemed to come to life, seized an arm of each of us affectionately and began enunciating platitudes volubly. Whilst standing listening to him I caught sight of the cause of his sudden animation, two familiar figures among those entering – George Lewes and George Eliot.

She was dressed in a long black silk jacket and dark-toned skirt, also a bonnet – one of those highly-respectable erections worn by elderly ladies at that period – of what shape or material no human being could afterwards have remembered or described, save that it was painfully unbecoming, and her dark straight hair, drawn in two lines on either side of her colourless face, did not assist the bonnet. She always gave one the impression of not caring in the least about her appearance.[2] She and George Lewes had come to see the pictures in the new Exhibition, and to judge these solemnly according to their lights.

Lady Lindsay had greeted the couple rapturously, and they were slowly making their way towards us, when the surging crowd almost thrust us into their arms; and the next moment we were all talking together – Robert

Browning and that quaint couple, the cynosure of all eyes. That plain-faced woman, then at the height of her fame – one could not but listen to every word she said and be astonished at its simple commonplaceness! Soon she was again claimed – claimed on every side simultaneously. Her position at that time was anomalous; yet here in the most fashionable place in all London that day there was not one who would not have given much to be seen speaking to her. ...

Mr. Lewes asked my husband what sculpture he was showing and the latter thereupon led him up to a beautiful group he had sent[3] and asked him to draw his wife's attention to it as he should value her opinion. But the next instant we were pushed aside by other claimants on her attention. She made conscientious efforts to fulfil the intention with which she had come – to study the works of art – but she had no chance of doing this, so great was the crowd pressing round her; and I realised more fully than I had done before what a grip she now had on London society. Yet she was a most unattractive woman – nothing could disguise that fact; and Lewes seemed to do most of the talking, indeed he talked with so much confidence and self-assertion, that although one knew that what he said was probably correct, it was none the less irritating.

Stirling, *Victorian Sidelights*, pp. 162–4 (Stirling's ellipses)

NOTES

Born in Scotland, Marion Jean Catherine (Mrs John) Adams-Acton (1846–1928, *ODNB*) was known as Jeanie Hering at the time of this recollection. She wrote literature for children, and also modelled for painters in St John's Wood, where she lived near the Priory.

1. 'The Minister's Garden', 184.2 cm × 275 cm, by Cecil Gordon Lawson (now in the Manchester Art Gallery, no. 1883.6). It was not in the 1877 opening exhibition, as Adams-Acton says, but featured the following year (*Grosvenor Notes 1877*, ed. by Henry Blackburn [London: Chatto and Windus, 1877?], pp. 3–8; *Grosvenor Notes: With Facsimiles of Sketches by the Artists*, ed. by Henry Blackburn (London: Chatto and Windus, 1878), pp. 7, 12–13). Descriptions of both exhibitions are in 'The Grosvenor Gallery', *Art Journal*, 39 (1877), 244, and 40 (1878), 155.

2. Of GE and GHL out strolling Adams-Acton says that 'they always gave the impression of being rigged up in the first old thing that came to hand and with a total disregard of the fashion of the day!' (*Victorian Sidelights*, p. 77). She also has a gossipy account of the 'ghastly failure' and 'nightmare evening' of the Priory housewarming on 24 November 1863, ending with GE in tears at so few guests and the implied social snub (pp. 78–9). GE and GHL, however, wrote of the occasion as a success (*Letters*, IV, 115, 116).

3. John Adams-Acton is recorded as exhibiting not in 1877 but in 1878, when he sent only a marble bust of the Prince of Wales (*Grosvenor Notes 1877*, p. 8; *Grosvenor Notes* (1878), pp. 56, 58).

DINNERS AT THE GOSCHENS'

I
John Bright

Dined with Mr. and Mrs. Goschen [on 15 May 1877]. Lord Lorne and the Princess Louise[1] were there; Professor Huxley; Mr. and Mrs. Lewes (George Eliot, author of so many famous novels); Capt. Burnaby, author of the 'Ride to Khiva.' Took in Mrs. Lewes to dinner. She looks old and worn, but is very pleasant in talk, thoughtful and good. She asked me about oratory, and if orators are not often moved by something of an overmastering feeling under which they must speak, etc.

We spoke of poetry, especially of Wm. Morris of *The Earthly Paradise*, and of Lewis Morris, of whose new poem *The Epic of Hades* she had not heard. In conversation she spoke against Women's Suffrage,[2] as did Mr. Huxley, though he had once been disposed to favour it.

The Diaries of John Bright (London: Cassell, 1930), p. 393

II
Lyon Playfair

I have just returned from the most charming dinner at Mr Goschen's [on 31 May 1878], the late First Lord of the Admiralty. The dinner was given to the Crown Prince and Princess of Germany.[3] ... Though I took George Eliot down to dinner, she never found out my name till the end. Then she became gushing, and said she had lost the evening, and asked me to go and see her often.[4] However, we had spoken a good deal, and she was quite as clever and agreeable as I expected to find her from her novels. She was much interested with some of my American experiences, especially with the lunatic lady at Washington who took me in so completely.[5]

Wemyss Reid, *Memoirs and Correspondence of Lyon Playfair*
(New York and London: Harper, 1899), p. 276

NOTES

A radical statesman and one of the most eloquent speakers of his time, John Bright (1811–89, *ODNB*) retired from politics in 1870. 'Bright took her down to dinner', GHL reported of this occasion, 'and charmed her' (*Letters*, VI, 374). The chemist Lyon Playfair, 1st baron (1818–98, *ODNB*), was MP 1868–92. GHL had known him in the late 1850s.

1. 'Instead of asking that Polly should be presented to her', GHL gleefully noted in his diary, 'she asked to be introduced to Polly, and was taken up to her!' (*Letters*, VI, 372–3).

2. According to GHL, 'Princess Louise interposed with, "But you don't go in for the superiority of women, Mrs. Lewes?" "No." – "I think," said Huxley, "Mrs. Lewes rather teaches *the inferiority of men*"' (vi, 394).
3. Frederick William and Victoria, who 'opened the talk by saying, "You knew my sister Louise" – just as any other slightly embarrassed mortal might have done. The only complaint one had to make was that she never sat down till quite late in the evening – a sore trial to plebeian legs and backs' (vii, 30).
4. Compare Dante Gabriel Rossetti, who found GE 'modest and retiring, and amiable to a fault when the outer crust of reticence had been broken through' (T. Hall Caine, *Recollections of Dante Gabriel Rossetti* (London: Stock, 1882), p. 282).
5. Playfair had visited an asylum near Washington, DC, where he met a woman who seemed so healthy that he agreed to help secure her release. She then told him that all the telegraph wires in the United States centred in her body. 'I left the asylum', he recorded, 'a humbler but a wiser man' (*Memoirs*, pp. 244–5).

THE WAGNERS' VISIT

I
Francis Heuffer

Altogether he [Richard Wagner] liked to mix in the society of English people; and I remember more especially an interesting evening at Mr. Dannreuther's house, when he was the life and soul of a large and distinguished gathering, including, amongst others, George Eliot and Mr. G.H. Lewes.[1] Madame Wagner, who speaks English perfectly, served as interpreter, and her conversation with the great English novelist – who took a deep interest in music, although her appreciation of Wagner's music was of a very platonic kind – was both friendly and animated.[2] "Your husband," remarked George Eliot, with that straightforwardness which was so conspicuous and so lovable in her character, "does not like Jews; my husband is a Jew."[3]

> *Half a Century of Music in England 1837–1887: Essays towards a History* (London: Chapman and Hall, 1889), pp. 71–2

II
Moncure Daniel Conway

Before the concerts began, Wagner was entertained by the Dannreuthers, the guests being not only musical artists but painters and writers. G.H. Lewes and his wife were present, and I remember a display of enthusiasm by George Eliot. Wagner performed on the piano a piece just composed, unknown I believe to his nearest friends.[4] It was a song, and in it were one or two passages that one might suppose beyond the compass of any voice; but Materna mastered them one after the other, the composer's face reddening with excitement until the last note sounded, when he leaped up and seized the hands of the singer. Then George Eliot moved quickly forward to shake hands with her, though whether Materna was aware of the distinction of the woman who congratulated her was doubtful. For George Eliot, who could probably not have been drawn into so large a company by any less attraction than Wagner, had sat in her usual reserve until this brilliant performance by Materna.

Autobiography, II, 372

NOTES

The music critic Francis Hueffer (1845–89, *ODNB*), born in Germany and naturalized in 1882, was a frequent caller at the Priory (Blind, p. 205). For Moncure Daniel Conway, see Part I. Another recollection by him appears in 'A Few Good Friends', above.

1. From 1 May to 4 June 1877 the Wagners were in London for the Albert Hall Wagner Festival, with six performances (May 7, 9, 12, 14, 16, 19) by a 200-strong orchestra behind vocalists from the Bayreuth Festival (*Musical World*, 55 (1877), 209). GE and GHL left town on 19 May but saw the Wagners frequently in the preceding two weeks. Stewart Spencer has published Chariclea Dannreuther's memoir of their visit in 'Wagner's Addresses in London,' *Wagner*, 26 (2005), 33–51 (pp. 44–51).

2. When they met at the Priory on 6 May, GE made 'einen edlen und angenehmen Eindruck', 'a noble and pleasant impression' (*Cosima Wagner: Die Tagebücher*, ed. by Martin Gregor-Dellin and Dietrich Mack, 2 vols (Munich: Piper, 1976–77), I, 1048; *Cosima Wagner's Diaries*, trans. by Geoffrey Skelton, 2 vols (New York and London: Harcourt Brace Jovanovich, 1978–80), I, 962). GE in turn found her 'a rare person, worthy to see the best things, having her father's (Liszt's) quickness and breadth in comprehension' (*Letters*, VI, 368). By the 18th GHL was declaring their love for her (VI, 374) – but not, evidently, for her husband. According to Charles Villiers Stanford, GE said '"She is a genius. He is an *épicier* [grocer]!"' (*Pages from an Unwritten Diary* (London: Arnold, 1914), p. 180). As for his music, GHL noted in 1870 that it was 'not for us', but 'hours of noise and weariness' (*Letters*, V, 85 *n.* 4a). Seven years later he held to his opinion, at least on the 'monotony of the recitative' (VI, 370 *n.* 8); but Cosima Wagner observed GE's appreciation of *Tannhäuser*: 'The poetical parts seemed to affect her especially, and she wept plentifully over the heavenly scene between *Siegmund* and *Brünnhilde*' (Charles L. Graves, *Hubert Parry: His Life and Works*, 2 vols (London: Macmillan, 1926), I, 178).

3. Ashton, pp. 355–6, discusses the canard that GHL was Jewish. For Liszt it somehow grew to embrace GE as well. In a letter to the *Gazette de Hongrie*, he classed her with Disraeli and Crémieux as 'trois Israélites de haut parage [three Jews of high repute]' (*Franz Listz's Briefe*, ed. by La Mara [Marie Lipsius], 2 vols (Leipzig: Breitkopf & Härtel, 1893), II, 346).

4. And to Wagner scholars. I wish to thank Stewart Spencer for his assistance with this reference.

THE TELEPHONE OFFICE

Kate Field

Only once did I succeed in luring her away from The Priory, and that was to see the telephone, about which she was very curious. Yes, she would come with Mr. Lewes, provided no one else was present. So one afternoon [21 March 1878] George Eliot visited the office of Bell's Telephone in the city and for an hour tested its capacity – "It is very wonderful, very useful," she said – "What marvellous inventions you Americans have!"

'Recollections by Kate Field', *New-York Daily Tribune*,
24 December 1880, p. 5

NOTE

Mary Katherine Keemle Field (1838–96), an American journalist, first met GE in Italy in 1860. Another recollection by her appears in 'The Continent', below.

MUSIC AT MME MOSCHELLES'S

I

Mary Gladstone Drew

28 March 1878

Wretched day of snow & darkness & cold. At 4 went to tea with Mme. Moschelles an ancient widow of the composer's, dear old lady found myself in a tiny room stuffed with musical celebrities, & <[?]> in the twinkling of an eye, found myself on a sofa talking amicably with Geo. Elliot & very soon listening to Henschell's glorious Handel singing – he accompanied himself all through in a masterly manner, showing himself equally great in the fiery & the quiet passages.[1] he sang a good many of his own songs, some extremely good. was introduced to him & Miss Redeker, etc. Miss Friedlander sang to Brull's accompaniment very finely tho' too loud for that little room – meanwhile my neighbour with her great strong face, (a mixture of Savonarola and Dante), <then –> impressed me deeply with the gentleness & earnestness of her manner both in speaking & listening.[2] there *is* something a little like affectation sometimes, but I don't expect its it. Mr. Lewes was rather obtrusively enthusiastic I thought, & is a comic sight with his long dishevelled hair.

Diary, BL, Mary Gladstone Papers, Add. MS 46,258, fol. 42[r], reproduced with permission of the British Library Board; publ. with alterations in *Mary Gladstone (Mrs. Drew): Her Diaries and Letters*, ed. by Lucy Masterman (London: Methuen, 1930), pp. 134–5

II

John Callcott Horsley

Our dear friend Mrs. Moscheles, in her widowhood, occasionally had "musical afternoons," to which we had the entrée. At one of these [3 May 1878?] Mr. and Mrs. George Lewes ("George Eliot") were present. Henschel, the admirable singer, was there, and when asked to sing, to my delight he chose the great scena from *St. Paul*, the most passionate appeal for mercy and forgiveness of sin ever written, the music being as thrilling as the holy words. Henschel is not only a great singer, but a good all-round musician, and the great advantage of his being, on this occasion, his own accompanist was intensely appreciated by the audience, as well as the noteworthy taste and expression with which he sang, and by none more than by the couple I have named. They evidently were acquainted with the noble composition.[3] When Henschel began they were seated at some distance from the piano. After the introduction, so full of pathetic harmony, they rose from their seats, and in the gentlest fashion – I might add with the humblest step – they moved across the room and stood at Henschel's left hand, not more than a foot away from the piano, Lewes a little to the rear. I could observe them to the end without being seen myself, and they never changed their attitude of riveted attention, and quietly left the room the moment the music was over.

Recollections of a Royal Academician,
ed. by M. Alice Helps (London: Murray, 1903),
pp. 159–60

NOTES

Mary Gladstone, later (Mrs Harry) Drew (1847–1927, *ODNB*), the daughter and private secretary of W.E. Gladstone, was a miscellaneous writer and editor. John Callcott Horsley (1817–1903, *ODNB*) was a painter, the son of composer William Horsley.

1. 'We have been having much musical pleasure of late, this being the time of Joachim's visit to England. Also, a great baritone singer, Henschel, has taken up his abode in London and stirs one's soul by singing fine Handel and other songs' (*Letters*, VII, 18).
2. The year before, as Mary Gladstone watched GE at a rehearsal of *Tristan und Isolde*, her face seemed 'repulsively ugly' (*Mary Gladstone (Mrs. Drew)*, p. 124).
3. This is the Mendelssohn oratorio GE found so distasteful forty years earlier when John Braham was performing in it; see J.W. Cross's third recollection in Part I. The passage Henschel chose is 'O God, Have Mercy Upon Me', which ends Scene 3 of Part I.

DOULTON'S POTTERY WORKS

George Tinworth

THESE VISITORS COME INTO MY ROOM [on 4 June 1878] WHEN MODELING THIS PANEL GEORGE. ELIOT AND AND MR G. LEWIS AND SIR H COLE OF SOUTH KENSINGTON WITH SIR H DOULTON H COLE SET DOWN IN FRONT OF THIS PANEL AND SAID, IT IS NOT VERY ORIGHNAL, NOT AN ORIGHNAL SUBJECT, THEN. G. ELLIOT, COME AND SPOKE TO ME, SHE HAD RATHER A PLAIN FACE BUT YOU FORGOT ALL ABOUT

HER FACE WHEN YOU HAD BEEN IN HER COMPANY 5 MINUTES SHE
WANTED TO SEE HOW I HAD TREATED THE RELEASE OF BARRABUS, BUT
I COULD NOT FIND THE SKETCH. SHE TOLD ME NOT TO VEX MY SELF
AT THE MOMENT, MR G. LEWIS WAS LOOKING AT A SKETCH OF MINE
RAISING OF LAZARUS AND HE SAID I HAD GIVEN POWER TO ONE OF
THE FIGURE, WHICH I COULD NOT GET FROM A MODEL. SIR HENRY
<TOLD ME THAT> SAID THAT GEORGE ELLIOT WAS THE SHAKESPERE
AMONG WOMAN.

MS Autobiography, Southwark Local History Library, 920 TIN,
fol. 133, reproduced with kind permission of the Southwark Local
History Library; publ. photographically in Peter Rose, *George Tinworth*
(Los Angeles: C.D.N., 1982), p. 29 (fig. 9)

NOTE

George Tinworth (1843–1913, *ODNB*), a potter and sculptor, joined the Doulton
works in Lambeth in 1867. Thanking Henry Doulton after her visit, GE asked him
to tell 'the interesting Tinworth' that meeting him had been a 'cheering benefit'
(*Letters*, vii, 53).

Eton, Cambridge, and Oxford

ETON

Oscar Browning

They walked down with me to the playing fields in the morning, where a
cricket match was in progress.[1] Both dined at table with the boys in my house,
and had an opportunity of seeing how Harold Transome looked when he was
an Eton boy. In the afternoon they drove with me into Windsor Park, and
enjoyed to perfection that loveliest of all views of Windsor from the green
sward in front of Cranbourne Tower, a prospect now made less lovely by the
too exuberant growth of trees. In the evening we rowed up the river, and
George Eliot talked to me of her Spanish journey, and compared Windsor
with Granada.[2] I have been told by those who knew her long that she was
awkward in her early womanhood, and had not acquired that repose and dignity which characterized her later years.[3] I remember on this visit seeing some
traces of the old "Maggie," the recollection of which is very precious to me.

Browning, pp. 96–7

NOTES

At this time, June 1867, the historian Oscar Browning (1837–1923, *ODNB*) was
a housemaster at Eton. He had met GE and GHL the preceding year. In 1875 he

returned to Cambridge, where he had been a student. Other recollections by him appear in this section, in 'The Countryside', and in 'Vignettes', all below.

1. 'At one Winchester match I remember seeing Miss Evans (George Eliot), who had come as the guest of one of the masters, and whose presence created quite a sensation' (George Greville, *Memories of an Old Etonian: 1860–1912* (London: Hutchinson, [1919]), p. 96).
2. A tour of forty days, beginning in late December 1866, with a week in Granada.
3. George Jacob Holyoake, who had known GE in her *Westminster Review* days, saw her *c*.1878 and 'was astonished at the stately grace she had acquired' (*Bygones Worth Remembering*, 2 vols (London: Unwin, 1905), I, 67).

CAMBRIDGE, FEBRUARY 1868

Oscar Browning

I travelled down with them in the train, the journey giving me the impression that railway-travelling was irksome to her. She reiterated, I remember, strong warnings against reading in the train, a mode of study in which I have spent many happy hours. We dined in the evening, a small party, in Mr. Clark's rooms. I sat next to her, and she talked to me solemnly about the duties of life, about the shallow immorality of believing that all things would turn out for the best, and the danger of fixing our attention too much on the life to come, as likely to distract us from doing our duty in this world. The next day she breakfasted with me in my rooms in college. I shall not readily forget her exquisite courtesy and tenderness to the ladies whom I had invited to meet her. This was the first of several visits to Cambridge, which always gave her great pleasure. At a later period she was on several occasions the guest of Dr. Jowett, at Oxford. I asked her once what struck her as the most salient difference between the society of the two universities, and she replied that at Cambridge they all seemed to speak well of each other, whereas at Oxford they all criticized each other.

Browning, p. 99 (where the visit is misdated 1869)

NOTE

For Oscar Browning, see just above. Other recollections by him appear in this section, and in 'The Countryside' and 'Vignettes', all below.

OXFORD, MAY 1870

Mrs Humphry Ward

I

It was at one of the Sunday suppers.[1] George Eliot sat at the Rector's right hand. I was opposite her; on my left was George Henry Lewes, to whom I took a prompt and active dislike. He and Mrs. Pattison kept up a lively conversation in which Mr. Bywater, on the other side of the table, played full part. George Eliot talked very little, and I not at all. The Rector was shy or tired, and George Eliot was in truth entirely occupied in watching or listening to Mr. Lewes. I was disappointed that she was so silent, and perhaps her quick eye may have divined it, for, after supper, as we were going up the interesting old staircase, made in the thickness of the wall, which led direct from the dining-room to the drawing-room above, she said to me: "The Rector tells me that you have been reading a good deal about Spain. Would you care to hear something of our Spanish journey?" – the journey which had preceded the appearance of *The Spanish Gypsy*, then newly published. My reply is easily imagined. The rest of the party passed through the dimly lit drawing-room to talk and smoke in the gallery beyond. George Eliot sat down in the darkness, and I beside her. Then she talked for about twenty minutes, with perfect ease and finish, without misplacing a word or dropping a sentence, and I realized at last that I was in the presence of a great writer. Not a great *talker*. It is clear that George Eliot never was that. Impossible for her to "talk" her books, or evolve her books from conversation, like Madame de Staël. She was too self-conscious, too desperately reflective, too rich in second-thoughts for that. But in tête-à-tête, and with time to choose her words, she could – in monologue, with just enough stimulus from a companion to keep it going – produce on a listener exactly the impression of some of her best work.[2] As the low, clear voice flowed on in Mrs. Pattison's drawing-room, I *saw* Saragossa, Granada, the Escorial, and that survival of the old Europe in the new, which one must go to Spain to find. Not that the description was particularly vivid – in talking of famous places John Richard Green could make words tell and paint with far greater success; but it was singularly complete and accomplished. When it was done the effect was there – the effect she had meant to produce. I shut my eyes, and it all comes back – the darkened room, the long, pallid face, set in black lace, the evident wish to be kind to a young girl.

Two more impressions of her let me record. The following day, the Pattisons took their guests to see the "eights" races from Christ Church meadow.[3] A young Fellow of Merton, Mandell Creighton, afterward the beloved and famous Bishop of London, was among those entertaining her on the barge, and on the way home he took her and Mr. Lewes through Merton garden. I was of the party, and I remember what a carnival of early summer it was in that enchanting place. The chestnuts were all out, one splendor from top to toe; the laburnums; the lilacs; the hawthorns, red and white; the new-mown grass spreading its smooth and silky carpet round the college walls; a May sky overhead, and through the trees glimpses of towers and spires, silver gray, in the sparkling summer air – the picture was one of those that Oxford throws before the spectator at every turn, like the careless beauty that knows she has only to show herself, to move, to breathe, to give delight. George Eliot stood on the grass, in the bright sun, looking at the flower-laden chestnuts, at the distant glimpses on all sides, of the surrounding city, saying little – that she left to Mr. Lewes! – but drinking it in, storing it in that rich, absorbent mind of hers. And afterward when Mr. Lewes, Mr. Creighton, she, and I walked back to Lincoln, I remember another little incident throwing light on the ever-ready instinct of the novelist. As we turned into the quadrangle of Lincoln – suddenly, at one of the upper windows of the Rector's lodgings, which occupied the far right-hand corner of the quad, there appeared the head and shoulders of Mrs. Pattison, as she looked out and beckoned, smiling, to Mrs. Lewes. It was a brilliant apparition, as though a French portrait by Greuze or Perronneau had suddenly slipped into a vacant space in the old college wall. The pale, pretty head, *blond-cendrée* [ash-blond], the delicate, smiling features and white throat; a touch of black, a touch of blue; a white dress; a general eighteenth-century impression as though of powder and patches – Mrs. Lewes perceived it in a flash, and I saw her run eagerly to Mr. Lewes and draw his attention to the window and its occupant. She took his arm, while she looked and waved. If she had lived longer, some day, and somewhere in her books, that vision at the window and that flower-laden garden would have reappeared. I seemed to see her consciously and deliberately committing them both to memory.

> *A Writer's Recollections*, 2 vols (New York and London: Harper, 1918),
> I, 144–7

II

It is one of the happy memories of my life to have seen and talked with George Eliot. When I think of her I seem still to see her under the blossoming chestnuts of Merton Gardens, or in the old rooms of Lincoln College where I first met her; and when I look back upon my various meetings with her, I am conscious of something very human and womanly, which seems still to lay an appealing hand upon one, as though it asked above all for sympathy – and to be understood. She was abnormally, pitifully dependent upon sympathy; it explains the false step of her life.[4] But it also explains the infinitely receptive and plastic temper which was the source of her best art. She who craved for sympathy had first given it in good measure – poured down and running over – to the human life about her.

> 'The Coventry Celebration: Interesting Letters',
> *Coventry Herald*, 7–8 November 1919,
> suppl., p. 8

III

W.L. Courtney

We were asked to assemble in one of the Common rooms, if I remember right, of Balliol College.[5] The celebrated novelist was sitting in the centre of an eager group, who were very anxious to exchange a few words with the author of "Silas Marner" and "Adam Bede." The lady herself was at her most gracious. I think she had come to Oxford for one purpose only, which was to study the character of an undergraduate. At all events, she seemed to be much more interested in the younger members of the gathering and cared but little for the dons and tutors. When we were introduced to her, a few ordinary expressions of courtesy and congratulation passed without leaving any definite memory on the mind. She made a rather wonderful figure nevertheless. The face was that of a tired woman, the large features being remarkable for only occasional flashes of inspiration. It was in some senses a disappointing face. It gave the idea of a woman who had passed through so many different phases of experience that there was little or nothing left for her to learn. But her eyes were a different matter. They were wonderful eyes – eyes that now and again seemed to flash a message or analyse a personality. The eyes had something of all that she had stood for in the course of her life. However patient the face might look, the eyes were perpetually in activity, keen and eager, though occasionally sorrowful.

When I had the honour of talking to her, she obviously was not listening, or, rather, her eyes were roving to find that of which she was in search. What was it? The answer was obvious. When a young undergraduate who had just come up to Balliol, and whose name I forget, was introduced to her, then at once the face lit up with animation and she probed the young man with questions – questions to which he found it very difficult to reply.

George Eliot was evidently sounding the depth of his nature and discovering for herself what was the charm of a young academician and what purposes and objects he had come to Oxford to promote. Or, in other words, George Eliot was making her first study of Fred Vincy. You will remember that in "Middlemarch" there is a characteristic young man, very well drawn, with a figure clearer to the eye than some of the other personalities of the story: just an ordinary young man with the brightness and agility of an athlete combined with all that light-hearted charm which an undergraduate can express with such consummate ease.

Perhaps we have wondered how it was possible that so serious a thinker as George Eliot should be able to analyse the soul of a young man. But when I looked at her talking to the undergraduate who had just been presented to her, I seemed to understand how real sympathy combined with an eager analysis can make discoveries even in the most unpromising material.

The Passing Hour (London: Hutchinson, [1925]), pp. 119–21

NOTES

Born in Tasmania, Mary Augusta (Mrs Thomas Humphry) Ward, née Arnold (1851–1920, *ODNB*), was the author of *Robert Elsmere* (1888), one of the most popular novels of the nineteenth century. At the time of the meeting recalled here, she was living with her family in Oxford and educating herself at the Bodleian with the help of Mark Pattison (1813–84, *ODNB*), Rector of Lincoln College. Born in India, William Leonard Courtney (1850–1928, *ODNB*) was a scholar of University College when he met GE, then Headmaster of Somerset College before returning to Oxford to teach philosophy. Later he became a journalist in London.

1. The dinner was on Wednesday, 25 May 1870 (*Journals*, pp. 139–40). Benjamin Jowett, invited to supper on the 27th, reported that GE was 'a very pleasing person in manners & has evidently great abilities. I am told that she has gone through some ceremony of marriage, though she can hardly be said, in the language of the Vicar of Wakefield, to "be made an honest woman of". The ladies here don't seem to object to her' (*Dear Miss Nightingale: A Selection of Benjamin Jowett's Letters to Florence Nightingale 1860–1893*, ed. by Vincent Quinn and John Prest (Oxford: Clarendon Press, 1987), p. 188). In Chapter 31 of Oliver Goldsmith's novel *The Vicar of Wakefield* (1766), Arabella Wilmot, finally married, 'was now made an honest woman of', that is, made virtuous (ed. by Michael Macmillan (London: Macmillan, 1897), who glosses the clause in question, p. 246). The marriage ceremony between GE and GHL was only a rumour, but a persistent one.
2. In 1888 Sir James Knowles said of Mrs Humphry Ward herself that she 'easily wakes up to enthusiasm in talk on *subjects* – & in this respect – as in many others reminds me more or less of George Eliot' (Priscilla Metcalf, *James Knowles: Victorian Editor and Architect* (Oxford: Clarendon Press, 1980), p. 322).
3. On Friday, 27 May (*Journals*, p. 140), the famous race in which Cambridge, J.H.D. Goldie (St John's) as stroke, ended Oxford's nine-year reign. '"George Eliot" was present', Sir Robert Edgcumbe recalled, 'and we [Cambridge] undergraduates were interested to know what she thought of it all. When we learnt that the only observation she let fall was, "all human joys are transient," she somewhat fell in our estimation' (*The Works of Arthur Clement Hilton* [ed. by Robert Edgcumbe] (Cambridge: Macmillan and Bowes, 1904), p. 81).
4. Her living with GHL.
5. Since GE does not mention a Balliol Common Room during her 1870 visit to Oxford, and since she began visiting Jowett at Balliol in 1873, Haight assigns this meeting to the latter year (*Letters*, IX, 100 *n*. 9). I have dated it 1870 because Courtney was an undergraduate from 1868 to 1872 and is not entirely certain where it took place. Further, GE had begun *Middlemarch* in 1869, then set it aside, so in May 1870 it is possible, as Courtney later suggests, that she was mentally forming Fred Vincy. By 1873 *Middlemarch* had appeared.

CAMBRIDGE, MAY 1873

I

Reginald Baliol Brett

George Eliot was more than an interesting visitor. Her presence has hallowed the place.[1] Her low sweet voice thanked me for giving her tickets for the Choir Festival at King's [on 20 May], to which she, interested in every or any religious service, took her husband, who had not entered a church for years.

He told us how she had been into some Roman Catholic church abroad and sat there watching the women and children praying round her.

Journals and Letters of Reginald Viscount Esher, ed. by Maurice V. Brett, 4 vols (London: Nicholson & Watson, 1934–38), I, 8–9

II

Henry Jackson

On Monday night and again last night I went to supper with the Myers' to meet George Eliot and her husband. The assembled multitude worshipped in a very amusing way, but I confess to being rather bored by the stiff way in which she wraps up platitudes in stilted language delivered in a peculiar, formal manner in a low voice.[2]

Letter to Frances Jackson, his mother, in R. St John Parry, *Henry Jackson, O.M.: Vice-Master of Trinity College & Regius Professor of Greek in the University of Cambridge: A Memoir* (Cambridge: University Press, 1926), p. 28 (where the letter is misdated 1893)

III

Richard Claverhouse Jebb

It would be most natural to begin by telling you of the ordinary May Term doings, perhaps, but another subject is uppermost in my thoughts just now, – an event in any life, and a large event in mine. I have met 'George Eliot' (Mrs Lewes) again, and found such great happiness in knowing her better. Friendship is a word varying in largeness of sense with the largeness of the nature; and her friendship means a great deal. She and her husband came to Cambridge for a few days with one of my oldest friends, Mr Frederic Myers.[3] I had known Mrs Lewes before; but acquaintanceship sprang into friendship by one of those impulses which cannot be explained except by some hidden law asserting itself in a moment; ... one of the things which brought our minds closest together was a talk about criticism: I was saying (*à propos* of Pater's essays on the Renaissance) that the 'precious' school seemed to be destroying everything – their finesses and small affectations blinding people's eyes to the great lineaments of the great creative works, – blinding them to the mind which speaks from these faces: – the creators, if they could revive, would never know their own thoughts under this veil of finikin yet thoroughly opaque ingenuities. Her face lit up in a moment, and she said, 'It is such a comfort and a strength to hear you say that' – and then she said why, so eloquently. I asked her how Sophocles had influenced her: – (we had been talking about him, and she had said that she first came to know him through a small book of mine): – and her answer certainly startled me. Probably all people, – or most people who have any inner life at all – sometimes write down things meant for no eye but their own. Long ago I was putting down in this way some things that had been passing through my mind about Sophocles, and this among the rest, – that George Eliot was the modern dramatist (in the large sense) most like him, and that he had told upon her work probably *in the outlining of the first emotions.* Her answer to my question was – 'in the delineation of the great primitive emotions.' *Verbally* this was an accident; but hardly in substance. Of course I did not tell her. But was it not curious? ... Her husband is very delightful: – he is accomplished, and he has a good heart. What I admire in him is his faithfulness in laying everything – knowledge, social power, reputation, all, at his illustrious wife's feet. ... We went together to the Choral Festival at King's, and as I was walking with her, I heard some people whisper – 'Mr Lewes is here; but is *she* here?' He was close behind, but I doubted whether he had heard it. When we came out, he quoted it to her. ...

Letter to Caroline Lane Slemmer, later his wife, in Caroline Jebb, *Life and Letters of Sir Richard Claverhouse Jebb* (Cambridge: University Press, 1907), pp. 154–6 (Jebb's ellipses)

NOTES

Reginald Baliol Brett, Viscount Esher (1852–1930, *ODNB*), later a government official, was at this time a student at Trinity College. Another recollection by him appears in this section, below. Henry Jackson (1839–1921, *ODNB*), a classical scholar, was an assistant tutor at Trinity and later Regius Professor of Greek, succeeding Sir Richard Claverhouse Jebb (1841–1905, *ODNB*), also a fellow of Trinity. By 1873 Jebb had published editions of Sophocles' *Electra* and *Ajax*, and in that year brought out his *Translations into Greek and Latin Verse.* A recollection by his wife appears in Part VI.

1. '"We were invited ostensibly to see the boat-race,"' GE wrote, '"but the real pleasure of the visit consisted in talking with a hopeful group of Trinity young men"' (Browning, p. 116). Elsewhere Brett noted that she and the Trinity men 'walked and talked in the college grounds and cloister' (*Ionicus* (London: Murray, 1923), p. 50). The Choral Festival was held for the Choir Benevolent Fund (programme in *Musical World*, 51 (1873), 374). For an entertaining description of Cambridge's social and intellectual life at this time, see Edward Lyttelton, *Memories and Hopes* (London: Murray, 1925), pp. 48–66.

2. Jackson held to his opinion. In 1904 he felt 'a little dismayed' that Lord Acton had made GE 'into a sort of Goddess'; although admitting that she was 'a considerable personage', he insisted upon 'the ephemeral quality of her work' (Parry, *Henry Jackson*, pp. 124, 126).

3. Myers sent Jebb a Pindaric ode to announce her arrival. An excerpt: 'For men say that there is a woman now | Man-named, anonymous, known of all, George Eliot, wiser than the wise, | Her too, methinks, my subtle net shall bear within the academic wall: | Her too in season thou must see' (Jebb, *Life and Letters*, p. 154).

OXFORD, JUNE 1873

I

Herbert Henry Asquith

After he was settled in the [Balliol] Master's Lodge, it was Jowett's practice during term-time to have what would now be called "week-end parties," at which the guests were drawn from diverse quarters of the outside world. ... A few privileged undergraduates used to be invited to come in on Sunday nights, and it was in this way that I first had a glimpse of Tennyson and George Eliot. It is not easy for the average English reader of the twentieth century to realize the hero-worship which was given in the eighteen-seventies to this illustrious pair. ...

George Eliot was a more frequent visitor, with her husband G.H. Lewes. He had a most versatile mind, and was one of the best and most accomplished critics of his time. I remember Jowett asking him at table, after the ladies had gone, whether an ordinary reader ought to have guessed from internal evidence, that "Adam Bede" and "The Mill on the Floss" were written by a woman. Lewes replied that he had always thought there was one thing which ought to have betrayed the author's sex: that no man with such fine observation and intimate knowledge of the country and of country life would have been so totally indifferent to sport in all its aspects.

After dinner I was privileged to have a talk with the Great Oracle herself – for she looked and spoke like a Sibyl, though with all imaginable courtesy to a raw and insignificant undergraduate. This must have been in the year 1873 or 1874, and she asked me whether the Church had still much hold on the intellectual elite of young Oxford. I replied that it had very little, and that little was on the wane. She answered: "I am getting an old woman, and you are a very young man, but unless my vision is at fault, you – though not I – will live to see a great renascence of religion among thoughtful people." I asked her what Church or community would profit by it. She answered without hesitation: "The Roman Catholic Church."

That was more than fifty years ago, and it is, I think, an interesting illustration of the hazards of prophecy.

Memories and Reflections: 1852–1927, 2 vols
(London: Cassell, 1928), I, 35–6

II

Almeric FitzRoy

The memory of Jowett's dinners embalms recollections of George Eliot and G.H. Lewes, Sir R. Morier, Professor Huxley, Swinburne, and Bishop Colenso. Of the first-named I recall an interesting discourse on the methods followed in the creation of her characters: she repudiated any conscious portraiture, but attributed their being to the gradual accumulation of impressions, a point here and a trait there, which finally emerged under the guise of an organic whole.[1] Lewes's vanity was such that he was always seeking to absorb the interest of the company by drawing attention to himself instead of allowing it to concentrate on the lady whose leonine countenance was in curious contrast to the softness of her voice.

Memoirs, 2 vols (London: Hutchinson, 1925), I, p. vii

III
William Wordsworth

... I was to hand out to dinner a particular lady, but her name was not mentioned to me, or at least I did not catch it. She, however, was told that I was a grandson of Wordsworth. 'Oh,' said she, 'I began to read Wordsworth when I was fifteen, and have gone on ever since with continually increasing pleasure;'[2] and then her talk flowed on with such strength and power, and showed such elevation of mind and such grasp and mastery of all learning, that I was certain she could be no other than Mrs. Lewes. So I asked her if she was not the author of "Middlemarch," and she said she was. In the drawing-room afterward she showed herself on the same level with Greek scholars and men of science, with whom she talked, filling with wonder all who listened.[3]

Ellis Yarnall, *Wordsworth and the Coleridges: With Other Memories Literary and Political* (London and New York: Macmillan, 1899), p. 101

NOTES

Herbert Henry Asquith, 1st earl (1852–1928, *ODNB*), was elected a fellow of Balliol in 1875 and was Prime Minister 1908–16. Sir Almeric William FitzRoy (1851–1935, *ODNB*), at this time studying history, was later a civil servant and author. William Wordsworth (1835–1917), who as GE noted 'had spent much time in India' (*Journals*, p. 143), returned to Mumbai as principal of Elphinstone College until 1890.

1. Frederic Burton also recalls hearing GE speak on this topic: 'she thought out characters, put them in certain circumstances & then they had to act according to their nature' (*Lady Gregory's Diaries*, p. 249). According to Frederick Locker-Lampson, GE similarly told a friend of his 'that, when she was arranging for a new novel, she first sketched in the characters, and then they gradually and naturally fell into certain positions in life and evolved the story' (*My Confidences: An Autobiographical Sketch Addressed to My Descendants* [ed. by Augustine Birrell] (London: Smith, Elder, 1896), p 311).
2. On her twentieth birthday GE purchased 'Wordsworth at full length' (the six-volume 1836–37 Moxon edn): 'I have never before met with so many of my own feelings, expressed just as I could <wish> like them' (*Letters*, I, 34) – a remark, according to Cross, which 'entirely expresses the feeling she had to him up to the day of her death' (*Life*, I, 61).
3. David Hunter Blair briefly recalls meeting GE on this visit in Charles Reade's rooms (*In Victorian Days and Other Papers* (London: Longmans, Green, 1939), pp. 104–5). Since GE herself does not mention seeing Reade, Haight, p. 466, finds Blair's recollection doubtful.

OXFORD, MAY 1875

Benjamin Jowett

Mrs. Lewis wished to form a character in which the greatest enthusiasm should be united with the most perfect wisdom & tolerance.

———

thought that Music & poetry were analogous[1]

———

agreed in the notion that simple ideas lay at the root of morality[2]
Notebook, 3 – 1873–75,[3] Balliol College Library, Oxford University, MS I/H24, fol. 45ʳ, reproduced with kind permission of the Jowett Copyright Trustees

NOTES

Benjamin Jowett (1817–93, *ODNB*), classical scholar and master of Balliol College, first met GE at Oxford in May 1870. She then saw him at Weybridge around the Christmas holidays, and from 1873 to 1878 paid almost annual visits to Balliol. 'My particular friend', she called him: 'I get on with him delightfully' (*Letters*, VI, 427; IX, 138). 'Some of the most pleasant recollections of my life at Oxford', Jowett later wrote, 'have been her visits' (letter to J.W. Cross, 27 January 1885, Yale). Other recollections by him appear in 'The Countryside', below, in Part III, and in Parts V–VII.

1. In an 1869 essay on versification, GE says that 'in both verse & music rhythmic & tonic relations are used as a means of moving men's souls by the adjustment of those relations to the bias of passionate experience, i.e. to the accumulated associations of certain modes of sound with ease & struggle, consent or resistance, joy or sorrow, awe or triumph, calmness or rage' (*George Eliot: A Writer's Notebook 1854–1879 and Uncollected Writings*, ed. by Joseph Wiesenfarth (Charlottesville: University Press of Virginia, 1981), p. 287). For the Victorian habit of using poetic and musical terms interchangeably, see Phyllis Weliver, 'Introduction', in *The Figure of Music in Nineteenth-Century British Poetry*, ed. by Phyllis Weliver (Aldershot: Ashgate, 2005), pp. 1–24 (esp. pp. 4, 19).
2. 'The fundamental antitheses of *right* and *wrong*, of what we *ought* and *ought not* to do; the great abstractions of Duty and Virtue; the august Ideas of Justice and Truth ... These are some of the ideas which lie at the root of Morality...' (William Whewell, *Lectures on Systematic Morality* (London: Parker, 1846), pp. 64–5).
3. Dated by Evelyn Abbott. From their location in the notebook, these notes seem to have been made after GE's 1875 visit, but it is possible that they were made after her visit in 1873.

OXFORD, MAY 1877

I

A.G.C. Liddell

I was determined to have a talk with 'George Eliot,' so taking advantage of the male hesitation in leaving the dining-room, I bolted upstairs, not looking back till I had landed myself beside her. She has a noble face of the equine type, with fine grey eyes, not large but deep-set thoughtful and kind. She asked if I was a north countryman, saying that my stature agreed with my being a Northumbrian, who were all tall men. I felt flattered, but was afraid of showing my weakness before such an analyst. She then asked for a specimen of the dialect, which I gave her. The talk next passed to circuit, which she said must be interesting from the opportunity of hearing such a variety of cases, and seeing so many types of humanity. I answered that there was too much sameness about the cases, and then went on to tell her how from my habit of sketching in Court I was struck with the constant reproduction of similar types of face and figure. She said that the forms of Nature were really few. I remarked how similarity of form was often accompanied by similarity of voice, movement and character. We then got on to the effect of a peculiarity of speech in conversation, and the part it played in arresting the attention. She said that some men's talk always seemed worth listening to, while others, who really talked better, could obtain no hearing, and that one reason why Scotsmen's talk often seemed more intellectual, was in a great measure due to the effect of their dialect in arresting attention, giving Carlyle as an example. She remembered a ludicrous effect in the conversation of the late Lord Lytton, who was deaf, and who would go on murmuring for a time, and then suddenly burst out for a sentence or two in a very loud key. The English always dropped their voices at the end of a sentence, and were much averse to any other form of talk than a *tête-à-tête* and in illustration she pointed out all the various persons *tête-à-têting* around us. Frenchmen had none of the English shyness, which did not arise from superior mental endowments, but from a peculiar sensibility to outward surroundings, which an Englishman had not. A Frenchman in conversation almost always reproduced in words the scene before him, or remarked upon it, even to its most trivial details.

I continued that I had not met many good talkers, but thought Professor Owen the best I had heard. She said he was a particularly charming talker, and excelled greatly in narrative and description.

We talked a good deal about the Professor, and she asked if I was the son of a Mrs. Liddell, whom she remembered Owen mentioning as a beautiful woman. This shows she must have a good memory, as it must have been said a long time ago.

In talking about the Professor, I remarked what a good reader he was and how (illustrating what she had said a few moments before), his Lancashire accent helped him. She said that Tennyson's reading was greatly improved by his Lincolnshire pronunciation, which had the good effect of making his vowels very sonorous, the reverse of which was the usual defect of English reading. I quoted 'mouthing out his hollow oes and aes,'[1] as to what Tennyson's own notion of good reading was, which she seemed to think apposite. She then spoke of the difference of Owen's son to his father. I said he was a complete contrast. She said that often was the case, and was going on to talk of the connection between parents and children, when her husband came up with Mr. Spottiswoode, and I thought I ought to retire. I felt that she had been very good-natured to talk so much to an 'ordinary mortal,' and to look so kindly out of her grey eyes. Spottiswoode began to talk to her of a Frenchman who had solved theoretically the problem of turning up and down motion into circular, the usual method in vogue being only an approximation to the theoretically perfect way.[2] I could only hear now and then scraps of the talk. They got on to 'spiral vortices,' and then 'imaginary geometry,' after which I understood not one word. George Eliot said she supposed that this science consisted in a system of reasoning from abstractions still purer than the ordinary geometrical ones.

Notes from the Life of an Ordinary Mortal: Being a Record of Things Done, Seen and Heard at School, College, and in the World during the Latter Half of the 19th Century (London: Murray, 1911), pp. 156–8

II
Benjamin Jowett

Mrs. Lewes:

―――

thought that we must accept certain bases of life resting on the facts of human nature[3]

―――

admitted that Darwinism used H Spencer, etc, but genus omne tended to impair the moral sense[4]

―――

Origin useless, vague, conjectural[5]

―――

was evidently for standing for the highest – the highest possible for humanity – separating the human from the physical & animal

―――

Detested Schopenhauer.[6]

―――

Any positive element however imperfect she would nurse & cherish.

―――

We must begin with the best which we have
Spoke of the extraordinary pleasure which she felt in being present at an assembly moved by a common feeling –
She has the strongest feeling of right & wrong
Men & women of genius from their greater sensibility often show in a higher degree the common tendencies of humanity

Notebook, *10 – April 1877*, Balliol College Library, Oxford University, MS I/H31, fols 11ʳ, 10ᵛ, reproduced with kind permission of the Jowett Copyright Trustees

NOTES

Educated at Eton and Balliol, Adolphus George Charles Liddell (1846–1920, *ODNB*) was called to the bar in 1871 and practised on the north-eastern circuit. In 1886 he left the law to become a civil servant. For Benjamin Jowett, see above in this section. Other recollections by him appear in 'The Countryside', below, in Part III, and in Parts V–VII.

1. 'The Epic' (1842), line 50.
2. Although the problem as Liddell phrases it here is to turn reciprocating motion into circular motion, not vice versa, presumably the Frenchman is Charles-Nicholas Peaucellier, whose 'inversor' linkage, based on mathematical properties of lines and circles, was the first to convert circular motion precisely into straight-line motion. In January 1874 the noted mathematician J.J. Sylvester, whose career GE followed (see *Letters*, VI, 162 *n.* 8), delivered a lecture on Peaucellier's discovery ('Professor Sylvester on Conversion of Motion', *Notices of the Proceedings at the Meetings of the Members of the Royal Institution of Great Britain*, 7 (1873–75), 179–98). I wish to thank Roger Cooke and John Hooker for their assistance with this reference.
3. GE elaborated *c.*1874 upon the limits imposed by human shape, movement, and senses; see K.K. Collins, 'Questions of Method: Some Unpublished Late Essays', *Nineteenth-Century Fiction*, 35 (1980), 385–405 (esp. pp. 387–90).
4. Spencer insisted upon the emotional basis of moral intuitions, but held that they evolved from accumulated experiences of utility, and so had no apparent relation to one's personal experiences of what might be useful and pleasing (*The Data of Ethics*, 2nd edn (London: Williams & Norgate, 1879), p. 123). For GE this view may have been relatively acceptable, but, like other evolutionary views, it may have seemed to appeal too readily to the explanatory power of animal behaviour; see K.K. Collins, 'G.H. Lewes Revised: George Eliot and the Moral Sense', *Victorian Studies*, 21 (1978), 463–92. J.A. Symonds recalls talking with GE during her May 1876 Oxford visit upon 'the fundamental truths of ethics & the way of adjusting the scientific instinct to sentiments sacred', but he gives no details (*The Letters of John Addington Symonds*, ed. by Herbert M. Schueller and Robert L. Peters, 3 vols (Detroit: Wayne State University Press, 1967–69), II, 417).
5. Startling judgements in 1877, although in 1859, when *Origin of Species* appeared, GE found it 'ill-written and sadly wanting in illustrative facts', adding that 'the Development theory and all other explanations of processes by which things came to be, produce a feeble impression compared with the mystery that lies under the processes' (*Letters*, III, 227). Sally Shuttleworth says that at first GE probably missed the implications of Darwin's theory of natural selection, but that strands of Darwinian thought broadly conceived may be traced in her fiction at least from *The Mill on the Floss* onwards (*Companion*, pp. 87–9); elsewhere Shuttleworth observes that like many thinkers of her time GE 'simply assimilated' Darwin's theories 'into a pre-established framework of developmental thought' (*George Eliot and Nineteenth-Century Science: The Make-Believe of a Beginning* (Cambridge: Cambridge University Press, 1984), p. 15). For Gillian Beer, GE had 'fully assimilated the implications of evolutionary ideas' by the time she wrote *Middlemarch* and *Daniel Deronda* (*Darwin's Plots: Evolutionary Narrative in Darwin, George Eliot and Nineteenth-Century Fiction* (London: Routledge & Kegan Paul, 1983), p. 158).
6. Still, as John Rignall notes, GE's 'increasing pessimism about social life and her elevation of music' have been linked to Schopenhauer's thought (*Companion*, p. 365).

CAMBRIDGE, MAY–JUNE 1877

I

Reginald Baliol Brett

I spent four hours this afternoon in the society of George Eliot. She talks like the best parts of her books, the parts where she analyses without dissecting, the parts out of which compilers get her "wise, witty, and tender" sayings.[1] She is wonderfully thoughtful even in trifles. She shut up George Lewes when he tried to talk about her. She does not seem vain. She adores Charles Darwin, because of his humility. I suppose it is an event to have spent the day in her company.

Journals and Letters, I, 40

II

Jane Ellen Harrison

And then last, but oh, so utterly first, came George Eliot. It was in the days when her cult was at its height – thank heaven I never left her shrine! – and we used to wait outside Macmillan's shop to seize the new instalments of *Daniel Deronda*. She came for a few minutes to my room, and I was almost senseless with excitement. I had just repapered my room with the newest thing in dolorous Morris papers. Some one must have called her attention to it, for I remember that she said in her shy, impressive way, "Your paper makes a beautiful background for your face."[2] The ecstasy was too much, and I knew no more. Later, in London, I met, of course, many eminent men, but there never came again a moment like that.

Reminiscences of a Student's Life (London: Hogarth Press, 1926), pp. 45–6

III

J.A. Fuller Maitland

Mr and Mrs Lewes were his [Henry Sidgwick's] guests for a week-end, and Lawrence Jones and I were singled out for the honour of being present, though only at a side-table, at the Sunday luncheon. We listened with all our ears for the "wise, witty, and tender" sayings that were to be expected; but all we caught was the remark addressed to Lewes, "But surely, my dear, you do not *really* like that heavy Bayrisch beer?" uttered with all the tragic air of a Siddons, though in a low and persuasive voice. After luncheon I was even luckier, for I had a few minutes' conversation with her, in the course of which I could feel that she was reading me like a book. I found myself giving her all sorts of confidences, and I have no kind of doubt that she really exercised some mesmeric power over susceptible people which in old times would have been taken for witchcraft.

A Door-Keeper of Music (London: Murray, 1929), pp. 54–5

IV
Frederick W.H. Myers

I remember how, at Cambridge, I walked with her once in the Fellows' Garden of Trinity, on an evening of rainy May; and she, stirred somewhat beyond her wont, and taking as her text the three words which have been used so often as the inspiring trumpet-calls of men, – the words *God, Immortality, Duty,* – pronounced, with terrible earnestness, how inconceivable was the first, how unbelievable the second, and yet how peremptory and absolute the third. Never, perhaps, have sterner accents affirmed the sovereignty of impersonal and unrecompensing Law. I listened, and night fell; her grave, majestic countenance turned toward me like a sibyl's in the gloom; it was as though she withdrew from my grasp, one by one, the two scrolls of promise, and left me the third scroll only, awful with inevitable fates. And when we stood at length and parted, amid that columnar circuit of the forest-trees, beneath the last twilight of starless skies, I seemed to be gazing, like Titus at Jerusalem, on vacant seats and empty halls, – on a sanctuary with no Presence to hallow it, and heaven left lonely of a God.[3]

'George Eliot', *Century*, 23 (1881), 57–64 (p. 62)

V
Oscar Browning

The authoress was more tender, more dignified, and more impressive than ever, showing especial delight in the details of my new home and life. I remember the interest she showed in an American type-writing machine, which had recently been given to me, expressing at the same time, with some archness, the fear lest the type-writer should not only reveal its utterances in print, but should multiply them after the manner of a printing-press, thus adding to the number of worthless books. Mr. Edmund Gurney and his wife were of the party, and Mr. Fuller Maitland delighted George Eliot with music, especially in his performance of Beethoven's Lichnowski Sonata. A rather large party had been asked to meet them, and as most of the guests had never met George Lewes and his wife before, there was some excitement to hear the words which might fall from their lips. The silence was broken by Lewes saying to her, "Why, my dear, you surely don't like that heavy black Bavarian beer, do you?" an unexpected beginning of memorable table-talk.[4]

Browning, pp. 125–6

NOTES

For Reginald Baliol Brett and Oscar Browning, see above in this section. Jane Ellen Harrison (1850–1928, *ODNB*), a student of Greek art and religion, later a noted scholar, went up to Newnham College, Cambridge, in 1874. John Alexander Fuller Maitland (1856–1936, *ODNB*) entered Trinity College in 1875 and was active in the university's musical society. He was later a music critic. Frederic William Henry Myers (1843–1901, *ODNB*), a poet and essayist, entered Trinity in 1860 and was a fellow from 1865 to 1874. By 1877 he had begun research into psychical phenomena.

1. A reference to Alexander Main's *Wise, Witty, and Tender Sayings in Prose and Verse, Selected from the Work of George Eliot* (1871, with many new edns).

2. 'George Eliot spoke like a true aesthete; one of the principles of the [Pre-Raphaelite] movement was that a person should harmonize with the décor' (Annabel Robinson, *The Life and Work of Jane Ellen Harrison* (Oxford: Oxford University Press, 2002), p. 43).

3. This is probably the most often quoted and reprinted recollection of GE. Ashton, p. 334, finds it a caricature, 'with calculated expressions, metaphorical and exaggerated' not typical of GE's speech. For Lord Acton, Myers 'insists on the aggressive attitude of negation. ... I do not know whether many of her friends would have the same experience as his' (letter to J.W. Cross, 24 April [1884], Yale). After this walk Myers wrote to GE trying to explain his 'deep-seated instincts' in favour of personal immortality and suggesting that she had been 'splendidly deceived' (*Fragments of Prose & Poetry*, ed. by Eveleen Myers (London: Longmans, Green, 1904), pp. 34–7 (pp. 35, 37)). Later GE assured him that she had 'no controversy with the faith that cries out and clings from the depths of a man's need' but wanted 'to help in satisfying the need of those who want a reason for living in the absence of what has been called consolatory belief' (*Letters*, IX, 201). Later still Sir Edward Marsh recalled a dinner party at the Jebbs' where Myers disclosed 'the social gossip of the next world, about which he had exclusive information: George Eliot, he understood, had lately been seeing a great deal of Wordsworth' (*A Number of People: A Book of Reminiscences* (London: Heinemann, 1939), p. 36). (This is one of several unearthly recollections of GE. See also E. Katharine Bates, *Psychical Science and Christianity: A Problem of the XXth Century* (London: Laurie, 1909), where GE says, 'after passing to the other side of life, "If you and others could only see the dark and malign influences surrounding you, under which you have to fight your life's battle, you would lose heart and courage entirely"' (p. 105); A.M.W. Stirling, *Life's Little Day: Some Tales and Other Reminiscences* (London: Butterworth, 1924), where she visits Katherine Macquoid on the fly just after dying (p. 226); Eleanor Sidgwick, 'A Contribution to the Study of the Psychology of Mrs. Piper's Trance Phenomena', *Proceedings of the Society for Psychical Research*, 28 (1915), i–xix, 1–652, where GE meets Adam Bede, Homer, Chaucer, Shelley, et al., hears Rubinstein play with a sort of disembodied philharmonic, and tries to deliver a message to Myers in a haunted house in Scotland (pp. 491–513); and Albert Durrant Watson, *The Twentieth Plane: A Psychic Revelation* (Philadelphia: Jacobs, 1919), where – on 7 July 1918 – she defends her craft against the modernists: 'I wrote the full picture, not as recent novelists write, not mere lines, dabs and question marks' (p. 71).)

4. Given Fuller Maitland's recollection, above, the only reasonable inference is that either GE or GHL said it to the other.

OXFORD, JUNE 1878

Benjamin Jowett

Mrs. Lewis agreed that Browning was infinitely greater in Paracelsus than in his later works

– very good & kind but not sympathetic
– not a master of thought but of external observation
– has not the right feeling of a man of genius towards the present intentions
of language which he mauls & abuses in various ways[1]

___

– had read Wolfe & was strongly for the natural growth of the Homeric
poems

___

spoke of the fallacy of Mr Muller's lectures – his antedating the infinite[2]

___

spoke of the importance of gradations of manner – of the necessity of a little
flattery to enable the world to go on.
E[vans].L[ewes].
most extraordinarily sensitive, pathetic, & sympathetic emotions. This is the
secret of her not writing until she was 40 years of age. So deeply affected by
what is said of her & therefore unable to read criticisms – which as far as possible are kept from her: She acknowledges the weakness & folly of this but it
is physical & may be passion; it cannot be overcome – says that she would
never have written anything, but for the kindness of her husband.

She has the clearest head I have ever known & is the gentlest kindest &
best of women – she throws an interesting light on any subject of which
she speaks. – She seems to me just right about philosophy, quite clear of
materialism – women's rights idealism &c

Notebook, *12 – Jan 1 1878*, Balliol College Library, Oxford University,
MS I/H33, fols 75ʳ, 78ʳ, reproduced with kind permission of the
Jowett Copyright Trustees; last paragraph publ. with misreadings in
Evelyn Abbott and Lewis Campbell, *The Life and Letters of Benjamin
Jowett, M.A.: Master of Balliol College, Oxford*, 2nd edn, 2 vols
(London: Murray, 1897), II, 144

NOTES

For Benjamin Jowett, see above in this section. Other recollections by him appear in
'The Countryside', below, in Part III, and in Parts V–VII.

1. *OED* editor Sir James A.H. Murray remarked that 'Browning constantly used words
without regard to their proper meaning. He has added greatly to the difficulties of the
Dictionary' (K.M. Elisabeth Murray, *Caught in the Web of Words: James A.H. Murray and
the 'Oxford English Dictionary'* (Oxford: Oxford University Press, 1979), p. 235).
2. 'What I hold is that with every finite perception there is a concomitant perception, or, if that word should seem too strong, a concomitant sentiment or
presentiment of the infinite; that from the very first act of touch, or hearing, or
sight, we are brought in contact, not only with a visible, but also at the same
time with an invisible universe' (Friedrich Max Müller, *Lectures on the Origin
and Growth of Religion as Illustrated by the Religions of India* (London: Longmans,
Green; Williams and Norgate, 1878), p. 45). GE admired Müller's *Lectures on the
Science of Language* (1861, 1864) (*Letters*, IV, 8; VII, 335) but disputed his 'circuitous

tracing of etymological derivations' and his emphasis upon the originary roles of abstraction and metaphor (Collins, 'Questions of Method', pp. 390, 397).

CAMBRIDGE, c.1885

Arthur Compton-Rickett

Then there was that amazing personality, Oscar Browning, not too well loved by his brother dons, but regarded by most of the undergraduates with affectionate amusement. Despite his well-known weakness for emperors and princes, whom he collected as some men collect butterflies, he was most entertaining. One had, of course, to allow for the "frills," which were harmless enough. "Yes, yes, reading George Eliot, are you? A great friend of mine ... between ourselves I am the original of Lydgate in *Middlemarch*. A most fascinating woman – one of the most emotional women I ever met. Lewes found her rather trying ... though he was devoted to her. Mistake to think she was over-intellectual. There you have her tragedy – emotional, passionate and dependent. Clever? Of course, damnably clever; but it wasn't her cleverness that appealed to you – it was her tremendous power of sympathy, and along with this power an extraordinary helplessness in managing her own life and a diffidence – quite unnecessary – about her own judgment. Her wonderful voice drew out all your confidences. ... I remember once talking to the Kaiser about English fiction – a most stimulating companion."

Here he would break off to greet another undergraduate guest. "Ah, Rupert, you're looking amazingly fit. What's the secret? You must sing that little song of yours this afternoon; I've forgotten what it was about, but I know it was charming." Then back to George Eliot. "Ah! I was speaking of George Eliot. Yes, I used to call her my mother-confessor. I was a young master at Eton in those days. No one gave me better advice than she did.[1] But perhaps you've read my life of her. ... Yes, it's pretty good. ... What do I think of Cross's *Life*?" A gentle, deprecating smile. "Ah, well, the poor man was handicapped."[2] Then he would break off to play with one finger a passage from "The Moonlight Sonata."

As I Look Back: Memories of Fifty Years (London: Jenkins, 1933),
pp. 55–6 (Compton-Rickett's ellipses)

NOTES

An alumnus of Christ's, Arthur Compton-Rickett (1869–1937) was an educator, biographer, editor, literary historian, and playwright.

1. He wrote 'on matters of education and literature', but lost her replies (Browning, p. 97).
2. Possibly a reference to Cross's honeymoon illness in Venice (see Caroline Jebb's recollection in Part VI), but probably a sly reiteration of a point from his *Life of George Eliot*, where Browning says that although Cross got the facts straight, he was no literary critic and therefore could not portray both 'the woman and the author' (p. 13).

The Countryside

HARROGATE

Charles D. Lockwood

In the summer of 1868 I was staying at Harrogate,[1] and while walking one day in the Cheltenham Gardens, my wife said, "I believe I have just met Marian Evans." "Why," I answered, "did you not ask her, and be sure about it? There can be no harm in speaking to her." My wife left me, but returned after a while, saying, "It is she, you must come to be introduced to her." I went willingly, and was duly presented to Mr. and Mrs. Lewes. I sat between them for more than an hour, although it seemed a very short time to me. I was too busy listening to talk much, as I was anxious to hear her speak of her writings, although at the time I had read very few of them. She did not hesitate to do so, and when I asked which of her works she thought the best she replied, *The Spanish Gypsy*.[2] In stature she appeared about the middle height. Her face was long, her features pronounced, and her complexion pale and rather sallow. Her hair was dark and abundant. When in repose her countenance had rather a melancholy expression, but when she spoke with a smile her expression was charming.

Of course I afterwards asked my wife how she brought about the recognition. When they met she begged to be excused in asking if her name was once Marian Evans. Mrs. Lewes, bowing coldly, said, "Yes." "I see that you do not know me." "I do not." "Do you not remember Jane M — [Mitchell] at Miss Franklin's school, at Coventry?" In a moment her countenance changed, all reserve was gone. She apologized, and explained that so many strangers introduced themselves to her wherever she went, that it was often positively painful to her. She was then out of health and wanted rest and quiet. Much conversation took place between them before I was summoned to the presence of the celebrated authoress.

I cannot give much account of my wife's recollections of their intercourse at school beyond the fact that Marian Evans many a time assisted her when her exercises, &c, were extra difficult, that she was a long way ahead of every girl in the school, and that her governesses almost stood in awe of her marvellous talents. She learned without an effort, her themes were faultless, and she played brilliantly on the piano. She was occasionally depressed in spirits and was sometimes hysterical.

My conversation with Mr. G.H. Lewes was chiefly of a physiological character, as I was suffering from paralysis, and he had not long ago lost a son, who died from a similar complaint. Mr. Lewes was certainly eccentric in appearance. His complexion was far from fair; his hair was dark, and hung over the collar of his coat He wore a soft, wide-brimmed hat, and a loose coat trimmed with fur, although the weather was decidedly warm. A gushing lady meeting him at a matinee at St James's Hall in London exclaimed, "Oh, you dear picturesque man." This truly described his outer man.

We met them once or twice after the first interview. The last time was on "The Stray," when my wife gave her a small book, *The Gates Ajar*, which she had not read. Of the four who then parted I am, alas! the only one left on this side the grave.

C[harles] D[ay] L[ockwood], 'A Glimpse of George Eliot and
George Henry Lewes', *City News Notes and Queries*, ed. by
J.H. Nodal, v (1883–84), 118; first publ. in *Manchester City News*,
11 August 1883, p. 2

NOTES

Charles Day Lockwood ran a stone quarry in Doncaster. He was the father of the lawyer and politician Sir Frank Lockwood.

1. It was the summer of 1870. GE and GHL arrived on 1 July and left on the 18th. On Saturday the 16th she 'recognized an old schoolfellow who brought her husband to be introduced' (GHL's diary, Yale). *The Spanish Gypsy* was published in 1868; Lockwood's remembering that GE mentioned it may have led him to date the encounter in that year.
2. GE is said to have asked Frederick J. Furnivall 'what poets had become famous after their death, and he was greatly amused when he recollected that her recent poems had been unsuccessful' (*Frederick J. Furnivall: A Volume of Personal Record* [ed. by John J. Munro] (London: Oxford University Press, 1911), p. 18).

ISLE OF WIGHT

Matilda Betham-Edwards

In the early winter of that terrible year 1870 Madame Bodichon took a furnished house near Ryde and invited me to join her. George Eliot and George Henry Lewes coming for Christmas, as the former wrote to her friend, "to weep together over the sorrows of France."[1]

In some respects the pleasant plan failed. Not for years had weather so severe visited the traditionally mild little island. Instead of finding roses and violets in Ventnor gardens, sunshine and balminess everywhere, skating, snow, and a bitter north wind were the order of the day. Our abode, too, a recently built commodious High Church rectory, in spite of tremendous fires in every room and passage, could not be made snug and warm as a second "Priory." Poor Lewes sometimes looked blue with cold, and although the pair delighted in the society of their friend, and in the absolute quiet and such glimpses of natural scenery as could be obtained, the arctic visitation and awful calamities of France kept down high spirits.

I well remember their arrival. As the hostess entered the drawing-room with her friends, George Eliot bent almost ecstatically over an exquisite flower on the centre table, what flower it was I have forgotten. The lovely bloom, the delicious fragrance brought out that radiance in her face I have before alluded to, a luminosity (no other word seems applicable) as transforming as it was evanescent. "Why, oh, why," she cried in her peculiar sighing voice, a voice that was often indeed a sigh, "not pray to such lovely things as these?" and she hung over the flower in an attitude of positive adoration. It was this intensity, alike of feeling, conviction, and aspiration, that characterised her as I suppose it characterises most sovereign natures.[2]

The pair had brought a little work with them, and the Vicar's handsome study was assigned to Lewes as a study. But on the second morning he joined George Eliot in hers, a smaller, less cheerless breakfast-room. The work, I think, consisted only of proof correcting, whilst for holiday reading they had brought surely the strangest book in the world, namely, Wolff's "Prolegomena." The volume possessed certainly one attraction. It did not at all bear on the painful events of the day. After dinner George Henry Lewes would tell us the most wonderful stories or his companion would sit down to the piano.[3]

"What shall it be, dear little boy?" she would ask as she turned over the contents of the music waggon; and the dear little boy – I loved to hear these terms of endearment among the great – generally demanded Beethoven. One Sonata she played to us was Op. 14, No. 2, containing the slow, plaintive Andante in C Major, ever one of my favourites.

She played correctly, conscientiously, but not with the *entrain* [drive] and charm of far inferior musicians. It is not geniuses, it is the merely talented people who can be universally brilliant, shine in everything, dazzle by parade of mere accomplishments. And listening to George Eliot's pianoforte playing, one could but feel here as ever the deep-seated melancholy that had not, as some suppose, her own life for its cause, but the life of all humanity. On her shoulders seemed to rest the material and spiritual burdens of the universe. ...

We always all breakfasted together, and on Christmas morning there was the usual round of good wishes. "A merry Christmas to you, Ann, and a marry New Year!" was Lewes's greeting to his hostess's staid, middle-aged parlourmaid. In spite of dyspepsia and other drawbacks to existence, he remained captivatingly genial and pranksome. When we sat down to our Christmas dinner, and Ann with extraordinary flourish deposited a huge covered dish on the table, he rubbed his hands, smiling at the mistress of the house.

"You will, I am sure, Barbara," he said, "excuse the liberty taken by an old friend. I have ventured to add a little delicacy to your bill of fare. Ann, remove the cover!"

We all started back with a scream. Something like a snake lay there, rebounding as it uncoiled. It was indeed the Vicar's scourge which Lewes had unhooked from its nail in the study, and which, doubtless, often served the purpose of self-flagellation.[4]

... I regret now that I did not journalise that historic week at Swanmore Parsonage.[5] One well-remembered conversation arouses reflection.

The topic was literary excellence and literary fame, or perhaps I should rather say, recognition, and the criterion of both.

"There is the money test," George Eliot said, and paused, as she often did before continuing a train of thought. Would she have uttered that sentence now? could the money test be accepted as a criterion when she spoke?[6] I played the part of listener, but have often dwelt on the words since.

The money test! But compare the sum paid for a consummate work of art, perhaps the most perfect romance (I here use the word romance as implying something quite distinct from the novel) ever written, to wit, "The Scarlet Letter," with the price say of a "Trilby"![7]

No, George Eliot's criterion fails here! Her next utterance will commend itself to all real lovers of literature.

"Then," she said in her slow, deliberate, conscientious way, and speaking from another point of view, that of literary excellence rather than of public acknowledgment – "then there is the test of sincerity."[8] ...

I happened at this time to have a whitlow on the thumb of my right hand, which for some days after lancing had to be carefully bandaged. On Christmas morning, when breakfast salutations were unusually cordial, George Eliot fancied that she had hurt my invalid thumb.

"I *always* do that sort of thing!" she cried, with a look of positive pain; and it was with no little difficulty that I could convince her to the contrary. The notion of having inflicted pain seemed intolerable. One can understand the sadness underlying a nature so sensitive.[9] ...

Our High Church rectory adjoined the church, and on Christmas morning Madame Bodichon carried off her friend to hear the fine musical service, Mass I feel inclined to call it. ...

George Eliot hearkened with subdued rapture, the clear, shrill voices of the choir, the majestic swell of the organ, evidently evoking a religious mood, none the less pure or deep because unallied with formulary or outward observance.[10]

The midnight service was proposed, but "No, dear, I would not on any account keep George up for us so late," said the great visitor, unlike her hostess in one respect. Whilst Madame Bodichon never had enough of the thing she loved, whether good company, downright enjoyment, or aesthetic impression, her feverish energy always craving expansion, George Eliot's nature needed repose. She did not, in French phrase, go out of her way in search of emotion.[11]

Reminiscences, pp. 146–8, 150–4

NOTES

For Matilda Betham-Edwards, see 'A Few Good Friends', above. She published other accounts of this holiday in 'A Week with George Eliot' and *Mid-Victorian Memories*. Another recollection by her appears in 'Out and About in London', above.

1. In the Franco-Prussian war: 'It was about this time that took place those terrible scenes outside Paris in which Henri Regnault, the brilliant young artist, – and how many other brave fellows – perished after indescribable sufferings and heroism' ('Week', p. 226).

2. 'In spite of her warm human sympathies and the keenness of her desire to enter into the feelings of others, her manner at first awed, perhaps even repelled. It was so much more difficult for her than for Mr. Lewes to quit her own world of thought and speculation, and enter into that of the common joys and sorrows and aspirations of humanity. Yet few delighted more in gathering her friends together. "From my good father I learned the pleasure of being hospitable," she once said to me with a glow of feeling. "He rejoiced ever to receive his friends, and to my eyes now the pleasure wears the shape of a duty"' ('Week', pp. 227–8).

3. Or 'George Eliot would read aloud something interesting, and then the subject would be discussed. She read to us one of Waterton's quaint essays with no little enjoyment' (p. 229, where Betham-Edwards also remarks that GE alluded to Wolf's *Prolegomena* 'just as any one else would allude to the last new novel'). One evening Betham-Edwards told them of a meeting of the International, Karl Marx presiding: 'Now this sort of experience was quite out of Mr. and Mrs. Lewes's way. Their world was the world of the intellectual elite, not of "the man in the street," the hewers of wood and drawers of water. So to the least little particular I could give, all paid the utmost attention' (*Mid-Victorian Memories*, p. 49).

4. GHL describes the incident in *Letters*, v, 126–7 (where he says, incidentally, that they usually breakfasted alone).

5. *Mid-Victorian Memories* includes a conversation on governments omitted in the *Reminiscences* account: '"A time will of course come, dear Barbara," said George Eliot, in her slowly enunciated, thoughtful way, "when royalties will disappear" (I believe the word "caste" was also used, but am not sure). "Kings and queens will be pensioned off, with cushions for their feet"' (p. 65).

6. In 1857 GE remarked to Sara Hennell that she believed 'almost all the best books in the world have been written with the hope of getting money for them' (*Letters*, ii, 377).

7. The sense here is 'little or nothing' for the first and 'a very great deal indeed' for the second. Hawthorne got no money from the English publishers of *The Scarlet Letter* (1850) (C.E. Frazer Clark, Jr, 'Hawthorne and the Pirates', *Proof*, 1 (1971), 90–121 (p. 90)), while du Maurier's large advance for *Trilby* (1894) was much publicized. Betham-Edwards's distinction between novel and romance comes from Hawthorne, who associated the first with 'a very minute fidelity, not merely to the possible, but to the probable and ordinary', and the second with 'truth under circumstances, to a great extent, of the writer's own choosing or creation' (Preface, *The House of the Seven Gables, a Romance* (Boston: Ticknor, Reed, and Fields, 1851), p. iii).

8. 'Then she went on to say that by sincerity the permanent value of a work must be judged, alike by outsiders and by writers themselves, if they would honestly ascertain how they stand with the public' ('Week', p. 230).

9. 'I firmly believe that had George Eliot convicted herself of inflicting a grave injury on any living soul, remorse would have worn her out, killed her by inches.

Her super-sensitiveness in little things was painful to witness' (*Mid-Victorian Memories*, p. 54).

10. Soon afterwards GE wrote of the 'fine intoning of the service by a clear strong tenor voice, sweet singing from boys' throats, and all sorts of Catholic ceremonial in a miniature way' (*Letters*, v, 131).

11. '*Chercher des émotions*' (*Mid-Victorian Memories*, p. 51).

SHOTTERMILL

Alice Maude Fenn

We have often endeavored to glean some information regarding George Eliot's life at Shotter Mill [from 2 May through 31 July 1871], but she and Mr. Lewes lived in such seclusion that there was very little to be told. They seldom crossed their threshold during the day, but wandered over the commons and hills after sundown. They were very anxious to lodge at the picturesque old farm, ten minutes' walk beyond Brookbank, on the same road, which was our home for two years, but all available room was then occupied. However, George Eliot would often visit the farmer's wife, and, sitting on a grassy bank just beside the kitchen door, would discuss the growth of fruit and the quality of butter in a manner so quiet and simple that the good country folks were astonished, expecting very different conversation from the great novelist. All the vegetables eaten at Brookbank were sent from the farm, and we have heard the old lady in speaking of it say: "It were wonderful, just wonderful, the sight o' green peas that I sent down to that gentleman and lady every week." They evidently knew what was good! Our old friend the farmer, who owns a neat horse and trap, was employed to drive them two or three times a week. They occasionally visited Tennyson, whose house is only three miles distant, though a rather tedious drive, since it is up-hill nearly all the way. George Eliot did not enjoy the ride much, for the farmer told us that, "withal her being such a mighty clever body, she were very nervous in a carriage – allays wanted to go on a smooth road, and seemed dreadful feared of being thrown out."

George Eliot was writing "Middlemarch" during her summer at Brookbank, and the term for which they had the cottage expired before they wished to return to London. The Squire was away at the time, so they procured permission to use his house during the remainder of their visit.[1] In speaking of them to us he said:

"I visited Mr. and Mrs. Lewes several times before they went back to town, and found the authoress a very agreeable woman, both in manner and appearance; but her mind was evidently completely absorbed in her work; she seemed to have no time for anything but writing from morning till night. Her hand could hardly convey her thoughts to paper fast enough.[2] It was an exceptionally hot summer, and yet through it all Mrs. Lewes would have artificial heat placed at her feet to keep up the circulation. Why, one broiling day I came home worn out, longing for a gray sky and a cool breeze, and on going into the garden I found her sitting there, her head just shaded by a deodora on the lawn, writing away as usual. I expostulated with her for letting the midday sun pour down on her like that.

"'Oh,' she replied, 'I like it! To-day is the first time I have felt warm this summer.'[3] So I said no more, and went my way."

One person volunteered the information that "as how I've heerd say as Mrs. Eliot couldn't eat Dunce's bread" (Mr. A. Dunce being the baker as well as the miller of Shotter Mill), and no wonder! We well recollect the pang with which we saw one of those solid "quarterns" on the dinner-table, on our arrival at the farm.

And thus nearly all we could learn about George Eliot was that she loved to bask in the sun, and liked green peas. She visited some of the cottagers, but only those living in secluded places, who knew nothing of her.

'The Borderlands of Surrey', *Century*, 24 (1882), 483–95 (pp. 487–9)

NOTES

Alice Maude Fenn, 'the American lady' cited by Mathilde Blind as having interviewed Shottermill residents (p. 188), wrote miscellaneous and literary essays. Her father was the Surrey-born artist Harry Fenn; his illustration of Brookbank appears on p. 487 of Alice's article.

1. Cherrimans, where they stayed throughout August: 'a brick and stone, two-storey house with a strikingly long, high, sloping red tile roof' (Robert M. Cooper, *The Literary Guide & Companion to Southern England*, 2nd edn (Athens: Ohio University Press, 1998), p. 220). Its owner was James Simmons IV, known as 'Squire Jimmy' (Greta A. Turner, *Shottermill: Its Farms, Families and Mills*, 2 vols (Headley Down: Smith, 2004–05), II: *1730 to the Early 20th Century*, p. 108).
2. 'During this long summer at Shottermill Marian wrote with less torment from diffidence and self-mistrust than she had felt in many years' (Haight, p. 433).
3. 'Imagine me seated near a window, opening under a verandah', GE wrote in August, 'with flower-beds and lawn and pretty hills in sight, my feet on a warm water-bottle, and my writing on my knees' (*Letters*, V, 177).

EARLSWOOD COMMON

Roland Stuart

During the summer [June] of 1874 on our way to Scotland, where my mother and I went for my holidays, I had the honour of meeting Mrs. Lewes for the first time, and during the visit she asked me to send her a photograph of my mother. With all deference I should like to say how I was struck by Mrs. Lewes's wonderful personality.[1] Her figure was slight, and neither tall nor short; her hair was worn as in the etching by Rajon, which I believe is the only authorised portrait of her. Her voice can only be compared to that of Sarah Bernhardt – in her melting moods: its tones were so low and soft, and at the same time so musical, that once heard it could never be forgotten; but above all else it was her eyes which impressed you – and she possessed that magnetic power of looking down into your soul and of drawing you out and making you speak of yourself – at the same time giving you the impression that she was deeply interested in your doings and all that concerned you. I was a mere schoolboy at the time, but I can remember my intense pride in our friendship, and the feeling that one could open one's heart to her and tell her *everything*, being sure of being understood.

> *Letters from George Eliot to Elma Stuart, 1872–1880*,
> ed. by Roland Stuart (London: Simpkin, Marshall, Hamilton,
> Kent, 1909), p. 22

NOTE

Roland Stuart was the son of Elma Stuart, née Fraser (1837?–1903), who introduced herself to GE in 1872 by sending her an oak book-slide she herself had carved. The gift brought about a long correspondence.

1. He charmed her as well, and with GHL she took him to see a pantomime on 14 January 1878 (*Letters*, vii, 3–4). 'I shall never forget my pride at going to Drury Lane under such an escort,' he recalled, 'nor do I forget the smiling appreciation of my companions at my wide-eyed delight and wonder at the transformation scenes then in vogue on the stage' (p. 101). That season's production was E.L. Blanchard's *White Cat*, in which good triumphs over evil after a wicked old fairy interrupts a birthday festival. A sample transformation scene: '*Rapid music. VIOLENTA waves crutch, all the viands vanish, wine casks disappear at side, baskets of flowers appear filled with withered leaves, and PSYCHO, the Goblin Dwarf, appears seated in the midst of the banquet table*' (*The White Cat: Grand Comic Christmas Pantomime* (London: Tuck, 1877), p. 23).

SIX MILE BOTTOM, OCTOBER 1876

W.H. Hall

Nothing was more refreshing than her affectionate enthusiasm for her father's memory and calling, which would breathe out whenever she was thrown amongst rural scenes and associations which evoked his memory. The commonest things in connection with 'the land' had the deepest interest for her. It has more than once been the writer's privilege to conduct 'George Eliot' over farmyards and farm buildings, where she showed as intense a sympathy and intimate acquaintance with animal as with human nature. Little pigs, in their very earliest life-career, never failed to attract her minute attention, and in every litter she would pick out one as an especial favourite. On one occasion the writer took 'George Eliot' to view Kisber, a Derby winner, in a racing stable at Newmarket, and to the utter astonishment and surprise of the trainer, she drew attention to the fine points of the horse.[1]

'Death of "George Eliot"', *Daily News*, 24 December 1880, p. 5, an anonymous obituary featuring an unsigned letter, of which this is the first paragraph, by 'one of her intimate friends', namely Hall, who took GE and GHL to see Kisber on 5 October 1876 (*Letters*, VI, 292)

NOTE

William Henry Hall, formerly Bullock (1837–1904, *ODNB*), was a barrister and worker for farm labourers' rights who wrote several books on travel and history. GE and GHL first visited the Halls at their estate in Six Mile Bottom (so named for its distance from Newmarket) in September 1872.

1. GHL was fond of relating this incident. According to Francis Espinasse, he said of GE that 'after a slight scrutiny, she pointed out some physical defect or blemish in the steed, the existence of which was at once admitted by the groom-in-waiting, and great was his astonishment, the proud and happy Lewes declared, that a lady should have detected what had escaped the ken of male connoisseurs in horse-flesh' (*Literary Recollections and Sketches* (London: Hodder and Stoughton, 1893), pp. 296–7). Caroline Holland heard that GE 'looked at the animal for some time, and then said: "Hasn't he rather a sloping shoulder?" The groom exclaimed: "That's just what he has, but nobody seems to notice it!"' (*The Notebooks of a Spinster Lady 1878–1903* (London: Cassell, 1919), p. 75).

WITLEY, JUNE 1877

Edmund Evans

George Eliot came to live at Witley: she was a very pleasant neighbour, very fond of a garden, a passionate lover of flowers.[1] She first saw some single dahlias which we had raised from seeds given us by Mrs Gilbert Baker of Kew Gardens: they were very beautiful in shape, with lovely tones of pleasing colour, ranging from light yellow through pleasing varieties of orange to bright and dark red. George Eliot decided to obtain seeds from the nurserymen, but, to her great disappointment, she could not obtain any seeds of Single Dahlias from them: they were not known or cared for. ... I shewed George Eliot the original drawings I had for *Under the Window*, which she admired intensely, she fully appreciated the quaintness and prettiness of them. After it was published I wrote and asked her if she would write for me a little story of such a character that Kate Greenaway could and would be delighted to illustrate, but, I am sorry to say, she refused to do it.[2]

> *The Reminiscences of Edmund Evans*, ed. by Ruari McLean
> (Oxford: Clarendon Press, 1967),
> p. 66

NOTES

The wood-engraver and colour printer Edmund Evans (1826–1905, *ODNB*) had lived in Witley since 1864, one of the 'first colonists' to arrive there (A.R. Hope Moncrieff, *Surrey* (London: Black, 1906), p. 185).

1. After purchasing the Heights in December 1876, she and GHL moved in at the beginning of June 1877, returning to the Priory in late October. By the time they arrived,
   Witley (with Hindhead close by) 'began to be so much affected by literary and scientific people that the nickhame *Mindhead* was suggested' (Moncrieff, p. 195).
2. GE admired Greenaway's work but explained to Evans that she wrote only from
   'inward prompting': 'I could never say "I will write this or that" until I had myself
   felt the need to do it' (*Letters*, VII, 215).

WITLEY, LATE 1870s

Arthur Paterson

It was at Witley in the 'seventies. George Eliot had called to see Mrs. Allingham,
to find that she was away. The children, however, were at home, and George
Eliot's quick eye noticing wistful glances directed at her pony carriage,
proposed a drive, with the nurse in the front seat.[1] This woman, a shrewd
country girl, and well aware who "Mrs. Lewes" was, hereafter became filled
with pride at her experience, but she was awed as well.

"Do you know, ma'am," she said to Mrs. Allingham, "when I looked at the lady as we got in I thought to myself she was
the ugliest I'd ever seen. But not when I got out! She talked to me the same
as if I were her friend, and as she talked never did I see such wonderful eyes,
nor so sweet a smile, and her voice like an organ – only it was low and gentle.
She was beautiful then. I'll not forget the light in her face as long as I live."

George Eliot's Family Life and Letters, pp. 32–3

NOTE

For Arthur Paterson, see 'Other Personal Meetings', above.

1. Elizabeth Haddon, later Graham Robertson's housekeeper (*Time Was: The
   Reminiscences of W. Graham Robertson* (London: Hamilton, 1931), p. 294). This is
   the Mrs (Harry) Cave quoted by Blanche Colton Williams: '"Plain she was, miss,
   but when she hopened 'er mouth you forgot heverything helse"' (*George Eliot:
   A Biography* (New York: Macmillan, 1936), p. 3).

THE HEIGHTS, WITLEY, OCTOBER 1877

Benjamin Jowett

E[vans].L[ewes]. talked charmingly with a grace & beauty that I shall always
remember.[1] Said, she was not a Comtist at all though she acknowledged
a debt to him as to every other great thinker – but she would not write &
contradict this at a time when every one was gibing at them. She gives the
impression of great philosophical power. She wanted to have an Ethical
System founded upon Altruism She argued that there was no such thing
as doing any <thing> action because it was right or reasonable <with> but
only because it accorded with one's better feelings towards others. <but>

She seemed however to admit that there might be such a form of thought given by teaching & acknowledged that practical moral philosophy should not be confined to one form.[2] One character was more suited to Utilitarianism etc. Her idea of action seemed to be 'doing good to others'

Said that she sometimes thought of writing about the history of moral philosophy. L did not wish her to write more – she suffered so much from writing[3] – she would not write anything dogmatic but might, perhaps, be induced to take as a subject "the Greek Moralists" Princess Louise said to her "Tell me who is Gwendolyn"[4] G.H.L. spoke of memory ...

E.L. spoke with enthusiasm of Turguenieff's novels: especially "Peres et Enfants"

Byron "a vulgar mind"[5] –

said that she was carried away by an admiration for some passages of poetry which she could not justify when she examined them & quoted as especially affecting her Wordsworth

"For action's life & noble origin

"Are breathed upon by hope's perpetual breath"[6]

Here the rhythm & the sentiment are fine but the image poor: What is hope's breath?

– could not understand how persons had found comfort & support in Browning

– spoke of her own self-criticism – she could find no medium – was always considering the different ways in which her words would be regarded –

– caught at the notion of a practical moral philosophy – said that so many duties were neglected – e.g. the duties of an author, the the [*sic*] minor morals were really the major

———

said that she would never condemn any body for acquiescing in the popular religion – (in reply to a remark of G.H.L. that the French Bishops were most to be blamed about the Lourdes Miracles because they knew that the girls to whom the visions were vouchsafed were in lunatic asylums)[7] because life was so complex – your own path was so unsatisfactory & uncertain in places that you could not condemn others.

She did not seem to object to remaining within an established religion with the view of elevating & purifying it.

Notebook, *10 – April 1877*, Balliol College Library,
Oxford University, MS I/H31, fols 80, 82ʳ, 83ʳ, reproduced
with kind permission of the Jowett Copyright Trustees;
first and last two paragraphs publ. with omissions and
alterations in Abbott and Campbell, *Life and Letters*, ii, 108

NOTES

For Benjamin Jowett, see 'Eton, Cambridge, and Oxford', above. Other recollections by him appear there, in Part iii, and in Parts v–vii.

1. Jowett 'stayed with us till 10', GHL recorded on 4 October, 'and left us knocked up' (*Letters*, IX, 196 *n.* 6).

2. Jowett later suggests, however, that GE also mentioned during this visit human motive as a common thread of interest across different 'forms' of philosophy (*Letters*, IX, 227).

3. '"Daniel Deronda" having recently been published with great success, I asked Lewes ... whether we might soon look forward to a new masterpiece from George Eliot's pen. "Never again," he replied. And on my asking why, he added, "Because she does not write unless I make her do it, and I dare not; it takes too much out of her"' (Lehmann, *An Artist's Reminiscences*, pp. 235–6).

4. Gordon S. Haight has traced the origin of *Deronda*'s Gwendolen Harleth to Byron's grandniece Miss Leigh, whom GE watched gambling at Bad Homburg in October 1872 ('George Eliot's Originals', in *From Jane Austen to Joseph Conrad: Essays Collected in Memory of James T. Hillhouse*, ed. by Robert C. Rathburn and Martin Steinmann, Jr (Minneapolis: University of Minnesota Press, 1958), pp. 177–93 (p. 193)). GE's description of the sight appears in *Letters*, V, 314. For GE's dinner with Princess Louise, see John Bright's recollection in 'Out and About in London', above.

5. Her very judgement in 1869 (see *Letters*, V, 57) in response to the controversy over Teresa Guiccioli's *Recollections of Lord Byron* (1869) and Harriet Beecher Stowe's reply to it, which revealed his mistreatment of his wife and his liaison with his half-sister ('The True Story of Lady Byron's Life', *Blackwood's*, 106 (1869), 24–33). K.M. Newton argues that Byron's effect upon GE's writing may have been more significant even than Wordsworth's, especially via the figure of the Byronic egotist (*Companion*, p. 44; *George Eliot, Romantic Humanist: A Study of the Philosophical Structure of Her Novels* (London: Macmillan, 1981), pp. 28–32).

6. 'Sonnets Dedicated to Liberty', XX, 'October, 1803': 'That every gift of noble origin | Is breathed upon by Hope's perpetual breath' (ll. 10–11). Two years later, after GHL's death, Jowett reminded GE of these lines in expressing his own hope that she might write again (*Letters*, IX, 284). See also *Life*, I, 176.

7. GHL's remark reflects some popular misperceptions. Only one young woman, Bernadette Soubirous (later St Bernadette of Lourdes), reported visions of the Virgin Mary, although her sister and a friend accompanied her on the first occasion (February 1858). None were in lunatic asylums, but Bernadette *took* lifelong asylum in a convent. (She was thought deranged upon reporting the apparitions, but four years later the Bishop of the diocese declared for their reality.) As late as 1872, however, a Parisian doctor announced that Bernadette had lost her mind and was shut up in a convent (J. Bricout, 'The Wonders of Lourdes', *Catholic World*, 89 (1909), 472–84, 615–23, 809–19 (p. 473)). More gently, Murray's *Handbook for Travellers in France*, 14th edn, 2 vols (London: Murray, 1877) noted that she 'subsequently became ill' and had to be 'taken care of' (I, 339).

SIX MILE BOTTOM, OCTOBER 1877

I

James Stuart

I was, of course, very greatly interested in meeting George Eliot, and so were the rest of us who were there. There were one or two Cambridge men besides myself, among whom was Sedley Taylor, and as he was one of the party it can be well believed that during our stay there many amusing stories of wit and humour were told. Of all these George Eliot was a very interested listener, and I think she thoroughly enjoyed good humour, but I noticed (as we all did in comparing notes afterwards) that, much as she seemed to appreciate a humorous story, she never during the whole four days told one herself. Her conversation was very interesting but perhaps rather stately, and she laid down the law somewhat. In appearance her features bore a strong resemblance to those of Savonarola, and I think she must have had a Jewish ancestry.[1]

Reminiscences (London: Cassell, 1912), p. 123

II
Sedley Taylor

I have come in from Six Mile by early train to do a day's work and go back again this evening to stay till Monday. Whom should I find there but 'George Eliot' and Mr. Lewis. I shall reserve my opinion of them until I have had a more adequate acquaintance with them, but as far as first impressions go, they are unprepossessing as regards her, & *repulsive* as regards him.

Our penny reading (proceeds to Indian Famine fund £2 odd[2]) went off very well. Mrs. Hall and the Schoolmistress (the latter has an *unusually* good voice & musical capacity) sang duetts and songs, Hall and I read & Lewis "recited".[3]

My 'Giles'[4] was a complete success & equally delighted the country folks and their entertainers. The authoress and Lewis were particularly struck by it and eager to know who was the writer, which I would not tell them. Of course I played the accompaniments, a March by way of overture and "God Save the Queen" as finale. ...

Our party at Six Mile consisted, besides those you know of already, of Mr. John Cross,[5] <Mr.> Dr. Bridges (an Oxford man and Inspector I think of Lunatic Asylums or something of that kind) & Professor Stuart.

I must say we were a lively lot and the number of stories, epigrammatic sayings and bons-mots that were recounted was something wonderful. Lewes is a capital rac<c>onteur (? *one c* or *two*) and acts his stories as well as telling them. He seems to have an unexhaustible supply and an extremely accurate memory. Yet somehow or other he is a man from whom I have an instinctive shrinking: this is not on account of any preconceived <antip> hostility but from something antipathetic in our respective natures. He is inordinately conceited, always talks about what *we* are doing, calls Mrs. Lewes "Madame" – in short clever and interesting and flowing over with knowledge as he is I find him quite insupportable. Mrs. Lewes (Stuart tells me they *are* married now[6]) has a rather drawly satiny voice and uses the most superfine phraseology, as "I should be inclined to express the distinction thus: the coexistent objective realism contrasted with a eurificatory,[7] if perhaps illusive organic totality &c &c". She says extremely well balanced clearly enunciated things, but they are not witty and always couched in the language of an ultra scientific book. She always waits till everybody else has said his say and then sums up in the style of the presiding Judge, though with an ultra feminine softness of voice and manner.

... I had a little opposition of sentiment with the Ls and their friend Dr. Bridges while we were out for a walk. They maintained that profane stories if witty and told *for the sake of wit*, were unobjectionable. I maintained that any story associating low gross or grotesque notions with the idea of God were to be eschewed.[8] Mrs. Lewis said it seemed childish to suppose that all our stories could do God any harm or move his anger, but I answered that what I had in view was the lowering effect *on one's own mind*. The "subject dropped" but Stuart who heard the discussion said to me the next evening that though at first inclined to side the other way he had on consideration come to think me in the right and was very glad I said what I did. I also tackled Lewes on the question whether it is right to buy a great bargain from a tradesman who does not know the value of what he is selling. Here I was only following in Stuart's wake who took the generous line in the strongest way. ... Hall and the Crosses adore Mrs. L. in the most unlimited degree, and regard L. as a sort of king consort. I am very glad to have had a good opportunity of seeing both of them, but shall not be at all chagrined if it turns out to be the last. One result of it will be that I shall have a stock of new stories for you. One you shall have at once. Some scientifically minded lady had been endeavouring to explain with much volubility to a highland shepherd the midnight sun in Norway. The man listened quite patiently to the end and then remarked that people "would make leddies believe *anything*".

Letters to Mrs George Taylor, his mother, 27, 29, and 31 October 1877,
CUL Add. MSS 6255/91–3, reproduced with kind permission of the
Syndics of Cambridge University Library

NOTES

Born in Scotland, James Stuart (1843–1913, *ODNB*) was a fellow of Trinity College, Cambridge's first professor of mechanism and applied mechanics, and an educational reformer. GE met him on her visit to Cambridge in June 1877 (*Letters*, VI, 380). Sedley Taylor (1834–1920, *ODNB*), a music scholar, resided in Trinity College without an official post. He was also a member of Girton College, which he had helped plan in the 1860s.

1. See Moncure Daniel Conway's recollection, *n.* 3, in 'Out and About in London', above.

2. GHL notes that Hall arranged the reading 'for the farm servants etc.' (*Letters*, VI, 413). The Indian Famine Fund, a response to the widespread famine of 1876–78, was a matter of national concern at the time.

3. 'I recited "Chestnut Horse", "Garrick and the Cock" and the Frenchman at the station' (*Letters*, vi, 413). In the anonymous poem 'Modern Logic; or, The Chestnut Horse', a schoolboy's prideful logic-chopping permits his uncle to reward him with a 'chestnut horse' that turns out to be a horse chestnut (*Routledge's Comic Reciter*, ed. by J.E. Carpenter (London: Routledge, n.d.), pp. 173–4). In 'Garrick and the Man of Rags', another anonymous poem, a shabby man astonishes David Garrick by embracing him and asserting that they once acted together; Garrick asks on what occasion; '"Lord!" quoth the fellow, "think not that I mock – | "When you play'd *Hamlet*, sir, – I played the cock"' (William Oxberry, *The Actor's Budget of Wit and Merriment* (London: Simpkin and Marshall, [1820]), p. 285). The third item may refer to 'The Frenchman and the Boxes', an anonymous recitation partly set in a Dover and London coach station in which a Frenchman explains in fractured English how Charles Mathews (who had a stage routine on this subject) conspired to confuse him by exploiting the different meanings of the word 'box' (*Routledge's Comic Reciter*, pp. 17–22; see also Anne Jackson Mathews, *Memoir of Charles Mathews, Comedian*, 4 vols (London: Bentley, 1838–39), iv, 172–3). Evidently 'the Schoolmistress' is GE.
4. Untraced.
5. Cross's sister Elizabeth, who died in 1869, was Hall's first wife.
6. They were not married.
7. A coinage hard to decipher; it may be 'eunficatous' or 'eunficatory'.
8. From this visit GHL records three such stories: 'The difference between Universalists and Unitarians. The one think God too good to d–n people, the other think themselves too good to be d—d. | Three men on a raft being swept down Niagara. "Can no one sing a hymn?" "No." "Nor a prayer?" "No." "We must do something religious – let's make a *collection*." | An old man left his property to his nephew but with a life rent of it to an old woman of 80, bedridden. When the will was read the Nephew rose and said, "I take ye all to witness that I'll bide the Lord's time"' (*Letters*, vi, 412–13).

THE HEIGHTS, WITLEY, AUGUST 1878

T.A. Trollope

I am afflicted by hardness of hearing, which shuts me out from many of the pleasures of society. And George Eliot had that excellency in woman, a low voice.[1] Yet, partly no doubt by dint of an exertion which her kindness prompted, but in great measure from the perfection of her dainty articulation, I was able to hear her more perfectly than I generally hear anybody. One evening Mr. and Mrs. Du Maurier joined us. The Lewes's had a great regard for Mr. Du Maurier, and spoke to us in a most feeling way of the danger which had then recently threatened the eyesight of that admirable artist.[2] We had music; and Mr. Du Maurier sang a drinking song, accompanying himself on the piano. George Eliot had specially asked for this song, saying, I remember, "A good drinking song is the only form of intemperance I admire!" ...

... Lewes told us in her presence, of the exclamation uttered suddenly by some one to whom she was pointed out at a place of public entertainment – I believe it was at a Monday Popular Concert in St. James's Hall. "That," said a bystander, "is George Eliot." The gentleman to whom she was thus indicated gave one swift, searching look and exclaimed *sotto voce*, "Dante's aunt!" Lewes thought this happy, and he recognised the kind of likeness that was meant to the great singer of the *Divine Comedy*. She herself playfully disclaimed any resemblance to Savonarola. But, although such resemblance was very distant – Savonarola's peculiarly unbalanced countenance being a strong caricature of hers – some likeness there was.

Her speaking voice was, I think, one of the most beautiful I ever heard, and she used it *conscientiously*, if I may say so. I mean that she availed herself of its modulations to give thrilling emphasis to what was profound in her utterances, and sweetness to what was gentle or playful. She bestowed great care too on her enunciation, disliking the slipshod mode of pronouncing which is so common. I have several times heard her declare with enthusiasm that ours is a beautiful language, a noble language even to the ear, when properly spoken; and imitate with disgust the short, *snappy*, inarticulate way in which many people utter it. ...

... Her nature was at once stimulated and steadied by Lewes's boundless faith in her powers, and boundless admiration for their manifestation. Nor was it a case of sitting like an idol to be praised and incensed. Her own mental attitude towards Lewes was one of warm admiration. She thought most highly of his scientific attainments, whether well foundedly or mistakenly I cannot pretend to gauge with accuracy. But she also admired and enjoyed the sparkling brightness of his talk, and the dramatic vivacity with which he entered into conversation and discussion, grave or gay. And on these points I may venture to record my opinion that she was quite right. I always used to think that the touch of Bohemianism about Lewes had a special charm for her. It must have offered so piquant a contrast with the middle-class surroundings of her early life. I observed that she listened with great complacency to his talk of theatrical things and people. ...

What I Remember, ii, 292, 296–7, 298–9

NOTES

Thomas Adolphus Trollope (1810–92, *ODNB*), the brother of novelist Anthony Trollope (see Part v), was a writer, historian, and authority on Italy. Other recollections by him appear in 'The Continent', below.

1. See George Smith's recollection, *n*. 1, in 'Publishers', above.
2. In 1857 du Maurier lost sight in his left eye, evidently from a detached retina; after that his remaining eye troubled him occasionally, but it began failing only in the late 1880s (Leonée Ormond, *ODNB*). On the evening recalled here, du Maurier told of consulting a heartless Belgian oculist when his first eye failed (for the story, see *Letters*, vii, 60–1).

WITLEY, SEPTEMBER 1878

William Allingham

1881

Sunday, October 16. ... In passing [the Heights] I call and ask Charles Lewes if he will walk? He has a cold. He lends me my own *Songs, Ballads*, etc., the copy I gave to George Eliot in May 1877.

As I sit on the tree trunk at Buss's Corner I take out the book and turn its leaves. Up this very path, on the edge of which I am sitting, George Eliot, G.H. Lewes and myself walked one fine autumnal afternoon, September 25, 1878. I had come over from Shere, where we had a cottage for the season; called, stayed for luncheon; and they both, when I started to walk home, came with me down their garden, into the little lane, across the railway line, to this corner where I sit, over Hambledon Hill, and up the hollow road; at the end of which we parted, talking at the last moment of Carlyle.[1] Sitting on the log and looking up the path eastwards, I recollect distinctly that just here we talked of death, and George Eliot said, 'I used to try to imagine myself dying – how I should feel when dying, but of course I could not.'

I said that when a child I firmly believed I should in some way escape dying.

George Eliot. – 'You cannot think of yourself as dead.'

G.H. Lewes was deeply silent at all this. I suspected him at the time of thinking the topic frivolous and uninteresting, but now I think he perhaps avoided it as painful. Charles Lewes has told Helen that his father could not bear to think of George Eliot's dying first. That September walk was my last sight of Lewes. Both are gone. And here I sit turning over my own book and looking at her pencil markings.

She wrote me a letter, which I have, on receiving this book.[2] I put it in my pocket and walk on.

> *William Allingham: A Diary*, ed. by H. Allingham and D. Radford
> (London: Macmillan, 1907), pp. 313–14

NOTES

Born in Ireland, the poet and critic William Allingham (1824–89, *ODNB*) was a frequent caller at the Priory from 1870. In June 1881 he and his wife Helen, née Paterson (1848–1926, *ODNB*), an artist and good friend of GE's, went to live at Sandhills, near Witley.

1. Allingham visited Thomas Carlyle frequently and preserved notes of their conversations.

2. GE acknowledged the gift in a letter of 22 May 1877 and then, on 22 August, wrote Allingham of her 'feeling of spiritual kinship' while reading the book: 'That tremendous tramp – "Life, Death; Life, Death," makes me care the more, as age makes it the more audible to me, for those younger ones who are keeping step behind me' (*Letters*, VI, 402). The quoted line is the refrain from 'The General Chorus'.

SIX MILE BOTTOM, OCTOBER 1878

I
Oscar Browning

In October, 1878, I was asked to meet her, Mr. Lewes, and the Russian novelist, Turguenieff, at the hospitable country house of Mr. Bullock Hall, at Six-Mile Bottom, near Newmarket. The only others present were the late Mr. Munro, the editor of Lucretius, and Mr. Sedley Taylor. They had driven in the afternoon to see the races at Newmarket, and George Eliot was full of admiration for the beautiful horses. Dogs were her favourite animals, but she had plenty of affection to spare for other species of our dumb companions. As we all sat together in the closing twilight, she made Turguenieff repeat to us, in his slow, broken English, what he had already related to George Eliot in private, the story of a play which he had seen in Paris,[1] the reception of which by a French audience threw, as he considered, a strong and unfavourable light on the French character. A woman in early life had married a scamp, who deserted her, leaving two children, a son and a daughter. She fled with them to the lake of Geneva, where she united herself with a wealthy merchant with whom she lived for twenty years, the children being brought up as his. At last her husband discovered her retreat, came unexpectedly to the home, and revealed to the son that he was his father. The merchant, afterwards entering, saluted his supposed daughter with the customary kiss. The son immediately struck him on the face and cried, "You have not the right to do that," upon which the audience applauded loudly, as if he had done an heroic action. Turguenieff alone stood up in his box and hissed. George Eliot hung eagerly upon his words as he told the tale. Lewes sat at some distance. Such was the French view of marriage, preferring the shadow to the substance, the legal tie to the bond of custom, affection, and gratitude. The party broke up deeply stirred, and Lewes said that the English would have behaved just as badly. It seemed to me strange that George Eliot should insist on hearing for a second time every detail of an imaginary story, which appeared to touch so nearly the deepest problems of her own life.

At dinner Lewes proposed Turguenieff's health, in an admirable speech, as the greatest living novelist. Turguenieff replied, repudiating the compliment and transferring it to George Eliot.

Browning, pp. 128–9

II
Sedley Taylor

This morning I had a long talk with G. Elliot about Erckmann-Chatrian and found she had just the same admiration for them that we have. She said she thought <them> their delineations of character the finest things since Walter

Scott and that the Blocus de Phalsbourg was absolutely perfect in every respect. Like myself she had been so struck by this work that she had tried to go round to see Phalsbourg [in July 1873] but had not been able to manage it.

We had one very odd[2]

Letter to Mrs George Taylor, his mother, 23 October 1878, CUL, Add. MSS 6255/100; reproduced with kind permission of the Syndics of Cambridge University Library

NOTES

For Oscar Browning, see 'Eton, Cambridge, and Oxford', above. Another recollection by him appears in 'Vignettes', below. He wrote of the evening recalled here again in *Memories of Sixty Years at Eton Cambridge and Elsewhere* (London: Lane, 1910), pp. 275–6. For Sedley Taylor, see above in this section.

1. Emile Augier's *Madame Caverlet* (1876) (Patrick Waddington, *Turgenev and England* (London: Macmillan, 1980), p. 232; for a detailed account of GE's visit, see pp. 229–38).
2. The remainder of the MS is missing.

The Continent

FLORENCE, 1860 OR 1861

Andrew Carnegie

A friend told me that a lady friend of hers, who was staying at the hotel in Florence where George Eliot was, made her acquaintance casually without knowing her name.[1] Something, she knew not what, attracted her to her, and after a few days she began sending flowers to the strange woman. Completely fascinated, she went almost daily for hours to sit with her. This continued for many days, the lady using the utmost freedom, and not without feeling that the attention was pleasing to the queer, plain, and unpretending Englishwoman. One day she discovered by chance who her companion really was. Never before, as she said, had she felt such mortification. She went timidly to George Eliot's room and took her hand in hers, but shrank back unable to speak, while the tears rolled down her cheeks. "What is wrong?" was asked, and then the explanation came. "I didn't know who you were. I never suspected it was *you!*" Then came George Eliot's turn to be embarrassed. "You did not know I was George Eliot, but you were drawn to plain me all for my own self, a woman? I am so happy!" She kissed the American lady tenderly, and the true friendship thus formed knew no end, but ripened to the close.

An American Four-in-Hand in Britain (New York: Scribners, 1883), pp. 142–3

NOTE

A firm admirer of GE's fiction, Andrew Carnegie (1835–1919, *ODNB*), the Scottish-born American industrialist and philanthropist, toured Coventry sites related to her in June 1881, six months after her death. This recollection comes from his description of that tour.

1. On their first trip to Florence (17 May–1 June 1860), GE and GHL stayed in the Hôtel de la Pension Suisse, away from 'the stream of English and Americans' (*Letters*, III, 294). On their second stay (4 May–7 June 1861), they began at the Hotel de l'Europe but soon moved to L'Albergo della Vittoria (III, 411, 413). Both Carnegie's friend and her friend have remained untraced.

FLORENCE, MAY 1860

Kate Field

It was at Villino Trollope that we first saw the wonderfully clever author, George Eliot.[1] She is a woman of forty, perhaps, of large frame and fair Saxon coloring.[2] In heaviness of jaw and height of cheek-bone she greatly resembles a German; nor are her features unlike those of Wordsworth, judging from his pictures. The expression of her face is gentle and amiable, while her manner is particularly timid and retiring. In conversation Mrs. Lewes is most entertaining, and her interest in young writers is a trait which immediately takes captive all persons of this class. We shall not forget with what kindness and earnestness she addressed a young girl who had just begun to handle a pen, how frankly she related her own literary experience, and how gently she *suggested* advice. True genius is always allied to humility, and in seeing Mrs. Lewes do the work of a good Samaritan so unobtrusively, we learned to respect the woman as much as we had ever admired the writer. "For years," said she to us, "I wrote reviews because I knew too little of humanity."[3]

'English Authors in Florence', *Atlantic Monthly*, 14 (1864),
660–71 (p. 665)

NOTES

For Kate Field, see 'Out and About in London', above.

1. GE and GHL were visiting T.A. Trollope, whose recollections of their subsequent visits appear below. Field had been in Italy since 1859, writing travel articles for the *Boston Courier*.
2. Compare Moncure Daniel Conway: 'She is by no means corpulent, nor are there any suggestions of steaks and sirloins about her, but she is of large skeleton. She is not meager, either, but has the look of being made out of fine clay' ('Correspondence', *Round Table* (New York), 3 (1866), 346–7 (p. 347)).
3. On a similarly personal note, Field later reported GE as saying '"I am miserable when writing, but I am still more miserable when not writing"' ('Recollections of Kate Field', *New-York Daily Tribune*, 24 December 1880, p. 5; see also 'A Chat

with Kate Field', *Gazette* (Baltimore), 3 May 1880, p. 4). Haight, certain that GE would not have shared something so personal, says that Field 'fancifully embroidered' this account (p. 326 *n*. 1). There are reasons for scepticism, not least Field's own remarks the day after she met GE: 'They say she converses finely, she is very retiring – and talked all the evening to Mr. Trollope' (*Kate Field: Selected Letters*, ed. by Carolyn J. Moss (Carbondale: Southern Illinois University Press, 1996), p. 19). Still, several others – among them Emily Davies, Elizabeth Malleson, Philip Gilbert Hamerton, and Justin McCarthy, all above – recall confidences about GE's work. Walter Bagehot too remembers discussing with her 'what she designated "the pain of composition"' (Emilie Isabel Barrington, *Life of Walter Bagehot* (London: Longmans, Green, 1918), p. 377).

CAMALDOLI AND LA VERNIA, ITALY, JUNE 1861

T.A. Trollope

The first stage of our rough ride was to the little hill town of Prato Vecchio on the infant Arno, and close under the lofty peaks of Falterona, in the flanks of which both the Arno and the Tiber rise. The path, as it descends to the town, winds round the ruins of an ancient castle, beneath the walls of which is still existent that Fontebranda fountain, which Adam the forger in the *Inferno* longed for a drop of, and which almost all Dantescan scholars and critics mistake for a larger and nowadays better known fountain of the same name at Siena. On pointing it out to George Eliot, I found, of course, that the name and the whole of Adam the forger's history was familiar to her; but she had little expected to find his local habitation among these wild hills; and she was unaware of the current mistake between the Siena Fontebranda, and the little rippling streamlet before us.

The little *osteria*, at which we were to get some breakfast, was a somewhat lurid dwelling in an uninviting back lane. But the ready and smiling good-humour with which the hostess prepared her coffee and bread, and eggs and bacon, availed much to make up for deficiencies, especially for guests far more interested in observing every minute specialty of the place, the persons, and the things, than they were extreme to mark what was amiss. I remember George Eliot was especially struck by the absence of either milk or butter, and by the fact that the inhabitants of these hills, and indeed the Tuscans of the remoter parts of the country generally, never use them at all – or did not in those days. ...

Had our party consisted of men only, we should have been received in the convent, where there was a very handsome suite of rooms reserved for the purpose. But females could not enter the precincts of the cloister. ...

And this requirement brought us to the consideration of our accommodation for the night. The humble little *forestieria* at Camaldoli was not built for any such purpose. It never, of course, entered into the heads of the builders that need could ever arise for receiving any save male guests. ... I had warned my friends that they would have to occupy different quarters; and it now became necessary to introduce George Eliot to the place she was to pass the night in.

At the distance of about twenty minutes' walk above the convent, across a lovely but very steep extent of beautifully green turf, encircled by the surrounding forest, there is a cow-house, with an annexed lodging for the cowherd and his wife. And over the cow stable is – or was, for the monks have been driven away and all is altered now![1] – a bedchamber with three or four beds in it ... I have assisted in conveying parties of ladies up that steep grassy slope by the light of a full moon, when all the beds had to be somewhat more than fully occupied. But fortunately George Eliot had the whole chamber to herself – perhaps, however, not quite fortunately, for it was a very novel and not altogether reassuring experience for her to be left absolutely alone for the night, to the protection of an almost entirely unintelligible cowherd and his wife! G.H. Lewes did not seem to be quite easy about it; but George Eliot did not appear to be troubled by the slightest alarm or misgiving. She seemed, indeed, to enjoy all the novelty and strangeness of the situation; and when she bade us good-night from the one little window of her chamber over the cows, as we turned to walk down the slope to our grand bedrooms at the convent, she said she should be sure to be ready when we came for her in the morning, as the cows would call her, if the cowherds failed to do so.

The following morning we were to ride up the mountain to the Sagro Eremo. Convent hours are early, and soon after the dawn we had convoyed our female companion down the hill to the little *forestieria* for breakfast, where the *padre forestieraio* gave us the best coffee we had had for many a day. George Eliot declared that she had had an exceptionally good night, and was delighted with the talk of the magnificently black-bearded father, who superintended our meal, while a lay brother waited on us. ...

At the Sagro Eremo – the sacred hermitage – is seen the operation of the Camaldolese rule in its original strictness and perfection. ... Each brother ... inhabits his own separately built cell, consisting of sleeping chamber, study, wood-room, and garden, all of microscopical dimensions. ... There is a library tolerably well furnished with historical as well as theological works. But it is evidently never used. Nor is there any sign that the little gardens are in any degree cultivated by the occupants of them. I remarked to George Eliot on the strangeness of this abstinence from both the two permitted occupations, which might seem to afford some alleviation of the awful solitude and monotony of the eremitical life. But she remarked that the facts as we saw them were just such as she should have expected to find! ...

Then followed another night in the cow-house for George Eliot and for us in the convent, and the next morning we started ... for La Vernia ... which most keenly interested and impressed her. She was in fact under the spell of the great and still potent personality of Saint Francis, which informs with his memory every detail of the buildings and rocks around you. Each legend was full of interest for her. The alembic of her mind seemed to have the secret of distilling from traditions, which in their grossness the ordinary visitor turns from with a smile of contempt, the spiritual value they once possessed for ages of faith, or at least the poetry with which the simple belief of those ages has invested them.[2] Nobody could be more alive to every aspect of natural beauty than she showed herself during the whole of this memorable excursion. But at La Vernia the human interest over-rode the simply aesthetic one.

What I Remember, ii, 271–2, 275, 276–8, 279–80, 281, 282–3

NOTES

For Thomas Adolphus Trollope, see 'The Countryside', above. Another recollection by him appears below.

1. In consequence of the dissolution of the monasteries in 1866; for GE's view of this measure, see Emily Davies's second recollection in 'Some Younger Women', above.

2. Compare Trollope's metaphor earlier in this recollection: 'Never, I think, have I met with so impressionable and so delicately sensitive a mind as that of George Eliot! I use "sensitive" in the sense in which a photographer uses the word in speaking of his plates. Everything that passed within the ken of that wonderful organism, whether a thing or combination of things seen, or an incident, or a trait revealing or suggesting character, was instantly reproduced, fixed, registered by it, the operating light being the wonderful native force of her intellect. And the photographs so produced were by no means evanescent. If ever the admirably epigrammatic phrase, "wax to receive and marble to retain," was applicable to any human mind, it was so to that of George Eliot. And not only were the enormous accumulations of stored-up impressions safe beyond reach of oblivion or confusion, but they were all and always miraculously ready for co-ordination with those newly coming in at each passing moment!' (pp. 268–9).

SWITZERLAND, JUNE 1864(?)

Emma Nason

Once, when in Switzerland, [Charlotte Eastman] had the pleasure of meeting George Eliot. The famous authoress sat in the garden of her hotel, reading aloud, in French, the story of *Romola* to a little girl at her side. As Mrs. Eastman approached, she paused a moment to listen to the musical voice of the reader. "Do you understand me?" asked Mrs. Lewes, graciously. "Pardon me," replied Mrs. Eastman; "I was only listening to your sweet voice." "Do you like it?" said Mrs. Lewes, as her face lighted with pleasure. Then, taking the hand of the American lady in her own, she said: "I thank you. I would much rather you would compliment my voice than my *Romola*."

Old Hallowell on the Kennebec (Augusta, Maine: [n.p.], 1909), p. 135

NOTE

Emma (Mrs Charles H.) Nason, née Huntington (1845–1921), was an American poet, local historian, and writer of children's literature. An earlier version of this recollection ('Enjoying the Enjoyable', *Literary World* (Boston), 21 May 1881, p. 181) has Montreux as the location, just after the publication of *Romola* (1862–63). I have found no record of GE in Montreux at this time, but the year after *Romola* appeared she was in Switzerland – Bellinzona, Airolo, Lucerne, and Basle – on her way back from Italy.

PAU, FRANCE, JANUARY 1867

Nina Lehmann

I

There is such a gentle graciousness about Mrs. Lewes, one must love her, and she seems to adore him. He is worn out and thin and languid, has lost his old spirits, but they'll come back with change and rest. I made myself pretty in my grey silk and lace *kragen* [collar], and they admired my dress so much. When I got up to play, Mrs. Lewes said, "I am inclined to quarrel, do you know, with Mr. Rudolf Lehmann about a portrait of you I saw at his house. It does not do you justice." I told her she was the first person who said so, as it was usually thought, and *I thought*, it flattered. (Do you remember Aunt J —'s [Janet's], "It's much too pretty – why it's quite a handsome woman," before me, the unhappy original?) I played to them, and wound up with "Adelaida" by particular request, Mr. Lewes having told her that I played such a beautiful arrangement! Arrangement? Why I never knew it was arranged, and if it is, it's certainly my own.[1] They are coming to-day to breakfast at twelve. ... I felt I must make an effort, because they told me it was solely on *my account* they came to Pau. "We look upon you as a sort of heroine, dear Mrs. Lehmann, parted so long from your husband and your home, and take a deep interest in you," for which I thanked her, and felt inexpressibly soothed in the idea that somebody at last had found out I was a heroine, which I had been suspecting all along myself. ... The Lewes's were enchanted with Chang. They say he is a real Maltese; they like Deutsch. He is the *brightest* German (always excepting you, I trust and believe) they ever saw. That is a nice little word for his hop-sparrowishness, I daresay, but they like him. He likes De Mussy too, and she said she was so anxious to see him (I can't tell why) that she did a rude thing at the theatre and turned round and stared at him when he was with us once. I am sure he did not remark it, and if he had, would have been flattered.

II

The Lewes's are gone after two delightful cosy days. I have got to know her as I never should have done in years in London, and I think she loves me – we are sworn friends. What a sweet, mild, womanly presence hers is – so soothing, too, and *elevating* above all. It is impossible to be with that noble creature without feeling *better*. I have never known any one like her – and then her modesty, her humility. A modesty, too, that never makes her or you awkward, as many modesties do. I am full of her. She makes a great impression on me, and I long to see more of her and be with her. She said, without my asking it, she would write me from Barcelona to tell me how it went with "George," and if they were going on as they now intend. They don't go to Madrid, but Seville, Cordova, Granada, &c. When she went away last night I said something of hoping she would like me, and we should be friends. She said, "I do; I love you better every hour." She said it so sweetly with her soft penetrating voice, it did not sound as such a compliment would from any other lips. How they like you, Doochen. This was such a tie between us – and she thinks you so handsome. I can't remember the word she used for your head. I had to give her the "head-medallion" photo of yours, so send me another; she didn't like the one she had, and admired this so much. ... She made me tell her the whole story of our courtship and marriage, which seemed to interest her intensely. In fact, she was like a dear, loving elder sister to me the whole time. I gave them a nice little dinner; first, a light lunch at twelve – then he went and rejoiced poor Mr. Savage's heart by a visit, whilst I walked in the garden and told her my love-story. I wanted to take them a drive, the day was so perfect – not a voiture to be had of any kind, a *chasse* [hunt] going on. Provoking, wasn't it? We had a long physiological talk afterwards, and of course I brought in the guillotine question again![2] Nina said her little poem of Goethe to them to-day, sweetly. My dear, she, Mrs. L., was so sweet, so attentive to Matilda! Often brought her gently into our conversation by talking of Germany, and appealing in her charming, gentle way to the delighted Tilla. ...

Here it is sirocco again to-day – like going into a hot-house when you go out. The valley was full of a seething mist over which the mountains towered clear and serene. George Eliot in looking at this mist said, "I love to see that mist – it is beautiful – it looks as if creation were going on underneath." ... Mrs. Lewes asked me if there was anything characteristic here to take home. I said, "Hardly!" then went to my drawer and pulled out a beautiful large beaded rosary of the box-root, which perfectly *enchanted* her. She said it was strange; she had longed for a rosary, and had never seen anything more charming than those beads made of a root. I also gave her a knitted wool shawl, in which she much rejoiced.

Letters to Frederick Lehmann, her husband, 22 and 23 January 1867, in *Familiar Letters: N.L. to F.L. 1864–1867*, ed. by R.C. L[ehmann] ([Edinburgh]: Ballantyne, Hanson, 1892), pp. 69–72, 73–5, 77–8

NOTES

Jane Gibson Lehmann, née Chambers (1830–1903), called Nina, of the Edinburgh publishing family, had known GHL as a girl and through him first met GE in 1864.

In the winter of 1866–67 she was staying in Pau for her health. A recollection by her husband appears in 'Other Personal Meetings', above.

1. Beethoven's 'Adelaide' (op. 46, 1797), 'that ne plus ultra', in GE's words, 'of passionate song' (*Letters*, III, 365), was arranged as a piano transcription, by Liszt (LW A58, 1840). What Nina Lehmann actually played remains untraced.
2. Presumably whether sentient awareness continues after the spinal cord is severed. GHL had cited cases of persistent heartbeat after decapitation in *The Physiology of Common Life*, 2 vols (Edinburgh and London: Blackwood, 1859–60), I, 336.

RICORBOLI, ITALY, MARCH 1869

T.A. Trollope

... [I have] the abiding conviction that she was intellectually by far the most extraordinarily gifted person it has ever been my good fortune to meet. I do not insist much on the uniform and constant tender consideration for others, which was her habitual frame of mind, for I have known others of whom the same might have been said. It is true that it is easy for those in the enjoyment of that vigorous health, which renders mere living a pleasure, to be kindly; and that George Eliot was never betrayed by suffering, however protracted and severe, into the smallest manifestation of impatience or unkindly feeling. But neither is this trained excellence of charity matchless among women. What was truly, in my experience, matchless, was simply the power of her intelligence; the precision, the promptitude, the rapidity (though her manner was by no means rapid), the largeness of the field of knowledge, the compressed outcome of which she was at any moment ready to bring to bear on the topic in hand; the sureness and lucidity of her induction; the clearness of vision, to which muddle was as impossible and abhorrent as a vacuum is supposed to be to nature; and all this lighted up and gilded by an infinite sense of, and capacity for, humour, – this was what rendered her to me a marvel, and an object of inexhaustible study and admiration. ...

Another very prominent and notable characteristic ... was the large and almost universal tolerance with which George Eliot regarded her fellow creatures.[1] Often and often has her tone of mind reminded me of the French saying, "*Tout connaitre ce serait tout pardonner!* [To know everything would be to forgive everything!]" I think that of all the human beings I have ever known or met George Eliot would have made the most admirable, the most perfect father confessor. I can conceive nothing more healing, more salutary to a stricken and darkened soul, than unrestricted confession to such a mind and such an intelligence as hers. Surely a Church with a whole priesthood of such confessors would produce a model world.

And with all this I am well persuaded that her mind was at that time in a condition of growth. Her outlook on the world could not have been said at that time to have been a happy one. And my subsequent acquaintance with her in after years led me to feel sure that this had become much modified. She once said to me at Florence that she wished she never had been born! I was deeply pained and shocked; but I am convinced that the utterance was the result, not of irritation and impatience caused by pain, but of the influence exercised on the tone of thought and power of thinking by bodily malady.[2] ...

[Lewes was] an incomparable companion, whether a gay or a grave mood were uppermost. He was the best *raconteur* I ever knew, full of anecdote, and with a delicious perception of humour. ... But George Eliot's sense of humour was different in quality rather than in degree from that which Lewes so abundantly possessed. And it was a curious and interesting study to observe the manifestation of the quality in both of them. It was not that the humour, which he felt and expressed, was less delicate in quality or less informed by deep human insight and the true *nihil-humanum-a-me-alienum-puto* [I consider nothing belonging-to-man strange to me] spirit than hers, but it was less wide and far-reaching in its purview of human feelings and passions and interests; more often individual in its applicability, and less drawn from the depths of human nature as exhibited by types and classes. And often they would cap each other with a mutual relationship similar to that between a rule of syntax and its example, sometimes the one coming first and sometimes the other.

What I Remember, II, 285–6, 287–8, 289–90

NOTES

For Thomas Adolphus Trollope, see 'The Countryside', above. Another recollection by him appears in the present section, above.

1. 'I am not in any sense one of the "good haters"', GE wrote in 1873; 'on the contrary, my weaknesses all verge towards an excessive tolerance and a tendency to melt off the outlines of things' (*Letters*, V, 367).
2. During this visit she suffered daily from sore throat and headache (V, 20–1).

ROME, APRIL 1869

J.W. Cross

It was during this journey that I, for the first time, saw my future wife at Rome. ... I have a very vivid recollection of George Eliot sitting on a sofa with my mother by her side, entirely engrossed with her. Mr Lewes entertained my sister and me on the other side of the room. But I was very anxious to hear also the conversation on the sofa, as I was better acquainted with George Eliot's books than with any other literature. And through the dimness of these fifteen years, and all that has happened in them, I still seem to hear, as I first heard them, the low, earnest, deep musical tones of her voice: I still seem to see the fine brows, with the abundant auburn-brown hair framing them, the long head broadening at the back, the grey-blue eyes, constantly changing in expression, but always with a very loving, almost deprecating, look at my mother, the finely-formed, thin, transparent hands, and a whole *Wesen* [being], that seemed in complete harmony with everything one expected to find in the author of 'Romola.'

Life, III, 81–2

NOTE

For John Walter Cross, see Part I. Other recollections by him appear in Parts V and VI.

PARIS, JUNE 1873

I

Candace Wheeler

After the Lowells and Mr. Holmes were gone a scholarly-looking Englishman and his wife came one day to the little hotel.[1] A "horse-faced" Englishwoman, my daughter characterized her. They were Mr. and Mrs. Lewes (George Eliot). Mr. Lowell had told us of their coming long before, saying that he had introduced us to her and he wished us to verify the introduction. When my daughter saw them at the luncheon-table and recognized Mrs. Lewes's face and style from Mrs. Lowell's description, she made ready to speak to her immediately after luncheon, but was somewhat delayed by an American friend who came late to the table, bringing with her a book she had borrowed from us, and explaining volubly how much she liked it. It was *Daniel Deronda*,[2] and as even enthusiastic criticism might be disastrous in the presence of the author, my daughter made haste to get over the introduction of herself; it ended by Mrs. Lewes proposing to visit her at once in her own room in order to prolong the conversation.

It proved to be, in fact, a lengthy interrogation, and in recounting it to us afterward my daughter said she felt like a turned-out glove. It covered minutely the days of a school year in a French pension, then a housekeeping year of her married life in Paris, and in fact every incident of her Paris experiences – little minutiæ of the domestic menage, of the servants and their privileges and ways, stopping hardly short of an inventory of the copper saucepans.

"I did not get much from her," she said, "in the way of intellectual sensation, but she got lots from me in the way of domestic experiences. I wonder what she wanted to do with them?" And at this melancholy conclusion we all laughed.

"It is just one of the ways in which authors get their facts," said my husband.

We found the Leweses very pleasant, but self-absorbed and unsympathetic, as we count the outgiving of human kindness. Still, it was a worthwhile experience to have seen and talked with Mrs. Lewes, and it helped to make an interesting winter.

Yesterdays In a Busy Life (New York and London: Harper, 1918),
pp. 206–8

II
Candace Wheeler Stimson

[We] found her very sociable. She is a gentle-mannered English woman, elderly and very *plain* – but of course we are very happy to have seen her. She
talked servants, prices of beef and housekeeping in as quiet and natural a
way as if she had never heard of Adam Bede or Romola – It was very funny,
the first night she was here. Miss St. John (a New York girl in the house) and
I discussed Middlemarch in the most unembarrassed manner right under
her nose without a suspicion of who she was. But I remembered afterward
seeing her turn to her husband with a quiet smile during the performance.

Letter to Henry Stimson, her husband's brother, 29 June 1873,
in Philip M. Stimson, 'A Poetic Souvenir: The Crossing of Pathways in
Memorable Lives', *Yale University Library Gazette*,
43 (1968), 85–90 (p. 89)

NOTES
Candace (Mrs Thomas Mason) Wheeler, née Thurber (1827–1923), was an American
textile and interior designer. Her daughter Candace (Mrs Lewis Atterbury) Stimson
(1845–76) had been in France for her health since 1871.

1. The Hôtel de Lorraine (*Letters*, v, 423).
2. It was *Middlemarch*, as her daughter's letter says; *Deronda* appeared in 1876.

Vignettes

Margaret Oliphant

I had a peep of George Elliot in George Street. The face has haunted me
<every> ever since – how profoundly sad it is – I do not remember to have
been equally impressed with any portrait. It may look foolish to pity a
woman who most likely scorns pity, but somehow one's heart weeps over
those eyes – I cannot get them out of my mind –

Letter to Julia Blackwood, [1861], NLS, Blackwood Collection, MS
4163, fol. 118, reproduced with kind permission of the Trustees of the
National Library of Scotland

NOTE
The novelist and biographer Margaret Oliphant (1828–1897, *ODNB*) almost met
GE in June 1876, but never again had the chance (see Porter, *John Blackwood*,
pp. 292–3; *Letters*, vi, 263). Here she reflects upon Samuel Laurence's 1860
chalk drawing, which hung in the back parlour of Blackwood's Edinburgh office

(Haight, p. 339). (It is now in the British Museum, with a preliminary version in Girton College, Cambridge; illustrations in Haight, frontispiece, and Ashton, no. 16, respectively.) Hearing a description of the portrait before buying it, John Blackwood remarked that 'the pensive sad look struck me the very first time I ever saw her' (*Letters*, III, 343).

Frederic Leighton

Miss Evans (or Mrs. Lewes) has a very striking countenance. Her face is large, her eyes deep set, her nose aquiline, her mouth large, the under jaw projecting, rather like Charles Quint; her voice and manner are grave, simple, and gentle. There is a curious mixture in her look; she either is or seems very short-sighted. Lewes is clever. Both were extremely polite to me; her I shall like much.

Letter to Dr Frederic Septimus Leighton, his father, 22 May 1862, in Emilie Isabel Barrington, *The Life, Letters and Work of Frederic Leighton*, 2 vols (London: Allen, 1906), II, 95

NOTE
At the time of this letter, the painter Frederic Leighton (1830–96, *ODNB*) had just met GE upon being commissioned to illustrate *Romola* for *Cornhill Magazine*. Years later, at a Priory reception, Matilda Betham-Edwards observed that Leighton 'seemed oblivious of everything around him, his eyes fixed' on his hostess: 'After a mechanically uttered phrase or two he burst out – a lover's voice could hardly have been more impassioned: "How beautiful she is!"' (*Mid-Victorian Memories*, p. 44).

Mary Gillies

... Mr. and Mrs. Lewes ... are people not easily come-at-able – & there is something about her that with all her tenderness & sweetness to those she knows & loves puts her up out of the reach of any familiar intercourse to the world besides – She has a quiet sort of queenly dignity about her ...

Letter to Richard Hengist Horne, 18 May 1865, Mitchell Library, State Library of New South Wales, R.H. Horne Papers, MS HM 2410, vol. 4, fol. 304

NOTE
Mary Gillies (d. 1870), who met GE through her friend Gertrude Lewes, wrote juvenile fiction and history. To GE she was 'a most gentle-hearted, refined woman' (*Letters*, V, 112).

Oscar Browning

I called upon them one morning [in autumn 1865] and was asked to stay to luncheon, and I shall not readily forget my emotions at seeing George Eliot at the head of the table with her majestic arm carving a leg of mutton.

Memories of Sixty Years, p. 111

NOTE
For Oscar Browning, see 'Eton, Cambridge, and Oxford', above. Another recollection by him appears in 'The Countryside', above.

Charles Dickens

[Dickens gave] an excellent description of Mr. and Mrs. Lewes. The latter he finds most interesting 'with her shy manner of saying brilliant things'.

James T. Fields, *Biographical Notes and Personal Sketches*, ed. by Annie Fields (London: Sampson Low, 1881), p. 153

NOTE
The novelist Charles Dickens (1812–70, *ODNB*), who knew GHL already, met GE in November 1859, after the anonymous publication of *Adam Bede*. They saw each other occasionally afterwards, including several times at the Priory during the last months of Dickens's life. His recorded comments on GE are brief and fragmentary. By report he said that GE and GHL '"really are the ugliest couple in London"', and also spoke of GE's '"lofty intellect"' (*Dickens: Interviews and Recollections*, ed. by Philip Collins, 2 vols (London: Macmillan, 1981), II, 284, 347). James T. Fields (1817–81) was a partner in a prominent Boston publishing house and editor of the *Atlantic Monthly*. A recollection by Annie Fields, his wife, appears in 'Sunday Gatherings at the Priory', above (see *n.* 1).

Edmund Yates

A slight presence, of middle height, as the height of women goes; a face somewhat long, whose every feature tells of intellectual power, lightened by the perpetual play of changing expression; a voice of most sympathetic compass and richness; a manner full of a grave sweetness, uniformly gentle and intensely womanly, which proclaims the depth of the interest taken in ordinary and obscure things and people; conversation which lends itself as readily to topics trivial as to topics profound, and which is full of a humour – as, indeed, are her writings – that is redeemed from sarcasm by its ever-present sympathy: such is a rough and imperfect sketch of George Eliot ...

'George Eliot', *World*, 2 February 1876, pp. 10–12 (p. 11)

NOTE
Born in Edinburgh, Edmund Hodgson Yates (1831–94, *ODNB*), a journalist and novelist, met GE in March 1869, but had known GHL for years. In 1874 Yates founded *The World: A Journal for Men and Women*, and is identified as the author of this unsigned piece by GHL (*The Letters of George Henry Lewes*, ed. by William Baker, English Literary Studies Monograph Series, 64–5, 79, 3 vols (Victoria: University of Victoria, 1995, 1999), II, 219).

Edmond Schérer

Un peu forts, un peu lourds dans leur cadre d'abondante chevelure, les traits de George Eliot graduisaient l'âme qui se possède, la grande intelligence restée bonne. On sentait la timidité qui se replie sur elle-même unie à un affectueux besoin de sympathie. Tout l'ensemble de la personne doux, distingué, gagnant la confiance et inspirant le respect. [A little pronounced, a little heavy in the frame of her abundant hair, George Eliot's features were a reflection of a self-possessed soul, of the great intelligence that remained good. One could sense the shyness that withdraws into itself conjoined with an affectionate need for sympathy. The whole person gentle, distinguished, earning trust, and inspiring respect.]

'George Eliot', *Études sur la littérature contemporaine*, 10 vols
(Paris: Lévy, 1866–95), VIII, 187–242 (pp. 229–30); translated
by Véronique Maisier

NOTE

The French theologian and literary critic Edmond Schérer (1815–89) here reflects upon Rajon's engraving of GE, which he found 'aussi ressemblant que peut l'être la reproduction d'une physionomie singulièrement expressive [as lifelike as the reproduction of a singularly expressive physiognomy can be]' (p. 229). Schérer met GE in 1866 and 1876 (*Letters*, IV, 328; VI, 292). He 'does not talk in ready-made epigrams, like a clever Frenchman', she wrote, 'but with well-chosen moderate words intended to express what he really thinks and feels' (IV, 348).

Robert Buchanan

She posed behind a curtain, and Lewes acted as showman. No one could approach the oracle save with reverence, fear, and bated breath. If she was 'composing' she must not be disturbed; if she descended from the tripod, it was a godlike condescension; if she deigned, in that deep voice of hers, to make a remark about the weather, it was celestial thunder; if she joked, which she did 'wi' difficulty,' as we say in Scotland, her joke was summer lightning on Minerva's brow.

Harriet Jay, *Robert Buchanan: Some Account of His Life*
His Life's Work and His Literary Friendships
(London: Unwin, 1903), p. 108

NOTE

The poet, novelist, and critic Robert Williams Buchanan (1841–1901, *ODNB*) made 'a favorable impression' when he met GHL and GE in 1863 (*Letters*, IV, 122), but in 1871 his notorious attack on Dante Gabriel Rossetti, 'The Fleshly School of Poetry', led GHL to break off relations. Buchanan later published 'A Talk with George Eliot' in *A Look Round Literature* (London: Ward and Downey, 1887), pp. 218–26. It is omitted here on account of its length (almost 2,500 words) and its being, according to Buchanan, not 'a literal report of George Eliot's words' but 'a mere transcript from memory' (p. 226).

James Adderley

I have been told that George Eliot was in a railway-carriage once with a friend, and there was a "muscular Christian" sort of parson conversing with them about all the topics of the day. The reverend gentleman got out at a certain station, and the friend remarked enthusiastically: –

'Ah! that's the sort of parson I like. No nonsense about him!'

'Is he the sort of parson you would like to have at your deathbed?' said George Eliot.

'Oh no!' said the lady.

In Slums and Society: Reminiscences of Old Friends
(London: Unwin, 1916), p. 226

NOTE

James Granville Adderley (1861–1942, *ODNB*) was a Church of England clergyman and Christian Socialist.

Edith Simcox

An incident [from May 1875] in the composition of *Daniel Deronda* well illustrates the conscientious care with which every detail in her works was elaborated. It will be remembered that Deronda was to sacrifice academical honours to his friendship for Hans, and her first thought was that the latter had been rusticated for some piece of mischief – an Hogarthian caricature of the college authorities – but on satisfying herself that in these days men were usually 'sent down' for uninteresting breaches of discipline calling for little sympathy, she at once sacrificed the incident – which in itself could not but have been admirably done (she had paid a visit to the 'Hogarths' at the National Gallery on purpose), on the ground that 'when one has to invoke the reader's sympathy, anything equivocal in the probabilities is a deadly defect' – and substituted the unnoticeable explanation that Hans caught cold in his eyes by travelling third class for economy after some bit of extravagance.[1]

'George Eliot', *Nineteenth Century*, 9 (1881),
778–801 (p. 798)

NOTE

For Edith Simcox, see Part III. Another recollection by her appears in Part VII.

1. Hogarth's art may have survived the sacrifice; Hans's 'bit of extravagance' is paying too much for 'an old engraving which fascinated him' (p. 154 (Book II, Chapter 16)).

Robert Leighton

[Robert Leighton] told me yesterday (which I never knew before) that he knew George Eliot quite well in the last three years of her life. He says she was very pleasant and charming to talk to, very approachable and more like a horse than anyone he ever met. She wasn't a bit early Victorian or old-fashioned, and when nearly sixty used to wear straw hats with blue flowers, and blue ribbons tied under her chin! She was very fond of blue.

Vera Brittain, Letter to Winifred Holtby, 21 June 1921,
in *Selected Letters of Winifred Holtby and Vera Brittain*
(1920–1935), ed. by Vera Brittain and Geoffrey Handley-Taylor
(London: Brown, 1960), p. 7

NOTE

A journalist, Robert Leighton (1859–1934) wrote a series of popular stories for boys. He is not mentioned in GE's letters or journals. Vera Brittain (1893–1970, *ODNB*), a writer and feminist, is best known for her autobiographical *Testament of Youth* (1933).

Peter Bayne

She was indeed a reserved and silent woman. I have been with her and Lewes alone; and I know how she conversed in the privacy of her own fireside. Little, indeed, did she ever say, and what she did say was (as they phrase it in Scotland) *in print*: every word clean cut and perfectly enunciated. She asked questions (like Miss Dartle) and carefully received the answers.

'George Eliot', *Literary World* (Boston), 26 February 1881, p. 90
(attributed to Bayne by John P. Anderson, 'Bibliography',
in Browning, Appendix, p. vii)

NOTE

A Scottish author and journalist, Peter Bayne (1830–96, *ODNB*) called at the Priory on 9 December 1877, and after GHL's death wrote a gratifying letter praising his criticism (*Letters*, IX, 266 and *n*. 9). Ten years earlier Bayne had written an essay tracing GE's 'inexpressible sadness' to her lack of Christian faith ('George Eliot', *British Quarterly Review*, 45 (1867), 141–78 (p. 177) (attributed to Bayne in *The Wellesley Index to Victorian Periodicals*, ed. by Walter E. Houghton and others, 5 vols (Toronto: University of Toronto Press; London: Routledge & K. Paul, 1966–89), IV, 156–7).

Lord Acton

I

... [She had] suspiciousness of accustomed praise rather than the wish for it, and that impatience of unintelligent admiration which all who knew her must have observed. If she accepted without rebuke the terms in which I spoke of her genius it was because I attempted to define the sphere in which I thought her unapproached, I mean her power of vividly and adequately examining not only state of mind, but every form of thought.[1] It was what she had heard a thousand times from better judges, but it was the utterance of a sincere and not a passing conviction.

> Letter to John Walter Cross, 9 February 1881,
> Yale, reproduced with kind
> permission of Lord Acton

II

Sated with praise, and conscious of lofty aims and extraordinary talents, content with her present success, she became, in her latter years, anxious about the stability of her fame. It was in her system to look far ahead, to fix her eye on a future generation – not because she had exhausted the tribute of contemporary praise, or <from> believed Diderot's questionable theory, that posterity does not erect statues to crime[2] – but from her belief that genuine <service is that which cannot be> <has> merit escaped reward.

Cross saw my first note [immediately above] and exclaimed: Nobody can understand her who does not see this. She was intensely ambitious. Doubted as to her own fame. Cared only for the future, but cared for it with meaty interiority. Would have been shocked if others had doubted.

> CUL, Add. MSS 5019/115, 702, reproduced
> with kind permission of Lord Acton and
> the Syndics of Cambridge University Library

NOTES

For Lord Acton, see Part I.

1. On 15 April 1878, the day after he first called at the Priory, Acton wrote to GE: 'But I am persuaded that if you chose you could make not only characters of men reveal their secrets to the world more fully than they are known to themselves, but all manner of doctrines and persuasions display themselves in their strength and attraction more faithfully and more vividly than they appear to their own exponents' (*Letters*, IX, 225). As he later told Cross, Acton believed that 'the second place in English Literature belongs to her and that in one supreme quality of power' – the examination of mental life – 'she was not second even to Shakespeare' (letter of 25 January 1881, Yale).

2. Acton seems to blend two references here. In *Rameau's Nephew* (*c*.1761–74), Diderot's protagonist argues that sooner or later all nations erect statues to geniuses as 'benefactors of the race' ('*Rameau's Nephew' and Other Works*, trans. by Jacques Barzun and Ralph H. Bowen (Indianapolis: Bobbs-Merrill, 1964), p. 13).

Conversely, in his article on 'The Encyclopedia' (1755), Diderot asserts that one who has been so honoured and then does wrong 'would be obliged to shatter his own statue with his own hands' (p. 301).

Frederic W. Farrar

After the ceremony, the chief guests went into the Jerusalem Chamber for the signing of the register.[1] ... I had to find Mr. Tennyson ... and steer him to the book. He was short-sighted; and the Jerusalem Chamber, always some-what dark, was still more so from its densely crowded condition. As I held his arm and led him along, a lady held out her hand with a warm, –

"How are you, Mr. Tennyson? I am glad that you got in just in time."

"Oh, how do you do?" he answered. "I have not the least idea who you are!"

"I am Mrs. Lewes," she said, with a smile.

It was his friend and neighbor, "George Eliot;" but (as he stopped to explain) he could hardly distinguish her features in the crowd and dim light of the ancient famous Chamber, and had not, at the moment, recognized her voice. This was the only time that I had the pleasure of seeing "George Eliot."

Men I Have Known (New York: Crowell, 1897),

pp. 37–8

NOTE

Frederic William Farrar (1852–1928, *ODNB*) was appointed a canon of Westminster in 1876. He was also a novelist and philologist, and later Dean of Canterbury.

1. For the marriage in Westminster Abbey of Lionel Tennyson and Eleanor Locker, in February 1878, 'a large and fashionable wedding, with thirty policemen to control the crowds outside' (Robert Bernard Martin, *Tennyson: The Unquiet Heart* (Oxford: Clarendon Press, 1980), p. 522). The Tennysons arrived just as Farrar pronounced the two man and wife.

James Bryce

To me personally the regretful thought often arose how little we had known of the desire for affection and the comprehensive kindliness which were the notes of her character. I do not mean that we did not feel in her presence her graciousness sweetness and friendliness, but that my reverence for her intel-lectual power always kept me from saying to her what I now feel I might have said, and from going half as often to see her as I would have gone.

Letter to John Walter Cross,

21 March [1885], Yale

NOTE

Born in Belfast, James Bryce, Viscount Bryce (1838–1922, *ODNB*), was a jurist, historian, and politician. When he called on GE remains uncertain, but GHL read and recom-mended Bryce's *Transcaucasia and Ararat* when it appeared in 1877 (*Letters*, VI, 429).

George Meredith

I

In the *George Eliot* I could not have refrained from touches on the comic scene of the Priory – with the dais, and the mercurial little showman, and the Bishops about the feet of an erratic woman worshipped as a literary idol and light of philosophy. No stage has had anything so poignant for satire.[1]

> To Sir Leslie Stephen, 18 August 1902, in *The Letters of George Meredith*, ed. by C.L. Cline,
> 3 vols (Oxford: Clarendon Press, 1970), III, 1460

II

"George Eliot had the heart of Sappho; but the face, with the long probiscis, the protruding teeth as of the Apocalyptic horse, betrayed animality." What of Lewes? "Oh, he was the son of a clown, he had the legs of his father in his brain."[2]

> Edward Clodd, quoting Meredith, in *Memories*, 3rd edn
> (London: Chapman and Hall, 1916), p. 157

NOTES

The novelist and poet George Meredith (1828–1909, *ODNB*) knew GE from her *Westminster Review* days, succeeding her in writing its 'Belles Lettres' section. She favourably reviewed his *Shaving of Shagpat* (*Leader*, 5 January 1856, pp. 15–17), but later remarked of one of his serially published novels that 'she had only discovered one admirer of it, a very eminent man as it happened, and even him she had convicted of missing two whole numbers without noticing a gap' (John Morley, *Recollections*, 2 vols (London: Macmillan, 1917), I, 48).

1. For the description of GE's receptions in Stephen's *George Eliot* (1902), see 'Sunday Gatherings at the Priory', above.
2. Not GHL's father John Lee Lewes but his grandfather Charles Lee Lewes was a comic actor (Ashton, *G.H. Lewes*, pp. 6–10). Meredith said of Grillparzer's play *Sappho* (1819): 'Love is all that Sappho's nature yearns for: all her inspirations are kindled from that one desire' (*The Notebooks of George Meredith*, ed. by Gillian Beer and Margaret Harris, Salzburg Studies in English Literature: Romantic Reassessment, 73:2 (Salzburg: Institut für Anglistik und Amerikanistik, Universität Salzburg, 1983), p. 22).

Part V
Mrs Lewes Alone 1878–80

'A GENERAL EXTREME CORDIALITY'

Robert Browning

But you are mistaken in supposing me to have been "intimately" acquainted with George Eliot: deeply impressed by her genius I could not fail to be, and some particular acts of personal kindness, beside a general extreme cordiality endeared her much to me, – still I only began to know her on returning to England after a long absence – during which her relation with Lewes had been entered into, under circumstances I really am all but quite ignorant about.[1] Lewes I had a slight acquaintance with, many years before: and it was on the occasion of his being reported to me as the writer of an article which greatly obliged me by its sympathy that I called on him and was introduced to her: He would permit me to add, I am sure, that I was greatly struck at what seemed to me the disappearance of certain little touches of unnecessary self-assertion even intolerance which prevented his society from being so attractive as it afterwards became.[2] I never conversed with either of them on any matters of deeper importance than the news of the day, literary or political.[3] The death of poor Lewes came with a shock the more sensible that I had supposed, – from a clever gay letter which he addressed to Leighton, some few days only before, – that his health was re-established: and, in answer to the few words I could not but address to George Eliot, I received an invitation to the Funeral which I obeyed with more than willingness.[4] The effect of the bereavement was described to me as overwhelming at first: I have since ascertained that composure is returning, and that the necessity of completing the unfinished works of Lewes will be a sufficient restorative in the end: so let us hope!

Letter to Mary Gladstone Drew, 17 December 1878, BL, Mary Gladstone Papers, Add. MS 46,251, fols 51–52, reproduced with kind permission of The Provost and Fellows of Eton College and the British Library Board; publ. with omissions and misreadings in *Some Hawarden Letters 1878–1913: Written to Mrs. Drew (Miss Mary Gladstone) Before and After Her Marriage*, ed. by Lisle March-Phillipps and Bertram Christian (London: Nisbet, 1917), pp. 44–5

NOTES

The poet Robert Browning (1812–89, *ODNB*) first called on GE on 12 December 1862 (Haight, p. 371). The following July he presented her with a photograph of his deceased wife, the poet Elizabeth Barrett Browning, which GE hung in her room (*Journals*, p. 118). In October 1865, Browning showed GE 'the objects Mrs. Browning used to have about her, her chair, tables, books etc. An epoch to be remembered' (*Journals*, p. 126).

1. Browning returned to England after his wife's death in 1861. He had been away fifteen years. The idea that he and GE were close was one he also disputed with Moncure Daniel Conway (see *Dearest Isa: Robert Browning's Letters to Isabella Blagden*, ed. by Edward C. McAleer (Austin: University of Texas Press, 1951), p. 167).

2. Browning thought the change in GHL 'astounding!' (*Dearest Isa*, p. 147); Ashton, p. 267, mentions others who found his rough edges smoothed. The sympathetic article may have been GHL's 'Robert Browning and the Poetry of the Age', *British Quarterly Review*, 6 (1847), 490–509, or 'Browning's New Poem', *Leader*, 27 April 1850, 111. GE also reviewed Browning favourably ('Belles Lettres', *Westminster Review* (1856), repr. in *Essays*, pp. 349–57, and in *Writings*, pp. 234–42).

3. One wonders. George W. Smalley remarks that Browning 'was content with those nearest him till he had a proposition in metaphysics or a theory of music to announce, and when that moment came it was useless to compete with him; nor did many men try; or not twice' (*Anglo-American Memories*, 2nd series (New York and London: Putnam, 1912), p. 281). This comment provides background for something GE said to William Allingham in April 1873, when they were discussing several writers, including Ralph Waldo Emerson, who had suggested the specifically conceptual (and perhaps divine) origin of language. 'Emerson would have liked to hear some of Browning's opinions', GE told William Allingham. 'Have *you* ever heard any of Browning's opinions?' (*William Allingham: A Diary*, ed. by H. Allingham and D. Radford (London: Macmillan, 1907), p. 222).

4. In his note to GE Browning mentioned how much he had valued GHL's sympathy (*Letters*, vii, 86). GHL's letter to Frederic Leighton has remained untraced.

FRIENDS' FACES

James Sully

Not long after George Lewes's death, Charles told me that his mother (as he always called her) would like to see me, to talk over the plan of my assisting her in the revision of Lewes's posthumous volume of the "Problems of Life and Mind," as well as an article on Lewes's life and work which I was about to write for a review. It was a dark afternoon when I called, and the lamp was not yet lit. I found a stranger talking with George Eliot. Shortly afterwards he left, and I had my turn. I could see that she was very solicitous about my proposed article on Lewes, and it was a relief when, after I had sent her a proof of it, she wrote to assure me that she had "read the article with very grateful feelings."[1]

About this time Francis Galton was making experimental inquiries into variations of visualizing power among individuals. He told me he particularly wanted to get George Eliot's "co-efficient." I brought up the subject during my visit, and she at once said she could carry about so distinct a picture of the faces of her friends, that not only photographs, but nearly all portraits, disappointed her by their incompleteness.

This was the last time I saw George Eliot.

> 'George Eliot in the Seventies', in *My Life & Friends: A Psychologist's Memories* (London: Unwin, 1918), pp. 259–66 (pp. 264–5)

NOTE

For James Sully, see 'Sunday Gatherings at the Priory' in Part IV.

1. *Letters*, VII, 198 (10 September 1879). The article was 'George Henry Lewes', *New Quarterly Magazine*, n.s. 2 (1879), 356–76, for which GE gave Sully biographical information (see VII, 153–4).

THREE VISITS

William Allingham

1879

H[elen] and I called on George Eliot, North Bank, first time since Lewes's death. She seemed well and cheerful. Herbert Spencer there. He talked of Art – 'people don't know what to admire – the Old Masters – folly! The R.A. Exhibition better than all the Old Masters. The art of painting greatly advanced, etc. etc. St. Mark's a barbarous and unpleasing edifice.'[1] George Eliot denounced 'the rain, or perpetual drizzle of criticism under which we live.'[2]

– George Eliot called. Carlyle portraits: H[elen] wished to do *hers*: G.E. said she would 'consider.'[3]

1880

April 19 – I out in St. John's Wood, and call on George Eliot. She was looking well in a high cap and black silk dress. I told her of C[arlyle] and Othello – 'the red mountain and blue vapour.' 'Like an imaginative child's description,' she said.[4]

> *William Allingham: A Diary*, pp. 284, 286

NOTES

For William Allingham, see 'The Countryside' in Part IV. Neither Allingham nor GE notes the day of the first visit, but Spencer called on 30 March and 20 April (*Journals*, pp. 168, 171).

1. Spencer approved the work of the old masters only 'relatively to the mental culture of its age, which was characterized by crude ideas and sentiments and undisciplined perceptions' (*An Autobiography*, 2 vols (London: Williams and Norgate, 1904), II, 190). As early as 1861 GE perceived 'a great gulf fixed' between them on the subjects of 'art and classical literature' (*Letters*, III, 469).

2. A persistent theme in GE's thought. She wrote in 1871 that 'literature of the criticising sort ... seems to me seriously injurious: it accustoms men and women to formulate opinions instead of receiving deep impressions, and to receive deep impressions is the foundation of all true mental power' (*Letters*, v, 155).

3. Helen Allingham did a series of coloured sketches of Carlyle in 1875–79, exhibited at the Fine Art Society in 1881 (*Memoirs of the Life and Writings of Thomas Carlyle*, ed. Richard Herne Shepherd, 2 vols (London: Allen, 1881), ii, 315–16). Of GE she later wrote: 'I once asked her if she would allow me to try to make a portrait – but she – most kindly, but firmly, – said it could not be – (& I greatly doubt if I could have managed any thing at all satisfactory!)' (letter to Elinor Southwood Lewes Ouvry, 18 June [1925?], Yale).

4. Carlyle had described an audience's reaction to a speech in Shakespeare's *Othello* as 'a passionate burst of approval, the voices of the men rising – in your imagination – like a red mountain, with the women's voices floating round it like blue vapour, you might say. I never heard the like of it' (*William Allingham: A Diary*, p. 286).

A PRIVATE HOUR

Anthony Trollope

I called on her one day last week [21 May 1879] – just as she was about to leave town for Witley and sat with her for an hour. I found her cheerful, but she said nothing about her own book.[1] She never does.

To William Blackwood, 26 May 1879, in
The Letters of Anthony Trollope, ed. by N. John Hall,
2 vols (Stanford: Stanford University Press, 1983), ii, 828

NOTE

A close friend of GHL's before meeting GE, the novelist Anthony Trollope (1815–82, *ODNB*) left only a few personal comments on her, following his belief that 'she was one whose private life should be left in privacy, – as may be said of all who have achieved fame by literary merits' (ii, 892). In this same letter he says that 'though I was very intimate with George Eliot, she never spoke to me of her life before I knew her, nor, as far as I am aware did she to her other friends'.

1. *The Impressions of Theophrastus Such*, published by Blackwood on 19 May. Among Lord Acton's notes on GE: 'Trollope said she was the most unhappy woman he ever saw. Such depression' (CUL, Add. MS 5019/1564[r], reproduced with kind permission of Lord Acton and the Syndics of Cambridge University Library).

LOVE FOR LIFE

Barbara Bodichon

I spent an hour with Marian (5th June). She was more delightful than I can say, and left me in good spirits for her – though she is wretchedly thin, and looks in her long, loose, black dress like the black shadow of herself. She said she had so much to do that she must keep well – 'the world was so *intensely interesting.*' She said she would come *next year* to see me. We both agreed in the great love we had for life. In fact, I think she will do more for us than ever.

Letter to Alice Bonham Carter, her cousin,
12 June 1879, in *Life*, III, 367

NOTE

For Barbara Bodichon, see 'A Few Good Friends' in Part IV. Other recollections featuring her, by Matilda Betham-Edwards, appear in Parts II and IV.

SWINBURNE AND DOLLS

Lucy Clifford

She said she would come and see me, or would I go and see her? I should find her, probably alone, any week-day afternoon. The Sundays were no more. Of course I went, glad and thankful indeed.[1] Madame Belloc was there on the first occasion. Presently, when she had gone, Mrs. Lewes made a little sign that took me from the arm-chair on her right to a grey cushioned footstool by her side. She took off my hat, and so we sat, she talking and I listening. Now and then she put her wonderful hands on my hair, they sent a thrill through me – the memory does: even yet.

And I went several times after that first visit, yet not very often, for it was difficult. I wish I could recall many of the things she said; but it was so soon after the tragedy of my own life, memory had deserted me, and everything is blurred. I remember that once she talked about Swinburne; she considered *Bothwell* the finest of his long poems, and its second act a wonderful thing. She spoke of his prose, and that led her to allude to a paper he had written about her, and she became – though she never raised the low tone of her voice – almost vehement. 'He suggested,' she exclaimed, and angrily doubled the fist that rested on her knee, 'that I'd taken some things in *The Mill on the Floss* from a story by Mrs. Gaskell called *The Children on the Moor.*'[2] I forget other of the actual words she used, even on that surprising occasion; it is only the general effect that remains. Evidently she was very sensitive to criticism, for when George Henry Lewes was alive she never took up newspapers, after she had published a book, till he had first looked through them for possibly ungracious reviews.

Once, when I went to see her, the maid-servant let me in with a queer little smile on her face that I understood on entering the room, for there was George Eliot with a ring of chairs round her, just as on the Sunday afternoons of old; but instead of philosophers, poets and other Victorian giants sitting on them, there were dolls; and through an open window – it was early spring-time – came the sound of merry voices.

'Charles's children are in the garden,' she explained, smiling, but with a sad little shake of her head, 'they've brought their children to see me,' nodding to the dolls.[3] ...

The last time I saw her [19 April 1880] she was not alone – it was just a little while before her marriage to Mr. Cross. Leslie Stephen was there, and she talked chiefly to him, but she held my hand the while – she had the most wonderful and soothing touch of any woman I ever knew; and to feel your hand in hers was to be sensible of all the troubled ways in your life peacefully subsiding. I meant to stay behind, but Leslie Stephen offered to take me home and it was impossible to refuse. We asked her if we should see her again before she left London for her Surrey cottage. A happy smile that vaguely puzzled us came to her face while she answered, 'Oh, yes; I dare say you'll see me – or you'll hear of me.' We did – we all heard of her marriage to Mr. Cross. ...

She had a wonderful personality, and, with the exception of my husband, greater magnetism than anyone I ever knew.[4] Something indefinable looked out of her grave eyes and lurked in the fleeting smile; some knowledge often seemed to be waiting behind them that she would fain use to help you, to give you pleasure, but that she held back for some wise reason she could not yet make known to you: meanwhile she gave you understanding and sympathy and, if you needed it sorely, tenderness. If you desired it, too, out of the store of learning with which she sometimes smothered her genius, she gave you the help or the courage that, perhaps unconsciously, you sought.

'A Remembrance of George Eliot', *Nineteenth Century*,
74 (1913), 109–18 (pp. 116–18)

NOTES

For Lucy Clifford, see 'Sunday Gatherings at the Priory' in Part IV. Another recollection by her appears in 'Out and About in London' in Part IV.

1. GE wished to see Clifford because her husband had died early in 1879, a few months after GHL; the date of this first visit is probably June or July 1879.

2. He accused GE of using material from Gaskell's *Moorland Cottage* (1850) and not acknowledging the 'palpable and weighty and direct obligation' (*A Note on Charlotte Brontë* (London: Chatto & Windus, 1877), p. 31). In 1878 Sir Edmund Gosse recorded that somehow Swinburne had come to believe GE 'was hounding on her myrmidons to his destruction' (*Portraits and Sketches* (London: Heinemann, 1912), p. 16).

3. Charles Lewes's daughter Blanche recalled GE as 'very stately and dignified and always gracious and charming to us children. I particularly remember the enormous number of armchairs in the drawing-room at the Priory, which mother told me were there because George Eliot and Grandpapa didn't like to sit in armchairs

themselves unless everyone else in the room could do so too'. She also noted that GE kept two rag dolls for the children to play with, 'one dressed in scarlet, the other in royal blue'. Her sister Maud, who has a recollection below, remembered 'coloured jellies specially prepared for us' (all from Arthur Paterson, *George Eliot's Family Life and Letters*, p. 250).

4. In 'George Eliot: Some Personal Recollections', *Bookman*, 73 (October 1927), 1–3, Clifford describes that magnetism as 'extraordinary; the more sedate of the great ones – the philosophers especially – held themselves in bravely, but I always felt that there were those among them who, if they had been asked in the firm sweet voice to go and drown themselves in the near-by canal, or the more picturesque Regent's Park lake, which was not far off, would religiously have done it' (p. 2).

'IT ALL LOOKED SO LONELY'

Edward Coley Burne-Jones

and the day [16 September 1879] was a very nice one with George Elliot – she lives in a lovely country too, near Godalming, – with the garden on a steep slope which is always pretty – she met me at the gate and looked well – and in the afternoon we went a long drive[1] – it is a solitary life, but evidently that does not vex her – but is rather her choice than her fate – I asked about work but she is doing none of her own – only busily working on what her husband left – and there will be none of her own in that only careful editor's work – she seemed to like to talk about him and her face looked not a bit more sorrowful than it used to – nor was she changed in any way – we talked about your father and about Homer and about lost Greek poems, and many and many a thing[2] – I think she is working much at Jewish matters – for the table was covered with Hebrew books – when I say covered I mean there were two or three – but she said she was busy with that literature – there is no one living, do you know, better to talk to – for she speaks always carefully so that nothing has to be taken back or qualified in any way – and her knowledge is really deep – and her heart one of the most sympathetic to me I ever knew – but it all looked so lonely – and I wondered she cared to lie down or get up any more. I thought that if a very great misery were to happen to me, like that, of losing the very heart & soul of life and fountain of hope and desire, as she has, I should behave very badly and disappoint all who like me – I know what I should like to do, if it was lawful – and I think she does not in any least dim way hope to see him again. – so I came away not so much strengthened as wondering at other peoples strength –

Letter to Mary Gladstone Drew, October 1879, BL, Mary Gladstone Papers, Add. MS 46,246, fols 27–8, reproduced with permission of the British Library Board; publ. with alterations in *Some Hawarden Letters*, pp. 46–7, and *Memorials*, II, 94–5

NOTES

Sir Edward Coley Burne-Jones, 1st baronet (1833–98, *ODNB*), a Pre-Raphaelite painter, met GE in 1868. His work, she told him, 'makes life larger and more beautiful to us' (*Letters*, V, 391). GE was especially close to Burne-Jones's wife Georgiana ('Mignon'), for whom see 'A Few Good Friends' in Part IV and who has another recollection below.

1. To Hindhead (*Journals*, p. 181), some six miles distant, the second highest point of Surrey, at this time wild moorland. For a description of the unfolding landscape on a drive from Witley to Hindhead, see Thomas Wright, *Hind Head: Or the English Switzerland and Its Literary and Historical Associations* (London: Simkin, Marshall, Hamilton, Kent, 1898), pp. 1–10.

2. W.E. Gladstone had written on Homer; see Benjamin Jowett's recollections, *n.* 2, below.

STATIONS

W. Graham Robertson

I remember Burne-Jones telling me of a day spent at 'The Heights' with George Eliot, and of his departure thence on a pitch-black autumn evening.[1] The lady, who, in spite of her genius, was hopelessly vague in mundane affairs, bade him farewell at the door, and saying – "If you turn to the right you will get to the station" – shut him out into the darkness. He stumbled blindly down the drive and into the lane where, hearing the distant approach of the train, he turned to the right as directed (incidentally scrambling over a fence), and – sure enough – got to the station, but upside-down, much torn by brambles and considerably bruised, after having fallen and rolled down a fairly perpendicular bank about thirty feet high. This rather inconvenient vagueness of the great lady was probably fostered by the exaggerated care taken of her by G.H. Lewes, of which another of Burne-Jones's stories gives instance.

He came across her standing monumentally alone at Waterloo Station, and, as he talked with her, they walked for a short distance along the platform. Suddenly Lewes rushed up to them, panic pale and breathlessly exclaiming – "My God! You are HERE!" George Eliot gravely admitted it. "But," stammered Lewes, "I left you THERE!" That his precious charge should have walked by herself, without proper escort and chaperonage, for over ten yards was a portent almost beyond possibility.

Time Was: The Reminiscences of W. Graham Robertson (London: Hamilton, 1931), pp. 293–4

NOTE

Walford Graham Robertson (1866–1948, *ODNB*), a painter and theatre designer, lived at Sandhills, near Witley.

1. The only visit by Burne-Jones GE records is the one described in the previous recollection.

NOTES ON GEORGE ELIOT'S CONVERSATION

Benjamin Jowett

M[arian].E[vans].L[ewes].
said that she had been pleased by letters from America, & elsewhere written by persons who had derived benefit from her works: Two motives greatly influenced her. 1. She desires to do good to others & to diffuse herself – to pour into the lives of others more than was contained or could be contained in any single one.[1] 2. The dread of falling into dulness & not a calling – This last at present affects her most

Expression quite extraordinary & lovely notwithstanding plainness of feature

Asked about Thucydides, Plato & admired Tennyson & his boyish ways – said we might wish that a person should equally show himself on all sides & in all way prose, poetry, talking, speaking but that this was an unattainable ideal [.] Yet Wordsworth & Shelley had written well both in poetry & prose

M.E.L.
said how much harm had been done by making a religion of Consolation. Persons must believe such & such things of which they had no evidence because they were comforting: They should be taught that certain things should be borne & that would be a useful lesson. They must be told this from the first & not allowed to give way:

She seemed to think it impossible for her to write any more, because she could not get over the babble of tongues: The motive of doing good to others, diffusing her personal existence

Did not wish to write more, because so many persons had written too much e.g Wordsworth & Goethe

Urged strongly that common interests should be enough for us, not great ideals. There is somebody to whom we can be kind &c

M.E.L.
suggested to me that I should write for people generally 'an account of the limitations of Greek thought'

Some persons said: A great writer was not made, but born: – others a great writer was made – as well as born. Seemed to think that writing was a natural gift: there was a extraordinary subtlety in it which could not be acquired

Great intellectual antipathy to W.E.G. – was going to read Homeric studies for the light which they threw upon him[2]

Seemed to fear too much that her writing would not be appreciated

M.E.L.
spoke of the Darwinians – they had degenerated into teleology – they talked of insects as having knowledge – .[3]

Survival of the fittest did not mean survival of the best:

Urged very strongly that a person did not want a whole moral system. A single aspect or principle of morality was enough for them, if they held to it.

She said that she had read Homer in the Greek during the time of her trouble finding it absolutely necessary to get into an emotionally different sphere[4]

Spoke of the drinking habits of S & S & B.[5]

Remarked that the followers of Darwin[6]

Mrs. Lewes
spoke of Froude – thought that he had a false ring & that his reflections were very superficial[7]

She was always ready to absorb & never weary of reading. But was this right? You should absorb for the sake of diffusion. Remembering the letters that I had written to her she intended to write again. I must help her, if I can[8] – She must give up poetry, & essay writing & return to novels

Lord S[alisbury] used to claim about the man when he read Romola declaring that Tito was a genuine Greek

M.E.L.
was quite indignant at the falsehoods told by the Liberals of their opponents[9]

Notebook, *17 – 1879 Oct.*, Balliol College Library, Oxford University, MS I/H38, fols 20ʳ, 21, 22ʳ, 23ʳ, 48ʳ, 56ʳ, reproduced, as is the quotation in *n.* 4 below, with kind permission of the Jowett Copyright Trustees

NOTES

For Benjamin Jowett, see 'Eton, Cambridge, and Oxford' in Part IV. He probably visited GE at the Heights on 29 October 1879 (*Letters*, VII, 218 *n.* 4), and definitely saw her at the Priory on 16 December (*Journals*, p. 188), making these notes after one of these occasions. Other recollections by him appear in Part III, in 'The Countryside' in Part IV, and in Parts VI –VII.

1. I wish to thank Dr Penelope Bulloch for deciphering this sentence. In a subsequent letter to GE, encouraging her to begin writing fiction again, Jowett reminded her of her idea of diffusing herself for others' good (*Letters*, IX, 284).

2. W.E. Gladstone, *Studies on Homer and the Homeric Age*, 3 vols (Oxford: University Press, 1858). His translation of 'The Shield of Achilles' (*Contemporary Review*, 23 (1874), 329 –36) GE considered 'doggerel', an example of 'the fashion of indulging an imbecile literary vanity in high places' (*Letters*, vi, 22).

3. In *The Descent of Man, and Selection in Relation to Sex*, 2 vols (London: Murray, 1871), Darwin wrote non-teleologically of insects' 'intelligence' (i, 37–8). Other Darwinians enlarged the concept toward group 'knowledge' rather than individual intelligence; Herbert Spencer would later talk of a butterfly's 'consciously adjusting its actions', and propose 'that in a community of social insects there has arisen a mass of experience and usage into which each new individual is initiated; just as happens among ourselves' (*The Principles of Biology*, rev. edn, 2 vols (New York: Appleton, 1898), i, 684). GE may have found the suggestion of design or purpose implicit in the turn from intelligence to knowledge – if indeed she made the distinction. I wish to thank John S. Haller for his assistance with this reference.

4. 'I remember Mrs. Lewes telling me that in her great sorrow, when she lost her husband (that strange man to whom she was so deeply attached) feeling she must do something for herself she read through, in the Greek, the Iliad & Odyssey, because that most completely separated her from useless and painful thoughts' (letter from Jowett to 'Mrs. A' (untraced), 15 August 1886, Balliol College Library, Oxford University, MS I/F11/1, fol. 2). GE found the 'emotionally different sphere' valuable for her writing as well, once remarking that 'she always read some of the "Iliad" before beginning her work, in order to take out of her mouth the taste of the modern world' (Browning, p. 100).

5. Untraced.

6. Jowett's truncation.

7. What GE had in mind is not clear, but Froude's most recent writings were the third series of *Short Studies on Great Subjects* (1877) and *Science and Theology, Ancient and Modern* (1878).

8. After GHL's death Jowett urged GE to write again (see *Letters*, vii, 289 n. 1; ix, 286; and his recollection in Part vii).

9. 'Her wrath used often to be roused, in late years, by the increased bitterness in the language of parties, and by the growing habit of attributing, for political effect, the most shameful motives to distinguished statesmen' (*Life*, iii, 427); see also *Letters*, ix, 282, where GE singles out Gladstone as the originator of poisonous Liberal speeches.

AN UNSIGNED BIRTHDAY BOOK

Eleanor M. Sellar

I met her again in the autumn of 1879, suddenly and unexpectedly, in a picture-gallery. John Cross was with her, and she asked me and my daughter Eppie, who was with me, to go and see her at The Priory next afternoon, which we did. I love to think of the comfortable cosy hour we spent with her. It was the last time I saw this great writer and wonderful woman. Eppie asked her if she would write her name in a birthday book she had brought with her in the hope of securing this valuable autograph, and I remember the sweet smile with which she said, "My dear, I would like to do anything to give you pleasure, but I was obliged long ago to register a vow that I would never sign my name for such purposes; and if you only knew the number of books that have been sent me from all parts of the world, you would understand and forgive!"

Recollections and Impressions (Edinburgh and London: Blackwood, 1907), p. 293

NOTE

J.W. Cross's cousin Eleanor Mary (Mrs William Young) Sellar, née Dennistoun (1829–1918), first met GE at a Priory gathering in 1870. 'There were several people of more or less importance there', she recalled, and 'the very fact of my being an "unknown quantity" made her only the more gracious to me' (p. 292).

SOCIETY VERSES

Frederick Locker-Lampson

I saw George Eliot only two or three times after Lewes's death: on the first occasion she was shrouded with much weed, so I talked to her with bated breath, hardly venturing to initiate a subject; however, as I was leaving the room, I chanced to say something about Mrs. Langtry, just then sailing with supreme dominion on the buoyant wings of her beauty; upon this George Eliot pricked up her ears, and asked about her. I said that I had lately met Mrs. Langtry at Mrs. Millais's, and had had an amiable little letter from her about some verses which afterwards got into the *World*.[1] On this George Eliot became more and much more interested, and laughed, and asked me to repeat the lines.

This was one of the few occasions on which I had seen George Eliot entirely alone; it enabled me to know her better, and it made me feel sorry that she had not more sprightly and natural people about her – indeed, that she did not breathe a more healthy atmosphere; for unless Du Maurier sang, or W.K. Clifford talked, or Vivier, the horn-blower, gave one of his impersonations,[2] her *réunions* had somewhat of the solemnity of religious functions, with the religion cut out.

My Confidences: An Autobiographical Sketch Addressed to My Descendants [ed. by Augustine Birrell] (London: Smith, Elder, 1896), pp. 309–10

NOTES

The poet Frederick Locker (1821–95, *ODNB*), as he was known until 1885, met GE in 1869 or 1870 and saw her occasionally afterwards. Evidently the meeting described here was on 21 December 1879 (*Journals*, p. 189), more than a year after GHL's death.

1. 'For Mrs. Langtry': 'When youth and wit and beauty call, | I never walk away; | When Mrs. Langtry leaves the ball, | I never care to stay. | I cannot rhyme like Oscar

Wylde | Or Hayward (gifted pair!), | Or sing how Mrs. Langtry smiled, | Or how she wore her hair. | And yet I want to play my part, | Like any other swain; | To fracture Mrs. Langtry's heart – | And patch it up again' ('What the World Says', *World*, 3 December 1879, p. 9). The lines (by 'a well-known society versifier') were 'handed about' at the wedding reception for the Millaises' daughter on 28 November ('The Millais Wedding', p. 13).

2. In Germany GE knew the French horn player Eugène Vivier (*Journals*, pp. 44, 45, 239, 251), famous for his wit and practical jokes, and he may have come to the Priory. But Locker is probably punning on 'Vivian', a pseudonym once used by GHL, who sometimes 'blew his horn' by doing impersonations at the Sunday gatherings.

'IN ABRAHAM'S BOSOM'

Frances Horner

Then yesterday afternoon [22 November 1879] I went to see Mrs Lewes. When I went in there was no one there & I was a little shy at first – we talked about travelling & Algiers etc – then a man [came] in a Mr Jacobson & they plunged into Judaism & talked about Spinoza miles over <I> my head.[1] I got up twice to go but she wouldnt let me & at last she fairly sent away the man & began to talk to me, & she said some lovely things that I shall always remember. She thinks it such nonsense for girls to think they must have a vocation, & do something queer; isnt that a comfort She says yr real duties are to make the lives close about you happy, & she told me how dismal she had got when she was young because she had to give herself up entirely to an old papa & how she thought her life was all going drivelling by – & now how thankful she was of that more than of anything else that had come – & she said it was nonsense to think of revolutionizing society, about rich & poor I mean – what she thinks wrong is the *vulgar* use people put their wealth to – dinners & gowns & things – & she told me to try always & keep from miserable gossip, that she thinks ruins womens lives & minds, & to make people feel as if one were a pure fresh rill amongst them. She thinks one individual may change a whole house, & society of people that way – & she said she would like all young people to have hopefulness of what was waiting for them – something glorious or happy for wh everything they had to do every day would really fit them –

O me – she made one feel a minx that was the worst. I think she's much more like a man than a woman – but Mr B[urne]. J[ones]. says Im wrong. It seems to me such a very masculine & powerful mind –

I think she's much more a philosopher than an artist – & a philosopher of that school who have summed up the universe & made 0 of it She's very sad now – she says she feels quite hard & insensible & she's trying to work & to interest herself in every way – O it did look a dismal house rather & that poor thing quite alone in it –

I suppose she's had a luckier life than most people after all I was thinking all the time of that dismal Bronte life, & then George Elliots seemed very rich. I dont think she is moved by worship much – is that like a woman or like a man I wonder – I dont believe it touches her much –

She asked me to come & see her again, but I felt such a Minx I dont think its any good –

I daresay shed help one if she knew all about one – but then thats just it – no one ever can even if one wanted them to – if you would tell your heart I dont think you could & I wouldnt & couldn't –

Now is that all wearisome – its so difficult to repeat & it all sounds platitudes I know, & yet she talked very well & freshly – & she put her hands on my knees & her face quite close & looked with good eyes at me – but I felt rather as if she were in Abraham's bosom because of the intellectual gulf between wh nothing can really bridge over however much they long to come down to us –

I dont know if being in love does but nothing else short of that sympathy could Im sure —

Letter to Mary Gladstone Drew, BL, Add. MS 46,251, fols 53^r–56^v, reproduced with permission of the British Library Board; publ. with alterations and omissions in *Some Hawarden Letters*, pp. 42–4

NOTE

Frances Jane Horner, née Graham, Lady Horner (1854/5–1940, *ODNB*), was a society hostess and patron of the arts.

1. It was Joseph Jacobs (*Journals*, p. 186), whose recollection appears next. Algiers would have been of interest because Barbara Bodichon and her husband spent winters there.

GLOOM AND DEPRESSION

Joseph Jacobs

I saw her but once more [on 22 November 1879] after Lewes's death. I had sent her something I had published in the *Nineteenth Century*,[1] and she had written asking me to call. I did so, and found the house in gloom and herself in depression. On this occasion I was struck by the massiveness of the head as contrasted with the frailty of the body. When she was seated one thought her tall: such a head should have been propped up by a larger frame. The long thin sensitive hands were those of a musician. The exquisite modulations of the voice told of refinement in every well-chosen phrase. She had at least one of the qualifications one expects in an author; she did indeed 'talk like a book.' She spoke of one of her favourite themes, the appeal of the circle in which one is born even if one has in certain ways grown beyond or outside it. Before I left she asked me to find out for her the meaning of a Hebrew inscription on a seal which an old Russian Jew had given Tourgenief: he had sent her an impression, which she intrusted to me. 'You will be careful of it,' she said, 'I prize it as coming from him.' I thought of old Kalonymos and his similar caution as he hands the key of his family archives to Daniel Deronda. We parted, and I soon returned the impression with an explanation of the inscription.[2] She sent a few words of kindly thanks, and that was all till I received the final summons to Highgate Cemetery.

Literary Studies (London: Nutt, 1895), pp. xvi–xvii; first publ. 1891

NOTES

For Joseph Jacobs, see 'Sunday Gatherings at the Priory' in Part IV.

1. 'The God of Israel: A History' (Sept. 1879), repr. in *Jewish Ideals and Other Essays* (London: Nutt, 1896), pp. 24–60. In it Jacobs argues that Judaism is not only a religion but also a philosophy of history; as such, it has revealed God by continuing to do His work. 'I can see no meaning in history', Jacobs concludes, if Judaism, 'the richest product of humanity, which has shared in all the progressive movements in the history of man, shall not have within it germs of mighty thoughts and deeds' (p. 59).

2. Taken from Alexander Pushkin's signet ring, in Turgenev's possession, the inscription meant '"Simkha, son of the esteemed rabbi Joseph the elder of blessed memory"' (Patrick Waddington, *Turgenev and England* (London: Macmillan, 1980), pp. 279–80). Kalonymos hands over the key in *Daniel Deronda* with 'the monitory and slightly suspicious look with which age is apt to commit any object to the keeping of youth' (p. 618 (Book VIII, Chapter 60)). GE was sixty years old, on this very day; Jacobs, twenty-four.

'WISE AND SWEET AND HUMOROUS'

Bret Harte

I spent a delightful hour with George Eliot (Mrs. Lewes) on Sunday last [4 January 1880] at her house, I was very pleasantly disappointed in her appearance, having heard so much of the plainness of her features. And I found them only strong, intellectual, and *noble* – indeed, I have seldom seen a grander face! I have read somewhere that she looked like a horse – a great mistake, as, although her face is long and narrow, it is only as Dante's was. It expresses elevation of thought, kindness, power, and *humour*. It is at times not unlike Starr King's – excepting King's beautiful eyes. Mrs. Lewes's eyes are grey and sympathetic, but neither large nor beautiful. Her face lights up when she smiles and shows her large white teeth, and all thought of heaviness vanishes. She reminds you continually of a man – a bright, gentle, lovable, philosophical man – without being a bit *masculine*. Do you understand me?

Of course, her talk was charming. It was wise and sweet and humorous. It was like her books – or her written speech when she moralizes – but I thought it kinder and less hard than some of her satire.[1] She said many fine things to me about my work, and asked me to come again to see her, which was a better compliment, as she has since Lewes's death received no one.[2]

> To Anna Griswold Harte, his wife, 7 January 1880, in *The Letters of Bret Harte*, ed. by Geoffrey Bret Harte (Boston and New York: Houghton Mifflin, 1926), p. 163

NOTES

Bret Harte (Francis Brett Harte, 1836–1902) was an American journalist and writer best known for his morally pointed stories of local colour. Nicholas Trübner took him to meet GE (*Journals*, p. 194).

1. 'Then, though she had a very gentle voice and manner, there was, every now and then, just a suspicion of meek satire in her talk' (Locker-Lampson, *My Confidences*, p. 308).
2. Not of course strictly true. On the day after Harte's first visit (he returned at least twice), GE wrote that she was 'now seeing many other friends, who interest me and bring me reports of their several worlds' (*Letters*, vii, 241).

AT ODDS

Charles Waldstein

I

London. Jan. 1880. Had note from Mrs Lewes (G. Eliot) she would like to see me. Have been there this afternoon. She is looking very well. She received me in her gentle kind way. The type of English lady, soft voice, beautiful accent & intonation. I avoided recalling our past meetings, the absent dear Lewes & did not mention or wonder at her looking well. She wanted to know how I had been & where. Her face lighted up as I described my Greek travels. At any joke her face can smile so smilingly, while it is generally sad with all the world's woe on it. She said that Bret Harte had been there a little before. She liked him. She admired his early works very much: They e.g. Luck of Roaring Camp, showed how in lowest stage of civilisation laws which call forth subtle human qualities remain same. Now these rough men became gentlemen though before child & dead woman. I suggested that it also proved how such differentiated fruits of civilisation lie at deep foundations of human love. That the Gentleman rose out of loving man. – a fact frequently forgotten in later stages of civilization (as in State. Montesq[1]) We spoke abt. Am. Accent which she does not not [sic] like. It is provincial Engl, of puritanic time that has obtained in U.S. – did not dislike it in Provincial but in Am. exterior etc. was unprovincial thence discord. I wanted to convey to her that I was sorry Bret Harte had not outwardly, in his social position gained by social context, realised the point which his genius demanded. I wanted to say that he ought to stand socially as high as Longfellow & Sewell but was made little consul in Crefeld because of his debts etc. while Sewell ambassador.[2] This was a pity. I wanted to see poet (& he is true one) rank highest widely in America. This she would not understand – only point in which she is unsympathetic. Anything that throws any blame for irregularity in [?our] life on part of past or great intellect touches her sensitive nature subjectively & it is the only moment she fails in her great sympathy. She told me abt. poor proud & sensitive man who it appears she has been helping for some time & who is now out of work. Can write, but eye-sight failing. Family to sustain. Asked me whether I knew anything for him to do. Told her would try, perhaps write for me.[3] She was as tender to me as she was on several occasions 2 years ago & asked me to call soon again. (Jan. 5th 80).

II

Sunday Jan 18. Got up late. Wrote a few letters. Then had a visit from Kalm, then called on Mrs Lewes. A beautiful girl was there when I left. She left when I came in. I learnt afterwards that she had come to G.E. for moral support. The best priest to go to.[4] We spoke abt. mistaken ethics. She said how much harm was done by the idea "Love of God" irrespective of actions. It was a moral cancer in the flesh of Xians.[5] About the mistaken ways of girls that began to study. I told her my Spec. article.[6] How good [?she thought] it would be if these female students could learn the general connection between sciences & their bearing upon life. I suggested methodology as a term. Spoke between [sic] difference betw. actions & cognitions. Said that in ideal world, millions of years from now (if human race persisted till then) how it might be that there would not be the diff. between thought & action. No struggle. That cognition had so transfused us that we acted the true great & good without any effort. I told her the characteristic of Greek plastic mind. Diff. betw. Phidias & Michelangelo.[7] She agreed with me that Michelang. was the type of the great struggler. – She said that the East had been travelled over in Middle [A]ges [more] than we suppose. Spoke of the question with regard to influence of ritual on Buddhism. Whether from Xist. or Xian. from East. Said people needed extremes. Could not see similarity in two [several words illegible] that reciprocal influence. –

III

London Jan. 1880. I told her that I left her on last visit with discord in mood: 1st time that I had found her unsympathetic. Had not met me half-way in understanding as usual, but even not met me at all, with regard to Bret Harte. She said I spoke in generalities abt. individual cases & then difficult to understand me. This may be true. Told her again & she understood me. Asked whether she played still "Yes". Whether she wanted to play with me? "No" she drolely [sic] said. I asked her why – but I didn't want her to do anything disagreeable to her. I should really like to know why she does not want to when once *she* expressed the desire. – She also said in the course of conversat. that it was so difficult to make people with petty worlds understand the reality of the suffering that surrounds them.

Margaret Harris and Christopher Stray, 'Charles Waldstein Waits upon George Eliot', *GE-GHLS*, 44–5 (2003), 12–25 (pp. 16–17, 18–19); authors' brackets

NOTES

For Charles Waldstein, later Sir Charles Walston, see 'Sunday Gatherings at the Priory' in Part IV.

1. Evidently a reference to *The Spirit of the Laws* (1748), Book XXX, where Montesquieu treats the theory of feudal laws in relation to the establishment of the monarchy, tracing the origin of the aristocracy to rewards given for allegiance. I wish to thank Jeanne Holierhoek and Michelle Sikkes of the Montesquieu Institute for their assistance with this reference.

2. Harte had been made United States Consul in Crefeld, Rhenish Prussia, in 1878. Sewell seems to be an error for George Frederick Seward, US minister to China 1876–79, whose resignation was requested after threat of impeachment. Longfellow had been much celebrated in England, with honorary degrees from Oxford and Cambridge.

3. 'As emerges later in his diary, Waldstein did not follow through on the prospect of employing Robert Ripley, a clerk in whom Lewes had taken a particular interest and to whom George Eliot gave £10 about this time' (Harris and Stray, p. 16).

4. As Harris and Stray note, a 'Miss Streeter' called on this day (see *Journals*, p. 196). She may have been Florence Streeter, at this time eighteen years of age and the daughter of a nearby family (see Patrick Streeter, 'Florence Streeter and George Eliot', *GE-GHLS*, 56–7 (2009), 140). Kalm has remained untraced.

5. An idea elaborated in GE's 'Evangelical Teaching: Dr. Cumming', *Westminster Review* (1855), repr. in *Essays*, pp. 38–68, and in *Writings*, pp. 138–70.

6. 'Specialization as a Morbid Tendency of Our Time', *Minerva*, 1 (1880), 27–41 (Harris and Stray, p. 25).

7. Waldstein's first book was *Essays on the Art of Pheidias* (1885).

CRUSHED DAISIES

Caroline Lindsay

March 23rd 1880.
I have this afternoon returned from a visit to the Priory, my first since the death of Mr. Lewes. I found everything but little changed; the hostess, looking paler and more worn perhaps, and wearing a black and white cap, received me in her accustomed corner; the room was the same, a few visitors sat in the old places; I missed George Lewes and his cheery voice.[1] Mr. Tennyson came in; I had never made his acquaintance before; I had a long talk with him, which pleased me much. He was full of the fact that Ruskin had abused him for saying that a crushed daisy blushes red, i.e. that

it then shews the lower side of the petals. Mr. Ruskin had called this "a sentimental fallacy";[2] Mr. Tennyson averred that Mr. Ruskin had no knowledge of daisies. <Then> Now ensued a long conversation about flowers, in which our gentle-voiced hostess joined, too learnedly somewhat, as it appeared to me, to please Tennyson, who (I thought) was rather desirous to be amused than instructed. But perhaps he found some difficulty in understanding her, for Mrs. Lewes scarcely raises her voice above a whisper, and several times during his visit he repeated abruptly: 'I am very deaf, I am very deaf.'[3]

MS Diary, Tennyson Research Centre, fols 1–2, reproduced with kind permission of the Tennyson Research Centre; first publ. in 'The Diary of Lady Lindsay', *George Eliot Fellowship Review*, 17 (1986), pp. 62–3

NOTES

Caroline Blanche Elizabeth Lindsay, née FitzRoy, Lady Lindsay (1844–1912), was a writer and patron of the arts. With her husband Sir Coutts Lindsay (1824–1913) she founded the Grosvenor Gallery in 1877. (See the recollection by Marion Adams-Acton in 'Out and About in London' in Part IV.) This diary entry was copied out for Hallam Tennyson (who did not use it) when he was writing *Alfred Lord Tennyson: A Memoir by His Son* (1898).

1. In addition to Tennyson and Hallam, the guests included William Henry Hall, Charles Waldstein, Lady Lilford, and Thomas Littleton Powys, her son (*Journals*, p. 201).
2. Properly 'pathetic fallacy', coined by John Ruskin in *Modern Painters* III (1856) to denote the tendency to credit nature with human emotions. In *Sesame and Lilies* (1865) Ruskin had treated a passage from Tennyson's *Maud* (1855) – 'For her feet have touched the meadows | And left the daisies rosy' (ll. 434–5) – as an example of this fallacy.
3. In a subsequent paragraph, omitted here, Lady Lindsay notes that 'nobody talked about books' and wonders why it should be 'the lowest depth of bad manners, when conversing with a great literary light, to allude to his works' (fols 2, 3).

THE GIFT OF CONSCIENCE

Maud Southwood Lewes

It seemed so sad and quiet without him. The solemnity of the occasion left a lasting impression upon us, and I think George Eliot meant that it should be so, for she had got for me a medal with the head of Jan Huss. Drawing me up to her side she showed it to me, and gave in a few words the story of his life, and his death for conscience' sake. Then she put the medal into my hand and told me I was to keep it and to be prepared all through life to obey my conscience and do what was *right*. Her wonderfully beautiful, sad, deep voice made it all the more impressive, and I can hear it still.

Arthur Paterson, *George Eliot's Family Life and Letters*
(London: Selwyn & Blount, 1928), pp. 250–1

NOTE

Maud Southwood Lewes (1874–1931), later Mrs John Rowland Hopwood, was Charles Lewes's second daughter. The occasion recalled here may have been her sixth birthday, 30 March 1880 (*Journals*, p. 201).

'"ONLY A POOR WOMAN"'

Georgiana Burne-Jones

A few days before Edward left town we had a visit from George Eliot [on 23 April 1880], memorable because it was the last time we ever saw her. She came to say good-bye before going abroad, and after first sitting with Edward in the studio came down and talked with me.[1] Her manner was even gentler and more affectionate than usual, and she looked so unfit to do battle with daily life, that in spite of all her power a protecting feeling towards her rose in my heart. She seemed loth to go, and as if there was something that she would have said, yet did not. I have always remembered, though, the weariness she expressed of the way in which wisdom was attributed to her. "I am so tired of being set on a pedestal and expected to vent wisdom – I am only a poor woman" was the meaning of what she said if not the exact phrase, as I think it was.[2]

A fortnight later she wrote to tell us she was about to marry Mr. Cross.[3]

Memorials of Edward Burne-Jones, 2 vols (London: Macmillan, 1906),

II, 103–4

NOTES

For Georgiana Burne-Jones, see 'A Few Good Friends' in Part IV.

1. There is no record of their conversation, but a recollection by Anne Thackeray Ritchie, written in 1899, seems relevant here: 'Lady Burne-Jones ... says all her life she has made the greatest mistake of being too reserved. She said George Eliot once said to her, "Ah! say I love you, to those you love. The eternal silence is long enough to be silent in, and that awaits us all"' (*Thackeray and His Daughter: The Letters and Journals of Anne Thackeray Ritchie, with Many Letters of William Makepeace Thackeray*, ed. by Hester Thackeray Ritchie (New York and London: Harper, 1924), p. 270).

2. Also relevant, and also from Anne Thackeray Ritchie, who spoke with Charles Lewes just after GE's marriage: 'George Eliot said to him if she hadn't been human with feelings and failings like other people, how could she have written her books' (p. 196).

3. She wrote on 5 May (*Letters*, VII, 269) and married the next day. Florence Nightingale Eve, Cross's youngest sister, recalled GE at the ceremony: 'I had such a vision of her beautiful, radiant face this morning, as she came up that aisle in her elegant robes, looking like a queen, bless her' (letter to J.W. Cross, 7 May 1880, Yale).

Part VI
Mrs Cross
1880

A HONEYMOON LETTER

'Mrs S.'

In early youth Miss Evans had a keen sense of the ridiculous, but it wore away. ... To give you an idea how true this is, I will read you a phrase in one of the last letters she ever wrote. 'I am intensely happy. We (that is, Mr. Cross and herself) are sitting on the balcony overlooking the river. The scene is striking and impressive. Dark clouds are rising as if for a storm, yet everything is peaceful in the calm twilight. We are very happy. All we long for is the impossible. We wish that George Lewes was with us.'[1] When you consider that George Lewes was her first husband and only dead a year, and that 'we' includes a young and second husband, this phrase, which you can see in her own handwriting, is to me an evidence that she had no idea of the ludicrous, at any rate at this time of her life. ...

This was, I think, her worst fault – she was utterly lacking in impulse and did nothing on the spur of the moment. Now this is of course a virtue, but also, to my mind, a great defect, especially in a literary or artistic character.

R. Davey, 'Our London Letter', *Evening Mail*,
18 November 1881, p. 1

NOTES

Interviewed by Richard Davey and presenting herself as GE's lifelong friend, 'Mrs S.' has remained untraced. A recollection by Davey appears in 'Other Personal Meetings' in Part IV.

1. To my knowledge this letter has not been found. One is tempted to doubt it, except that Davey, a responsible journalist, clearly implies here that it was shown to him. Further, on their wedding journey through France and Italy, GE and Cross did go to places she had visited with GHL. From Grenoble she wrote to Charles Lewes: 'I had but one regret in seeing the sublime beauty of the Grande Chartreuse. It was, that the Pater had not seen it. I would still give up my own life willingly if he could have the happiness instead of me' (*Letters*, VII, 283).

THE INFLUENCE OF BEAUTY

Caroline Jebb

We found the Sidgwicks still staying on at Six Mile Bottom [on 5 September 1880], to our joy. The Crosses might have been too much for us in their new felicity. George Eliot old as she is, and ugly, really looked very sweet and winning in spite of both. She was dressed in a short soft dark satin walking dress with a lace wrap half shading the body – a costume most artistically designed to show her slenderness, yet hide the squareness of age. I thought of what Mrs. Lionel [Tennyson] had told me – how George Eliot had been seen at all the fashionable milliners & dressmakers in London, choosing her trousseau. Whatever money & taste could do, to make her look not too unsuitable a bride for a man of forty, had been done.[1] In the evening she made me feel sad for her. There was not a person in the drawing room, Mr. Cross included, whose mother she might not have been, and I thought she herself felt depressed at the knowledge that nothing could make her young again; to her we were all young and of a later generation. She adores her husband, and it seemed to me, it hurt her a little to have him talk so much to me. It made her, in her pain, <a> slightly irritated & snappish, which I did not mind, feeling that what troubled her was beyond remedy. He may forget the twenty years difference between them but she never can. I feel myself, sometimes, when with a lot of young people, <how> a vague sadness at the knowledge that they are increasing and I am decreasing, that they are just beginning a life almost over for me, which I found & still find very pleasant.[2] It must be a hundred times worse for George Eliot, who cares about success of all kinds a good deal more than I ever could. You can see by her books how much strength of intellect she devotes to showing the emptiness and heartlessness of beauty; and it is said by her friends that she never has heartily liked a pretty woman. If ever she did wrong in her life, I am afraid she will suffer enough now to make atonement; not that Mr. Cross is apparently not devoted to her, but such a marriage is against nature. She will never be happy when she sees him talking to other people, and she will constantly realize that no power on earth can make her a suitable wife for him. If power *could* do it, she would succeed. She has always cared much more for men than for women, and has cultivated every art to make herself attractive – feeling bitterly all the time what a struggle it was, without beauty, whose influence she exaggerates as do all ugly people. Mr. Cross I liked very much. He is tall, finelooking, a good talker, altogether an exceptionally interesting man. I don't now believe the story that Eleanor B. had heard, that he had tried to drown himself; and for all I could see, he is content enough.[3]

Letter to Ellen Reynolds DuPuy, her sister, [7 September 1880], MS Lady Caroline Lane Reynolds Slemmer Jebb Papers, Sophia Smith Collection,

Smith College, reproduced with kind permission of the Sophia Smith
Collection; publ. with alterations and omissions in Mary Reed Bobbitt,
With Dearest Love to All: The Life and Letters of Lady Jebb
(London: Faber, 1960), pp. 163–4.

NOTES

Caroline Lane Slemmer Jebb, née Reynolds, Lady Jebb (1840–1930), an American
of great beauty, probably met GE in Cambridge in 1877. A recollection by her
husband, Sir Richard Claverhouse Jebb, appears in 'Eton, Cambridge, and Oxford' in
Part IV.

1. Visiting GE three months later, Soph'ia V. Kovalevskaia gained a different impres-
   sion: 'She appeared even younger than before, although she clearly had not
   the slightest wish to look younger, no anxiety or care about her appearance'
   ('A Memoir of George Eliot', trans. and introd. by Miriam Haskell Berlin, *Yale
   Review*, 73 (1984), 533–50 (p. 547)). Other friends too found her 'a changed
   woman; she was more natural, more cheerful, happier' (Frederick Locker-Lampson,
   My Confidences: An Autobiographical Sketch Addressed to My Descendants [ed. by
   Augustine Birrell] (London: Smith, Elder, 1896), pp. 317–18) – for example,
   Caroline Holland, who lived near Witley and saw her playing lawn tennis with
   Charles Lewes's children (*The Notebooks of a Spinster Lady 1878–1903* (London:
   Cassell, 1919), p. 182). GE herself felt Cross's love and his family's affection as
   'wonderful blessing falling to me beyond my share after I had thought that my
   life was ended and that, so to speak, my coffin was ready for me in the next room'
   (*Letters*, VII, 291).
2. Lady Jebb was forty years old; GE was nearing sixty-one, and would die fifteen
   weeks later.
3. Eleanor B. is Eleanor Sidgwick (née Balfour); the story is that on his honeymoon
   in Venice Cross jumped into the Grand Canal, an item of gossip in its day later
   accepted by Haight, p. 544, on the basis of a note by Lord Acton. Recently Brenda
   Maddox has presented firm evidence – Venetian newspaper coverage and the
   police report – that the incident did in fact occur (*George Eliot: Novelist, Lover, Wife*
   (London: Harper, 2009), pp. 215–17). At the time the story acquired a life of its
   own. On Christmas Day 1880, three days after GE's death, the *Examiner* retailed
   it, adding that Cross 'survived, but only to be placed in a *maison de santé* [lunatic
   asylum]' ('Political and Social Notes', p. 1421). In March 1881 the story reached
   Cosima Wagner in yet another form: GE had married Cross because he tried to
   commit suicide from love of her, and after her death was having bouts of madness
   (*Cosima Wagners Briefe an Ihre Tochter Daniela von Bülow 1866–1885*, ed. by Max
   Freiherrn von Waldberg (Stuttgart and Berlin: Cotta, 1933), p. 173). Cross himself
   mentions being 'thoroughly ill' in Venice from 'continual bad air, and the complete and sudden deprivation of all bodily exercise' (*Life*, III, 408) – an explanation
   compatible, incidentally, with what Hallam Tennyson heard in Venice shortly after
   the incident and reported to his mother: 'Cross had caught a fever on the Lakes &
   he jumped into the Canal here according to our porters account to cool his fever &
   was not far off being slain' (letter to Emily Sellwood Tennyson, 23 June 1880,
   MS Alfred Tennyson Collection, Beinecke Rare Book and Manuscript Library, Yale
   University).

'A KIND OF SAINT'

Benjamin Jowett

Mrs. Cross
– no trace of laxity of any kind in her conversation.
– sad & isolated in a crowd.[1]
– very sensitive to public opinion & the "Babel of voices" – she seemed as if she
wanted to keep herself from that – never read what was written of her.
– she was a kind of saint without a definite creed
a sweet voice & soft sad humour – quite capable of 'biting' but never doing
so homely but motherly features[2]

Notebook, *19 – 79–80 80–1*, Balliol College Library,
Oxford University, MS I/H40, fol. 62^r, reproduced with kind
permission of the Jowett Copyright Trustees

NOTES

For Benjamin Jowett, see 'Eton, Cambridge, and Oxford' in Part IV. Other recollections
by him appear in Part III, in 'The Countryside' in Part IV, in Part V, and in Part VII.

1. I have found no record of a meeting between GE and Jowett after 16 December
   1879 (*Journals*, p. 188), when she was not yet 'Mrs. Cross'. This reference to a
   crowd may indicate that they met at the London performance by Oxford undergraduates of Aeschylus's *Agamemnon* on 17 December 1880. In a letter to Arthur
   Penrhyn Stanley, 29 December 1880, Jowett notes that she was there (MS I/F5/16,
   fol. 2), but of course Cross may have told him that.
2. One of GE's obituaries has a similar description: 'A remarkable motherliness of
   look was, indeed, what most distinguished her personal appearance: and this alone
   gave to her a certain beauty, in spite of the large, massive, homely features of her
   face' ('George Eliot', *St James's Gazette*, 24 December 1880, pp. 3–4 (p. 4)). The
   anonymous writer was probably Frederick Greenwood, who founded the *Gazette*
   in May 1880 and had known GE since *c*.1866.

'THANK YOU'

Violet Greville

Another time my aunt took me to see George Eliot.[1] Her fame was great, and
she was at the zenith of her reputation, having just married Mr. Cross, her new
husband. I thought her face rather like that of a horse, and her manner stiff and
cold. Presently she seemed distraite, and kept looking out of the window. "That,"
she said, pointing to the winding walk leading up from the valley, "that is the
way the beloved one comes." She sighed with content. It seemed to my innocent
young mind rather a foolish speech for a woman of genius to make. ...

On this fateful interview my aunt suggested that as George Eliot was very
fond of music, I should sing her something. I was very nervous, but managed

to get through a little song by Lord Henry Somerset, whose music was very popular in drawing-rooms, and was set to words by Miss Christina Rossetti, beginning: "When I am dead, my dearest, sing no sad songs for me."[2] I sang rather prettily and hoped to hear a few words of praise. George Eliot made no remark except "Thank you." Altogether, I don't think I was a success that day, and though I wrote her a nice little letter thanking her for seeing me and saying how much I adored and appreciated her work, she never sent me a line in return. I was very much disappointed, for in my youthful ardour I had almost deified her as an author.

Vignettes of Memory (London: Hutchinson, [1927]), p. 143

NOTES

Lady Beatrice Violet Greville, née Graham (1842–1932), was a novelist and miscellaneous writer best known for her book *The Gentlewoman in Society* (1892).

1. Sabine Matilda (Mrs Richard) Greville lived in Milford Cottage, near Witley. The date of the visit recalled here is uncertain, but GE noted a visit by Mrs Greville on 16 September 1880 (*Journals*, p. 211).

2. The first two lines of her 'Song', perhaps 'oftener quoted, and certainly oftener set to music' than her other verse (William Michael Rossetti, *The Poetical Works of Christina Georgina Rossetti* (London: Macmillan, 1928), pp. 477–8).

RECOLLECTIONS OF MARRIED LIFE

J.W. Cross

I

We generally began our reading at Witley with some chapters of the Bible, which was a very precious and sacred Book to her, not only from early associations, but also from the profound conviction of its importance in the development of the religious life of man. She particularly enjoyed reading aloud some of the finest chapters of Isaiah, Jeremiah, and St Paul's Epistles. With a naturally rich, deep voice, rendered completely flexible by constant practice; with the keenest perception of the requirements of emphasis; and with the most subtle modulations of tone, – her reading threw a glamour over indifferent writing, and gave to the greatest writing fresh meanings and beauty. The Bible and our elder English poets best suited the organ-like tones of her voice, which required, for their full effect, a certain solemnity and majesty of rhythm. Her reading of Milton was especially fine; and I shall never forget four great lines of the "Samson Agonistes" to which it did perfect justice –

> "But what more oft in nations grown corrupt,
> And by their vices brought to servitude,
> Than to love bondage more than liberty, –
> Bondage with ease than strenuous liberty." [ll. 268–71]

The delighted conviction of justice in the thought – the sense of perfect accord between thought, language, and rhythm – stimulated the voice of the reader to find the exactly right tone. Such reading requires for its perfection a rare union of intellectual, moral, and physical qualities. It cannot be imitated. It is an art, like singing – a personal possession that dies with the possessor, and leaves nothing behind except a memory. Immediately before her illness we had read, together, the First Part of "Faust."[1] Reading the poem in the original with such an interpreter was the opening of a new world to me. Nothing in all literature moved her more than the pathetic situation and the whole character of Gretchen.[2] It touched her more than anything in Shakspeare. During the time that we were reading the "Faust," we were also constantly reading, together, Shakspeare, Milton, and Wordsworth: some of Scott's novels and Lamb's essays too, in which she greatly delighted. For graver study we read through Professor Sayce's 'Introduction to the Science of Language.' Philology was a subject in which she was most deeply interested; and this was my first experience of what seemed to me a limitless persistency in application. I had noticed the persistency before, whilst looking at pictures, or whilst hearing her play difficult music; for it was characteristic of her nature that she took just as great pains to play her very best to a single unlearned listener, as most performers would do to a room full of critical *cognoscenti*. Professor Sayce's book was the first which we had read together requiring very sustained attention (the 'Divina Commedia' we had read in very short bits at a time), and it revealed to me more clearly the depth of George Eliot's mental concentration. Continuous thought did not fatigue her. She could keep her mind on the stretch hour after hour: the body might give way, but the brain remained unwearied.

Her memory held securely her great stores of reading. Even of light books her recollections were always crisp, definite, and vivid. On our way home from Venice, after my illness, we were reading French novels of Cherbuliez, Alphonse Daudet, Gustave Droz, George Sand.[3] Most of these books she had read years before, and I was astonished to find what clear-cut, accurate impressions had been retained, not only of all the principal characters, but also of all the subsidiary personages – even their names were generally remembered. But, on the other hand, her verbal memory was not always to be depended on. She never could trust herself to write a quotation without verifying it.

II

During our short married life, our time was so much divided between travelling and illness that George Eliot wrote very little, so that I have but slight personal experience of how the creative effort affected her. But she told me that, in all that she considered her best writing, there was a "not herself" which took possession of her, and that she felt her own personality to be merely the instrument through which this spirit, as it were, was acting. Particularly she

dwelt on this in regard to the scene in [Chapter 81 of] 'Middlemarch' between Dorothea and Rosamond, saying that, although she always knew they had, sooner or later, to come together, she kept the idea resolutely out of her mind until Dorothea was in Rosamond's drawing-room. Then, abandoning herself to the inspiration of the moment, she wrote the whole scene exactly as it stands, without alteration or erasure, in an intense state of excitement and agitation, feeling herself entirely possessed by the feelings of the two women.[4] Of all the characters she had attempted, she found Rosamond's the most difficult to sustain. With this sense of "possession," it is easy to imagine what the cost to the author must have been of writing books, each of which has its tragedy.

III

She was keenly anxious to redress injustices to women, and to raise their general status in the community. This, she thought, could best be effected by women improving their work – ceasing to be amateurs. But it was one of the most distinctly marked traits in her character, that she particularly disliked everything generally associated with the idea of a "masculine woman." She was, and as a woman she wished to be, above all things feminine – "so delicate with her needle, and an admirable musician."[5] She was proud, too, of being an excellent housekeeper – an excellence attained from knowing how things ought to be done, from her early training, and from an inborn habit of extreme orderliness. Nothing offended her more than the idea that because a woman had exceptional intellectual powers, therefore it was right that she should absolve herself, or be absolved, from her ordinary household duties.

It will have been seen from the letters that George Eliot was deeply interested in the higher education of women, and that she was amongst the earliest contributors to Girton College.[6] After meeting Mr and Mrs Henry Sidgwick, in September 1880, when they had gone to reside at the new hall of Newnham College for a time, she was anxious to be associated in that work also, but she did not live to carry out the plan herself. The danger she was alive to in the system of collegiate education, was the possible weakening of the bonds of family affection and family duties. In her view, the family life holds the roots of all that is best in our mortal lot; and she always felt that it is far too ruthlessly sacrificed in the case of English *men* by their public school and university education, and that much more is such a result to be deprecated in the case of women. But, the absolute good being unattainable in our mixed condition of things, those women especially who are obliged to earn their own living, must do their best with the opportunities at their command, as "they cannot live with posterity," when a more perfect system may prevail. Therefore George Eliot wished God-speed to the women's colleges. It was often in her mind and on her lips that the only worthy end of all learning, of all science, of all life, in fact, is, that human beings should love one another better. Culture merely for culture's sake can never be anything but a sapless root, capable of producing at best a shrivelled branch.

Life, III, 419–22, 424–5, 427–9

NOTES

For John Walter Cross, see Part I. Other recollections by him appear below in this part, in 'The Continent' in Part IV, and in Part V.

1. She suffered a renal attack (one of many) on 19 September 1880, but within two months began to regain strength (*Journals*, p. 213).
2. The climax of Part I of Goethe's *Faust* portrays the seduction and abandonment of an uncultured woman by a man socially and intellectually her superior, followed by her imprisonment for infanticide and her death. Richard Simpson early noted the parallels with Hetty Sorrel in *Adam Bede* ('George Eliot's Novels', *Home and Foreign Review* (1863), repr. in *Critical Heritage*, pp. 221–50). The influence of *Faust* upon GE's fiction has been traced extensively; see Gerlinde Röder-Bolton, *George Eliot and Goethe: An Elective Affinity* (Amsterdam: Rodopi, 1998), esp. pp. 99–162.
3. GE's journals and letters cite titles only for George Sand, whose work she knew well.
4. Examining the MS, Jerome Beaty finds that GE planned this chapter just as she did others and revised it 'in all stages of its evolution and in almost all its aspects: timing, content, point of view, characterization, tone, and outcome' (*'Middlemarch' from Notebook to Novel: A Study of George Eliot's Creative Method*, Illinois Studies in Language and Literature, 47 (Urbana: University of Illinois Press, 1960), p. 123). The fiction of GE's 'perfect' manuscripts was popular both before and after Cross's *Life*. An example: 'One day Lewes took me into his library to show me her manuscripts ... They were written without a single erasure, in a very small neat handwriting, and Lewes told me her method with her work was to think out a chapter and then write it straight off, and no corrections were necessary' (Maria Theresa Earle, *Memoirs and Memories* (London: Smith, Elder, 1911), pp. 285–6).
5. Othello's description of Desdemona in Shakespeare's *Othello*, IV.1.
6. In March 1868 she contributed £50 (*Letters*, VIII, 414).

THE LOGIC OF DEATH

Soph'ia V. Kovalevskaia

After her marriage, George Eliot moved to a different house.[1] The room in which she now received me [in December 1880, some two weeks before her death] was wonderfully cosy, as though intended for quiet, intimate conversations. Half study, half library, with some soft, very comfortable armchairs and many books and prints on the table, on shelves hanging on every bit of free wall space – this room was incomparably more suitable to her than the formal, rather banal salon in which I had first met her. She told me that this was their favorite room in the house, and that she and her husband spent their whole day here reading, working, or talking. Indeed, they gave the impression of two good friends with common tastes, habits, and occupations, where the younger completely admires the older.

Our conversation touched on literature in general and then turned to George Eliot's work. She told me that each time she begins to publish a new novel she is besieged with masses of letters from people unknown to her; some give advice on how to develop the plot, on how to resolve various complex situations; others assure her that they recognize themselves and their acquaintances among her heroes and heroines. "For example," she said, "when I published *Middlemarch*, three young women paid me the compliment of suggesting that I had divined their most secret thoughts and put them into the mouth of my Dorothea. I asked each of these interesting ladies to send me her photograph. Alas, how little they resembled, at least in appearance, the heroine as I had imagined her myself. There was also a happy father who assured me that I must have met his two daughters somewhere, otherwise I could not have described the egotistical Rosamund with such truth and precision."

I pointed out to George Eliot that I was always struck by one characteristic feature in her novels: all her heroes and heroines die at an appropriate time, just at the very moment when the psychological intrigue is becoming complex, reaching the point of maximum tension. When the reader wants to know how life will unravel the consequences of this or that action, a sudden death unties the knot. ...

All this I said to George Eliot.[2] She listened to me very seriously and then responded. "In what you say there is an element of truth; I will ask you only one question. Have you not noticed that in life this is the way it really happens? I personally cannot refrain from the conviction that death is more logical than is usually thought. When in life the situation becomes strained beyond measure, when there is no exit anywhere, when the most sacred obligations contradict one another, then death appears; and, suddenly, it opens new paths which no one had thought of before; it reconciles what had seemed irreconcilable. Many times it has happened that faith in death has given me the courage to live."

'A Memoir of George Eliot', trans. and introd. by Miriam Haskell Berlin, *Yale Review*, 73 (1984), pp. 547–8, 550 © 1984 by The Yale Review; reproduced with permission of Blackwell Publishing Ltd

NOTES

For Soph'ia Kovalevskaia, see 'Other Personal Meetings' in Part IV. Another recollection by her appears in 'Sunday Gatherings at the Priory' in Part IV.

1. 4 Cheyne Walk, Chelsea, on 4 December 1880. William Bell Scott, who lived nearby, lovingly describes the 'idyllic life' of the neighbourhood at this time, 'in many respects like a quiet country town': 'The old woman who called watercresses; the groggy old gentleman whom the boys waylaid, and induced to chase them

with his brandished stick; and the ancient barber, too, who actually still had daily customers whom he shaved, was to be met on his beat, with brush, comb, etc., peeping out of the pocket of his snow-white apron' (*Autobiographical Notes of the Life of William Bell Scott*, ed. by W. Minto, 2 vols (New York: Harper, 1892; repr. New York: AMS Press, [1970]), II, 247–8).

2. Kovalevskaia mentions the difficult circumstances resolved by the ending of *The Mill on the Floss*, by Casaubon's death in *Middlemarch*, and by Grandcourt's death in *Daniel Deronda*.

FINAL ILLNESS AND DEATH

J.W. Cross

On the afternoon of Friday the 17th December, we went to see the "Agamemnon" performed in Greek by Oxford undergraduates.[1] The representation was a great enjoyment – an exciting stimulus – and my wife proposed that during the winter we should read together some of the great Greek dramas. The following afternoon we went to the Saturday Popular Concert at St James's Hall. It was a cold day. The air in the hall was overheated, and George Eliot allowed a fur cloak which she wore to slip from her shoulders. I was conscious of a draught, and was afraid of it for her, as she was very sensitive to cold. I begged her to resume the cloak, but, smiling, she whispered that the room was really too hot.[2] In the evening she played through several of the pieces that we had heard at the concert,[3] with all her accustomed enjoyment of the piano, and with a touch as true and as delicate as ever. On Sunday there was very slight trouble in the throat, but not sufficient to prevent her from coming down-stairs to breakfast as usual. In the afternoon she was well enough to receive visits from Mr Herbert Spencer and one or two other friends. ...

Little more remains to be told. On Monday the doctor[4] treated the case as one of laryngeal sore throat; and when Dr Andrew Clark came for consultation on Wednesday evening, the pericardium was found to be seriously affected. Whilst the doctors were at her bedside, she had just time to whisper to me, "Tell them I have great pain in the left side," before she became unconscious. Her long illness in the autumn had left her no power to rally. She passed away, about ten o'clock at night, on the 22d December 1880.

She died, as she would herself have chosen to die, without protracted pain, and with every faculty brightly vigorous.[5]

Life, III, 437–9

NOTES

For John Walter Cross, see Part I. Other recollections by him appear above in this part, in 'The Continent' in Part IV, and in Part V.

1. In St George's Hall, London, on the 16th, 17th, and 18th; first mounted in June at Balliol College by Francis Robert Benson (New College), who took the role of Clytemnestra. Six students played the separate parts, while fourteen others performed the choruses, abridged and 'divided amongst the performers; some bits were chanted Gregorian-wise, others solemnly recited; and so ingeniously was the whole managed, that there was no apparent weariness in an audience of which at least a quarter were ladies professedly ignorant of Greek, while two-thirds of the remainder were actually in much the same condition' ('The Antiquary's Note-Book', *Antiquary*, 3 (1881), 86–8 (p. 86)).
2. Sir Edmund Gosse, who sat just behind her, recalls in contrast that the room was chilly, and describes her 'in manifest discomfort, drawing up and tightening round her shoulders a white wool shawl' (*Aspects and Impressions* (London: Cassell, 1922), p. 2).
3. Her beloved Beethoven's Sonata No. 4 in E flat major, op. 7, with an encore of Chopin's Nocturne in E flat major, op. 55, no. 2, the only works for solo piano, played by Eugen d'Albert. The full programme, including performers, appears in 'Musical Intelligence: Saturday Popular Concerts', *Musical Standard*, n.s. 19 (1880), 401.
4. George Welland Mackenzie, an old pupil of Clark's (*Letters*, VII, 351 *n*. 2; Haight, p. 548).
5. Cross's sister Emily Helen Otter wrote to him on 27 December: 'What a comfort she had no pain, also that it was not a long lingering illness a death in life, which she had such a horror of the darling I truly loved her and am so thankful we had that time with her here, her words & her music keep ringing in my ears' (Yale). GE and Cross had visited the Otters at Ranby four months earlier (*Journals*, pp. 210–11).

'SURELY AN EXTRAORDINARY WOMAN'

Henry James

I paid John Cross a longish visit some little time since and sat in his poor wife's empty chair, in the beautiful little study they had just made perfect, while he told me, very frankly, many interesting things about her. She was surely an extraordinary woman – her intellectual force and activity have, I suspect, never been equalled in any woman. If, with these powers, she had only been able to see and know more of life, she would have done greater things. As for the head itself, it was evidently of the first order – capable of almost *any* responsibilities. She led a wonderfully *large* intellectual life – and Cross said that her memory and her absolute exemption from the sense of fatigue, were more amazing the more he knew her.[1] He, poor fellow, is left very much lamenting; but my private impression is that if she had not died, she would have killed him.[2] He couldn't keep up the intellectual pace – all Dante and Goethe, Cervantes and the Greek tragedians. As he said himself, it was a cart-horse yoked to a racer ...

To Alice James, his sister, 30 January 1881, in *Henry James Letters*, ed. by Leon Edel, 4 vols (Cambridge, Mass.: Belknap Press of Harvard University Press, 1974–84), II, 337

NOTES

For Henry James, see 'Other Personal Meetings' in Part IV. He reviewed Cross's *Life* in *Atlantic Monthly* (1885), repr. in James's *Partial Portraits* (London: Macmillan, 1888), pp. 37–62, and in *Critical Heritage*, pp. 490–504.

1. '[Cross] was talking to Fanny Kemble the other day about George Eliot and her wonderful genius. He said that her mind was always on the stretch, and the only recreation she seemed to require was a change of subject for thought and talk' (*Echoes of the 'Eighties: Leaves from the Diary of a Victorian Lady*, intro. by Wilfred Partington (London: Nash, 1921), pp. 18–19). Kemble herself reportedly said that a day with GE and GHL wore her '"to a thread"' (Lucy Walford, *Memories of Victorian London* (New York: Longmans, Green; London: Arnold, 1912), p. 145); but for her spirited defence of GE's personal life, see Augustus J.C. Hare, *The Story of My Life*, 6 vols (London: Allen, 1896–1900), v, 454.

2. Sir Edward Marsh recounts James's 'pensive answer to someone who asked what he supposed George Eliot's husband, J.W. Cross, to have felt when she died: "Regret ... remorse ... RELIEF"' (*A Number of People: A Book of Reminiscences* (London: Heinemann, 1939), p. 118).

Part VII
Postscripts
1880–81

'MOST DISMAL DAY'

James Thomson

With T.R.W. & Percy to George Eliot's funeral.[1] Most dismal day, drizzle settling into heavy rain – 3/4 hour waiting at the grave: we secured footing on a plank; other outsiders on swampy clay & drenched clay-sward. No arrangements for comfort save broken red brick up path to grave, & sawdusted planks for mourning-coach intimates & reporters.[2] For distinguished people present see newspapers.[3] Dr Sadler conducted service in Chapel & mumbled something over grave – scarcely a word to be caught at two yards' distance. Coffin polished oak, covered with camellias & a few violets & lilies of the valley. Brick sarcophagus, to be lidded. It struck me no pauper's funeral could be more dismal. Nothing to see but expanded umbrellas.

Journal, 29 December 1880, in Tom Leonard, *Places of the Mind:*
The Life and Work of James Thomson ('B.V.') (London: Cape, 1993), p. 245

NOTES

James Thomson, formerly Thompson (1834–82, *ODNB*), a Scottish poet who published under the pseudonym 'B.V.', was best known for 'The City of Dreadful Night' (1874). When he sent it to GE, she told him that she admired its 'distinct vision and grand utterance', but hoped for 'a wider embrace of human fellowship' in his future work (*Letters*, VI, 53).

1. On 29 December 1880 in Highgate Cemetery. Thomson's friends Theodore R. Wright and Percy Holyoake accompanied him.

2. Moncure Daniel Conway reported that the cemetery 'became a sticky bog ... and some ladies fell prostrate in the mud while trying to get near the grave. There were about four hundred persons ... [and] only a hundred could crowd into the little gothic chapel' ('London Letters', *Cincinnati Commercial*, 14 January 1881, p. 4). Oddly, Oscar Browning remarks both that the crowd was 'orderly and respectful' (Browning, p. 138) and that it 'demonstrated' against the doctors' 'apparent negligence' (*Memories of Sixty Years at Eton Cambridge and Elsewhere* (London: Lane, 1910), p. 291). John Tyndall observed that the crowd was 'reverent' (John Fiske, *Life and Letters of Edward Livingston Youmans: Comprising Correspondence with Spencer, Huxley, Tyndall, and Others* (London: Chapman & Hall, 1894), p. 366).

3. For example, 'Funeral of "George Eliot"', *Daily News*, 30 December 1880, p. 2, which includes Thomas Sadler's address. Haight, pp. 549–50, lists the most famous persons attending.

'SHE SEEMED TO LIVE UPON AIR'

'An intimate friend'

... I am absolutely convinced of this, that no one of her younger friends – I might almost add, of her acquaintances – failed to feel in her presence, that they were for the time, at all events, raised into a higher moral level, and that none ever left her without feeling inspired with a stronger sense of duty and positively under the obligation of striving to live up to a higher standard of life.[1] George Eliot's personality was fully as great and as remarkable as her books. In every line of her face there was power, and about the jaw and mouth a prodigious massiveness, which might well have inspired awe, had it not been tempered by the most gracious smile which ever lighted up human features, and was ever ready to convert what otherwise might have been terror into fascination. Whatever George Eliot's religious opinions may have been – and it may perhaps surprise those who did not know her intimately to learn that the "De imitatione Christi" was one of her favourite books, found by the writer lying on her table by her empty chair after her death[2] – she possessed to a marvellous degree the divine gift of charity, and of attracting moral outcasts to herself, whose devils she cast out, if I may be permitted the expression, by shutting her eyes to their existence. In her presence you felt wrapped round by an all-embracing atmosphere of sympathy and readiness to make the least of all your shortcomings, and the most of any good which might be in you. But great as was her personality, she shrank with horror from intruding it upon you, and, in general society, her exquisitely melodious voice was, unhappily for the outside circle, too seldom raised beyond the pitch of something not much above a whisper. Of the rich vein of humour which runs through George Eliot's works, there was comparatively little trace in her conversation, which seldom descended from the grave to the gay. But although she rarely indulged in conversational levity herself, she was most tolerant of it, and even encouraged its ebullition in others, joining heartily in any mirth which might be going on. George Eliot's sensibility on the subject of her own works was so exquisite that she would not tolerate the faintest allusion to them in general society. An extraordinary delicacy pervaded her whole being. She seemed to live upon air, and the rest of her body was as light and fragile as her countenance and intellect were massive.

'The Late George Eliot', *Daily News*,
27 December 1880, p. 3[3]

NOTES

The anonymous writer of this recollection avows to have been GE's 'intimate friend' for twelve years before her death. Among the persons who met her *c.*1868, perhaps the most likely candidate is Margaret Holland (see Part III), but there is no real evidence.

1. In her obituary of GE, Edith Simcox offers a refreshing variation upon this often-sounded theme of her ability to inspire others: 'To love her was a strenuous pleasure', Simcox says, 'for in spite of the tenderness for all human weakness that was natural to her, and the scrupulous charity of her overt judgments, the fact remained that her natural standard was ruthlessly out of reach, and it was a painful discipline for her friends to feel that she was compelled to lower it to suit their infirmities' ('George Eliot', *Nineteenth Century*, 9 (1881), 778–801 (p. 785)).

2. A claim causing some commotion in the newspapers; see K.K. Collins, *Identifying the Remains: George Eliot's Death in the London Religious Press*, English Literary Studies Monograph Series, 94 (Victoria: ELS Editions, 2006), pp. 33–47. Cross presented a copy of the *Imitation* to GE on their wedding day (now in the Beinecke Rare Book and Manuscript Library, Yale University), and C. Kegan Paul says that in December 1880 he sent GE a copy of his new edition of the work only to learn that it 'reached the house in time to be laid on her coffin' (*Memories* (London: Paul, Trench, 1899), p. 337). (Edith Simcox, however, reports seeing it marked in GE's hand (*Shirtmaker*, p. 160).) The book plays a significant role in *The Mill on the Floss*, where Maggie Tulliver's incomplete understanding of its meaning leads her to believe that renunciation can bring happiness (Volume II, Book Fourth, Chapter 3).

3. For the record, eleven main-entry recollections in previous parts of this volume come from obituaries of GE or newspaper or journal items published shortly after her death: in Part I, these are by Alfred L. Scrivener, 'the child of a schoolmate', and 'a correspondent'; in Part II, by Susanna Chapman and Noah Porter; in Part III, by Janet Ruutz-Rees; and in Part IV, by Julia Wedgwood, Kate Field, Edith Simcox, W.H. Hall, and Peter Bayne. George W. Smalley's recollection, next, also comes from an obituary. Four other obituaries of GE contain brief personal accounts of her, omitted here because they add no new information or insight: 'George Eliot', *Christian World and News of the Week*, 30 December 1880, p. 869; 'The Late George Eliot', *Truth*, 30 December 1880, pp. 852–3; 'George Eliot', *Academy*, 8 January 1881, pp. 27–8; and 'George Eliot', *Blackwood's Edinburgh Magazine*, 129 (1881), 255–68 (p. 267).

SCORN AND HUMILITY

George W. Smalley

She was tall, gaunt, angular, without any flowing ease of motion, though with a self-possession and firmness of muscle and fibre which saved her from the shambling awkwardness often the characteristic of long and loose-jointed people. There was no want of power in her movements nor in the expression of her elongated visage, to the lower part of which went plenty of jaw and decision of contour. She was altogether a personage whom at first sight the beholder must regard with respect, and whom, upon further acquaintance, it was perfectly possible to find attractive, not from her talk only, which was full, but from her mere external appearance and still more from her expression and the animation of her face. Her eyes were, when she talked, luminous and beautiful, dark in colour and of that unfathomable depth and swift changefulness which are seldom to be seen in the same orbs, except in persons whose force of character and force of intellect are both remarkable. They could be very soft, and she smiled with her eyes as well as with that large mouth of hers; and the smile was full of loveliness when it did not turn to mocking or mark that contemptuous mood which was not, I gather, very infrequent with her.[1] In conversation which did not wake this demon of scornfulness, born of conscious intellectual superiority, the face was full of vivacity and light, whether illuminated by a smile or not. I have seen it, when she was talking on a subject that moved her, irradiated and suffused with deep feeling.

She had her humble moods too. Boldly controverting everybody else, leading the talk, often monopolising it, always confident, sometimes despotic, she bowed herself before Lewes in a humility that on occasions was positively distressing to her friends.[2]

'George Eliot', in *London Letters and Some Others*, 2 vols (London: Macmillan, 1890), I, 282–90 (pp. 289–90); first publ. in *New-York Daily Tribune*, 9 January 1881, p. 5

NOTES

An American journalist, George Washburn Smalley (1833–1916) worked in London from 1867 until 1895. He says that although he never called at the Priory, he 'met George Eliot perhaps a dozen times' (p. 283).

1. Blind notes that a 'keen observer of human nature' (unidentified) thought that Laurence's portrait of GE 'conveyed no indication of the infinite depth of her observant eye, nor of that cold, subtle, and unconscious cruelty of expression which might occasionally be detected there' (pp. 207–8). See also Sir Leslie Stephen's recollection in 'Sunday Gatherings at the Priory' in Part IV.
2. Louise Chandler Moulton reports being told by GE's friends that 'she never argued any point directly' with GHL but instead shaped her disagreement 'as a question, a suggestion, never with the positiveness of an assertion' (*Ourselves and Our Neighbors: Short Chats on Social Topics* (Boston: Roberts, 1894), p. 84).

HARNESSED PASSION

Edith Simcox

Her character seemed to include every possibility of action and emotion: no human passion was wanting in her nature, there were no blanks or negations; and the marvellous thing was to see how, in this wealth of impulses and desires, there was no crash of internal discord, no painful collisions with other human interests outside; how, in all her life, passions of volcanic strength were harnessed in the service of those nearest her, and so inspired by the permanent instinct of devotion to her kind, that it seemed as if it were by their own choice they spent themselves there only where their force was welcome. Her very being was a protest against the opposing and yet cognate heresies that half the normal human passions must be strangled in the quest of virtue, and that the attainment of virtue is a dull and undesirable end, seeing it implies the sacrifice of most that makes life interesting. She was intolerant of those who find life dull as well as of those who find their fellow-creatures unattractive, and both for the same reason, holding that such indifference was due to the lack of vital energy and generosity in the complainer, since the same world held interests enough for those who had enough impulses and affections of their own whereby to entangle themselves in its affairs.

'George Eliot', *Nineteenth Century*, 9 (1881), 778–801 (pp. 785–6)

NOTE

For Edith Simcox, see Part III. Another recollection by her appears in 'Vignettes' in Part IV.

'THIS SAD LOSS'

Benjamin Jowett

Those who knew her only from her books have but a faint idea of her character. *'Elle était plus femme* [She was more of a woman]' & had more feminine qualities than almost any body whom I have ever known. She was so kind & good & so free from vanity & jealousy of all sorts very religious without definite beliefs: and with a sad humour & sense of humour, which was very singular & attractive. It would have been a great pleasure to me to introduce you to her. I did not at all disapprove of her marriage, for Mr Cross is a most worthy & intelligent man who was devoted to her & she could scarcely live without some one to take care of her. She needed to be sheltered from the world to be out of the Babel of voices as she would have called it. She had intended to write one more great novel & if her life had been spared would, I think, have gone on writing to the end.[1] There was a time when she greatly desired to write something for the good of women. But she thought that there were circumstances in her own life which unfitted her for this task. The accident of poverty about twenty years ago led her at Mr. Lewes' suggestion to try & write a story – this story was Amos Barton. She told me that if it had not been for the kindness of her husband that she would have never written anything. She also told me that she was never a Comtist, but as they were a poor & unfortunat[e] sect she would never finally renounce them. She was a regular student & had a great knowledge of numerous subjects about which she felt as well as thought, without in any degree losing her power of judgment.

I do not know whether you are too far off to be interested in this sad loss to the world & to her friends, which deeply affects us in England. I never

heard this remarkable woman say a word against others, or a word which
I should wish unsaid. ...

Letter to Sir Robert Morier, minister at Madrid,
15 January 1880 [i.e. 1881], Balliol College
Library, Oxford University, MS III/M/90, fol. 2ᵛ, reproduced, as is the
quotation in *n*. 1 below, with kind permission of the Jowett Copyright
Trustees; publ. with alterations in Evelyn Abbott and Lewis Campbell,
The Life and Letters of Benjamin Jowett, M.A.: Master of Balliol College,
Oxford, 2nd edn, 2 vols (London: Murray, 1897), II, 181–2

NOTE

For Benjamin Jowett, see 'Eton, Cambridge, and Oxford' in Part IV. Other recollections
by him appear in Part III, in 'The Countryside' in Part IV, and in Parts V–VI.

1. 'Mr. Cross tells me that she had intended to write one more great work of fiction'
(Jowett to Arthur Penrhyn Stanley, 29 December 1880, MS I/F5/16, fol. 2).

THE PRIORY ON SALE

Elizabeth M. Bruce

We found the home an unpretending structure, surrounded by a pretty
garden-plat – the grounds enclosed by a high fence from the street. A notice
being on this outer wall that "This very desirable residence, with frontings
on two roads, affording room for studios, stabling, &c., is to be sold," we
found an easy entrance. A servant was in charge who had been for years
with the family,[1] and we, therefore, were able to ask all the questions which
a reverent curiosity prompted.

There were five rooms on the first floor – a small reception room, two
drawing-rooms, Mr. Lewes's study and the dining-room. On the second floor
three rooms, two of them bed-rooms, the other the room made sacred by the
use of the great authoress. Herein were the many wonderful books written.
We felt within it as pilgrims at a shrine may feel. We were moved by an
impulse to enter with unsandalled feet.

It is by no means a pretentious room, not large, nor more than nine feet
high. It has two windows on the front, looking down into the garden. Before
one of these, during her occupancy, stood the desk at which she sat to write.
A small fire grate, with white marble mantle and enclosure, was on the side
of the room at right angles with, and near where the desk stood. There were
two book-cases in the room, one between the windows, the other and larger
one on the wall opposite. The paper on the wall was green, with a dull red
dado. The doors and mopboards are painted yellow and grained. ...

We were told that no effort was spared in the household to keep her safe
from interruption. Her hours for writing were held very sacred. She went

to her desk immediately after breakfast, 8 o'clock A.M., and remained until 1 o'clock lunch; after which, if the day was fair, she went usually to ride. If it was stormy she returned to her writing until the evening dinner hour. ... She was not disturbed by household cares, being provided with a housekeeper who was charged with the entire oversight. In the words of the servant, "she never knew what was to be for dinner until she came down to it." The kitchen arrangements were all in the basement, she being thereby spared from their contiguity, and her lyrics not set to the jingle of pots and pans.

'Communications: England's Holy Ground',
Christian Leader (New York),
27 October 1881, p. 3

NOTE

For Elizabeth Meugens Bruce, see Part I.

1. Presumably Mrs Gibson, who may have been hired *c*.1871 but is mentioned in GE's letters only in 1879–80.

LAST WORDS

Lydia Paget

The more one thinks of her, and her deep affection for your father, the more one feels how she stood alone, amid the many friends he has won. I never can think of her without a strange feeling of jealousy over her, a kind of true regard and admiration I can't describe. She was so gentle, so generous, so affectionate, so charitable in her spirit towards others.

Letter to Stephen Paget, her son, a few weeks after GE's death,
in *Memoirs and Letters of Sir James Paget*, ed. by Stephen Paget,
2nd edn (London: Longmans, Green, 1901), p. 402 *n*. 1

NOTE

Lydia Paget, née North, Lady Paget (1815–95), met GE *c*.1869. Her husband, the surgeon Sir James Paget, 1st baronet (1814–99, *ODNB*) treated GHL's son Thornton in his last illness.

Index

Page numbers in **bold** refer to a recollection by the person named and/or a pertinent biographical head-note. For an explanation of how this index works, see p. xxii.

---

immortality, 67, 122, 155, 156;
muscular Christianity, 191; no
definite, 219; pantheism, 23; piety
in youth, 6, 11, 12; Roman Catholic
Church, 146, 148, 164, 180–1,
with GE called priest or confessor,
158, 184, 212; rosary, 183; services,
11–12, 18, 145, 162, 164; *see also*
Judaism; morality
residences: 4 Cheyne Walk, Chelsea
(3–22 Dec. 1880), 223, 224, 225,
226; 8 Park Shot, Richmond
(3 Oct. 1855–5 Feb. 1859), 49,
50–2; 8 Victoria Grove Terrace
(now Ossington St), Bayswater,
(Apr.–May 1855), 46; 21 Cambridge
St, Paddington (18 Oct. 1853–20
July 1854), 41; 142 Strand (8 Jan.
1851–8 Oct. 1853), 26, 27–30,
36–41; Bird Grove, Foleshill
Road, north of Coventry (17 Mar.
1841–12 June 1849), 'a substantial
semidetached villa' (John Rignall
in *Companion,* p. 158), 13–14, 16,
17–21; Griff (1820–17 Mar. 1841),
'a spacious, comfortable, red–brick
farmhouse' (Margaret Harris in
Companion, p. 145) on the road
between Nuneaton and Coventry,
1, 2, 6, 9, 10, 11, 16; Holly Lodge,
South Fields, Wandsworth
(Feb. 1859–Sept. 1860), a 'delightful
ridge' (Solly, *'These Eighty Years'*
(1893), II, 89), 46–7, 53–4; Plongeon
and Geneva (25 July 1849–18 Mar.
1850), 22, 23; *see also* Priory; Witley
science: fatalism of modern, 70; and
female students, 212; and GHL,
174; knowledge of, 10, 39, 110,
149; of language, 221; language
contaminated by, 172; proper end
of, 222; and religious sentiments,
153; in school, 6; and Spencer, 58;
women in, 100; *see also* Darwin
speech: accent and inflection, 80,
106, 211; diction and syntax, 40,
70–1, 90, 146, 171–2; measured,
precise, 16, 56, 68, 89, 116, 192;
not calculated or metaphorical,
156; showy, 23, 172; *see also*

conversation; voice; speech *as
main entry*
spiritualism, 23, 97
shopping, 122
strangers, impositions of, 106, 159
translations, *see* Feuerbach; Spinoza;
Strauss
travels abroad: France and Germany
(1873), 186–7; France and Italy
(1869) 80, 184–6 (1880), 216; France
and Spain (1867), 140, 142, 182–4;
Geneva (1849–50), 21–3; Germany
and Switzerland (1868), 98, 99; Italy
(1860, 1861), 177–81; Switzerland
(1864?), 181–2; Weimar and Berlin
(1854–55), 43–6
travels in Britain: London (Aug. 1838),
11–12; Bagginton (July 1839), 12;
Birmingham (Sept. 1840), 12–13;
Cambridge (Feb. 1868), 141 (May
1873), 145–7 (May–June 1877),
154–6; Clapton (May–June 1846),
29; Earlswood Common (June
1874), 165–6; Edinburgh (Oct.
1852), 31, 32; Eton (June 1867),
140–1; Harrogate (July 1870),
159–60; Oxford (May 1870), 141–5
(June 1873), 148–9 (May 1875), 150
(May 1877), 150–3 (June 1878),
156–8; Ryde, Isle of Wight (Dec.
1870), 160–4; Shottermill, near
Haslemere (May–Aug. 1871), 164–5;
Six Mile Bottom (Oct. 1876), 166–7
(Oct. 1877), 170–3 (Oct. 1878),
176–7 (Sept. 1880), 217–18;
Weybridge (Dec. 1872), 150
visits, unable to make, 97
voice: angelic, 79; beautiful, 56, 81,
86, 98, 214; charming, 73, 96, 107,
131; clear, 72, 142; complimented,
xix, 181; contralto, 33, 60; delicate,
111; delicious, 105; drawly, 171;
earnest, 185; emotional, 109;
feminine, 111, 172; firm, 102, 121;
full-toned, 93; gentle, 33, 115,
188, 211, 214; grave, 188; in anger,
200; like a whisper, 214, 229, an
organ, 168, 220, Bernhardt's, 165;
measured, 120; marvellous, 105;
mellow, 90; modulated, 56, 93, 107,

124, 145, 149, 197, 198, 203, 205,
207, 208, 209, 211, 213, 214, 215,
219, 220, 223, 226
Jowett, Benjamin, **50–1**, 141, 145, 148,
150, **152–3**, **156–8**, **168–70**, **204–6**,
219, **232–3**: letter in Quinn and
Prest, eds (q.v.), 145; MS letters to
Morier, 232–3, to Stanley 219, 233;
MS notebooks, 51, 150, 152, 157, 169,
205, 219
Judaism, 113, 208, 210; *see also* Jews;
Daniel Deronda under Eliot, George:
writings
Juggernaut, *see* Car of Juggernaut

Kaiser: presumably Wilhelm II
(1859–1941), German emperor and
grandson of Queen Victoria, 158
Kalm, 212, 213
Kant, Immanuel (1724–1804), German
philosopher, 26, 27, 44
Kelly, John, 127
Kemble, Frances Ann or 'Fanny'
(1809–93), actress, 227
Kew, 300-acre Royal Botanic Gardens of
west London, 58, 167
King & Co., Cornhill publishing house
of Henry Samuel King (d. 1878),
where C. Kegan Paul worked as editor
and manager, 111
King, Thomas Starr (1824–64), celebrated
American Unitarian preacher, 210
King's College, *see* Cambridge University
Kingsley, Charles (1819–75), clergyman,
novelist, and social reformer,
Westward Ho! (1855), 3
Kingsley, Rose G. (1846–1925), daughter
of Charles Kingsley, 'GE's County'
(1885), 14, 20
Kisber, first Hungarian-bred horse to
win Derby, in 1876 (Whitaker's 1906
Almanack, p. 412), 166, 167
Kleist, Heinrich von (1777–1811),
German poet, met Varnhagen (q.v.) in
1810, 45
Knowles, James Thomas (1831–1908),
145
Knox, Thomas W. (1835–96), American
journalist and writer of boys' books,
130

Kovalevskaia, Soph'ia V., **80–1**, 83,
99–100, 218, **223–5**: 'Memoir of GE'
(1885, trans. 1984), 81, 83, 100, 218,
224
Krasiński, *see* Cook, Martha

La Vernia or Alvernia, Italy, in Tuscan
Apennines, monastery est. 1214 by
St Francis of Assisi, where he received
stigmata, 180–1
Lamb, Charles (1775–1834), essayist
(pseud. 'Elia'), 55, 221
Lambeth, inner London borough on
South Bank, 140
Lamont, L.M., 112
Landseer, Edwin (1802–73), painter
specializing in animal subjects, 106
Langtry, Lillie: popular name of Emilie
Charlotte (Mrs Edward) Langtry, née
Le Breton (1853–1929), society beauty,
mistress of Prince of Wales, 207, 208
language: beauty of English, 174; origin
of, 197; and philology, 221
Latin, maxim in, 88: *see also* education
and studies *under* Eliot, George;
Horace
Laurence, Reginald Vere (1876–1934), 83
Laurence, Samuel (1812–84), painter,
chalk drawing of GE (1860), 187, 231
Lawson, Cecil Gordon (1849–82),
painter, 'The Minister's Garden'
(1878), 134
Leader, The (London, 1850–60), radical
weekly est. by GHL and Thornton
Hunt, 29, 44, 46, 195, 197
Lecky, (William) Edward Hartpole
(1838–1903), historian whose
History of ... Rationalism (1865) GE
reviewed, 88
Leeds Mercury (1738–1939), 11
Lehmann, Frederick, **76–7**, 127, 128,
183: *Memories* (1908), 76
Lehmann, John (1907–87), *Ancestors and
Friends* (1962), 77
Lehmann, Nina, xviii, xxi, 77, **182–4**:
letter to Frederick Lehmann in
Familiar Letters (1892), 183
Lehmann, Nina, daughter of Frederick
and Nina Lehmann, *c.* six years old,
183

Lightning Source UK Ltd.
Milton Keynes UK
UKOW07n2252260215

246965UK00005B/62/P